# Suicide Prevention
## *Toward the Year 2000*

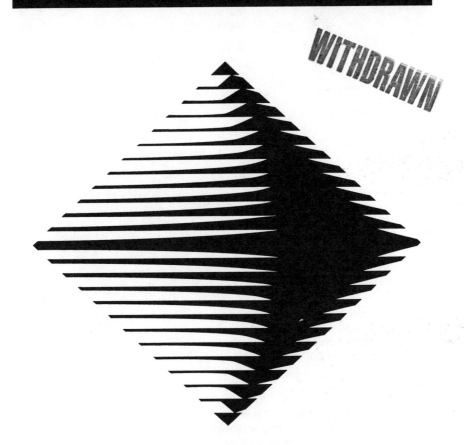

# Morton M. Silverman, M.D., and
# Ronald W. Maris, Ph.D., Editors

**THE GUILFORD PRESS**

New York                    London

© 1995 The American Association of Suicidology
Published by The Guilford Press
A Division of Guilford Publications
72 Spring Street, New York, NY 10012

This volume was published simultaneously as *Suicide and
Life Threatening Behavior*, Volume 25, Number 1, Spring 1995

ISBN 0-89862-803-2

Last digit is print number:   9   8   7   6   5   4   3   2   1

Printed in the United States of America

# SUICIDE PREVENTION
# TOWARD THE YEAR 2000

## Editors
### Morton M. Silverman
### Ronald W. Maris

# Editorial

It does not seem that long ago that I sat in a small hotel room in Albuquerque and assumed the editorship of *SLTB* from my mentor and long-time friend, Edwin S. Shneidman. Now, 14 years later, I suspect I have some of the same feelings Ed had back in 1981 — fatherly pride in the young adult development and the simple perseverance of *SLTB*, deep gratitude to the many consulting editors, staff, and authors over the years who have been and are the heart and soul of the journal, relief that I will no longer have to worry about soliciting enough papers to put out yet another issue, and yes, sadness that my own editorial run with *SLTB* is finally over.

Occasionally I have regrets that I did not seize the opportunities and write more editorials on timely self-destructive topics (like Jonestown, Waco, Vince Foster, Kevorkian, Kurt Cobain, etc.). For better or worse, I have tended to let the journal, its authors' ideas, and their data, speak for themselves.

In 1981 when I assumed the *SLTB* editorship my presidential address to the American Association of Suicidology was on "rational suicide." Although I still believe that in rare and limited circumstances suicide can be appropriate; the vast majority of the time suicide is simply a waste, a tragic inability to keep on trying, biopsychosocial deficiencies giving rise to a bankruptcy of hope and resources. Accordingly, as my last editorial offering, Mort Silverman and I have focused on suicide prevention. Premature, unnecessary death that causes lifelong heartache for surviving loved ones is nothing to be proud of, although it is forgivable and understandable.

Thanks for your trust and confidence in my editorship over all these years and thanks to Ed Shneidman for giving me this opportunity. May your life, luck, and love be good enough to see you through.

Ronald W. Maris, Ph.D.
Editor-in-Chief

Postscript:

Editor-elect Alan L. Berman accepted the Executive Directorship of the American Association of Suicidology. This means that he will *not* become Editor of *SLTB*. Instead the AAS Board of Directors has asked me to remain Editor of *SLTB* until May 1, 1996.

Ronald Maris is Editor-in-Chief of *Suicide and Life-Threatening Behavior*. Address correspondence to the author at the Center for the Study of Suicide, University of South Carolina, 228 Callcott Bldg., Columbia, SC 29208.

# Preface

There already exists a body of literature on the prevention of suicide, suicidal behaviors, and those disorders that are closely linked to suicide (e.g., depression) (Berman, 1990; Diekstra, 1988, 1992; Leenaars & Wenckstern, 1991; Munoz & Ying, 1993; Pfeffer, 1989; Richman, 1993; Shaffer, Garland, Gould, Fisher, and Trautman, 1988; Wilmotte & Mendlewicz, 1982). However, a close examination of these articles and texts reveals that there is very little, if any, systematic and conceptual discussion of the evolution of prevention theory and practice. Furthermore, and most importantly, the existing literature lacks an integrated explication of how existing prevention theories, concepts, and technologies are applicable to the range of human behaviors that concern suicidologists. All too often, existing prevention techniques are "lifted" from their applications in one arena (e.g., alcohol and other drug abuse) and hastily (and inappropriately) applied to problems of suicidal behaviors. The "fit" is not always compatible. Few, if any, modifications are made to adopt one set of concepts and interventions to a different set of behaviors or disorders. Rarely are suicidologists with specific subspecialty expertise asked to elucidate those preventive interventions most likely to be successful in addressing their specialty areas. This is a major intent of the present monograph.

Our monograph is organized to reflect the "essential ingredients" of suicide prevention, with a focus on epidemiology, modifiable risk and protective factors, theoretical and conceptual foundations of preventive interventions, specific settings for interventions, and identification of high-risk populations. In any undertaking such as this, it is inevitable that certain topics do not receive the attention they may be due. This effort is no exception. Had we had the luxury of time and page allocation, we would have included a discussion of state-level prevention efforts (Males, 1994), prevention activities addressing additional special populations (e.g., military, incarcerated, medically ill, disabled) (Bonner, 1992; Hendin & Haas, 1991), and children under the age of 12 (although here the suicide rates are known to be relatively low) (Pfeffer, 1989).

We chose the title of this monograph to reflect the resurgence in interest of reducing suicidal behaviors worldwide by the year 2000. We were aware of a series of national and international efforts to set guidelines and goals for the reduction of suicidal behaviors in target populations through the application of preventive intervention techniques (APHA, 1991; Department of Health and Human Services – DHHS, 1991, 1992; World Health Organization – WHO, 1979, 1981, 1982). Our reading of these documents led us to realize that this monograph was needed to provide practical guidelines and examples of interventions and techniques that currently work and techniques that are in the process of development and study. It is our hope that this effort will contribute in some way to these broader designs and applications.

The remainder of this Preface provides summaries of the individual papers.

Morton M. Silverman is with the University of Chicago. Ronald W. Maris is with the University of South Carolina.

## Silverman and Maris—The Prevention of Suicidal Behaviors: An Overview

Morton Silverman and Ronald Maris provide an overview of the multiple issues involved in conceptualizing the range of suicidal behaviors from the perspective of developing potential preventive interventions. They provide a context for understanding the current evolution of prevention activities and briefly review and compare four models of risk reduction as they relate to suicidal behaviors. They conclude with a discussion of future trends in suicide prevention.

## Mościcki—Epidemiology of Suicidal Behavior

Eve Mościcki begins with a discussion of the field of epidemiology and the limitations of comparing international suicide rates; she discusses the limitations on estimating the range of suicidal behaviors (attempts) due to problems with inconsistent definitions and data collection. She discusses age, gender, and race differences, as well as cohort and period effects. She discusses the important distinctions between suicidal completions and suicide attempts along the continuum of age, gender, and lethal methods used. In the process, she identifies the most salient distal and proximal risk factors for suicide completion and suicide attempts. These risk factors include biological, psychological, familial, and situational factors. Mościcki addresses the myths of sexual identity, adolescent stress, and physical illness as risk factors for suicidal behavior. She concludes by stating that mental disorders are a necessary cause for suicide, and that mental and addictive disorders are the most powerful of the multiple risk factors for suicide in all age groups. Since risk factors for suicide rarely occur in isolation, she argues that preventive interventions must address multiple risk factors.

## Diekstra—On the Nature, Magnitude, and Preventability of Suicidal Behaviors: An International Perspective

Rene Diekstra reviews three lines of research to answer the questions on the increased risk for suicide in adolescents and adults, the reasons for the increased risk, and what can be done to prevent suicidal behavior in these populations. Dr. Diekstra engages us in a discussion of definitions of terms used to describe the range of suicidal behaviors, including attempts, ideation, and parasuicide. He focuses on secular trends in suicidal behavior by identifying three separate populations: (1) those with depressed mood and suicidal ideation, (2) parasuicides, and (3) completed suicides. He emphasizes how little we really know for sure about the roles of secular trends, age, and gender in the etiology and expression of suicidal behaviors. He attempts to answer, from an international perspective, the critical question of why depressive disorders and suicide mortality are increasing among adolescent and young adult populations in the 20th century.

## Canetto and Lester—Gender and the Primary Prevention of Suicide Mortality

Sylvia Canetto and David Lester review the limitations of reporting data from a unique perspective of gender as a demographic variable and risk factor. They suggest that cultural factors are a strong influence on underreporting of suicidal behaviors, particularly completions for women. They provide a rich international analysis of suicide rates holding gender constant while focusing on gender differences regarding: (1) age, (2) social class, (3) employment status, (4) personal relationships (including marital status), (5) methods used, and (6) presence of mental disorder. Such an analysis provides new insights into the role of gender as it relates to suicidal behaviors. Their recommendations for preventing suicidal behaviors in women are focused on sociocultural factors.

### Felner—Theoretical and Conceptual Foundations of Prevention

Robert Felner highlights the evolution of theoretical and conceptual thinking in prevention. He emphasizes that populations, not individuals, are the targets of preventive interventions. He delineates the preventive approaches that best fit with the available knowledge base regarding suicidal behaviors. He synthesizes the current approaches to preventive interventions and links them to populations at risk for the expression of suicidal behaviors.

### Potter, Powell, and Kachur— Suicide Prevention from a Public Health Perspective

Lloyd Potter, K. E. Powell, and S. P. Kachur clearly distinguish the difference between public health and mental health approaches to suicide prevention through a discussion of Freudian vs. Durkheimian approaches to understanding suicidal behaviors. They argue that public health is concerned with social and environmental factors that influence suicidal behavior in populations, not individuals. They outline a sequence of efforts that are essential for the foundation of preventive interventions: (1) health-event surveillance, (2) epidemiological analysis, (3) intervention design and evaluation, and (4) program implementation. They discuss the limitations of the accuracy of surveillance for suicide and discuss existing surveillance mechanisms. They outline the Centers for Disease Control Youth Suicide Prevention Program as a viable public health approach to the prevention of suicide in a specific population.

### Felner and Silverman—Conceptual and Practical Models

Robert Felner and Morton Silverman identify the existing preventive intervention models that are applicable to the study of suicidal behaviors. They offer a synthesis of various approaches and suggest that the future of preventive inter-

vention development may best follow the model of Robert Gordon (1983) and the recent work of the Institute of Medicine (1994).

### Tanney—Suicide Prevention in Canada: A National Perspective Highlighting Progress and Problems

Bryan Tanney outlines an approach to suicide prevention from a national perspective that takes into account various sociopolitical factors and economic factors that determine the degree of effectiveness of such programs. Drawing upon his work with the World Health Organization in developing guidelines for community action, Tanney outlines approaches to community-based prevention for specific high-risk populations.

### Kalafat and Elias—Suicide Prevention in an Educational Context: Broad and Narrow Foci

John Kalafat and Maurice Elias focus on youth suicide attempters and review broad- and narrow-focused programs in school settings. They call for multidimensional, noncategorical prevention programs aimed at reducing all risk-taking behaviors that are commonly seen in school-based populations. They offer practical explanations of what constitutes essential ingredients and components of successful programs, including training, implementation, and assessment and evaluation. They: (1) review needs and conceptual bases for prevention programs and educational contexts, (2) propose appropriate objectives and cost-effective strategies for achieving objectives, and (3) review formative and summative evaluations of existing prevention programs.

### Litman—Suicide Prevention in a Treatment Setting

Robert Litman takes an individual focus rather than a population-based approach to address the prevention of suicide from a clinical perspective. He reviews the literature on clinical prediction and the role of existing biological therapies. He emphasizes the lack of demonstrated techniques and tools to prevent individuals from actually inflicting self-harm. Against the backdrop of studies suggesting that inpatient treatment for the prevention of suicide are not successful, Litman offers a drastic strategy: relinquish our reliance on psychiatric hospitalization to protect and cure suicidal patients. In its place, we should accept the inevitability of risk for suicide in the outpatient setting. Consequently, the prevention of suicide in an outpatient setting requires increased recognition, assessment, treatment, and monitoring of risk factors and risk behaviors over time. He proposes a continuum care model that include an emphasis on consultation and a team approach to the outpatient management of suicidal patients. He predicts the role of technology (particularly computers) in advancing: (1) the accurate identification of at-risk individuals in need of care, (2) training of primary care providers, (3) providing continuity of care, (4) improving consultation, and (5) evaluating the effectiveness and efficiency of specific interventions.

### Berman and Jobes—Suicide Prevention in Adolescents

Alan Berman and David Jobes discuss the rising tide of adolescent suicide in the last few decades. They suggest why risk factors for male suicide are higher than those for females. They critically review the Centers for Disease Control Youth Suicide Prevention Programs, which contain eight strategies for preventing youth suicide. They offer a model with an emphasis on preventing predisposing factors and strengthening protective factors. Theirs is a focus on levels of intervention from primary through tertiary interventions.

### Lipschitz—Suicide Prevention in Young Adults, Ages 18–30

Alan Lipschitz emphasizes the significance of mood disorders in young adults

as being an exceedingly significant risk factor for the development of suicidal behaviors. He also identifies psychotic behavior (e.g., schizophrenia) as a psychiatric disorder with onset in young adulthood that can predispose individuals to suicidal behaviors. Lipschitz focuses on ethnic minorities as being at particularly high risk for suicidal behaviors in young adulthood. He emphasizes social and economic risk factors as well as cultural factors that may contribute to risk status. He concludes with a discussion of existing institutions that have an increased concentration of young adults and may represent appropriate settings for the implementation of preventive interventions, i.e., military, prisons, and institutions of higher education.

### Maris—Suicide Prevention in Adults (30–65)

Ronald Maris poses questions about how to capture an understanding of midlife suicidal behaviors by discussing midlife suicidal careers—a concept he originated. Maris focuses on various theories of midlife development, especially the work of Daniel Levenson, Farrell and Rosenberg, and Vaillant. He contrasts these developmental perspectives in terms of how they inform us about midlife suicidal behavior and suicidal assessment. Maris concludes with a discussion of broad-based preventive interventions that are focused on the risk factors in this midlife population.

### McIntosh—Suicide Prevention in the Elderly (65–99)

John McIntosh illustrates that older adults have the highest suicide rates in the United States. He explores issues of gender, race, and age of the late-life population contributing to this high suicide rate. Being white, male, and over the age of 65 increases the risk factors for suicide to a level of 42.7/100,000. McIntosh distinguishes between the "young-old" (65–74 years old) and the "old-old" (75 years of age and above). He describes a number of successful intervention programs that are sensitive and responsive to the specific needs of elderly populations. He offers secondary and primary preventive interventions across psychological, sociological, familial, and community domains.

### Hendin—Assisted Suicide, Euthanasia, and Suicide Prevention: The Implications of the Dutch Experience

Herbert Hendin, having recently returned from extended study abroad, shares new data that bear on the relationship of the incidence of suicide to the practice of euthanasia in the Netherlands. He provides another perspective on how we, as a society, approach mental illness, pain, suffering, and old age. He reports on Dutch studies into euthanasia and assisted suicides as practiced by Dutch physicians. He argues for a halt to such practices until such time as we have a better understanding of all the dynamics and mechanisms involved in the desire to terminate one's life.

We hope you will enjoy our joint efforts and welcome your comments.

Morton W. Silverman, M.D.
Ronald W. Maris, Ph.D.
October 14, 1994

## REFERENCES

American Public Health Association (APHA). (1991). *Healthy communities 2000: Model standards* (3rd ed.). Washington, DC: Author.

Berman, A. L. (Ed.) (1990). *Suicide prevention: Case consultations.* New York: Springer.

Bonner, R. L. (1992). Isolation, seclusion, and psychosocial vulnerability as risk factors for suicide behind bars. In R. W. Maris, A. L. Berman, J. T. Maltsberger, & R. I. Yufit (Eds.), *Assessment and prediction of Suicide* (pp. 398–419). New York: Guilford Press.

Department of Health and Human Services (DHHS). (1991). *Healthy people 2000: National health promotion and disease prevention objectives* (DHHS Publ. No. (PHS) 91-50212). Washington, DC: U.S. Government Printing Office.

Department of Health and Human Services. (1992). *The third national injury control conference* (DHHS Publ. No. 1992-634-666). Washington, DC: U.S. Government Printing Office.

Diekstra, R. F. W. (1988). Towards a comprehensive strategy for the prevention of suicidal behavior: A summary of recommendations of national task forces. *Crisis, 9*(2), 119–126.

Diekstra, R. F. W. (1992). The prevention of suicidal behavior: Evidence for the efficacy of clinical and community-based programs. *International Journal of Mental Health, 21*(3), 69–87.

Gordon, R. S. (1983). An operational classification of disease prevention. *Public Health Reports, 98,* 107–109.

Hendin, H., & Haas, A. P. (1991). Suicide and guilt as manifestations of PTSD in Vietnam combat veterans. *American Journal of Psychiatry, 148*(5), 586–591.

Institute of Medicine (1994). Reducing risk for mental disorder: frontiers for prevention intervention research. Washington, D.C.: National Academy of Physicians.

Leenaars, A. A., & Wenckstern, S. (Eds.). (1991). *Suicide prevention in schools.* New York: Hemisphere.

Males, M. (1994). California's suicide decline, 1970–1990. *Suicide and Life-Threatening Behavior, 24*(1), 24–37.

Mrazek, P. J., & Haggerty, R. J. (Eds.). (1994). *Reducing risks for mental disorders: Frontiers for preventive intervention research.* Washington DC: National Academy Press.

Munoz, R. F., & Ying, Y. W. (1993). *The prevention of depression: Research and practice.* Baltimore, MD: Johns Hopkins University Press.

Pfeffer, C. R. (Ed.). (1989). *Suicide among youth: Perspectives on risk and protection.* Washington, DC: American Psychiatric Press.

Richman, J. (1993). *Preventing elderly suicide.* New York: Springer.

Shaffer, D., Garland, A., Gould, M., Fisher, P., & Trautman, P. (1988). Preventing teenage suicide: A critical review. *Journal of the American Academy of Child and Adolescent Psychiatry, 27,* 675–687.

WHO. (1979). *Formulating strategies for health for all by the year 2000.* Geneva: World Health Organization.

WHO. (1981). *Development of indicators for monitoring progress towards health for all by the year 2000.* Geneva: World Health Organization.

WHO. (1982). *Plan of action for implementing the global strategy for health for all.* Geneva: World Health Organization.

Wilmotte, J., & Mindlewicz, J. (Eds.). (1982). *New Trends in Suicide Prevention* (Bibliotheca Psychiatrica No. 162). New York: S. Karger.

# Notes on Contributors

**Alan L. Berman, PhD**, is director of the National Center for the Study and Prevention of Suicide at the Washington School of Psychiatry and editor-in-chief-elect of *Suicide and Life-Threatening Behavior*. He is a past president of the American Association of Suicidology and is coauthor of *Adolescent Suicide: Assessment and Intervention*.

**Silvia Sara Canetto, PhD**, is assistant professor of psychology at Colorado State University. She has doctoral degrees from the University of Padova, Italy, and Northwestern University Medical School, Chicago; and an MA degree from the Hebrew University of Jerusalem. Dr. Canetto has published on gender, aging, life-threatening behaviors, and couple/family processes.

**Rene F. W. Diekstra, PhD**, is professor of clinical and health psychology and dean of the Faculty of Social Sciences at the University of Leiden, the Netherlands. He is directing a research group on the social epidemiology of depressive disorders and suicidal behaviors, and has extensively published in the field of suicidology and adolescent psychology. He also worked for a number of years for the World Health Organization, Geneva, as manager of the Programme on Psychosocial and Behavioral Aspects of Health and Development. Among his recent publications are *Suicide and Depression in Late Life* (with D. DeLeo, Hogrefe International Publishers, 1991) and *The Anatomy of Suicide*, a treatise on historical, social, psychological, and biological aspects of suicide behaviors and their preventability (Boston/Dordrecht: Kluwer Academic Publishers, 1994).

**Maurice J. Elias, PhD**, is professor of psychology and coordinator, Internship Program in Applied, School, and Community Psychology at Rutgers University, and cofounder of the Consortium on the School-Based Promotion of Social Competence. His school-based life skills development and problem behavior prevention programs have been recognized as national models by the National Mental Health Association and the Program Effectiveness Panel, U.S. Department of Education's National Diffusion Network.

**Robert Felner, PhD**, is professor of psychology, education, and social service at the University of Illinois at Champaign–Urbana, as well as being the director of the Center for Prevention Research and Development. He has published widely in the areas of marital disruption, at-risk youth assessment and intervention, prevention theory and practice, evaluation techniques, and suicide prevention.

**Herbert Hendin, MD**, is the executive director of the American Suicide Foundation and professor of psychiatry at New York Medical College. His books on suicide include *Suicide and Scandinavia*, *Black Suicide*, and *Suicide in America*, a new edition of which has recently been published. For the past few years, he has been studying assisted suicide and euthanasia in this country and in the Netherlands; the article in this issue of *Suicide and Life-Threatening Behavior* is the outgrowth of that work.

**David A. Jobes, PhD**, is associate professor of psychology at the Catholic University of America and is a member of the clinical faculty. He is also assistant director of the National Center for the Study and Prevention of Suicide at the Washington School of Psychiatry. Dr. Jobes' major research and teaching interests are in suicidology, and he has published numerous journal articles, book chapters, and two books in the field. He is also a board member of the American Association of Suicidology (AAS), a consulting editor to *Suicide and Life-Threatening Behavior*, and is the 1995 recipient of the AAS Shneidman Award (in recognition of early career contributions to the scholarly literature in suicidology).

**S. Patrick Kachur, MD, MPH**, is an Epidemic Intelligence Service Officer assigned to the Division of Violence Prevention at the National Center for Injury Prevention and Control of the Centers for Disease Control and Prevention. He is a graduate of Kent State University and the Northeastern Ohio University College of Medicine. He completed a preventive medicine residency at the Mary Imogene Bassett Hospital and the Johns Hopkins University School of Hygiene and Public Health.

**John Kalafat, PhD**, is professor of psychology at Spalding University in Louisville, Kentucky. He is cochair of the School Committee of the American Association of Suicidology and coauthor of *Lifelines: A School-Based Adolescent Suicide Response Program* as well as a number of articles and chapters on youth suicide prevention.

**David Lester, PhD**, has doctoral degrees from Brandeis University (in psychology) and the University of Cambridge (in social and political science). He has written over 350 scholarly articles and books on suicide, and is currently president of the International Association for Suicide Prevention.

**Alan Lipschitz, MD**, is associate director for research at the American Suicide Foundation, and assistant professor in the department of psychiatry at New York

Medical College, and medical director at Value Behavioral Health.

**Robert E. Litman, MD, PhD**, is clinical professor of psychiatry at the UCLA School of Medicine. Dr. Litman has practiced psychiatry and psychoanalysis in Los Angeles since 1950. With Dr. Shneidman and Dr. Farberow, he helped found the Los Angeles Suicide Prevention Center, and he was chief psychiatrist of the center for more than 30 years. He was the first director of Psychiatric Inpatient Services at Cedars–Sinai Hospital, Los Angeles, and a founding member and past president of the American Association of Suicidology.

**Ronald W. Maris, PhD**, directs the Center for the Study of Suicide at the University of South Carolina (Columbia), where he is a professor of (medical) sociology and adjunct professor of psychiatry. Maris is past president of the American Association of Suicidology and editor-in-chief of its official journal, *Suicide and Life-Threatening Behavior*. Maris is an active consulting forensic suicidologist and a fellow in the American Academy of Forensic Sciences. He is currently coauthoring a comprehensive textbook on suicidology and suicide prevention with J. John Mann, MD (Columbia University), and Alan L. Berman, PhD (Washington School of Psychiatry). Maris has authored or edited 13 other books on suicide and numerous journal articles.

**John L. McIntosh, PhD**, is professor of psychology at Indiana University South Bend. He is immediate past president of the American Association of Suicidology. McIntosh has published 5 books on suicide and over 40 journal articles and book chapters on the topic. He is senior author of the most recent book, *Elder Suicide: Research, Theory, and Treatment*, published in 1994 by the American Psychological Association. McIntosh was the 1990 recipient of the American Association of Suicidology's Shneidman Award.

**Eve K. Mościcki, ScD, MPH,** is an epidemiologist, chief of the Prevention Research Branch at the National Institute of Mental Health (NIMH), and chair of the NIMH Suicide Research Consortium. Her numerous publications and presentations on the epidemiology of suicide and suicidal behaviors have been widely recognized. She is on the editorial boards of *Suicide and Life-Threatening Behavior* and the *American Journal of Epidemiology*, and is listed in *Who's Who in Science and Engineering* and *American Men and Women of Science*.

**Lloyd B. Potter, PhD, MPH,** is the leader of the Suicide Prevention Team in the Division of Violence Prevention, National Center for Injury Prevention and Control, Centers for Disease Control and Prevention. He is a graduate of Texas A&M University and of the University of Texas at Austin with specializations in sociology and demography; and holds an MPH from Emory University School of Public Health.

**Kenneth E. Powell, MD, MPH,** is associate director for science in the Division of Violence Prevention, National Center for Injury Prevention and Control, Centers for Disease Control and Prevention. He holds an undergraduate degree in chemistry from Harvard University, is a graduate of Northwestern University Medical School, and received his MPH in epidemiology from Harvard School of Public Health. He has worked at the Centers for Disease Control and Prevention in various positions, encompassing general infectious disease; tuberculosis; heavy metal, pesticide, and other environmental contaminants; physical activity and other health-related behaviors; and violence. He has produced more than 60 publications on various topics from enzyme kinetics to violence prevention.

**Morton M. Silverman, MD,** is associate professor of psychiatry at the University of Chicago and director of the Student Counseling and Resource Service. Dr. Silverman is a special issue editor for *Suicide and Life-Threatening Behavior*. Dr. Silverman has published in the areas of prevention, youth suicide, alcohol and other drug abuse, and forensic suicidology.

**Bryan Tanney, MD,** is professor of psychiatry at the University of Calgary in Alberta, Canada. Dr. Tanney has published in the areas of biological psychiatry and risk assessment. He is the founder of the Suicide Information and Education Centre (SIEC).

# I. Epidemiology and Risk Factors

## 1
## The Prevention of Suicidal Behaviors: An Overview

Morton M. Silverman, MD, and Ronald W. Maris, PhD

The authors discuss the development of the concept of prevention as it has evolved from the public health and mental health fields. Concepts of epidemiology, treatment, and community mental health are defined in terms of their contributions to the evolution of prevention thinking. Four models of prevention are presented and critiqued: the public health model, the operational model, the antecedent conditions model, and the injury control model. Essential ingredients for implementing effective preventive interventions are presented, as well as examples of practical preventive interventions.

A suicide is, by definition, not a disease, but a death that is caused by a self-inflicted, intentional action or behavior. Not all suicides have the same etiology, pathogenesis, and expression (e.g., different methods are utilized). Suicidal behaviors are actions that place an individual at high risk for self-destruction. Often it is not the observed behaviors that are critical for our understanding of the etiology of suicide but, rather, the largely unobservable, internal mechanisms (values, beliefs, attitudes, knowledge, neurochemistry, feelings, perspectives). These "hidden" mechanisms are not necessarily suicidal "behaviors" but result in the expression of behaviors that, to the observer, are classified as self-destructive in nature. These psychological mechanisms can be influenced by genetics, biology, society, family, economics, politics, and so on.

Hence, when we think about preventing suicide, we must first distinguish between suicidal behaviors (gestures, threats, attempts) and suicidal ideation (thoughts) and intent. When we think about prevention, we must be perfectly clear about what are to be the targets of our interventions—ideas, intent, attempts, or completions. Although often conceived of as a continuum of suicidal behaviors (from ideation to completion), in fact, it is yet to be demonstrated that this continuum is continuous for every individual in every situation. Assuming that suicidal ideation is relatively common and rarely progressive or constant, most suicidologists interested in prevention have focused their energies on preventing suicidal behaviors. Lacking a clear etiologic or pathogenic pathway toward self-injury or self-destruction, suicidologists have often looked elsewhere for inspiration and ideas to assist in conceptualizing a science of prevention for the range of suicidal behaviors.

## STEPS IN THE DEVELOPMENT OF SUICIDOLOGY

There have been a number of revolutions and identifiable evolutionary steps in the

Morton M. Silverman, MD, is with the Student Counseling and Resource Service, University of Chicago. Ronald W. Maris, PhD, is with the Center for the Study of Suicide and Life-Threatening Behavior, University of South Carolina.

Send reprint requests to Morton M. Silverman at 5737 S. University, Chicago, IL 60637.

field of suicidology over the last century. Many of these advances have come as a result of advances in the related fields of public health and mental health (Albee, 1982; Cowen, 1983; Pardes, Silverman, & West, 1989). Our understanding of suicidal behaviors has evolved alongside our understanding of disease entities and conditions as defined by public health and mental health researchers, theoreticians, clinicians, and epidemiologists. Although there remains some debate about how many revolutions have occurred, and in which order, we can safely say that as they impact on suicidology, the major revolutions in our "sister" fields that relate to our understanding of the range and scope of suicidal behaviors are:

1. Epidemiology – the definition and classification of disease processes; the identification and elaboration of risk factors; the modeling of causal relationships between and among risk and demographic variables
2. Treatment – the evolution of techniques and technologies to effectively and efficiently treat individuals demonstrating early (and sometimes late) signs and symptoms of distress and disorder
3. Community mental health movement – a recognition of the power and importance of the role of family, community, schools, and workplace on the etiology, maintenance, and exacerbation of individual and group disturbance; the recognition of the powerful roles of ecology and environment in the development, expression, and maintenance of disordered social systems that express themselves as beliefs, attitudes, and behavior (Rappaport, 1987)
4. Prevention – a coordinated and comprehensive set of specific interventions that are strategically linked to target populations at risk for the development of specific disorders and dysfunctions (Felner, Jason, Moritsugu, & Farber, 1983; Seidman, 1987).

Allow us to elaborate on some of these revolutions.

## Epidemiology

We are still in our infancy regarding the knowledge base for the definitions and classification of suicidal behaviors. The currently used terms and descriptors are too numerous and overlapping. There are too few studies that help us specifically identify who is at risk and who is at most risk. Because we are studying human behavior, we have difficulty in pinpointing or assigning relative weighting to factors contributing to cause-and-effect relationships. Are behaviors related to each other, and if so, in what ways? How do individuals move along a continuum from suicidal ideation (a thought), to plan (an intent), to attempt or completion? What are the facilitating (promotive) or inhibitory (protective) factors that contribute to this process? An important activity is surveillance – the accurate measurement and reporting of behavior in a defined population over time. This effort has assisted in elucidating different sets of risk (predisposing, precipitating, perpetuating) and protective factors (Felner & Silverman, 1989).

## Treatment

Although there is now a burgeoning literature on the treatment of suicidal individuals, we still lack a comprehensive treatment strategy and set of alternative approaches to the treatment of self-destructive behaviors. Again, we have drawn upon existing paradigms from other fields as well as modifying and adapting successful treatment strategies for disorders and dysfunctions that seem related to or associated with self-destructive behaviors (Ottosson, 1979). Such approaches include cognitive-behavioral interventions (Freeman & Reinecke, 1993; Linehan, Armstrong, Suarez, Allman, & Heard, 1991), family therapy (Richman, 1985), biological treatments (Goldblatt & Schatzberg, 1992; Maris, 1986) and dynamic therapies (Dulit & Michels, 1992). It still remains an open question whether the development and implementation of successful preventive interventions will eventually lead to a refinement or development of a set of specific treatment interventions for those already expressing self-destructive behaviors.

## Prevention

Prevention is predicated on prediction. None of us have proven to be good predictors of future human behavior. Our best predictions have been in the arena of violence prevention – i.e., human aggression perpetrated on another (Flitcraft, 1992; Marzuk, Tardiff, & Hirsch, 1992). Even here our best predictive indicators are a history of past violent behavior and a family history of being a victim of violence. The relationship between violence and self-destructive behaviors (violence turned inward) needs further study, although a history of prior nonfatal suicide attempts seems promising (Maris, Berman, Maltsberger, & Yufits, 1992, Chap. 17).

Our ability to predict future suicidal behavior is rather dismal (Gould, Shaffer, Fisher, Kleinman, & Morishima, 1992; Motto, 1965; Pokorny, 1983; 1992). Therefore, our ability to selectively identify those most likely to commit suicide or inflict self-injurious harm is rather poor. Furthermore, most of the interventions we have readily available (i.e., treatment) are expensive, time intensive, and not always effective. Nevertheless, prevention holds the promise of providing more good to more people, more effectively and more efficiently (Felner, Silverman, & Felner, in press).

The field of prevention has evolved from a conceptual framework that included only three factors (host, environment, agent) and three levels of intervention (primary, secondary, tertiary) to one that allows for multifactorial considerations and multiple levels of intervention without assigning hierarchical value to them (Mrazek & Haggerty, 1994). In fact, current prevention approaches as applied to the expression of self-destructive human behaviors include elements of more tradi-

tional prevention programming in addition to intervention and postvention strategies and techniques. Prevention has expanded to encompass both disease prevention and health promotion. It is in the arenas of health protection, health promotion, and health maintenance that human behavioral dynamics have become a focus of great interest and study.

One cannot begin to discuss the potential of prevention without understanding that our ability to intervene preventively is the final common pathway of prior revolutions. The science of prevention has evolved from the successes of prior and current health-related sciences. In fact, in order to effectively mount a successful preventive intervention program, it is incumbent to first measure the extent of the problem (epidemiology), identify who is at risk (risk assessment), decide how and where to target interventions (needs assessment), identify local resources and support networks (ecological assessment), and be prepared to provide immediate interventions for those identified at most risk (treatment) (Silverman & Koretz, 1989).

The last century has witnessed numerous attempts by many dedicated and concerned researchers, theoreticians, and clinicians to solve the mystery of suicide. In the beginning, these investigators and observers of human behavior lacked the technologies, the rigorous definitions, and the outcome studies to defend their conceptual models. In part, the major obstacle is that suicidal behaviors are complex behavioral expressions emanating from multiple etiologies (psychological, biological, genetic, sociological, economic, etc.). The suicidal behaviors that we observed are the expression of a culmination of multiple ingredients – all contributing their cumulative risk potential – that leads to a wide range of expressions that we categorize as suicidal behaviors. The knowledgeable reader knows that commonly agreed upon definitions for this range of suicidal behaviors still elude us (Maris et al., 1992, Chap. 4). It also is disconcerting that we understand little about the factors that move an individual along the continuum (if, in fact, there truly is such a linked continuum) from ideation, through intent and plan, to execution of a self-destructive or life-threatening behavior.

## PREVENTION MODELS

### Public Health Model

Well-intentioned investigators have looked to models from related fields of human study to serve as templates for conceptualizing, classifying, and categorizing these suicidal behaviors. The most commonly referenced model is the public health (or medical) model. Many investigators have attempted to understand the range of suicidal behaviors within this context (Blumenthal & Kupfer, 1988). The shortcomings of the model are that it best explains the mechanisms of causation and transmission of disease, not behavior. Suicide is a behavior, albeit a disordered one and one that may be secondary to an identifiable (and treatable) disease process. There has not been a "goodness of fit" between this available model of disease and the knowledge base of suicidal behaviors.

In order to intervene preventively using the traditional public health disease paradigm, one must first have clearly identified: (1) well-defined signs and symptoms, (2) incidence and prevalence statistics in specifically defined populations, (3) etiological factors that are linked to expression of the behavior, (4) modes of transmission (facilitation and inhibition), (5) natural history of the process, and (6) possible points of interruption/intervention along the pathological trajectory. Clearly this is not yet possible for most forms of suicidal behavior.

### Operational Model

The model offered by Robert Gordon (1983) has an intervention focus and is not based on causality or etiology. It defines preventive interventions as categories using an operational nomenclature and, thus, serves as an alternative to the traditional triad of primary, secondary, and tertiary prevention. His three categories of interventions are universal procedures, selective procedures, and indicated procedures. This organization is based on how the target groups are identified.

*Universal preventive interventions* are directed at an entire population and not specifically at subgroups presumed to be at greater risk. Health promotion and protection measures desirable for "essentially everybody" are classified here. *Selective interventions* are directed at individuals who are at greater risk for diseases or disorders than the general population. These measures can be reasonably recommended, in terms of "the balance of benefits against risk and cost," for a relatively large subgroup "whose risk of becoming ill is above normal." *Indicated interventions* are targeted at those relatively small groups who are found, by screening programs or other inquiries, to "manifest a risk factor, condition, or abnormality that identifies them, individually, as being at sufficiently high risk to require the preventive intervention." As a society moves from universal procedures to indicated procedures, the cost of providing these procedures increases in terms of staff needs, time, effort, and cost.

If we focus on suicidal behaviors, Gordon might agree that universal procedures include gun control and easy access to mental health facilities (community mental health centers, crisis centers, hotlines, etc.). Selective procedures would include treatment for associated behaviors such as substance abuse, decreasing general access to means of suicide (such as placing barriers on bridges), and increasing the number and availability of support networks for those individuals most at risk or who have already entered into self-destructive behavior. Such procedures would be providing easily accessible treatment for depression and hospitalizing serious suicide attempters. Indicated procedures would be seen as early secondary prevention or early treatment efforts.

## Antecedent Conditions Model

A paradigmatic shift occurred in our thinking about what should be the target of preventive interventions (Kuhn, 1970). This shift resulted in preventive intervention models that were based on modifying antecedent conditions that are related by correlation to an outcome rather than focusing exclusively on the outcome itself (Bloom, 1986). The assumption was that there is not a specific etiologic agent that is identifiable. This challenges the previously held concept of a universal, nonspecific vulnerability for illness. This model suggested that there are predisposing circumstances that are distal to the eventual outcome, and that these predisposing conditions place an individual in a category of being generally vulnerable to a specific outcome. It is only when more proximal or precipitating conditions or circumstances "interact" with the general state of vulnerability that an individual expresses a negative outcome.

There is tension between those who focus on specific risk factors as antecedents for psychopathology and those who do not support this specific etiology model. The latter group finds that "an antecedent-condition model applies across a wide range of emotional and behavioral dysfunctions. These observers argue that non-specific predisposing factors and precipitating conditions may be responsible for the expression of many disorders, moving away from the focus on specific risk factors to the possibility of a more universal potential for disturbance in various populations" (American Psychiatric Association Task Force, 1990). Felner and Silverman (1989) stated:

At this point, a key debate in the prevention literature becomes salient if we are to decide how and when to move from "risk factors" to programs. We need to be clear on how we answer the questions: (a) do we attempt to tailor primary prevention programs to the prevention of a specific disorder, or (b) do we develop programs which are effective in alleviating a number of conditions that are antecedent to a range of emotional and physical problems, including, but not limited to the target problem?

The "specific disorder prevention" model rests heavily in a classic medical–public health paradigm which views diseases as caused by specific conditions that interact with individual vulnerabilities, again, specifiable. In contrast, the antecedent condition model argues that at least for a wide range of emotional and behavioral disorders, particularly those related to stress and other elements of the normal life-course, the specific etiology model is not appropriate. (p. 25)

The focus of preventive interventions is on the mechanisms and processes that lead to the expression of disorder, not on the disorder itself, and not on the individual who may not be ill or expressing the problem. The assumption is that negative outcomes may be healthy adaptations to disordered environments. Such a radical rethinking of causal and correlational factors in the evolution of disease and disorder has resulted in a shift in emphasis to ecological, transactional, and social/environmental domains (Felner & Felner, 1989).

This model suggests that there are two distinct sets of conditions that are antecedent to the expression of suicidal behaviors – predisposing conditions and precipitating conditions (Felner and Silverman, 1989). These two conditions place an individual at increased risk and make them more vulnerable to suicidal behavior. Predisposing conditions are distal to the behavior itself but are necessary to place an individual at increased risk. Precipitating conditions are proximal conditions to the behavior and are often associated with the expression of the dysfunction in a temporal manner. Precipitating conditions alone, without the presence of predisposing conditions, often will not lead to the expression of the dysfunction.

This model suggests that there are two loci for intervention. One is a more societal or community approach that eradicates or diminishes predisposing conditions for the entire population. The second level of intervention is for those who have already been identified as having experienced predisposing conditions. For this "at-risk" population, the approach is to eliminate or ameliorate those precipitating conditions that are proximally or temporally related to the expression of the disease.

## Injury Control Models

William Haddon, Jr. (1968, 1980) first expanded the public health model of pathogenesis to include an injury control approach. Haddon (1967, 1968, 1980) set forth 10 unintentional injury control strategies to break the chain of injury causation. These strategies fall into the tripartite concept of primary, secondary, and tertiary prevention, and deal, respectively, with the preinjury, injury, and postinjury phases (Institute of Medicine – IOM, 1985; Department of Health and Human Services – DHHS, 1991).

The advantage of injury control modeling is that it allows for the identification of multiple causes that, in and of themselves, may be necessary, but not sufficient, to propel the individual to complete a suicidal act. Thus, one does not necessarily have to strongly believe in or defend any one particular cause, or limit one's interventions to only that cause. The modeling allows for the displaying of multiple causes and for an objective development and identification of the most cost-effective intervention. Furthermore, it allows for the identification of various methods to identify and break the chain of disease causation at its weakest link. The weakest link might be proximal or distal to the disorder and might involve passive or active countermeasures.

Only recently have those in the mental health field revisited these approaches and attempted to apply them to suicide prevention (DHHS, 1991). Under this conceptualization, suicide becomes the direct result of an injury that was not prevented. The beauty of this approach is that one can stratify the various actions that can be taken to address each of the various components that together become sufficient for the suicidal act to occur.

Table 1 outlines Haddon's injury control strategies, with our own examples that relate to issues of suicide prevention. This approach provides an elegant means of identifying testable hypotheses and developing preventive interventions that are specifically linked to a particular strategy in a particular phase or at a particular level of prevention, and allows for a means of evaluating the outcome.

One major conceptual problem in adapting the Haddon injury control model to the study of suicide prevention is the underlying assumption in injury control strategies that the "injury" is *unintentional*. The concept is that injuries are "accidents" that are not intended to occur. However, the prevailing perspective in the field of suicide is that suicidal behaviors are *intentional* and under the direct control of the individual involved. There is some interesting theoretical and practical discussion of whether injury control models can be applied to suicide attempts and suicide completions (DHHS, 1991). For purposes of this discussion, however, we will assume that a certain percentage of suicidal behaviors are amenable to injury control approaches.

Much research on suicide and on nonfatal self-injury has emphasized personal characteristics and methods of treating suicidal individuals. Changes in the physical and social environment, and their effect on suicide rates have been the subject of little research to date. "The validity of the widespread assumption that non-fatal suicide attempts represent a lack of desire to kill oneself and, therefore, involve the choice of less lethal means, should be subjected to scientific scrutiny; there is evidence that reducing the availability of popular means of committing suicide can cause a major reduction in the suicide rate" (IOM, 1985, p. 45).

One example of this approach might be the reduction of suicides by domestic gas inhalation (Lester & Abe, 1989). The causes for death were secondary to the chemical content of the gas that was used for domestic use (stoves in the kitchen). The gas was easily and readily available and accessible. Furthermore, the gas was

Table 1
Haddon's Injury Control Strategies: Applications to Suicide Prevention

Primary prevention (preinjury phase)
1. Prevent the initial creation of the hazard
   - Do not manufacture handguns for non-military or nonsecurity use
   - Reduce the toxic content of domestic gas
   - Reduce psychological stress
   - Improve social support networks
2. Reduce the amount of hazard that is created
   - Provide opportunities for all members of society to contribute (employment)
   - Allow only plastic bullets to be sold as ammunition for nonsecurity uses
   - Limit the number of pills per bottle sold of over-the-counter and prescription medications commonly involved in overdoses
   - Control the distribution (sales) and registration of firearms
3. Prevent the release of a hazard that already exists
   - Set standards for the purchasing of firearms
   - Limit access to alcohol (amount, frequency, timing)
   - Prevent access to illicit drugs
   - Promote responsible alcohol consumption
   - Require training in conflict resolution/anger management
   - Limit sales of toxic chemicals
Secondary prevention (injury phase)
4. Modify the rate of release or spatial distribution of the hazard from its source
   - Enforce judicious prescribing techniques (no automatic refills) of potentially dangerous medications
   - Individual tablet packaging of medications to prevent rapid consumption of large quantities
   - Implement a national firearms tracking system
   - Enforce seat belt use in all vehicles
   - Provide automatic ventilation systems or automatic engine cut-off valves in automobiles when toxic gases are detected
   - Provide psychological interventions (therapies) for the psychiatrically ill
5. Separate, in time or space, the hazard from persons to be protected
   - Develop laws to prevent the severely psychiatrically ill from gaining access to weapons
   - Separate ammunition from firearms
   - Confiscate firearms and all medications after suicide attempts

- Establish a uniform national waiting period between the application to purchase a firearm and its sale
6. Interpose a barrier between the hazard and person to be protected
   - Initiate "911" or emergency hotline numbers everywhere
   - Provide air bags that inflate automatically in automobile crashes
   - Keep hunting weapons and firearms in locked cabinets outside of the home
   - Develop additives for alcohol and other poisonous drugs that reduce or block absorption in the body at increased concentrations
   - Place high barriers and increased lighting on bridges and high buildings
7. Modify contact surfaces to reduce injury
   - Prevent access to rooftops of high buildings
   - Alter medications to reduce harmful side effects of drug ingestion (cardiovascular, CNS)
   - Redesign bullets to reduce injury severity
8. Strengthen the resistance of persons who might be injured by the hazard
   - Stress reduction and mutual support programs in the community
   - Health promotion and wellness programs in schools and the workplace
   - Early detection of distress, dysfunction, and disorder in institutional settings
   - Initiate psychoeducational programs throughout the community
Tertiary prevention (postinjury phase)
9. Move rapidly to detect and limit damage that has occurred
   - Improve medical knowledge and training in the assessment, diagnosis, and treatment of suicidal individuals
   - Provide emergency medical response teams and improved communications systems (telephones on bridges)
   - Provide postvention teams to work with survivors of suicide
   - Promote first-aid training for laymen
10. Initiate immediate and long-term reparative actions
   - Provide hospitalization and psychotherapy for suicide attempters
   - Support research on suicide prevention
   - Provide community mental health services (follow-up) for all behavioral problems seen in emergency rooms

Adapted and expanded from: Haddon and Baker (1981); Gerberich et al. (1985); Kellermann et al. (1991); Robertson (1986).

odorless and colorless, which allowed for the surreptitious use of the "method" without detection. As has been shown in a number of studies, the most cost-effective and cost-beneficial intervention was to detoxify the chemical content of the domestic gas. This has conclusively been shown to break the chain of death by suicide across many countries, especially in the United Kingdom (Kreitman, 1976; Lester, 1990).

Needless to say, this preventive intervention does not address motivation, psychological disorder, domestic disruption, socioeconomic disorder, or biological predilection. However, similar to the direct approach of placing barriers on bridges, this preventive intervention resulted in the control of self-injurious behaviors. Haddon (1980) has stated, "the analysis is not per se a means for choosing policy . . . but is rather an aid for identifying, considering, and choosing the various means by which policy might be implemented."

Three general strategies are available to prevent injuries (Robertson, 1975): (1) persuade persons at risk of injury to alter their behavior for increased self protection; (2) require individual behavior change by law or administrative rule; and (3) provide automatic protection by product and environmental design. Each of these general strategies has a role in any comprehensive injury control program; however, behavioral research suggests that the second strategy – i.e., requiring behavior change – is generally more effective than the first, and that the third – providing automatic protection – would be the most effective (Robertson, 1983). A fundamental reason for this is that members of high-risk groups tend to be the harder to influence with approaches that involve either voluntary or mandated changes in their individual behavior (IOM, 1985).

Although education has become a cornerstone for any public health or community-based program targeted at changing behavior, it has become clear over time that educational programs alone are not sufficient to substantially reduce the incidence and prevalence of the targeted disorder. Failure to use available information is found, not only in the people who may be the victims of this action, but also in decision makers who can influence the probability of injury to others. One problem with relying on educational approaches is the counterinfluence of the mass media in implicitly encouraging certain types of behavior. What is needed is more careful evaluation of educational efforts, advertising campaigns, incentive programs, and persuasion techniques to determine to what extent they are cost-effective and cost-beneficial.

In many ways, Haddon's contribution was to place "the fault" outside of the individual. He saw the environment as the variable that could be altered, manipulated, changed. He saw the protection of the individual *at risk* as being through the engineering of the environment. Of note is that community psychologists began their field through the recognition that the way toward better mental health (and physical health) was through social engineering – better schools, better living conditions, better jobs, greater self-esteem, better family relationships, and social support systems. The primary prevention of mental disorders was initially conveyed as a set of manipulations to the individual's external environment – in a mode analogous to the concept of "inoculation" and immunizations – providing individuals with essential ingredients to help them navigate exposure to risky settings, risky situations, and risky behaviors.

And so now we are on the verge of major rethinking in the *practical* nature of how to *protect* individuals from harm – intentional and unintentional self-injurious harm. We are developing interventions to protect individuals from their environments (man-made and natural disasters), from each other (violence), and from themselves. We are moving beyond the individual as the sole focus of our inquiry and our intervention to the greater circles of influence that impinge and affect their view of themselves and how the interact with familial, social, community, national, and even international realms of influence.

Even more excitement is now being generated by the ecological (Vincent & Trickett, 1983) and transactional–ecological models (Felner and Felner, 1989), which attempt to explain the emergence and continuance of multiple human behaviors that have commonalities. Here the emphasis is on the interactions and transactions between and among groups of individuals and their environments (family, school, community, workplace). Such a "paradigmatic shift" from focusing prevention efforts solely on biological disease entities to expressions of human behavior has evolved over the last quarter century (Bloom, 1986; Kuhn, 1970).

## FROM MODELING TO INTERVENTION: TOWARD THE YEAR 2000

One of the major functions of a model is to provide us with identifiable points of entry to insert preventive interventions. Table 2 outlines the who, what, when, where, and why questions needed to be answered in the process of developing preventive interventions directed at risk reduction for a specific disorder or dysfunction. As is readily apparent, the field of suicidology has not evolved to the point where it can provide rigorous answers to all these questions. Nevertheless, we do have some answers and some strong hunches based on empirical findings. Once the preventive interventions are developed and modified to fit the specific model, certain decision points arise in selecting those preventive interventions to be implemented (Table 3).

Implementing these interventions involves yet another set of strategies, techniques, and technologies, in addition to a conceptual framework for studying the effect of interventions on human behavior (Cole et al., 1993). Such an undertaking is not easy, nor should it be short-lived. Because suicide fortunately remains a relatively low base rate phenomenon, a preventive intervention program must be large in size and long in duration to document a statistically significant change in the rate of completed suicides in a specified population. Hence, the likelihood of seeing large-scale suicide prevention programs, per se, is not great. Rather, suicide prevention messages and programs must create new linkages with other prevention-oriented programs in order to get our messages heard by target audiences. In like manner, suicide preventionists can support those other public health and community efforts that do not directly address our immediate concerns but do have indirect effects in lowering the overall suicide rates in the population. Such programs might include the mandatory use of seat belts, subsidies to encourage the installation of electronic ignition gas ovens, legislation to promote the use of carbon monoxide detectors in homes and cars, promotion of research and development to design better safety features on firearms,

Table 2
Basic Questions in Developing Preventive Interventions

1. How to define the risk condition/behavior
2. Who is at risk
3. How to identify who is at most risk
4. Why an individual is at risk
5. When an individual is at most risk
6. What situations/settings/behaviors place an individual at most risk
7. What interventions lower risk status
8. What interventions raise risk protection
9. When interventions are to be applied to lower risk
10. Where interventions are most effectly received

## Table 3
## Decision Points in Selecting Preventive Interventions

- Which points in the causal chain are particularly vulnerable to interruption?
- Which interventions are likely to contribute to the prevention of a large proportion of a disorder?
- Which interventions are likely to be effective across different (but related) types of disorders?
- What sorts of interventions will result in *immediate* reductions in such disorders?
- What sorts of interventions will result in *long-term* reductions in such disorders?
- Which of the potential interventions are *feasible* and most readily *adopted*?
- What are the *costs* of the various promising interventions, relative to their likely *effectiveness?*

Adapted from: DHHS, *Third National Injury Control Conference* (1992).

support of healthy family functioning programs in the community, educational programs for physicians regarding prescribing practices for potentially lethal medications, development of national standards for nursing home care, and creation of community volunteer programs for the unemployed and retired.

The future reduction of suicidal behaviors will be dependent on a number of variables, not least of which will be political will and societal pressures to support large-scale, multidimensional, long-term efforts. Patience and persistence will be critical attributes for prevention programs and prevention professionals. Successful translation of theory and concepts into practical programs that are well received by target populations is critical (Kelly, Dassoff, Levin, Schreckengost, & Altman, 1988). Much will depend on the elegance and appropriate application of evaluation research and cost-effectiveness and cost-benefit analyses to the programs being administered. We are on the verge of clarifying concepts of risk reduction, risk factors, protective factors, cumulative effects of comorbidity, etiology and pathogenesis of maladaptive behaviors and sequences, and measurement of outcome variables over time (Mrazek & Haggerty, 1994). With such advances in the next few years, we will have available the necessary armamentarium to launch a full-scale attack on the incidence and prevalence of suicidal behaviors. We look forward to the year 2000.

## REFERENCES

Albee, G. W. (1982). Preventing Psychopathology and promoting human potential. *American Psychologist, 37,* 1043–1050.

American Psychiatric Association. Task Force on Prevention Research. (1990). Report of the APA task force on prevention research. *American Journal of Psychiatry, 147,* 1701–1704.

American Public Health Association (APHA). (1991). *Healthy communities 2000: Model standards* (3rd ed.). Washington, DC: Author.

Bloom, B. L. (1986). Primary prevention: An overview. In J. T. Barter and S. W. Talbott (Eds.), *Primary prevention in psychiatry: State of the art* (pp. 3–12). Washington, DC: American Psychiatric Press.

Blumenthal, S. J., & Kupfer, D. J. (1988). Clinical assessment and treatment of youth suicidal behavior. *Journal of Youth and Adolescence, 17,* 1–24.

Coie, J. D., Watt, N. F., West, S. G., Hawkins, J. D., Asarnow, J. G., Markman, H. J., Ramey, S. L. Shure, M. B., & Long, B. (1993). The science of prevention: A conceptual framework and some directions for a national research program. *American Psychologist, 48*(10), 1013–1022.

Cowen, E. L. (1983). Primary prevention in mental health: Past, present, and future. In R. D. Felner, L. A. Jason, J. N. Moritsugu, & S. S. Farber (Eds.), *Preventive psychology: Theory, research, and practice* (pp. 11–25). New York: Pergamon Press.

Department of Health and Human Services (DHHS). (1991). *Healthy People 2000: National health promotion and disease prevention objectives* (DHHS Publ. No. (PHS) 91-50212). Washington, DC: U.S. Government Printing Office.

Department of Health and Human Services. (1992). *The third national injury control conference* (DHHS Publ. No. 1992-634-666). Washington, DC: U.S. Government Printing Office.

Dulit, R. A., & Michels, R. (1992). Psychodynamics and Suicide. In D. Jacobs (Ed.), *Suicide and clinical practice* (pp. 43–54). Washington, DC: American Psychiatric Press.

Felner, R. D., Adan, A. M., & Silverman, M. M. (1992). Risk assessment and prevention of youth suicide in schools and educational contexts. In R.

W. Maris, A. L. Berman, J. T. Maltsberger, & R. I. Yufit (Eds.), *Assessment and prediction of suicide* (pp. 420–447). New York: Guilford Press.

Felner, R. D., & Felner, T. Y. (1989). Primary prevention programs in the educational context: A transactional–ecological framework and analysis. In L. Bond & B. Compas (Ed.), *Primary prevention and promotion in the schools.* Newbury Park, CA: Sage Publications.

Felner, R. D., Jason, L. A., Moritsugu, J. N., & Farber, S. S. (Eds.). (1983). *Preventive psychology: Theory, research, and practice.* New York: Pergamon Press.

Felner, R. D., & Silverman, M. M. (1989). Primary prevention: A consideration of general principles and findings for the prevention of youth suicide. In *Report of the secretary's task force on youth suicide.* Vol. 3: *Prevention and interventions in youth suicide* (pp. 23–30) (DHHS Publ. No. ADM 89-1623). Washington, DC: U.S. Government Printing Office.

Felner, R. D., Silverman, M. M., & Felner, T. Y. (in press). Prevention in mental health and social intervention: Conceptual and methodological issues in the evolution of the science and practice of prevention. In J. Rappaport & E. Seidman (Eds.), *Handbook of community psychology.* New York: Plenum Press.

Flitcraft, A. H. (1992). Violence, values, and gender. *Journal of the American Medical Association, 267*(3), 3194–3195.

Freeman, A., & Reinecke, M. (1993). *Cognitive Therapy for Suicidal Behavior.* New York: Springer.

Gerberich, S. G., Hays, M., Mandel, J. S., Gibson, R. W., & Van der Heide, C. J. (1985). Analysis of suicides in adolescents and young adults: Implications for prevention. In U. Laaser, R. Senault, & H. Viefhues (Eds.), *Primary health care in the making* (pp. 137–145). Berlin: Springer-Verlag.

Goldblatt, M., & Schatzberg, A. (1992). Medication and the suicidal patient. In D. Jacobs (Ed.), *Suicide and clinical practice* (pp. 23–42). Washington, DC: American Psychiatric Press.

Gordon, R. S. (1983). An operational classification of disease prevention. *Public Health Reports, 98,* 107–109.

Gould, M. S., Shaffer, D., Fisher, P., Kleinman, M., & Morishima, A. (1992). The clinical prediction of adolescent suicide. In R. W. Maris, A. L. Berman, J. T. Maltsberger, & R. I. Yufit (Eds.), *Assessment and prediction of suicide* (pp. 130–143). New York: Guilford Press.

Haddon, W., Jr. (1967). The prevention of accidents. In D. M. Clark & B. MacMahon (Eds.), *Preventive medicine.* Boston: Little, Brown.

Haddon, W., Jr. (1968). The changing approach to the epidemiology, prevention, and amelioration of trauma: The transition to approaches etiologically rather than descriptively based. *American Journal of Public Health, 58,* 1431–1438.

Haddon, W., Jr. (1980). Advances in epidemiology of injuries as a basis for public policy. *Public Health Reports, 95,* 411–421.

Haddon, W., Jr., & Baker, S. P. (1981). Injury control. In D. W. Clarke & B. MacMahon (Eds.), *Pre-*

*ventive and community medicine* (pp. 109–140). Boston: Little, Brown.

Institute of Medicine. (1985). *Injury in America: A continuing public health problem.* Washington, DC: National Academy Press.

Kellermann, A. L., Lee, R. K., Mercy, J. A., & Banton, J. (1991). The epidemiologic basis for the prevention of firearm injuries. *Annual Review of Public Health, 12,* 17–40.

Kelly, J. G., Dassoff, N., Levin, I., Schreckengost, S. P., & Altman, B. E. (1988). A guide to conducting prevention research in a community: First steps. New York: Haworth Press.

Kreitman, N. (1976). The coal gas story: United Kingdom suicides rates, 1960–71. *British Journal of Preventive and Social Medicine, 30,* 86–93.

Kuhn, T. S. (1970). The structure of scientific revolutions (2nd ed.). Chicago, IL: University of Chicago Press.

Lester, D. (1990). The effect of detoxification of domestic gas in Switzerland on the suicide rate. *Acta Psychiatrica Scandinavia, 82,* 383–384.

Lester, D., & Abe, K. (1989). The effect of restricting access to lethal means for suicide: A study of suicide by domestic gas in Japan. *Acta Psychiatrica Scandinavia, 80,* 198–182.

Linehan, M. M., Armstrong, H. E., Suarez, A., Allman, D., & Heard, H. L. (1991). Cognitive-behavioral treatment of chronically parasuicidal borderline patients. *Archives of General Psychiatry, 48*(12), 1060–1064.

Maris, R. W. (Ed.). (1986). *Biology of suicide.* New York: Guilford Press.

Maris, R. W., Berman, A. L., Maltsberger, J. T., & Yufits, R. I. (Eds.). (1992). *The assessment and prediction of suicide.* New York: Guilford Press.

Marzuk, P. M., Tardiff, K., & Hirsch, C. S. (1992). The epidemiology of murder–suicide. *Journal of the American Medical Association, 267*(23), 3179–3183.

Motto, J. A. (1965). Suicide attempts: A longitudinal view. *Archives of General Psychiatry, 13,* 516–520.

Mrazek, P. J., & Haggerty, R. J. (Eds.). (1994). Reducing risks for mental disorders: Frontiers for preventive intervention research. Washington, DC: National Academy Press.

Ottosson, J.-O. (1979). The suicidal patient – Can the psychiatrist prevent his suicide? In M. Schou & E. Stromgren (Eds.), *Origin, prevention and treatment of affective disorders* (pp. 257–267). New York: Academic Press.

Pardes, H., Silverman, M. M., & West, A. (1989). Prevention and the field of mental health: A psychiatric perspective. In L. Breslow, J. E. Fielding, & L. B. Lave (Eds.), *Annual review of public health,* Vol. 10 (pp. 403–422). Palo Alto, CA: Annual Reviews.

Pokorny, A. D. (1983). Prediction of suicide in psychiatric patients. Report of a prospective study. *Archives of General Psychiatry, 40,* 249–257.

Pokorny, A. D. (1992). Prediction of suicide in psychiatric patients: Report of a prospective study. In R. W. Maris, A. L. Berman, J. T. Maltsberger, & R. I. Yufit (Eds.), *Assessment and prediction of suicide* (pp. 105–129). New York: Guilford Press.

Rappaport, J. (1987). Terms of empowerment/exemplars of prevention: Toward a theory for community psychology. *American Journal of Community Psychology, 15*, 121–148.

Richman, J. (1985). Family therapy for suicidal people. New York: Springer Publishing Company.

Robertson, L. S. (1975). Behavioral research and strategies in public health: A demur. *Social Science and Medicine, 9*: 165–170.

Robertson, L. S. (1983). *Injuries: Causes, control strategies, and public policy.* Lexington, MA: Lexington Books.

Robertson, L. S. (1986). Injury. In B. A. Edelstein & L. Michelson (Eds.), *Handbook of prevention* (pp. 343–360). New York: Plenum Press.

Seidman, E. (1987). Toward a framework for primary prevention research. In J. A. Steinberg & M. M. Silverman (Eds.), *Preventing mental disorders: A research perspective* (pp. 2–19) (DHHS Publ. No. ADM 87-1492). Washington, DC: U.S. Government Printing Office.

Silverman, M. M., & Koretz, D. S. (1989). Preventing mental health problems. In R. E. K. Stein (Ed.), *Caring for children with chronic illness: Issues and strategies* (pp. 213–229). New York: Springer.

Vincent, T. A., & Trickett, E. J. (1983). Preventive interventions and the human context: Ecological approaches to environmental assessment and change. In R. Felner, L. Jason, J. Moritsugu, & S. Farber (Eds.), *Preventive psychology: Theory, research, and practice* (pp. 67–86). New York: Pergamon Press.

# 2

# Epidemiology of Suicidal Behavior

## Eve K. Mościcki, ScD, MPH

This paper presents the epidemiology of suicide and discusses the known risk factors for suicide within a framework designed to encourage a systematic approach to theory testing and prevention. Mental and addictive disorders are the most powerful of the multiple risk factors for suicide in all age groups. Since risk factors for suicide rarely occur in isolation, prevention efforts are more likely to succeed if multiple risk factors are targeted.

The purpose of this discussion of the epidemiology of suicide is, first, to describe the rates of occurrence for suicide mortality and morbidity and, second, to discuss the known risk factors for suicide within a framework that will permit a systematic approach to theory testing and prevention.

Epidemiologic and clinical research work in complementary fashion to increase our understanding of disease. Epidemiology is the basic science of prevention. It is the study of patterns of diseases and disorders in groups (Lilienfeld & Lilienfeld, 1980). Data from *descriptive epidemiology* are widely used by epidemiologists and nonepidemiologists alike to generate estimates of prevalence and incidence of diseases and disorders. Most epidemiologic research goes far beyond the mere description of the distribution of disease occurrence in the population, however. *Analytic* (including *experimental*) *epidemiology* focuses on the systematic investigation of causal relationships between risk factors, or exposures, and disease outcomes (Kleinbaum, Kupper, &

Morgenstern, 1982). The high methodologic standards mandated by epidemiologic paradigms permit rigorous hypothesis and theory testing using both simple and sophisticated statistical techniques. Epidemiologic designs in studies of both clinical and community populations make possible not only the identification of independent risk factors, but also a quantification of their relative contribution to the risk of disease or disorder (Mościcki, 1989). Recent epidemiologic studies have made important contributions to our knowledge of suicide and suicidal behavior (Brent et al., 1988; Henriksson et al., 1993; Mościcki, O'Carroll, Locke, Rae, Roy, & Regier, 1989; Rich, Young, & Fowler, 1986; Younger, Clark, Oehmig-Lindroth, & Stein, 1990).

## ISSUES IN THE CLASSIFICATION OF MORTALITY AND MORBIDITY

Information on incidence of completed suicide is derived from mortality data. There are no worldwide, standardized cri-

Eve K. Mościcki is with the National Institute of Mental Health.

Address correspondence to the author at the Prevention Research Branch, National Institute of Mental Health, Room 10-85, 5600 Fishers Lane, Rockville, MD 20857. Fax: 301/443-4045; e-mail: emoscick@aoamh2.ssw.dhhs.gov.

This work was supported in part by the cooperative agreements of the Epidemiologic Catchment Area Program (ECA): U01 MH34224, U01 MH33870, U01 MH33883, U01 MH35386, and U01 MH35865. The ECA is a series of five epidemiologic research studies performed by independent research teams in collaboration with NIMH. Portions of this paper were presented at the workshop on the Study of Suicide and Aging: Evolving Questions in a Life Course Perspective, July 1992, National Institute of Mental Health, Rockville, MD; at the annual meeting of the American College of Epidemiology, Bethesda, MD, September 1992; at the Second World Conference on Injury Control, Atlanta, GA, May 1993; and at the annual meeting of the American Association of Suicidology, New York, NY, April 1994.

teria for the classification and reporting of suicide deaths, however. Some nations report age-adjusted rates, others report crude rates, while still others report numbers of deaths but no death rates (World Health Organization – WHO, 1993). The quality of data on suicide and suicidal behaviors varies tremendously, and can affect estimates of occurrence within as well as between nations. The variability in data quality also affects the accuracy of information on risk factors, and thus decisions about preventive intervention strategies.

In the United States, national mortality data are based on standardized death certificate information. Criteria for classifying a death as a suicide differ based on the health jurisdiction reporting the data from each State. Reporting officials can range from an elected coroner who is also the village funeral director to a medical examiner with a medical degree, a highly sophisticated automated data system, and a university appointment. The objective determination of suicide can be complicated by the emotion and social stigma associated with the act of killing oneself, and by the impact a suicide death has on the family and community of the deceased. Numerous authors (e.g., Blumenthal, 1988) have therefore asserted that suicide deaths are vastly underreported, but without providing empirical evidence to support their claims. Population-based, epidemiologic studies of suicides that included a reexamination of death certificates (e.g., Brent, Perper, & Allman, 1987; Ford, Rushforth, Rushforth, Hirsch, & Adelson, 1979) have found that any underreporting has consistently been in far more modest proportions than has been claimed by some. Officially reported mortality data are considered reasonably sound and can be used to study risk factors and correlates of completed suicide (Monk, 1987; O'Carroll, 1989; Sainsbury & Jenkins, 1982). Recently, operational criteria for the classification of a death as a suicide have been established in the U.S. (Rosenberg et al., 1988), and their application is expected to resolve many classification issues.

The U.S. has no comparable system for classification and collection of data on suicide morbidity. The lack of a consistent definition has resulted in great variability in estimates of various suicidal behaviors. The most reliable data come from surveys of psychiatric morbidity in community samples (Andrews & Lewinsohn 1992; Garrison, McKeown, Valois, & Vincent, 1993; Meehan, Lamb, Saltzman, & O'Carroll, 1992; Mościcki, O'Carroll, Regier, Ray, Roy, & Locke, 1988; Paykel, Myers, Lindenthal, & Tanner, 1974) that contain questions about operationally defined suicidal behaviors, although even these need to be interpreted with caution. One major difficulty with collecting standardized data on suicide morbidity is the measurement of suicidal intent (Garrison 1989; Garrison, Lewinsohn, Marsteller, Langhinrichsen, & Lann, 1991; Meehan et al., 1992; Mościcki et al. 1988). Such information is of great importance, however, because self-inflicted injuries that are labeled as attempted suicides can range in severity from a "cry for help" to a genuine failed suicide. The use of medical lethality as an index of severity has been used in recent studies and appears to be an acceptable and objective method of distinguishing between failed suicides and cries for help (Andrews & Lewinsohn, 1992; Brent et al., 1987; Garrison et al., 1993; Meehan et al., 1992; Pedinielli, Delahousse, & Chabaud, 1989).

## COMPLETED SUICIDES

Suicide is the eighth leading cause of death in the United States. In 1991, the most recent year for which final mortality data are available, there were 30,810 suicide deaths, representing 1.4% of the total number of deaths (National Center for Health Statistics – NCHS, 1994). The age-adjusted suicide rate was 11.4/100,000, similar to the death rate from diabetes mellitus (11.8/100,000). These rates are substantially lower than the rates for the leading cause of death, diseases of the heart, at 148.2 /100,000. Suicide rates vary widely from state to state, and in

1991 ranged from 5.7/100,000 in the District of Columbia, and 6.6/100,000 in New Jersey, to 24.8/100,000 in Nevada. Traditionally, suicide rates have been highest in western states, with Vermont the single eastern exception among the top ten. Suicide, with homicide, is the third leading cause of years of potential life lost (YPLL) in the U.S. (Centers for Disease Control – CDC, 1993).

Overall, U.S. suicide rates tend to be lower than rates in many other industrialized nations in the world (*Statistical Bulletin*, 1990). The same nations tend to experience the lowest and highest suicide rates over time. Among industrialized nations, the lowest age-adjusted rates for both men and women are found in Greece, Mexico, and the Netherlands (WHO, 1993). The highest rates for both genders are in Hungary. The 1991 age-adjusted suicide rates for Hungarian men were 46.8/100,000; the rates for women were 13.8/100,000. In contrast, U.S. rates in 1991 were 18.8/100,000 for men and 4.3/100,000 for women. Figure 1 shows age-adjusted suicide rates for selected WHO member nations reporting for 1990 and 1991 (WHO, 1993).

In the United States, as well as worldwide, suicide rates differ by age, gender, race, socioeconomic status, and marital status. In general, suicide rates in most industrialized nations increase with age, with the highest suicide rates among persons over the age of 65. However, suicide is never among the leading causes of death among the elderly, who are far more likely to die from chronic and infectious diseases than from external causes. For example, in the United States, the 1991 suicide rates for persons 65–74 and 75–84 years of age were 16.9/100,000 and 23.5/100,000, respectively (NCHS, 1994). These rates are far lower than the death rate for diseases of the heart at 148.2/100,000 which is the leading cause of death for persons 65 years and over. (See McIntosh's paper in this issue for a fuller discussion of elderly suicides.) In contrast, the suicide rate for persons 15–24 was 13.1/100,000. Suicide is the third leading cause of death in this age group, following unintentional injuries and homicide.

Figure 2 shows 1991 rates of suicide in the U.S. by age, gender, and race. Men are much more likely to commit suicide than are women. The ratio of male to female suicide rates in the U.S. has increased gradually from 3.1 in 1979 to over 4.1 in 1991 (NCHS, 1994). Over 70% of all suicides in the U.S. are committed by white men (73% in 1991), with the highest suicide rates occurring among elderly white men

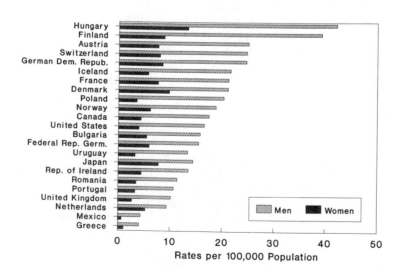

Figure 1.   Age-adjusted suicide rates per 100,000 population for men and women for selected member nations of the World Health Organization, 1990 and 1991.

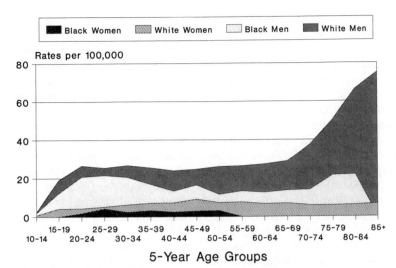

Figure 2.   Suicide rates per 100,000 population by 5-year age group, race, and gender, United States, 1991.

(75.1/100,000 for men 85 years of age and over in 1991) (NCHS, 1994). Nonwhite men are also at risk, however, with the risk being as high in the younger age groups (20–34 years) as it is in oldest age groups (75–84 years), with lower rates in the middle age groups. This pattern is comparable to that found among American Indians and Alaska natives, who have the highest rates of any ethnic group in the United States. The 1987–1989 running average rate for Indian and Alaska native men aged 15–24 was 64.0/100,000; the comparable rate in these groups for men 75–84 years of age was 4.3/100,000 (Indian Health Service – IHS, 1993).

Significant age effects are evident in suicide rates when period and cohort effects are controlled for. Manton, Blazer, and Woodbury (1987) found that suicide rates peaked for white men at midlife and again around age 80. This was in contrast to rates for white women, which peaked in midlife, and for nonwhite men and women, which peaked in young adult life. Period effects, controlling for age and cohort, indicated that suicide rates were highest in the 1970s and in general did not differ between race–gender groups. Cohort effects, controlling for age and period, also showed few differences between race–gender groups. However, cohort effects suggested that suicide rates are high for two

population groups: persons born before World War I who are now in the "oldest-old" group, or persons born after World War II, the "baby boomers."

## Method

Across all age groups, the most common method used to commit suicide in the United States in both genders is by means of firearms. Firearms consistently account for nearly 60% of all suicide deaths. It is the method of choice for both men and women, followed by drugs and medicaments for women, and hanging for men. Of all firearm suicides, nearly 80% are committed by white men. Between 1980 and 1986, the rate of suicide by firearms among men and women over 65 increased from 60% to 66% (Meehan, Saltzman, & Sattin, 1991). In the U.S., hanging is the second most common method of suicide in both age groups. Firearms are much less readily available to the public in other countries than they are in the United States. Where firearm availability is limited, hanging, suffocation, and poisoning are the most frequently reported methods of suicide.

## ATTEMPTED SUICIDE

Although completed and attempted suicides have common characteristics, there also are important differences, limiting the generalizability of findings between populations of completers and attempters. One important difference is that nearly 80% of suicide completers are men, while the majority of attempters are women. Another is that not all attempters injure themselves with the intent to die. Even when there is a strong intent to die, not all attempters injure themselves severely enough to cause death (Meehan et al., 1992). However it is defined (or not, in many studies), attempted suicide is an extreme form of behavior and an expression of distress that in and of itself merits study.

There are no national, population-based data on attempted suicide. Population-based data on attempted suicides in any age group are infrequently reported (Garrison, 1989; Mościcki, 1989). Estimates of lifetime prevalence of attempts in adults range from 1.1 to 4.3 per 100; estimates of 12-month prevalence of attempts range from 0.3 to 0.8 per 100 (Mościcki, 1988; Paykel et al., 1974; Ramsay & Bagley, 1985; Schwab, Warheit, & Holzer, 1972). Recent U.S. studies that have incorporated a measure of lethality report low estimates of lethal and/or intentional attempts among adolescents, ranging from 1.6 to 2.6 per 100 (Andrews & Lewinsohn 1992; Garrison et al. 1993; Meehan et al. 1992).

Petronis, Samuels, Mościcki, & Anthony (1990) analyzed data from the National Institute of Mental Health Epidemiologic Catchment Area Study (ECA), a landmark psychiatric survey of 18,571 adults in five communities. Data were collected in two waves, approximately 1 year apart. The rate of incident suicide attempts in the year prior to the baseline interview was 22/10,000; the rate in the year prior to the follow-up interview was 19/10,000. There were no significant gender or age differences. A comparison of these data with age-adjusted suicide mortality data suggests that there were approximately 18 attempts to 1 suicide completion in the early 1980s (the time period during which the ECA data were collected). When stratified by gender, how-

ever, the estimated ratio is 8:1 for men and 59:1 for women. The higher ratio of attempts to completions for women reflects the fact that, although incident attempt rates for men and women are similar, women have much lower rates of completed suicide than do men.

Andrews and Lewinsohn (1992) conducted a detailed study of psychiatric disorders in a representative cohort ($n = 1710$) of high school students in five communities in west central Oregon. The lifetime rate of attempted suicide at baseline was 7.1%; the rate for females, 10.1%, was significantly greater than the rate for males, 3.8%. At follow-up, 2.2% of females and 1.1% of males reported having attempted suicide in the 12-month period prior to interview, but the gender differences were not statistically significant. Thirteen (0.7%) of the attempts reported by 121 adolescents were considered medically lethal, and 6 (0.35%) were given the highest rating on intent to die. Lethality and intent were significantly correlated (0.67). There were no gender differences in lethality. Medical lethality and intent for the follow-up period were not reported.

In contrast to completed suicides, lifetime prevalence of attempted suicide is significantly more frequent among women and girls, regardless of race or ethnicity (Andrews & Lewinsohn, 1992; Garrison et al., 1993; Mościcki et al., 1988). Gender has not been found to be significantly associated with incident attempts, however (Andrews & Lewinsohn, 1992; Petronis, Samuels, Mościcki, & Anthony, 1990). Various explanations have been proposed to account for the differences in lifetime rates between males and females (Mościcki, 1994). It may be that females are better reporters of their health history, and therefore are more likely to recall salient lifetime events such as attempted suicides. Likewise, females are more likely than males to suffer from depression and may be more likely to use self-inflicted injury as an expression of distress and signal for help, which would be reported as a suicide attempt. On the other hand, males may attempt suicide with the same frequency as females, but with greater intent and lethality, thus resulting in differential mortality. (See Canetto and Lester, this issue, for an expanded discussion of gender issues.)

Attempts are reported more frequently among Whites than non-Whites (Garrison et al., 1993; Mościcki et al., 1988), although the reasons for the difference are not clear. Garrison et al. (1993) found that, although frequency of attempts was higher among White than among Black high school girls, attempts requiring medical treatment were reported most frequently among black girls. Mościcki et al. (1988) found that the risk of attempted suicide in the ECA was significantly lower in both black and Hispanic adults than in non-black/non-Hispanic adults. Medical lethality was not ascertained.

## Method

Little information on methods of attempted suicide is available from community studies. The most common method reported from hospital-based studies is self-medication and drug overdose, accounting for over 70% of all attempts (Andrus et al., 1991; Weissman, 1974). Andrews and Lewinsohn (1992) reported that the most common method used by adolescents to attempt suicide was ingestion of pills, followed by cutting of wrists or other parts of the body. It should be noted that these methods are distinct from the most common methods used in completed suicides, although ingestion of pills is also a frequent method of completed suicide among women.

## RISK FACTORS FOR COMPLETED AND ATTEMPTED SUICIDES

Systematic efforts to understand suicide began with Durkheim's classic work in the late 19th century (Durkheim, 1897/1951). An important indicator of how much progress we have made since then in our understanding of suicide and in suicide prevention is our scientifically based knowledge of risk factors. With increasingly rigorous research efforts, including the application of multivariate models in epidemiologic

studies of both completed and attempted suicide, has come increasing understanding of the multiple, interrelated risk factors for suicide. On one hand, the complex nature of suicide suggests that complex and elaborate interventions are necessary for prevention; on the other hand, it implies that preventive interventions can be targeted and tested at a number of points in a theoretical model.

There is evidence that the majority of suicidal behaviors occur on a continuum of severity that proceeds from less serious and more prevalent behaviors through increasingly severe and less prevalent behaviors. At one end are included behaviors such as casual ideation without specific plans. These behaviors may progress in some individuals through ideation that includes a plan, self-inflicted injury without intent to die, and, for a very small proportion of persons at the other end of the continuum, to failed suicide and completion (Andrews & Lewinsohn, 1992; Garland and Zigler 1993; Mościcki et al., 1989).

Information on risk factors and correlates of completed suicide and suicidal behaviors is derived from various sources, including analyses of national mortality data, population-based psychological autopsy studies from selected geographic areas, population-based surveys of psychiatric morbidity, and studies based on clinical populations. Because of the biases and lack of generalizability associated with nonepidemiologic studies of clinical populations (Feinstein, 1977), most of the findings reviewed here are from analytic epidemiologic studies, particularly population-based psychological autopsies and morbidity studies of representative samples, which used standardized psychiatric criteria (e.g., DSM-III-R: American Psychiatric Association – APA, 1987) and other measures. With a few notable exceptions (e.g., Runeson, 1989), the majority of such studies have been conducted in the United States.

### Framework for Risk Factors

For prevention purposes, the construction of a plausible epidemiologic framework for the many risk factors for suicide is as important as understanding the actual risk factors themselves. A framework will not only enhance our understanding of the contribution of various risk factors, but can also facilitate prevention efforts. One useful way to think about risk factors is in terms of *proximal* and *distal*. Distal risk factors represent the foundation upon which suicidal behavior is built. They represent a threshold that increases individual risk for later vulnerability to proximal risk factors. Distal risk factors are not limited to suicide but can produce multiple adverse physical and mental health outcomes. Their relationship to suicide is indirect; they are considered necessary, but not sufficient, for suicide to occur (Rich et al., 1986). Proximal risk factors, on the other hand, are those factors more closely associated with the suicide event itself. They are more closely related temporally to the suicidal event itself and can act as precipitants. In and of themselves, proximal risk factors are neither necessary nor sufficient for suicide. The combination of powerful distal risk factors with proximal events, however, can lead to the necessary and sufficient conditions for suicide.

Distal and proximal risk factors can be loosely grouped into psychiatric, biological, familial, and situational. These groupings are not mutually exclusive. Both distal and proximal risk factors can and do co-occur in individual, family, and environmental domains, and their co-occurrence is likely to be associated with the greatest risk for suicide (Henriksson et al., 1993; Rich & Runeson, 1992). It is important to note that many individuals may have one or more risk factors and not be suicidal; on the other hand, the likelihood of suicide or suicidal behavior increases with an increasing number of risk factors. Most psychiatric, biological, and familial risk factors associated with suicide can be thought of as distal. Many situational risk factors are proximal. Such "triggering" events are likely to differ with age, gender, ethnicity, and other sociodemographic factors. The conceptual distinction between distal and proximal risk factors assumes practical importance when planning prevention programs, since the strategies employed, and their potential effectiveness, are likely to differ depending on the nature of the targeted risk factors. (See Felner, this issue, for a broader discussion of risk factors.)

## Psychopathology

Mental and addictive disorders are central risk factors for suicide and suicidal behavior. Findings from psychological autopsy studies from the United States and Sweden indicate that more than 90% of completed suicides in all age groups are associated with mental or addictive disorders (Brent, 1987; Rich et al., 1986; Runeson, 1989). Likewise, a psychiatric disorder is the strongest observed risk factor for attempted suicide in all age groups (Andrews & Lewinsohn, 1992; Brent et al., 1988; Mościcki et al., 1988). Mental disorders are a necessary cause for suicide (Rich et al., 1986; Shaffer, Garland, Gould, Fisher, & Trautman, 1988). They are not sufficient, however, since the majority of individuals with mental disorders do not die by suicide. Mental and addictive disorders provide the major context for suicide and suicidal behavior, and an understanding of these as underlying risk factors is fundamental to the understanding, prediction, and prevention of suicide.

The most frequently found disorders in psychological autopsy studies of completed adolescent suicides are affective disorders, conduct disorder or antisocial personality, and substance abuse disorder (Brent et al., 1988; Rich et al., 1986; Shaffer et al., 1988). Behavioral disorders such as antisocial personality and conduct disorder are found in much larger proportions in adolescent suicides than in older suicides, which are dominated by mood disorders (Barraclough, 1971; Brent, 1987; Rich et al., 1986). Conwell (1991) suggests that the proportion of suicides associated with affective disorder increases with the age of the suicide. Depression, substance abuse, and aggressive behavior disorders have also been found to distinguish suicide attempters from nonattempters in controlled studies of youth (Andrews & Lewinsohn, 1992; Brent et al., 1993; Garrison et al., 1993).

Comorbid diagnoses—that is, more than one psychiatric diagnosis or co-occurrence of psychiatric and substance abuse disorder, and high levels of psychiatric symptoms in addition to a primary diagnosis—occur in a large proportion of suicides (Brent et al., 1988; Henriksson et al., 1993; Rich & Runeson, 1992; Rich et al., 1986; Shafii, Carrigan, Whittinghill, & Derrick, 1985). Hopelessness has been identified as a strong indicator of suicide potential (Beck et al., 1985, 1990). These findings, along with evidence from studies of suicide attempters (Mościcki, 1994), imply that suicidal behaviors are associated with more severe forms of mental illness. Andrews and Lewinsohn (1992), for example, found that, among adolescents with a DSM-III-R diagnosis of affective disorder, suicide attempters had significantly higher levels of psychiatric symptoms than did nonattempters even after symptoms related to suicide were eliminated.

Prior suicide attempts are strong risk factors for completed suicide (Rich et al., 1986; Robins, Murphy, Wilkinson, Gassner, and Kayes, 1959) and, in retrospective studies, may be the best single predictor of completed suicide (Shaffer et al., 1988).A history of attempts generally is not clinically reliable, however, in individuals at immediate risk for completed suicide, especially youth, since it will generate a large proportion of false positives. There are several explanations for this. First, the majority of suicide attempters do not intend to die (Meehan et al., 1992). Second, the ratio of attempted to completed suicides in children and adolescents is considerably higher than among older persons (Andrus et al., 1991; Mościcki, 1994), thus diluting the clinical predictability for completed suicides in the population. Third, outside of clinic-based studies, there is considerable inconsistency in defining attempted suicide. The need to apply standardized terminology in the study of suicidal behavior was identified in the literature nearly 20 years ago (Beck, Resnick, & Lettieri, 1974) but has re-mained largely unaddressed (Garrison, 1989; Garrison et al., 1991; Mościcki, 1989).

Interestingly, there is some evidence from clinical studies that attempted suicide may be a much stronger predictor of later suicide for elderly patients than it is for younger patients (Maris, 1992). Unlike younger attempters and completers, clinical and sociodemographic factors associated with elderly attempters closely resemble those associated with elderly completers (Frierson, 1991; Merrill & Owens, 1990). Unpublished data from the ECA indicate that the ratio of suicide attempts to completions is lower for persons over 65 than for any other age group (Mościcki, in press).

## Substance Abuse

Substance abuse plays a major role in suicide. It has been found in the majority of cases of completed and attempted suicide, and can act as either a distal or proximal risk factor (Andrews & Lewinsohn, 1992; Brent et al., 1987, 1988; Garrison et al., 1993; Rich et al., 1986; Shaffer et al., 1988; Shafii et al., 1985). It is associated with greater frequency and repetitiveness of suicide attempts, more medically lethal attempts, more serious suicidal intent, and higher levels of suicidal ideation (Crumley, 1990). History of abuse of alcohol or other drugs, with or without a comorbid mood disorder, is the most frequently identified form of substance abuse in completions and attempts (Andrews & Lewinsohn, 1992; Brent et al., 1987, 1988; Garrison et al., 1993; Rich et al., 1986). Multiple substance abuse has been found in most cases, usually alcohol coupled with cocaine and/or marijuana (Fowler, Rich & Young, 1986; Garrison et al., 1993; Marzuk et al., 1992). In addition, intoxication at the time of death, most frequently with alcohol, is a highly significant correlate of suicide and has been found in approximately half of youthful suicides (Fowler et al., 1986; Hlady & Middaugh, 1988; Hoberman & Garfinkel, 1988; Rich et al., 1986; Shaffer et al., 1988). Recent findings suggest that cocaine can also play a major role in suicides that occur in geographic areas where it is readily available (Marzuk et al., 1992), as well as independently increasing risk for attempted suicide (Petronis et al., 1990).

## Biological Risk Factors

Neurochemical studies of adult suicide attempters and completers have consistently found evidence of serotonergic dysfunction (Mann, Stanley, McBride, & McEwen, 1986). Postmortem studies of the brains of suicide completers report lower brainstem levels of serotonin (5-HT) and/or its metabolite, 5-hydroxyindoleacetic acid (5-HIAA) (Coccaro et al., 1989; Mann et al., 1986; Stanley & Stanley, 1989) and localized changes in $5\text{-}HT_2$ receptors in the prefrontal cortex. Clinical studies of serious suicide attempters also have found decreased levels of 5-HIAA (Asberg, 1989; Brown & Goodwin, 1986). The exact relationship between reduced serotonergic activity and suicide has not been elucidated. It is not clear whether the effect is direct, or whether it is mediated through specific psychiatric disorders. Stanley and Stanley (1989), for example, note that the association between serotonergic dysfunction and suicidal behavior crosses diagnostic categories. They speculate that two distinct conditions may be needed for suicide to occur: first, an underlying psychiatric diagnosis such as depression, schizophrenia, or personality disorder, and second, a disturbance in serotonergic functioning. Arango (Arango et al., 1990) and Cocarro (Coccaro et al., 1989), on the other hand, suggest that the observed serotonergic changes may not be specifically associated with suicidal behaviors, but with more general characteristics such as impulsivity or threshold for violence. It is not known whether the effect is state or trait dependent, nor whether it is consistent across all age groups.

## Familial Risk Factors

A family history of suicide and/or of mental or substance abuse disorder is a distal risk factor that has been associated with suicide or suicidal behavior in the index case (Egeland and Sussex, 1985; Roy, 1989; Shaffer et al., 1988). Effects of family history may be mediated through shared biological vulnerability or through a shared family environment that may produce adverse outcomes. If the risk is biological, it is not clear if there is a genetic predisposition for suicide per se or, more likely, a genetic vulnerability to mental disorder that underlies potential suicidal behavior (Roy, Segal, Centerwall, & Robinette, 1991). Some investigators have suggested that one genetic factor that may contribute to suicide may be related to impulsivity (Kety, 1986; Roy et al., 1991). Whether family history differentially affects suicidal behavior by age has not been addressed.

A disrupted family environment as defined by separation, divorce, widowhood, or family violence, has also been associated with suicide. In terms of marital status, much higher suicide rates have been found for divorced and widowed persons than for married persons in all age groups, with age-adjusted rates of 34.9/100,000 and 33.2/100,000, respectively (Smith, Mercy, & Conn, 1988). Rates were highest for young widowers between 15 and 34 years of age. The patterns are similar for both Whites and Blacks (Smith et al., 1988). The role of parents' disrupted marital status as a risk factor for completed suicide in the child has not been systematically examined; however, absence of the father in the home environment has been linked with an increase in an adolescent's risk for attempted suicide (Andrews & Lewinsohn, 1992).

Family violence and physical and sexual abuse have been associated with completed and attempted suicides among young people, and can act as distal or proximal risk factors (Briere & Zaidi, 1989; de Wilde, Kienhorst, Diekstra, & Wolters 1991). Many biological and environmental risk factors associated with the family are interrelated. For example, families in which there are high rates of mental disorder and/or substance abuse, or high levels of psychiatric symptoms, are more likely to be dysfunctional, disorganized, violent, and abusive than are families without these characteristics, thus increasing the risk for suicidal behavior in the child or adolescent.

## Situational Risk Factors

Many situational risk factors are proximal to the suicidal event. In and of themselves, they are not sufficient for suicidal behavior. However, in combination with strong distal risk factors such as mental or addictive disorders, they may create the necessary and sufficient conditions that lead to suicide.

In the United States, one of the strongest of the situational risk factors is the presence of a firearm in the home (Brent et al., 1988, 1991; Kellerman & Reay, 1986; Kellerman et al., 1992). Keeping one or more guns in the home independently increases the risk of suicide for both genders and across all age groups, even after other strong risk factors, such depression and alcohol and drug abuse, are taken into account (Brent et al., 1988, 1991; Kellerman et al., 1992). In a case–control study of young suicides compared with demographically similar suicidal and nonsuicidal inpatient controls, Brent and colleagues (1991) found that the risk of completed suicide increased independently if a firearm was present in the home. In addition, there was no difference in level of risk with respect to the type of firearm used, or whether the weapon and ammunition were stored in separate locations (Brent et al., 1991).

Recent, severe, stressful life events – for example, the death of a spouse, other profound interpersonal loss or rejection, loss of employment, finding oneself in jail, or being diagnosed with acquired immune deficiency syndrome (AIDS) (Marzuk et al., 1988) – may be associated with suicide. The most frequently identified stressors in young suicides are interpersonal loss or conflict, economic problems, and legal problems (Rich, Fowler, Fogerty, & Young, 1988). Stressors in elderly suicides, on the other hand, may be more difficult to isolate. For example, Clark (1993) did not find unusually high levels of stressors present in a population-based sample of elderly suicides. Instead, Clark has suggested that some individuals may not be able to tolerate the cumulative strain of "acute but ordinary life stressors of aging," and a sufficient magnitude of stressors concurrent with major depression and/or substance use disorder may trigger a suicide.

Exposure to the suicidal behavior of others may lead to suicidal behavior in a vulnerable individual. Exposures may include behaviors of family members or peers (Brent et al., 1989; Davidson, Rosenberg, Mercy, Franklin, & Simmons, 1989) or originate in the media (Gould & Shaffer, 1986; Schmidtke & Hafner, 1988), although the effect of media exposure as a vehicle of suicide contagion is controversial (Davidson et al., 1989; Kessler, Downey, Milavsky, & Stipp, 1988). Young people may be at much greater risk from exposure effects than are adults (Schmidtke & Hafner, 1988; Gould et al., 1990a, 1990b). Studies of time–space suicide clusters – that is, an unusually high number of suicides that occur within a small geographic area and brief time period – suggest that nearly all clusters occur among adolescents and young adults, with limited evidence for clusters beyond age 24 (Gould et al., 1990a, 1990b). Clusters are rare occurrences in the U.S. and vary considerably by State and year, with estimates ranging between 1% and 13% of all adolescent suicides (Gould et al., 1990a, 1990b).

Another risk factor that may affect younger persons differentially is incarceration (U.S. Department of Health and Human Services – USDHHS, 1990). Suicide is a leading cause of death in jails and lockups (Hayes, 1989; Kerkhof & Bernasco, 1990; USDHHS, 1990). It is not clear if the high suicide rates among the incarcerated reflect specific vulnerability of younger persons, or if this is the age group which is more likely to be arrested and detained.

The role prescription medications can play in suicide and suicidal behavior among the elderly needs to be examined more fully. On one hand, drugs and medicaments together are the second most frequent method of suicide for elderly women (Meehan et al., 1991). On the other hand, depression may conceivably be a side effect of a poorly coordinated medication regimen for some elderly persons, especially if several different physicians prescribe medications incompatible with each other, without taking complete histories from their elderly patients (Sorenson, 1991).

## CONTROVERSIAL ISSUES

There are some commonly held misperceptions about risk factors for suicide that need to be addressed. The first of these is physical illness. It has long been believed that physical illness as a stressful life event is a risk factor for suicide, and that suicide can be a rational "way out" for the terminally ill. There is no evidence from appropriately designed studies that included measures of psychopathology that supports the notion that chronic or terminal physical illness at any age is an *independent* risk factor for suicide outside the context of depression and/or substance abuse (Barraclough, 1971; Clark, 1993; Rich et al., 1986). Identification and appropriate treatment of depressive symptoms in physically ill individuals may therefore be an important step in preventing suicides, especially among the elderly. (See Hendin, this issue, for a discussion of euthanasia in the terminally ill.)

A second misperception is that gay and lesbian youth account for a large proportion of suicides, and that sexual orientation is a major risk factor. This hypothesis has not been tested in carefully designed studies. Research on this issue is complicated by the lack of accurate information on the true rate of homosexuality in the population and by the strong emotions it generates in many otherwise objective discussions. In the San Diego Suicide Study, to date the only published population-based study to examine sexual orientation among suicide completers, only 13 of 283 consecutive suicides were gay (Rich

et al., 1986). The investigators found that there were no differences between homosexual and heterosexual men on rates of psychiatric diagnosis, prior attempts, stressors, social isolation, or legal trouble. The dominant finding among both gay and nongay suicides was the high rate of mental disorder and substance abuse. Based on this evidence, sexual orientation does not appear to be an independent risk factor for completed suicide. There is limited evidence that sexual orientation may increase risk for attempted suicide (e.g., Harry, 1989; Remafedi, Farrow, & Deisher, 1991); it is not clear, however, whether it independently contributes to increased risk. Unfortunately, no information is available from unbiased samples. This area needs more careful, objective investigation to determine if sexual orientation significantly and independently contributes to suicidal behavior.

A third misperception about risk for suicide is represented in the philosophy espoused by many so-called suicide prevention programs aimed at youth. Too often, such programs teach that suicide and suicidal behaviors occur in response to the many stressors experienced by adolescents in the process of growing up. They fail to recognize the critical role of poor mental health and substance abuse (Garland, Shaffer, & Whittle, 1989). There is no credible evidence that stressors in and of themselves produce suicidal behaviors.

## IMPLICATIONS FOR PREVENTION

Many of the risk factors for suicide reviewed here have been known since Durkheim's work was published nearly 100 years ago (Durkheim, 1897/1951). Despite our knowledge, we have not been able to demonstrate that the occurrence of suicide can be reduced by addressing only one major risk factor, or even several specific risk factors, one at a time. The epidemiologic evidence has consistently shown that suicide has multiple, interacting causes, and risk factors that frequently co-occur. It is essential to recognize that suicide is a complex, long-term outcome that requires complex theoretical models for appropriate study and complex interventions for effective prevention.

The best method for preventing suicide is likely to be one that includes a long-term approach designed to address the major distal risk factors in an integrated manner, and that includes the individual as well as his or her physical and psychosocial environment. The highest likelihood of success lies in well-designed, comprehensive programs focused on mental health and substance abuse. The greatest hope for preventing suicide in all age groups is the prevention of mental and addictive disorders.

# REFERENCES

American Psychiatric Association. (1987). *Diagnostic and Statistical Manual of Mental Disorders*, 3rd ed. rev. (DSM-III-R). Washington, DC: Author.

Andrews, J. A., & Lewinsohn, P. M. (1992). Suicidal attempts among older adolescents: Prevalence and co-occurrence with psychiatric disorders. *Journal of the American Academy of Child and Adolescent Psychiatry, 31*, 655–662.

Andrus, J. K., Fleming, D. W., Heumann, M. A., Wassell, J. T., Hopkins, D. D., & Gordon, J. (1991). Surveillance of attempted suicide among adolescents in Oregon, 1988. *American Journal of Public Health, 81*, 1067–1069.

Arango, V., Ernsberger, P., Marzuk, P. M., Chen, J., Tierney, H., et al. (1990). Autoradiographic demonstration of increased serotonin 5-$HT_2$ and $\beta$-adrenergic receptor binding sites in the brain of suicide victims. *Archives of General Psychiatry, 47*, 1038–1047.

Asberg, M. (1989). Neurotransmitter monoamine metabolites in the cerebrospinal fluid as risk factors for suicidal behavior. In Alcohol, Drug Abuse, and Mental Health Administration, *Report of the Secretary's Task Force on Youth Suicide*, Vol. 2, *Risk Factors for Youth Suicide*, (pp. 193–212). (DHHS Publ. No. (ADM)89-1622). Washington, DC: U.S. Government Printing Office.

Barraclough, B.M. (1971). Suicide in the elderly. *British Journal of Psychiatry*, Special Supplement 6, 87–97.

Beck, A. T., Resnik, H. L., & Lettieri, D. J. (1974). *The Prediction of Suicide*. Philadelphia, PA: Charles Press.

Blumenthal, S. J. (1988). A guide to risk factors, assessment, and treatment of suicidal patients. *Medical Clinics of North America, 72*, 937–971.

Brent, D. A. (1987). Correlates of medical lethality of suicide attempts in children and adolescents. *Jour-*
nal of the American Academy of Child & Adolescent Psychiatry, 26, 87–89.

Brent, D. A., Johnson, B., Bartle, S., Bridge, J., Rather, C., Matta, J., et al. (1993). Personality disorder, tendency to impulsive violence, and suicidal behavior in adolescents. *Journal of the American Academy of Child and Adolescent Psychiatry, 32*, 69–75.

Brent, D. A., Kerr, M. M., Goldstein, C., Bozigar, J., Wartella, M., & Allan, M. J. (1989). An outbreak of suicide and suicidal behavior in a high school. *Journal of the American Academy of Child and Adolescent Psychiatry, 28*, 918–924.

Brent, D. A., Perper, J. A., & Allman, C. J. (1987). Alcohol, forearms, and suicide among youth, *Journal of the American Medical Association, 257*, 3369–3372.

Brent, D. A., Perper, J. A., Allman, C. J., Moritz, G. M., Wartella, M. E., & Zelenak, J. P. (1991). The presence and accessibility of firearms in the homes of adolescent suicides: A case–control study. *Journal of the American Medical Association, 266*, 2989–2995.

Brent, D. A., Perper, J. A. Goldstein, C. E., Kolko, D. J., Allan M. J., et al. (1988). Risk factors for adolescent suicide. *Archives of General Psychiatry*, 45, 581–588.

Briere, J. & Zaidi, L. Y. (1989). Sexual abuse histories and sequelae in female psychiatric emergency room patients. *American Journal of Psychiatry, 146*, 1602–1606.

Brown, G. L., & Goodwin, F. K. (1986). Cerebrospinal fluid correlates of suicide attempts and aggression. In J. Mann & M. Stanley (Eds.), *Annals of the New York Academy of Sciences: Psychobiology of Suicidal Behavior, 487*, 175–188.

Centers for Disease Control and Prevention. (1993). Years of potential life lost before age 65 – United States, 1990 and 1991. *Morbidity and Mortality Weekly Report, 42*, 251–253.

Clark, D. C. (1993). Narcissistic crises of aging and suicidal despair. *Suicide and Life-Threatening Behavior, 23*, 21–26.

Cocarro, E. F., Siever, L. J., Klar, H. M., et al. (1989). Serotonergic studies in patients with affective and personality disorders. *Archives of General Psychiatry, 46*, 587–599.

Conwell, Y. (1991). *Suicide in the elder*. Presented at the NIH Consensus Development Conference on the Diagnosis and Treatment of Depression in Late Life, Bethesda, MD.

Crumley, F. E. (1990), Substance abuse and adolescent suicidal behavior. *Journal of the American Medical Association, 263*, 3051–3056.

Davidson, L. E., Rosenberg, M. L., Mercy, J. A., Franklin, J., & Simmons, J. T. (1989). An epidemiologic study of risk factors in two teenage suicide clusters. *Journal of the American Medical Association, 262*, 2687–2692.

de Wilde, E., Kienhorst, I. C. W. M., Diekstra, R. F. W., & Wolters, W. H. G. (1991). The relationship between adolescent suicidal behavior and life events in childhood and adolescence. *American Journal of Psychiatry, 149*, 45–51.

Durkheim, E. (1951). *Suicide: A study in sociology* (G. Simpson, Ed.), Glencoe, IL: Free Press. (Originally published 1897)

Egeland, J. A., & Sussex, J. N. (1985). Suicide and family loading for affective disorders. *Journal of the American Medical Association, 254,* 915-918.

Feinstein, A. R. (1977). *Clinical biostatistics.* St. Louis: C. V. Mosby.

Ford, A. B., Rushforth, N. B., Rushforth, N., Hirsch, C. S., & Adelson, L. (1979). Violent death in a metropolitan county: II. changing patterns in suicides (1959-1974). *American Journal of Public Health, 69,* 459-464.

Fowler, R. C., Rich, C. L. & Young, D. (1986). San Diego suicide study: Substance abuse in young cases. *Archives of General Psychiatry, 43,* 962-965.

Frierson, R. L. (1991). Non-fatal suicide attempts by elderly persons. *Archives of Internal Medicine, 151,* 141-144.

Garland. A. F., Shaffer, D., & Whittle B. (1989). A national survey of school-based suicide prevention programs. *Journal of the American Academy of Child and Adolescent Psychiatry, 28,* 931-934.

Garland, A. F., & Zigler, E. (1993). Adolescent suicide prevention: Current research and social policy implications. *American Psychologist, 48,* 169-182.

Garrison, C. Z. (1989). The study of suicidal behavior in the schools. *Suicide and Life-Threatening Behavior, 19,* 120-130.

Garrison, C. Z., Lewinsohn, P. M., Marsteller, F., Langhinrichsen, J., & Lann, I. (1991). The assessment of suicidal behavior in adolescents. *Suicide and Life-Threatening Behavior, 21,* 217-230.

Garrison, C. Z., McKeown, R. E., Valois, R. F., & Vincent, M. L. (1993). Aggression, substance use, and suicidal behaviors in high school students. *American Journal of Public Health, 83,* 179-184.

Gould, M. S. & Shaffer, D. (1986). The impact of suicide in television movies. *New England Journal of Medicine, 31,* 690-694.

Gould, M. S., Wallenstein, S., & Kleinman, M. H. (1990a). Time-space clustering of teenage suicide. *American Journal of Epidemiology, 131,* 71-78.

Gould, M. S., Wallenstein, S., Kleinman, M. H., O'Carroll, P., & Mercy, J. (1990b). Suicide clusters: An examination of age-specific effects. *American Journal of Public Health, 80,* 211-212.

Harry, J. (1989). Sexual identity issues. In Alcohol, Drug Abuse, and Mental Health Administration: *Report of the secretary's task force on youth suicide,* Vol. 2: *Risk factors for youth suicide* (pp. 2-131-2-142). (DHHS Publ. No. (ADM)89-1624). Washington, DC: U.S. Government Printing Office.

Hayes, L. M. (1989). *Jail Suicide Update, 2*(2).

Henriksson, M. M., Hillevi, M. A., Marttunen, M. J., Isometsa, E. T., et al. (1993). Mental disorders and comorbidity in suicide. *American Journal of Psychiatry, 150,* 935-940.

Hlady, W. G., & Middaugh, J. P. (1988). Suicides in Alaska: Firearms and alcohol. *American Journal of Public Health, 78,* 179-180.

Hoberman, H. M. & Garfinkel, B. D. (1988). Completed suicide in children and adolescents. *Journal of the American Academy of Child and Adolescent Psychiatry, 6,* 689-695.

Indian Health Service. (1993). *Trends in Indian health-1993.* Rockville, MD: U.S. Department of Health and Human Services, Public Health Service.

Kellerman, A. L., Reay, D. T. (1986). Protection or peril? An analysis of firearm-related deaths in the home. *New England Journal of Medicine, 314,* 1557-1560.

Kellerman, A. L., Rivara, F. P., Somes, G., Reay, D. T., Francisco, J., et al. (1992). Suicide in the home in relation to gun ownership. *New England Journal of Medicine, 327,* 467-472.

Kerkhof, A. J. F. M., & Bernasco, W. (1990). Suicidal behavior in jails and prisons in the Netherlands: Incidence, characteristics, and prevention. *Suicide and Life-Threatening Behavior, 20,* 123-137.

Kessler, R. C., Downey, G., Milavsky, J. R., & Stipp, H. (1988). Clustering of teenage suicides after television news stories about suicides: A reconsideration. *American Journal of Psychiatry, 145,* 1379-1383.

Kety, S. (1986). Genetic factors in suicide. In A. Roy (Ed.), *Suicide* (pp. 41-45). Baltimore, MD: Williams & Wilkins.

Kleinbaum, D. G., Kupper, L. L., & Morgenstern, H. (1982). *Epidemiologic research: Principles and quantitative methods.* New York: Van Nostrand Reinhold.

Last, J. M. (1983). *A dictionary of epidemiology.* New York: Oxford University Press.

Lilienfeld, A. M., & Lilienfeld, D. E. (1980). *Foundations of epidemiology.* New York: Oxford University Press.

Mann, J. J., Stanley, M., McBride, P. A., & McEwen, B. S. (1986). Increased serotonin$_2$ and $\beta$-adrenergic receptor binding in the frontal cortices of suicide victims. *Archives of General Psychiatry, 43,* 954-959.

Manton, K. G., Blazer, D. G., & Woodbury, M. A. (1987). Suicide in middle age and later life: Sex and race specific life table and cohort analyses. *Journal of Gerontology, 42,* 219-227.

Maris, R. (Ed.). (1986). *Biology of suicide.* New York: Guilford Press.

Maris, R. M. (1992). The relationship of nonfatal suicide attempts to completed suicides. In R. A. Maris, A. L. Berman, J. T. Maltsberger, & R. I. Yufit (Eds.), *Assessment and prediction of suicide* (pp. 362-380). New York: Guilford Press.

Marzuk, P. M., Tardiff, K., Leon, A. C., Stajic, M., Morgan, E. B., & Mann, J. J. (1992). Prevalence of cocaine use among residents of New York City who committed suicide during a one-year period. *American Journal of Psychiatry, 149,* 371-375.

Marzuk, P. M., Tierney, H., Tardiff, K., Gross, E. M., Morgan, E. B., Hsu, M-A., et al. (1988). Increased risk of suicide in persons with AIDS. *Journal of the American Medical Association, 259,* 1333-1337.

Meehan, P. J., Lamb, J. A., Saltzman, L. E., & O'Carroll, P. W. (1992). Attempted suicide among young adults: Progress toward a meaningful estimate of prevalence. *American Journal of Psychiatry, 149,* 41-44.

Meehan, P. J., Saltzman, L. E., & Sattin, R. W. (1991). Suicides among older United States residents: Epidemiologic characteristics and trends. *American Journal of Public Health, 81,* 1198-1200.

Merrill, J., & Owens, J. (1990). Age and attempted suicide. *Acta Psychiatrica Scandinavica, 82,* 385-388.

Monk, M. (1987). Epidemiology of suicide. *Epidemiologic Reviews, 9*, 51-69.

Mościcki, E. K. (1989). Epidemiologic surveys as tools for studying suicidal behavior: A review. *Suicide and Life-Threatening Behavior, 19*, 131-146.

Mościcki, E. K. (1994). Gender differences in completed and attempted suicides. *Annals of Epidemiology, 4*, 152-158.

Mościcki, E. K. (in press). Epidemiology of suicide. *International Psychogeriatrics.*

Mościcki, E. K., O'Carroll, P., Locke, B. Z., Rae, D. S., Roy, A., & Regier, D. A. (1989). Suicidal ideation and attempts: The epidemiologic catchment area study. In Alcohol, Drug Abuse, and Mental Health Administration, *Report of the secretary's task force on youth suicide, Vol. 4: Strategies for the prevention of youth suicide* (DHHS Publ. No. (ADM)89-1624). Washington DC: U.S. Government Printing Office.

Mościcki, E. K., O'Carroll, P., Regier, D. A., Rae, D. S., Roy, A., & Locke, B. Z. (1988). Suicide attempts in the epidemiologic catchment area study. *Yale Journal of Biology and Medicine, 61*, 259-268.

National Center for Health Statistics. (1994). Advance report of final mortality statistics, 1991. *Monthly Vital Statistics Report*, Vol. 42, No. 2 Suppl. Hyattsville, MD: Public Health Service.

O'Carroll, P. W. (1989). A consideration of the validity and reliability of suicide mortality data. *Suicide and Life-Threatening Behavior, 91*, 1-16.

Paykel, E. S., Myers, J. K., Lindenthal, J. J., & Tanner, J. (1974). Suicidal feelings in the general population: A prevalence study. *British Journal of Psychiatry, 124*, 460-469.

Pedinielli, J.-L., Delahousse, J., & Chabaud, B. (1989). La "léthalité" des tentatives de suicide. *Annales Médico-Psychologiques, 147*, 535-550.

Petronis, K. R., Samuels, J. F., Mościcki, E. K., & Anthony, J. C. (1990). An epidemiologic investigation of potential risk factors for suicide attempts. *Social Psychiatry and Psychiatric Epidemiology, 25*, 193-199.

Ramsay, R., & Bagley, C. (1985). The prevalence of suicidal behaviors, attitudes and associated social experiences in an urban population. *Suicide and Life-Threatening Behavior, 15*, 151-167.

Remafedi, G., Farrow, J. A., & Deisher, R. W. (1991). Risk factors for attempted suicide in gay and bisexual youth. *Pediatrics, 87*, 869-875.

Rich, C. L., Fowler, R. C., Fogarty, L. A., & Young, D. (1988). San Diego suicide study: III. Relationships between diagnoses and stressors. *Archives of General Psychiatry, 45*, 589-592.

Rich, C. L., & Runeson, B. S. (1992). Similarities in diagnostic comorbidity between suicide among young people in Sweden and the United States. *Acta Psychiatrica Scandinavia, 86*, 335-339.

Rich, C. L., Young, D., & Fowler, R. C. (1986). San Diego suicide study: I. Young vs. old subjects. *Archives of General Psychiatry, 43*, 577-582.

Robins, E., Murphy, G. E., Wilkinson, R. H., Gassner, S., & Kayes, J. (1959). Some clinical considerations in the prevention of suicide based on a study of 134 successful suicides. *American Journal of Public Health, 49*, 888-899.

Rosenberg, M. L., Davidson, L. E., Smith, J. C., Berman, A. L. Buzbee, H., et al. (1988). Operational criteria for the determination of suicide. *Journal of Forensic Sciences, 33*, 1445-1456.

Roy, A. (1989). Genetics and suicidal behavior. In Alcohol, Drug Abuse, and Mental Health Administration, *Report of the secretary's task force on youth suicide*, Vol. 2, *Risk factors for youth suicide*, (pp. 247-262). (DHHS Publ. No. (ADM)89-1622). Washington, DC: U.S. Government Printing Office.

Roy, A., Segal, N. L., Centerwall, B. S., & Robinette, C. D. (1991). Suicide in twins. *Archives of General Psychiatry, 48*, 29-32.

Runeson, B. S. (1989). Mental disorder in youth suicide: DSM-III-R Axes I and II. *Acta Psychiatrica Scandinavia, 79*, 490-497.

Sainsbury, P., & Jenkins, J. S. (1982). The accuracy of officially reported suicide statistics for purposes of epidemiological research. *Journal of Epidemiology and Community Health, 36*, 43-48.

Schmidtke, A., & Hafner, H. (1988). The Werther effect after television films: New evidence for an old hypothesis. *Psychological Medicine, 18*, 665-676.

Schwab, J. J., Warheit, G. J., & Holzer, C. E. (1972). Suicide ideation and behavior in a general population. *Diseases of the Nervous System, 33*, 745-748.

Shaffer, D., Garland, A., Gould, M., Fisher, P., & Trautman, P. (1988). Preventing teenage suicide: A critical review. *Journal of the American Academy of Child and Adolescent Psychiatry, 27*, 675-687.

Shafii, M., Carrigan, S., Whittinghill, J. R., & Derrick, A. (1985). Psychological autopsy of completed suicide in children and adolescents. *American Journal of Psychiatry, 142*, 1061-1064.

Smith, J. C., Mercy, J. A., & Conn, J. M. (1988). Marital status and the risk of suicide. *American Journal of Public Health, 78*, 78-80.

Sorenson, S. B. (1991). Suicide among the elderly: Issues facing public health. *American Journal of Public Health, 81*, 1109-1110.

Stanley, M., & Stanley, B. (1989). Biochemical studies in suicide victims: Current findings and future implications. *Suicide and Life-Threatening Behavior, 19*, 30-42.

Statistical Bulletin. (1990). International comparison of mortality from suicide. *Statistical Bulletin, 71*, 22-28.

U.S. Department of Health and Human Services. (1990). *Healthy people 2000: National health promotion and disease prevention objectives* (DHHS Publ. No. (PHS) 91-50212). Washington, DC: U.S. Government Printing Office.

Weissman, M. M. (1974). The epidemiology of suicide attempts, 1960 to 1971. *Archives of General Psychiatry, 38*, 737-746.

World Health Organization. (1993). *1992 world health statistics annual*. Geneva: Author.

Younger, S. C., Clark, D. C., Oehmig-Lindroth, R., & Stein, R. J. (1990). Availability of knowledgeable informants for a psychological autopsy study of suicides committed by elderly people. *Journal of the American Geriatric Society, 38*, 1169-1175.

# 3

# On the Nature, Magnitude, and Causality of Suicidal Behaviors: An International Perspective

## Rene F. W. Diekstra, PhD, and Nadia Garnefski, M.A.

The central questions addressed in this paper are whether present generations of adolescents and adults worldwide are at greater risk of developing suicidal reactions than previous generations were and what the possible causal mechanisms involved are. On the basis of data from international and national data banks as well as an extensive review of the literature, it is concluded that a true increase in suicide mortality and morbidity has occurred over the larger part of this century among the White urban adolescent and young adult populations of North America and Europe, particularly among (young) males over the last three decades. Among the possible causal mechanisms identified are (1) the corresponding increase in the prevalence of depressive disorders; (2) the corresponding increase in the prevalence of substance (ab)use and substance abuse disorders, and a lowering of age of onset of (ab)use; (3) psychobiological changes, in particular the dramatic lowering of the age of puberty; (4) an increase in the number of social stressors with extensive consequences for youth; (5) changes in attitudes towards suicidal behaviors and the related increased availability of suicidal models.

Recent summaries of physical health status indicators have suggested an emerging trend of healthier adults and adolescents in developed countries (Irwin & Vaughan, 1988). A more comprehensive picture of the current state of health, however, seems to indicate otherwise. If parameters of health include mental and psychosocial conditions and behaviors having more long-term implications for health such as dropout from work or school, sexual activity, substance abuse, and inclination to violence, current data do not provide unequivocal support for the view of improving health and social well-being for the population. The purpose of this paper is to present and discuss the available evidence for, as well as the preventive implications of, a secular increase in one manifestation or sign of mental ill-health, namely self-destructive or suicidal behavior. The key question addressed is the following: Are today's adults and adolescents, worldwide, at greater risk for developing suicidal reactions as well as related conditions such as mental disorders and psychoactive substance abuse disorders in particular, than previous generations were? If so, why? And what are the implications of the causal mechanisms involved for prevention activities?

The literature that is available for answering these questions can be divided into three approaches or research lines (Diekstra, Kienhorst, & De Wilde, in press; Fombonne, in press; Petersen, Compas, & Brooks-Gunn, 1993); (1) depressed mood and suicidal ideation, (2) parasuicide or attempted suicide, and (3) suicide. Each of these approaches encompasses not only an emphasis on different aspects of suicidal phenomena but also a different theoretical and/or empirical tradition. The separate study of attempted or parasuicide for example has emerged from theory and research that suggests that such behavior

---

Rene F. W. Diekstra and Nadia Garnetski are with the Department of Clinical and Health Psychology, the University of Leiden, Wassenaarsweg 52, 2333 AK, Leiden, The Netherlands.

is different from suicide in terms of etiology, functionality, demography, and behavioral characteristics (Rutter, 1986).

Several studies (Petersen et al., 1993; see Weinstein, Noam, Grines, Store, & Schwab-Stone, 1990) suggest that a gradient of severity is implied from depressed mood via suicidal ideation, attempted suicide or parasuicide, to suicide. With regard to affect and cognitive characteristics there seems to be a great deal of similarity between the three. It has also often been suggested (see Maris, 1981) that developmental pathways exist that sequentially link suicidal ideation to parasuicide to suicide. Yet, little is known about the causes and patterns of recruitment from suicidal ideation to parasuicide and from parasuicide to suicide, and about the factors that precipitate or protect against these transformations. In the following we first discuss the issues of definition and operationalization or measurement of these concepts. Against that background we then review the available evidence on rising secular trends. The paper concludes with a discussion of possible causal mechanisms, and priorities for future research and public health care.

## DEFINITIONS

*Depressed mood* refers first of all to a loss of positive affect and emotional involvement with self, others, or situations. It is often also characterized, however, by the so-called cognitive triad (Beck, 1976) of thoughts of unworthiness and self-blame, feelings of helplessness to change the situation, and hopelessness about the future (Rutter, 1986). Depressed mood tends to be accompanied by inefficient coping with normal life demands and stressful events. In this, it is different form normal feelings of sadness, grief, or disappointment. It has been shown to be one of the main characteristics differentiating persons referred for clinical help from those not referred (Achenbach, 1991).

*Suicidal ideation* refers to cognitions that can vary from fleeting thoughts that life is not worth living, via very concrete, well-thought-out plans for killing oneself, to an intense delusional preoccupation with self-destruction (Goldney, Winefield, Tiggemann, Winefield, & Smith, 1989). These definitions imply that depressed mood and suicidal ideation are not synonyms and that the first is a necessary condition for the second. Suicidal thoughts might both be an aspect of depressed mood and a cognitive coping strategy with such a mood (e.g., Percy Walker in his film The Moviegoer: "It's the thought of suicide that keeps me alive"). Suicidal ideation, therefore, can be of a habitual or chronic as well as an acute nature.

The term *parasuicide* (or *suicide attempt*) covers behaviors that can vary from suicidal gestures and manipulative attempts to serious attempts to kill oneself. It refers to any deliberate act with nonfatal outcome that might cause or actually causes self-harm, or that without intervention from others would have done so, or that consists of ingesting a substance in excess of its generally recognized or prescribed therapeutic dose (Kreitman, 1977).

More and more authors on the subject prefer the term *parasuicide* to *attempted suicide* or *suicide attempt* since it makes no reference to intention. As Kreitman (1977) has pointed out, intention cannot be used as a criterion since the person's motive may be too uncertain or too complex to ascertain readily. When asked "Why did you do it?" most will deny (afterward) that they wanted to kill themselves. Many will reply "I just don't know." Since parasuicide, particularly during adolescence and young adulthood, is usually carried out at the height of an interpersonal crisis by an individual feeling desperate and confused, such obscurity of intent is not at all surprising. Moreover, approximately two thirds of the men and nearly half of the women who present as parasuicides have taken alcohol within a few hours of the act (Kreitman, 1977).

This points to another important aspect of the definition of parasuicide or suicide attempt: The act should be nonhabitual. A habitual user of excessive quantities of alcohol or a habitual user of dangerous quantities of (hard) drugs, if found unconscious as a result of an overdose (assuming that other information indicating suicidal intent such as a suicide note is not present), is not considered a parasuicide or suicide attempt. Nor is habitual self-mutilation (cutting, piercing, head banging) implied under these terms.

The term *suicide* refers to any death that is the direct or indirect result of a positive or negative act accomplished by the victim, knowing or believing the act will produce this result (Maris, 1991). This definition implies, first, that the term *suicide* should be applied only in case of a death. Second, risk taking that leads to death, if the indirect causal sequence can be specified and was intentional, is suicide. Indirect suicide is a common but neglected form of suicide. Some authors (Farberow, 1980) believe it is particularly common in adolescence and young adulthood, and that a considerable number of road traffic fatalities in young males are in actual fact suicides. Third, self-neglecting behavior, sometimes referred to as suicidal *erosion*, such as hunger strike or refusal to take life-preserving medication, if it results in death, is also considered suicide.

## MEASUREMENTS

An important obstacle to answering satisfactorily the question with regard to the prevalence of and trends in suicidal behaviours is the differences in quantity and in quality of the data available for each of the three categories of suicidal phenomena, both within and between countries. First, of all, suicide is the only category for which national statistics or registers are available, but only for a limited number of countries. For example, in the 1992 *World Health Statistics Annual* (World Health Organization – WHO, 1992) only 39 of the almost 180 member states of the United Nations are listed as reporting suicide mortality statistics to the World Health Organization. For those that do,

the issue whether the data reported indeed reflect the actual toll of suicidal deaths, seems largely unresolved. Surprising as this may sound, despite development of more sophisticated methods for psychological autopsy, the problem of underreporting recently has increased, particularly in highly developed countries such as the United States or the Netherlands. This is a consequence of the increase of "doctor-assisted" deaths such as in euthanasia and assisted suicide, which often for fear of legal persecution or other reasons do not enter into mortality statistics as suicides, although many of them actually are. In some countries such as the Netherlands, official suicide figures possibly have to be increased by one fifth to one fourth to account for these cases of suicide (Diekstra et al., in press).

Furthermore, nowhere do health surveillance systems exist, not even at a regional or local level, that allow for a monitoring of the prevalence of nonfatal suicidal phenomena over significantly long periods of time, such as several decades. The only exceptions are a few research centers that over several decades have collected all cases of hospital-admitted parasuicides in a well-defined catchment area (Diekstra et al., in press; Platt, 1988). The lower age limit for case identification in these centers, however, has been 15 years, so no data are available on early adolescence.

In the few countries where repeated national surveys of mental and behavioral health are carried out (such as the Monitoring the Future projects in the United States – see Bachman, Johnston, & O'Malley, 1986; and the Netherlands – see Diekstra, De Heus, Garnefski, de Zwart, & Van Praag, 1991), these concern only adolescent or young adult populations, and either measures of depression and suicidal reactions are not included (United States) or the studies are not long enough in place (the Netherlands) to allow for any solid conclusions with regard to secular trends. In addition, longitudinal studies of birth cohorts that could provide information on the life course proportional vul-

nerability for depressive and nonfatal suicidal conditions are not available yet (see
Fombonne, in press).

## PREVALENCE/INCIDENCE
## OF SUICIDAL BEHAVIORS

It is clear from what has been discussed in
the preceding paragraph that our "cartog-
raphy" of the territory of suicidal behavior
is still very incomplete, particularly if
seen from an international perspective. In
addition to the discrepancies/deficiencies
in data sources, data collection and measurement methods diverge widely, while
with regard to suicidal ideation and parasuicide there are also the issues of differences between studies in methods of sam-
pling, size and characteristics of samples,
and methods of data analysis that make
comparison hazardous (for a review of
these methodological issues, see Diekstra
et al., in press). The following overall conclusions with regard to point prevalence
and lifetime prevalence or lifetime risk of
suicidal behaviors should therefore be considered very tentative.

### Depressed Mood and
### Suicidal Ideation

What percentage of people suffer from episodes of depressed mood and/or suicidal
ideation during their lifetime? Stated as
such, the question might seem to be rather
trivial, at least with regard to depressed
mood, since it is a popular assumption
that episodes of depressed mood belong to
the normal developmental trajectories.
There are, however, no empirical data to
substantiate this assumption, at least not
if depressed mood is defined in the way described above. In order to settle the issue,
information would be needed on lifetime
prevalence of depressed mood. For obvious reasons, such information is available
neither for adults nor for children and adolescents.

The only more or less valid information
available on this point comes from community survey studies from a number of

countries such as the USA, Belgium, and
the Netherlands (see Fombonne, in press)
that looked into point prevalence of depressive mood among adolescents (age
group 11–18 years) and have come up with
rates ranging from about 22% (Kaplan et
al., 1984) to 50% (Schoenbach et al., 1980),
with a median rate of 36–39% (see also
Petersen et al., 1993). Relevant also is the
observation that the point prevalence of
depressed mood increases dramatically
during and following puberty but seems
to decline in adulthood. Findings are con-
tradictory, however, with regard to the
nature of the relationship between age and
prevalence of depressed mood in the adolescent period. Some studies indicate a
positive correlation with age, while others
do not. The majority of studies converge
on the conclusion that the (post)puberty
increase in considerably greater in girls
than in boys. While in prepuberty sex differences are negligible, during adolescence
there is a preponderance of depressed girls
(Petersen et al., 1993).

Similar puberty, age, and sex relationships have been clearly demonstrated for
depressive disorders. Community survey
studies that have looked into point prevalence of such disorders – mostly defined as
major depressive disorder although the
distinction with dysthymia sometimes
proves difficult to make (Fombonne, in
press) – indicate a range from about 2% to
8%, with a median rate between 3% and
4% (Fombonne, in press) and a ratio of
girls to boys of about 2:1. In contrast to
depressed mood, however, there are no indications of a possible decrease of point
prevalence of depressive disorders in
adult life. Lifetime prevalence rates for
depressive disorders among adolescents
are estimated to lie within a range of 8–
16% (Petersen et al., 1993).

If depressed mood appears to be a "self-
limiting" phenomenon over the course of
development from adolescence into adulthood in some adolescents, while in others
it not only proves to be a continuous phenomenon but might even develop into a diagnosable depressive disorder, the question arises as to what differences exist

between these two subgroups, in terms of both depressive symptomatology and etiology as well as individual and social comorbidity. Studies addressing this question are very scarce indeed, but according to some authors (De Wilde et al., 1992) the combination of depressed mood and suicidal behavior might indicate a more unfavorable prognosis than depressed mood without suicidal tendencies.

What has been stated with regard to depressed mood can *mutatis mutandis* be stated with regard to suicidal ideation also. There is no satisfactory answer to the question: What percentage of people have episodes of suicidal ideation during their lifetime. A review of community survey studies reveals the following: estimates of the prevalence of suicidal thoughts range from 3.5% (Kienhorst, De Wilde, Van den Bout, Diekstra, & Wolters, 1990a), through 14% (Canton, Gallimbertin, Gentile, & Ferraren, 1989), 15.4% (Pronovost, Cote, & Ross, 1990), 18.9% (Diekstra et al., 1991), 23.3% (Nagy & Adcock, 1990), 38% (Watanabe, Ninomiya, Shukutani, Aizawa, & Hasegawa, 1988), 52.1% (Smith & Crawford, 1986), to 52.9% (Harkavy Friedman, Asnis, Boeck, & DiFiore, 1987). To a large extent, the differences in rates reported can be explained by differences in definition of suicidal ideation and differences in period of reference. In some studies the subjects have been asked about "recent" suicidal thinking (Kienhorst et al., 1990a), in others about suicidal thoughts during the past year (Diekstra et al., 1991; Dubow, Kausch, Blum, Reed, & Bush, 1989; Nagy & Adcock, 1990), and again in others for suicidal ideation "ever" or "at least once" (Pronovost et al., 1990; Smith & Crawford, 1986; Harkavy Friedman et al., 1987). Not surprisingly, the longer the period of assessment (retrospectively), the higher the rate tends to be. If the reasonable assumption is made that measuring suicidal ideation "ever" or "at least once" can be equated with measuring lifetime prevalence rate, we find a range of about 15% to 53%, which proves it to be a phenomenon quite common indeed. Most of

the studies reviewed show a clear preponderance of suicidal women and girls. There is also some evidence of a positive correlation of prevalence of suicidal ideation and age, at least over the period of 12 through 17 years of age and more prominently in girls than in boys (Diekstra et al., 1991). No data are available on pre- and postpuberty differences with regard to the prevalence of suicidal ideation, but it seems safe to assume that such differences, similar to the ones found for depressed mood and depressive disorders, do exist.

## Parasuicide or Attempted Suicide

The answer to the question as to how common is parasuicide, varies considerably according to the data sources one uses, i.e., service utilization studies or community surveys. With regard to the first category there are currently two international studies, one completed and one in progress, that shed some light on this issue. The former (Diekstra, 1982) was carried out in 1976 in seven of the nine countries that constituted the European Economic Community (EEC) at that time. Using data provided by centers with well-defined catchment areas it was extrapolated that for the whole of the EEC (comprising about 200 million inhabitants at the time), approximately 430,000 episodes of deliberate self-harm were treated in either in- or outpatient facilities. This equals an averaged rate of 215 cases per 100,000 persons aged 15 years and older (162 for males and 265 for females). Between countries or centers, rates varied considerably (for males rates range from 26 to 353, for females from 82 to 527), a finding that can at least partially be explained by differences in referral and data-recording procedures.

The other study in this category is currently in progress and is being carried out under the auspices of the World Health Organization (WHO Multicentre Study on Monitoring Trends in Parasuicide, see Platt, Bille-Brahe, & Kerkhof, 1992). The first progress report, comprising data from 15 centers in 10 countries (Finland,

France, Hungary, Italy, the Netherlands, Norway, Spain, Sweden, Germany, Denmark), indicates that parasuicide rates (based on admission to health facilities for the year 1989) vary widely between centers. With regard to parasuicide among males the highest rate (414 per 100,000) was found in Helsinki (Finland) and the lowest (61 per 100,000) in Leiden (the Netherlands), a ratio in excess of 7:1. For females the rate was highest (595 per 100,000) in Pontoise (France) and lowest (95 per 100,000) in Guipuz Coa (Spain).

Although in most centers the general picture of higher parasuicide rates among females than among males was confirmed, there were exceptions to this rule, such as Helsinki, Finland, for example, where rates for males appeared to be remarkably higher. From both studies it appears that peak ages for parasuicides, in terms of both absolute numbers and rates per 100,000 of the particular age group, fall within the first half of the life cycle, i.e., between 15 and 44 years of age, although between countries and sexes there is considerable and unexplained variation in the age category (15–24, 25–34, 35–44) with the highest rate.

The results from studies in the second category, community surveys, shed considerable doubt upon the validity of the picture of magnitude and nature of the parasuicide phenomenon that emerges from studies using service utilization data. A review of community survey studies on both adult and adolescent samples in a number of countries published since the late 1960s shows estimates of year prevalence of parasuicidal acts to vary between 2.4% and 20% (CDC, 1991; Dubow et al., 1989; Nagy & Adcock, 1990; Pronovost et al., 1990; Rubinstein, Hearen, Housman, Rubin, & Stechler, 1989) while lifetime prevalence rates range from 2.2% to 20% (Andrews & Lewinsohn, 1990; Diekstra et al., 1991; Harkavy Friedman et al., 1987; Kienhorst et al., 1990a; Rubenstein et al., 1989; Smith & Crawford, 1986). On the one hand, the differences between studies in estimated incidence might be a valid reflection of

differences between the respective countries or regions in parasuicide rates. On the other hand, however, there are differences in data collection between studies that certainly have had a strong impact on their findings. All studies report a clear preponderance of women and girls but whether there is an age effect (in the adolescent period) remains obscure. Studies of clinical samples also provide controversial data with regard to the relationship between parasuicide rates and age, although a number of clinical studies support the existence of both a puberty and an age effect (see Andrus et al., 1991; Rey & Bird, 1991).

Both community survey studies and studies of clinical samples show that a considerable percentage of parasuicidal persons make repeated parasuicidal acts: between 14% (Hawton et al., 1982) and 51% (Mehr, Zeltzer, & Robinson, 1981, 1982), depending partially on length of follow-up period.

It appears that depressed mood or depressive disorder is a characteristic of a substantial proportion, but not all of parasuicides. Rates of depressive conditions (range about 20–55%) may vary depending upon the population studied, with the highest rates found in psychiatric samples and much lower rates in medical units and community samples (Spirito, Brown, Overholser, & Fritz, 1989). A problem here is that the assessment of depression is mostly made after the parasuicidal act.

## Suicide

Generally speaking suicide is a relatively rare event, although there is large international variation in death rates from suicide. Of the countries that report to WHO and whose suicide rates are published (WHO, 1992), the range of suicide rates spans from a low of almost zero suicides per million females in Malta to a high of over 600 per million males in Hungary. According to a multitide of authors (see Vaillant & Blumenthal, 1990) one of the most basic facts about suicide is that its risk increases as a function of age. Indeed, completed suicide is extremely rare in children under the age of 12 and becomes more common after puberty, with its incidence increasing in each of the adolescent years (Moens, 1990). From late adolescence/young adulthood onward, however, the age–mortality relationship starts to diverge between countries and between the sexes within countries. In some countries we observe a first peak in the life cycle in that developmental period (roughly between 24 and 35 years of age; e.g., in males in Iceland, females in Norway, females in Bulgaria, in the United States for both sexes), whereas in other countries suicide rates continue to rise till midlife (roughly between 45 and 54 or 64 years of age; e.g., both sexes in Hungary and Denmark): After that stage a dip occurs. In almost all countries the highest suicide rates are among elderly men (age category 75 +), while in quite a number of countries the highest suicide rates among females are found at a considerable younger age. This is particularly the case among women in Scandinavian countries (the peak age for women in Norway and Iceland is between 45 and 54 years of age, and for Finnish women between 55 and 64).

Nevertheless, there is a high correlation between suicide and age in the countries on the European and North American continents. For males the correlation between suicide rate and age ranges from 0.78 to 0.91 [exceptions are Iceland (0.51) and Ireland (0.26)]. For females the correlation ranges from 0.77 to 0.98 [the exceptions being Iceland (0.59), Norway (0.15) and Finland (0.10)].

There is, however, another way of analyzing the relationship between suicide and age, namely using proportional mortality rates. If we relate the rank order of suicide in the hierarchy of causes of death to age, it appears that with increasing age the ranking of suicide in that hierarchy decreases.

In most of the countries on the European and North American continents suicide ranks as the 9th or 10th cause of death all age groups taken together, ac-

counting for slightly more than (an averaged) 1% of all deaths in females and 2% in males. There are, however, substantial international differences. Some countries, such as Hungary and Denmark, have a suicide mortality three to five times as high as, for example, England and Wales and Ireland. There are also significant differences between age groups. In the age group 15–34 years the percentage of all deaths caused by suicide is 15 to 20 times the percentage in the 65–74 age category. Among the former, suicide constitutes the second or third most important cause of death, accounting for 1 of every 8 deaths among females and 1 every 6 among males. In some countries, such as Denmark, suicide is even the number one cause of death in the age group 25–34. Approximately 25% of all female deaths and 30% of all male deaths in this age category are by suicide. This hierarchical ranking is not simply a consequence of the fact that other causes of death, such as infectious and parasitic diseases, have to a large extent been brought under control or are almost completely eliminated, as we shall demonstrate later.

## SECULAR TRENDS IN SUICIDAL BEHAVIOR

### Depressed Mood and Suicidal Ideation

As stated earlier, there are no adequate data on secular trends in depressed mood or suicidal ideation for any country in the world. Indirect evidence for upward trends in these phenomena might be found in a number of studies that point to an increasing risk for depressive disorders among successive birth cohorts over the course of this century (Hagnell, Lanke, Rorsman, & Ojesjö, 1982; Klerman, 1985; Robins, Locke, & Regier, 1991; Weissman, Livingston Bruce, Leaf, Florio, & Hozer, 1991). The lifetime prevalence rates for depression appear to be higher for adolescents and young adults today than they were for their parents at that age, who in turn had higher rates during their adolescence or young adulthood than their parents had (see Figure 1).

One of the causes of this increase seems to be the lowering of the age of onset for depressive disorders, a phenomenon that has also been reported for a number of other disorders, such as substance abuse and delinquent behavior. There is reason to assume, however, that the increase is restricted to White populations living in the highly industrialized urban areas of North America and Northern Europe, since studies of identical design on other populations have not confirmed this finding (Canino et al., 1987, Karno et al., 1987).

The same studies that show an increase in risk for depression in younger birth cohorts also suggest a closing of the classical sex gap in depression in that the rise seems to be greater for young men than young women (Hagnell et al., 1982). In one study (Joyce, Oakley-Brown, Wells, Bushnell, & Hornblow, 1990) the prevalence rates among young men were even higher than among young women.

## Parasuicide

In the absence of adequate national statistics of parasuicide, locally based estimates provide the only data that can be used to estimate trends in a country as a whole. Only a few countries have centers that have been monitoring episodes of hospital- and/or general practitioner-treated parasuicide from defined populations for over at least one decade. The reports of those centers in countries such as the United Kingdom (Hawton, O'Grady, Osborn, & Cole, 1982; Kreitman, 1977; Platt, 1988) and the Netherlands (Diekstra, 1989) indicate that the incidence of parasuicide increased markedly in the period from the early 1950s till the mid-1970s or early 1980s. A similar development was noted in the United States (Weismann, 1974). Since then a decrease in parasuicide rates have been noted (see Diekstra, 1989a; Platt, 1988). This decline, however, was observed earlier in some countries (such as Great Britain from 1981 onwards) than in others (such as the Netherlands from 1983) and also earlier among women than in men.

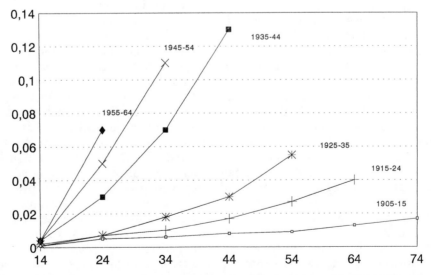

Figure 1.   Major depression: period–cohort effects and lifetime prevalence. (From the Epidemiologic Area Catchment Study, NIMH, adapted from Weissman et al., 1991.)

The decline in parasuicide rates also seems to be more marked among women than among men (all age groups). Of special relevance to the question of trends is the fact that the proportional change appears to be greatest among late adolescents and young adults (approximately 20–34 years old; see Platt et al., 1992). Both for males and for females in this age group the rates in 1988 were just above (males) or below (females) the level of 1970, while for the younger age group (15–19 years old) the rates in 1988 were still clearly above the level of 1970, but significantly more so for men than for women. One consequence of this development is that the ratio of females to males tends to fall over time.

## Suicide

In a number of developed countries, particularly European countries, suicide rates have been recorded for at least 100 years. This makes it possible to answer the question: What has been the trend in suicide over the course of the 20th century? Is suicide increasing and if so, is this similar for all age and sex groups? As Table 1 shows for 16 European countries, the answer depends on what countries one is looking at.

In nine countries the national suicide rate reached an all-time high during the last decade, whereas in seven countries the century's suicide peak occurred earlier, in most instances in the first part of the century. The latter development can also be observed in the United States, where the rate at the beginning of the century was 10.2 per 100,000, increased to 16.2 by 1915, then decreased sharply to again 10.2 in 1920. After 1925 it climbed steadily upward, to reach a maximum of 17.4 in 1932. Since then, the rate has stayed significantly below this level (13.3 in 1977 and 12.7 in 1987).

Despite these differences in trends between countries, it is noteworthy that the per period averaged rate for the 16 countries taken together has gone up over the course of the century significantly. What is even more noteworthy is that while the

average rate for Europe has gone up, the variation around the European mean has remained the same. This suggests that (1) although the prevalence of selfdestruction continues to vary in accordance with international differences in traditions, customs, religious convictions, social viewpoints, climactic conditions and other factors influencing human conduct, (2) the strength of these international differences is decreasing.

## Secular Trends in Suicide, Age, and Sex

As has been mentioned earlier, any analysis of trends in suicide risk among the younger age groups is hampered by the deficiencies in suicide mortality statistics on late childhood/early adolescence. The analysis of suicide rates by age categories 5–14, 15–24, and 25–34 years, and by sex, as reported in the *Statistics Annual* published by the World Health Organization over two decades (WHO, 1972, 1982, 1992) clearly shows that the crude suicide rate reported for children and early adolescents (5–14 years of age) in many European as well as non-European countries is (1) often very low and (2) sometimes not reported at all for reasons unknown (no cases or just not reported?). Those authors (see Moens et al., 1990) that nevertheless have tried to analyze trends for this age group have concluded that there appears to be a trend toward an increase of suicides among boys, at least up to 1984, in most European countries. If we limit ourselves to an analysis of secular trends for those aged 15 and over, the following conclusions appear to be warranted. First, there has been a real increase in suicide risk among adolescents and young adults over the past two decades in many European countries as well as in highly industrialized countries in other parts of the world. Figures 2 and 3 illustrate this by presenting age-specific suicides for the United States and the Netherlands as a percentage of total suicides in 5-year (United States) or 10-year (Netherlands) age groups, for the census years 1970 and 1987 (United States) or

Table 1
Suicide in Europe 1881–1988

| Country | 1881–1890 | 1921–1925 | 1951–1954 | 1961–1967 | 1972–1974 | 1982–1984 | 1987–1988 |
|---|---|---|---|---|---|---|---|
| Australia | 16.1 | 28.3 | 23 | 21.9 | 23.6 | 28 | 25 |
| Belgium | 11.4 | 13.4 | 13.6 | 14.1 | 15.5 | 23 | 22.5 |
| Denmark | 22.5 | 13.8 | 23.5 | 18.3 | 24.6 | 28.9 | 28 |
| Finland | 3.9 | 12.7 | 17.4 | 20.7 | 24.2 | 24.6 | 27.6 |
| France | 20.7 | 19.5 | 15.5 | 15.5 | 15.8 | 21.8 | 22.1 |
| Germany | 20.9 | 22.1 | 18.6 | 18.9 | 20.6 | 21.4 | 17.9 |
| Ireland | 2.3 | 2.8 | 2.3 | 2.5 | 3.4 | 7.5 | 6.9 |
| Italy | 4.9 | 8.8 | 6.5 | 5.4 | 5.6 | 5.3 | 8.3 |
| Netherlands | 5.5 | 6.2 | 6.3 | 6.5 | 8.7 | 11.6 | 11 |
| Norway | 6.8 | 5.8 | 7.1 | 7.5 | 9.4 | 14.4 | 15.5 |
| Portugal | – | 6.9 | 10.2 | – | 8.7 | 10.2 | 8.1 |
| Spain | 2.4 | 5.6 | 5.9 | 6 | 4.3 | 7.2 | 7.8 |
| Sweden | 10.7 | 14.4 | 17.2 | 18 | 20.4 | 19.4 | 18.5 |
| Switzerland | 22.7 | 23.1 | 21.8 | 18.1 | 19.6 | 24.7 | 22.7 |
| England and Wales | 7.7 | 10.1 | 10.6 | 11.8 | 7.8 | 8.7 | 8.5 |
| Scotland | 5.5 | 6.6 | 5.6 | 8.5 | 8.3 | 10.7 | 11.9 |

*Note*: Averaged rates per 100,000 of population over sample periods starting at 1881 and ending in 1988. Data from Cavan, 1926; Moens, 1990; and WHO. Data bank 1987/88 equals last year reported in *World Health Statistics Annual*, 1989; for some countries, last year is 1986.

1965–1969 and 1985–1987 (Netherlands). As can be seen, the rates of suicide in the younger age categories (roughly between 15 and 30–34) were substantially lower around 1970 than around 1987. The trend is just the opposite for older age groups (45 and over).

As Figure 4 shows for 19 selected countries throughout the world, there is a significant difference in trends between the

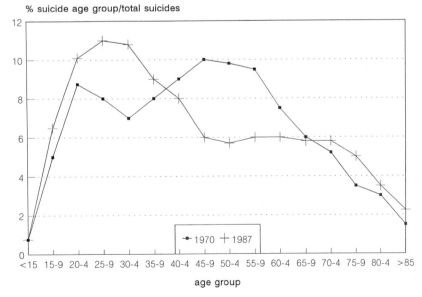

Figure 2. Percentage of all suicides per age group: United States, 1970–1987; 5-year age groups. (Source: Buda & Tsuang, 1990).

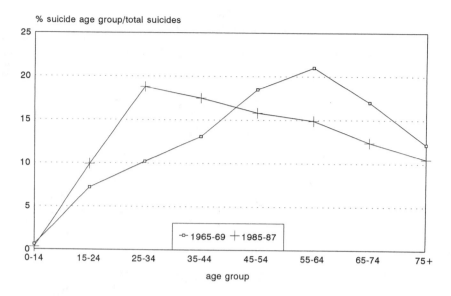

Figure 3. Percentage of all suicides per age group: The Netherlands, 1965–1987; 10-year age groups. (Source: WHO, *World Health Statistics Annual.*)

sexes over the period 1970 to 1986. In the majority of the countries there was an increase in suicide among males in all age groups, this trend being most pronounced in adolescents and young adults (a mean change of +70%). Among females the pic-

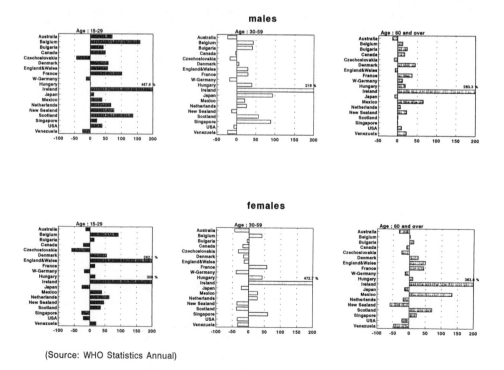

(Source: WHO Statistics Annual)

Figure 4. Suicides by gender, 1970–1986.

ture is different. In the age group 15 to 29 years, the majority of countries still show an increase (a mean change of +40%), but it is noteworthy that a number of countries with a significant increase in suicide in young males show a decrease in young females (e.g., Canada and the United States). (For the age categories 30–59 years and 60 years and older, only a minority of countries show a significant increase in suicide mortality among females.)

A number of studies of suicide trends in countries such as Canada (Barnes, Ennis, & Schober, 1986; Reed, Camus, & Last, 1985; Solomon & Hellon, 1980), the United States (Lester, 1984; Murphy & Wetzel, 1980), Australia (Goldney & Katsikitis, 1983), Germany (Häfner & Schmidtke, 1985), England and Wales (Murphy, Lindesay, & Grundy, 1986), Italy (Vecchia, Bollinni, & Imazio, 1986), Belgium and the Netherlands (Moens, 1990), and Sweden (Asgard, Nordström, & Raback, 1987), all applying birth cohort methodologies, have confirmed this picture of a shift toward younger ages over the course of this century as well as a relatively greater risk increase among young males. This is poignantly illustrated by Figures 5 through 7, presenting the suicide rates for the 15- to 24- and the 29-year-olds for the years 1900 through 1987 in the United States and the Netherlands.

In both countries there are two conspicuous peak periods in youth suicide mortality over the course of this century, one around 1980 and another in the beginning of the century, around 1910. This pattern has been observed in other European countries as well. In this respect, it is of more than just anecdotal relevance that the first scientific meeting on suicide ever held took place in Vienna in 1910. The meeting was organized by the Viennese Psychoanalytic Society and chaired by Alfred Adler. Sigmund Freud was one of the discussants. The special topic of the meeting was suicide among adolescents. Increased rates in youth suicide in Austria and other European countries, and several so-called school epidemics at that time,

had aroused public and professional concern.

Besides the similarities between the graphs for the United States and the Netherlands – after an all-time low around 1950, the rates rapidly rose until around 1980 they reached the level of the 1910 period and then broke through that barrier to climb to all-time highs – there are also some notable differences. For the Netherlands, in contrast to the United States, this is so only for the age group 20–29 years old, in both males and females. In the age group 15–19 the suicide rates remained below the level of the beginning of the century, although since 1950 we also observe a substantial increase in this age category.

The interaction between age and gender over time in overall suicide mortality appears to be different between the two countries. In the Netherlands the increase of young males in contrast to young females is accompanied by a decrease of this ratio for the older age groups taken together. This is not so for the United States (Diekstra et al., in press).

## Secular Trends in Depressive Disorders and Suicide Mortality: Preliminary Conclusions

The findings presented in the preceding paragraphs on secular trends in depressive disorders as well as in suicide mortality lend support to the hypothesis that a true increase in these phenomena has occurred over the larger part of this century among the White urban adolescent and young adult populations of North American and Europe. This conclusion is corroborated by the data on depressive disorders and suicide, which converge on the fact that this increase is particularly conspicuous among young males.

Of further relevance is evidence suggesting that the percentage of adolescent male suicides suffering from a depressive disorder at the time of death has increased over the past decades. In a comparison of psychological autopsies in two series of male suicides separated by 25 years, it

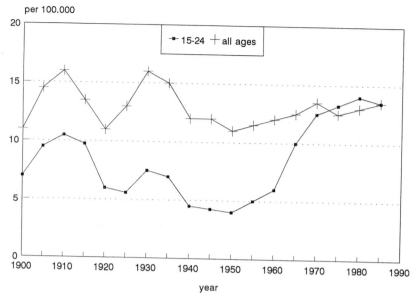

Figure 5. Suicide rates in the United States, 1900–1987. (Source: Buda & Tsuang, 1990.)

was found that the prevalence of depressive disorders was higher among young males in the more recent series (Carlson, Rich, Grayson, & Fowler, 1991).

It is difficult to assert whether the earlier age of onset observed for depressive disorders is also reflected in an increase of suicide mortality at a lower age, given the

problems with suicide statistics for early adolescence mentioned earlier, but there is indirect evidence to suggest that this might be the case. As described earlier, there have been a number of community survey studies assembling (retrospectively) data on lifetime prevalence of parasuicide among both the general and the high

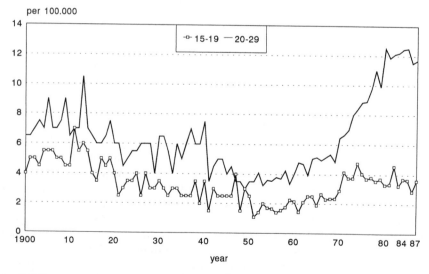

Figure 6. Suicide rates in the Netherlands, 1900–1987; until 1950, age groups are 16–20 and 21–29 years. (Source: Central Bureau of Statistics of the Netherlands; WHO *Statistics Annual.*)

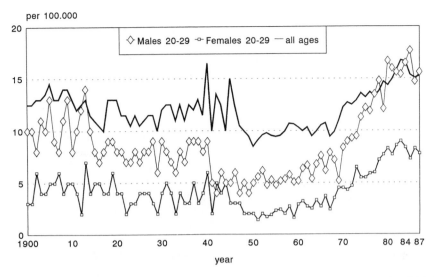

Figure 7.   Suicide rates for the Netherlands, 1900–1987; until 1950, age groups are 16–20 and 21–29 years. (Source: Central Bureau of Statistics of the Netherlands, WHO *Statistics Annual*.)

school student populations. Given the reasonable expectation that lifetime prevalence rates should increase with age since time augments risk, it is surprising that the lifetime parasuicide rates in general population studies do not exceed and sometimes even remain below the rates for high school students (Diekstra et al., in press). Assuming that recall of past episodes remains constant throughout the life span (an assertion still under heavy debate; see Fombonne, in press), one possible explanation for this finding is a lower age of first-ever parasuicidal acts in recent decades. Since parasuicide is an important, presumably the most important, precursor of suicide, a lower age for first-ever parasuicides can be expected to predict a lower age for suicides as well.

## SECULAR TRENDS IN DEPRESSION AND SUICIDE: THE SEARCH FOR CAUSAL MECHANISMS

The plausibility of the assertion that depressive disorders and suicide mortality have been increasing among the adolescent and young adult populations over the larger part of this century, raises a question as to the possible causes of these increases. We are dealing here with a very complicated issue. Depression and suicide are descriptive or phenotypical categories, and not etiological or genotypical concepts. It is highly probable that the observed secular increases can be attributed predominantly to a subgroup of the different causal pathways to, or genotypes of, depression and suicide. Although Maris (1981) more than a decade ago had already laid out the issue of the different pathways to suicide in a most convincing way, research addressing this question is still virtually nonexistent.

But even if we could identify which pathways to depression and suicide are more frequently seen today than in the past, we still would not automatically have explained secular changes. It is one thing to explain what causes a phenomenon to occur in the first place; it is quite a different thing to explain changes in that phenomenon. It may very well be, for example, that weather conditions are associated with a change in the incidence of road traffic accidents in a particular period compared to previous and following periods, but that does not imply that the weather causes road traffic accidents (nor does it necessarily mean that reduction of bad weather leads to reduction of road accidents in the long term).

In trying to explain secular trends, we must look for variables that have a known etiological and/or "control" function with regard to depression and suicide, and whose changes in a specified period can be empirically related to changes in the prevalence and incidence of depression and suicide in the same or a later period. No research programs are currently addressing these two issues in conjunction. By default we must resort to the "bits and pieces" method, which can only deliver very preliminary answers.

## Biological Changes

In the highly industrialized countries of Europe and North America a remarkable biological-developmental change has taken place over the course of the past 150 years. Around 1850 the average age of menarche was 16 years; in most countries today the average age is around 12½ years (Hamburg, 1989). A similar trend seems to apply to boys (age of spermarche) but is harder to document. A number of authors have tried to attribute secular changes in emotional disturbances in adolescence to this change (Hamburg, 1989; see also Fombonne, in press). Although earlier puberty might explain earlier onset of depressive conditions or earlier occurrence of suicidal behaviors— given the validity of the assumption that puberty contributes to risk, an issue not yet settled—it still does not automatically explain higher prevalence rates.

A more plausible explanation seems to be that the lower puberty age has caused a disjunction of biological development on the one hand and psychological and social development on the other. The brain does not reach a fully adult state of development until the end of the teenage years (Hamburg, 1989) and social changes dur-

ing two centuries, particularly during the last century, have postponed the end of adolescence—and of social dependence— until much later. This phenomenon of biopsychosocial dysbalance is a distinctly human evolutionary novelty (Hamburg, 1989) and might pose for many youngsters stresses and strains that overtax, at least for a number of years, their coping repertoires and those of families and educators. In most countries, too, the present average age of puberty coincides with another important developmental task for the early adolescent, the transition from elementary to secondary or high school (Petersen et al., 1993).

Some researchers hypothesize (see Fombonne, in press) that these processes particularly affect girls. This hypothesis seems to be substantiated by the fact that depressive disorders, suicidal ideation, and parasuicide are more prevalent in girls than in boys, but it also seems to be contradicted by the fact that the rise in depressive disorders and suicides is greater among boys than among girls.

## Psychological/Behavioral Changes

The lowering of the average age of puberty has been accompanied by the earlier use of various life-threatening or (mental) health-threatening substances. For example, over the past 30–40 years increasing percentages of young people have started to drink alcoholic beverages, their alcohol consumption has increased in quantity and frequency, and the age at which drinking starts has become lower (Perry, 1989; WHO, 1989). Problem drinking and alcohol-associated morbidity and mortality rates have increased among adolescents and are higher for boys than for girls, although the rise in alcohol use appears to be as strong for girls as for boys (Perry, 1989). Chronic excessive use of alcohol among adolescents is often a reaction to social problems, such as family difficulties or failure at school, and can also aggravate these problems. Acute intoxication often removes inhibitions that would otherwise prevent risky behaviors. It is especially implicated in aggression, crime, accidents, and, of particular relevance to this paper, suicidal behavior.

What applies to alcohol use applies, *mutatis mutandis*, to the use of other substances, such as tobacco, cannabis, cocaine, and psychopharmaca (prescribed or nonprescribed). The age of onset of use has lowered, and quantity and frequency of use in adolescence have generally increased. There is also growing evidence to suggest that the use of substances tends to cluster. Adolescents who are regular smokers have a higher probability of using alcohol regularly. Adolescents who drink regularly are more likely than others to use illicit drugs (WHO, 1989). Regular multiple substance use is associated with poorer performance at school, at work, at sports; and with a pessimistic future perspective.

From a sociocultural perspective it is important to note that the increase in substance use among adolescents – in particular the use of alcohol, tobacco, and psychopharmaca – is associated with greater availability of those substances both in the family and at the societal level (the supermarket substance shelves), and with an increased acceptability of their use by young people as portrayed in the media, for example.

The combination of increased availability and acceptability of chemical mind and mood changing substances in highly industrialized countries (Rose, 1990) is, from a behavioral perspective, particularly relevant to suicidal behaviors. In many countries, the majority of parasuicides in men and women, and the majority of suicides in women (in men a considerable minority) are by overdoses of drugs or (other) poisonous substances, often in combination with alcohol. Once people have taken to coping with life stresses and strains through the use of chemical substances, such as alcohol, there is a strong increase in the probability of the use of other chemical substances and their (combined with alcohol) abuse or overdosage, often labeled *parasuicide* in case of a non-

fatal outcome and *suicide* in case of a fatal outcome. If this is one of the pathways that explain (partially) the secular increases in suicidal behaviors, one would hypothesize that the incidence of both suicide and parasuicide should be high among psychoactive substance abusers, and that the correlation between changes in national suicide rates among adolescents and young adults and changes in national alcohol consumption should be high and positive. The available evidence lends support to both hypotheses (Diekstra, 1989b; Fremouw, De Perczel, & Ellis, 1990; Kreitman, 1977; Miles, 1977).

The role of substance abuse disorders in the secular increase of suicidal behaviors may, however, be greater in young men. In a case–control study of teenage suicides it was found (Gould, Shaffer, & Davies, 1991) that of the male suicides, 37% suffered from a substance abuse disorder (as against 7% of the normal group), whereas 5% of the female suicides had such a disorder (as against 7% of the normal group). From a behavioral perspective, another finding of that study is of considerable interest. Over a third of the adolescent suicides (41% in males and 33% in females) had a first- or second-degree relative who had attempted a parasuicidal act or committed suicide. This suggests that the probability of suicidal behavior is, among other things, a function of the availability of suicidal "models" in the present or past social network of the adolescent. Earlier studies (Kreitman, 1977) have demonstrated that the same relationship exists for parasuicides: Suicidal behavior was significantly more frequent among significant others (not necessarily people of kin) of parasuicidal persons than in representative samples of the general population. This imitation effect has also been observed with models not belonging to family or other immediate social networks (such as school). Public discussion (through television, radio, newsprint, and the like) of celebrities or noncelebrity young people (fictional or nonfictional) who have committed suicide often elicits an increase in suicides (Diekstra et al., in press), particularly among youth.

These findings render plausible the hypothesis that suicidal models within a society have a causative effect on the incidence of suicidal behavior among young people in that society. Although no studies have measured media coverage of (fictional or nonfictional) suicide cases over the course of this century, it seems safe to assume that an increase in coverage has occurred.

## Social Changes

It has been repeatedly shown that both depression and suicidal behaviors among adolescents and adults are associated with a variety of social conditions such as unemployment and economic hardship, interpersonal difficulties such as parental/marital discord and family conflicts, interpersonal losses (e.g., through parental divorce), parental mental disorders such as depression and psychoactive substance abuse, and physical and sexual abuse during childhood and/or adolescence (Diekstra et al., in press; Fombonne, in press; Petersen, Compas, & Brooks-Gunn, 1993). A number of reports indicate that these adverse social conditions have increased over the last three to four decades (Coleman & Husen, 1985; Preston, 1984). In their report for the Organization for Economic Cooperation and Development (OECD), Coleman and Husen (1985) concluded that although "the number of social changes in the highly industrialized countries with extensive consequences for youth . . . differ in different OECD countries, the pattern is so widespread that it can be regarded as a general change" (p. 8). If the prevalence of such social and interpersonal problems in the community in general has been rising, it may well be that the increasing rates of depression and suicidal behavior reflect in part the increasing presence of these social stressors. There are, however, very few studies carried out at an international level that shed some light on this issue (Diekstra et al., in press; WHO, 1982) and they have, for obvious reasons, focused exclusively on the

relationship between secular trends in some of these social conditions and secular trends in suicide (no such studies are available for depression or parasuicide).

Sainsbury and colleagues (WHO, 1982), in cooperation with the World Health Organization, investigated the relationship between certain social conditions and changes in suicide rates in 18 European countries after 1960. The social characteristics of countries in 1961–1963 associated with a subsequent increase in rates of suicide in the period 1972–1974 were: (1) a high divorce rate; (2) a low percentage of the population under the age of 15 years; (3) a high unemployment rate; (4) a high homicide rate; (5) a high proportion of women employed. Sainsbury and colleagues (WHO, 1982) also analyzed which changes in social conditions after 1960 were related to changes in national suicide rates. The results indicated similar but not identical factors associated with suicide trends. Increased suicide rates were associated with: (1) a reduction in population aged 15 and under; (2) an increase in the percentage of the populated aged 65 and over (the age group with the relatively highest suicide rate in European countries); (3) an increase in females in tertiary education, possibly an indicator of the changing status of women and of family structure. Sainsbury's study examined only the relationship between social factors and changes in total suicide rates, and therefore did not provide information on changes in rates among adolescents and young adults. Diekstra and coworkers, within the framework of the WHO Program on Preventive Strategies on Suicide (Diekstra et al., in press), carried out a similar analysis on the 15- to 29-year-old age group. Changes in suicide rates for this age group for the same European countries over the period 1960/61 to 1984/85 were related to proportional changes in a number of social variables (all age groups). The extent to which each of the (seven) variables investigated accurately predict observed changes in national suicide rates can be deduced from the fact that the multiple correlation between those seven variables and changes in suicide rates was 0.84. Five of these variables are identical or similar to the ones shown by Sainsbury's study to be associated with changes in national overall suicide rates. Unlike Sainsbury's findings, however, this study showed a positive relationship between the percentage of young people in the population and the suicide rate (see also, Holinger, Offer, & Zola, 1988). The two other variables related to change in youth suicide rates, the change in use of liters of pure alcohol per head of population and the proportional change in church membership (nine countries only), an indicator of secularization, require some additional comments. First, the change in use of alcohol has the highest single correlation (0.70) with change in suicide rate. This seems to substantiate what we previously discussed about the relationship between the increasing emergence of a pattern of behavior involving the use or abuse of psychoactive substances to cope with life problems and depressive and/or suicidal reactions.

The association between the proportional change in church membership and change in suicide rate suggests a change in moral values and hence in attitudes toward suicide and the frequency with which it occurs. It might also be seen as an indicator of decreasing social integration, since churches have for centuries also functioned as social havens.

In conclusion, the results from the two studies seem to indicate that societies, communities, or social groups increasingly and simultaneously subject to such conditions as economic instability or deprivation (unemployment), breakdown of traditional primary or family group structure, greater intragenerational pressures and competition, interpersonal violence and increase in criminal behavior, secularization and (possibly) more permissive attitudes toward suicide, and increasing substance use and abuse are at a high risk for an increase in suicide mortality.

The exact nature of the association between each of these conditions separately and suicide mortality remains, however, rather obscure. At the individual level, unemployment, for example, appears to be related to depression and suicidal behavior in a number of ways (Fombonne, in press). Unemployment of a family member, particularly the father, is associated with both depressive conditions and suicidal reactions in children and adolescents, but the association is moderated by a number of other variables, such as the presence or absence of other problems in the family, for example, poverty, marital disruption, and parental mental illness (Rutter, Graham, Chadwick, & Yule, 1976). Furthermore, parental unemployment appears to be a risk factor of unemployment in adolescent children, a phenomenon sometimes labeled "transgenerational problem transmission." Unemployment of the adolescent or young adult is also, independent of parental unemployment, associated with elevated risk of suicidal behavior and presumably also depression (Platt, 1984). The interpretation of this latter association is uncertain. Unemployment might be a "stadium" on a pathway leading to depression or suicidal behavior, but the reverse might also be true; depressive or suicidal reactions causing poor functioning at work, continued absence from work, and loss of job. The associations between other social problems, such as parental divorce and the risk of depression and suicidal behavior in adolescents, are of similar complexity. There appears to be growing consensus in the literature that the associations between social problems and mental illhealth are generally stronger among adolescents than among adults (Platt, 1984; Rutter, 1980); that is, adolescents are more vulnerable to social and interpersonal adversities than are adults. Illustrative of this are the results of a study on attitudes toward suicide and age (Diekstra & Kerkhof, 1989). In a factor analysis of the answers to a suicide attitude scale taken from two samples of the general population, two principal factors were found that could be interpreted as follows:

1. Respondent's ability to imagine any circumstances at all in which he or she might commit suicide
2. Estimated probability of physical and social

problems as reasons or motives for committing suicide by respondent or others

Relevant for the present discussion are the findings on the relationship between age and factor scores on the second factor. The older and younger age groups showed no differences in estimated probability of suicide (by self or others) under conditions such as incurable or terminal illness or chronic mental illness. They did, however, differ very strongly in estimated probability of suicide under adverse social conditions such as loss of job, breaking off of a (love) relationship, unwanted pregnancy, and the like. The adolescents and young adults rated the probability that they or others would commit suicide under such circumstances much higher than the older age groups.

## CONCLUSION

To develop oneself is to work on one's self and to be worked on by other persons and by nonpersonal processes and events. Developmental stress is, therefore, a form of work stress and vice versa. The most recent and best-substantiated models or schemes of work stress – often labeled as *interactional* or *relational* models – explain this and its emotional and physical consequences as the outcome of the interaction between five sets of factors:

1. Task demands (their number, natures, and patterning)
2. The available social support (both emotional/affective, informational and behavior-regulatory) for meeting those demands
3. The available resources (material, financial, technical) for meeting those demands
4. The available personal (coping) skills and attitudes relevant to the task demands
5. The socioecological context in which demands have to be met

If one inserts the word *developmental* before the words *task demands* in item (1), it immediately becomes clear that this scheme might be as applicable to developmental stress as to work stress in *sensu stricto*. Developmental stress and related emotional disorders can thus be seen as resulting from the discrepancies between developmental task demands, on the one hand, and available support, resources, personal skills, and environment measure up to those demands. If the assumption is valid that over the past 100 years or so the developmental tasks of adolescence and young adults have grown not only in number but also in complexity, the key question is whether available support, resources, skills, and suitability of the developmental context have grown or changed in similar ways, or alternatively have lagged behind for certain subgroups of the population.

The data on secular trends in depression and suicide as presented and discussed in this paper seem to suggest that the number of disadvantaged has grown in most industrialized countries. Despite a general rise in standard of living and physical health, it remains doubtful whether the quality of mental life and of social well-being for many has improved. It also remains doubtful whether those at the lower end of the social continuum today are better off than their peers 50 or 100 years ago.

There are no clear signs that social inequity in health, particularly in mental health, is decreasing in most countries, and it cannot be ruled out that it has instead been increasing over the past decades and that the increase will continue in the next decades (WHO, 1989). In the opinion of the authors the priorities of the future public health and research agendas, in particular as far as adolescents and young adults are concerned, should be: (1) a precise identification of the developmental tasks in contemporary society; (2) a careful description of the conditions, both material and physical, psychological and social, for their successful completion in adolescence and young adulthood; and (3) a clear delineation of who is to be held responsible for the fulfillment of those conditions during the second and third decades of life.

Surprising as it may sound, national public health policies and research programs have not, as far as these three goals are concerned, reached adolescence, let alone adulthood, in the countries of Europe and North America. They are still in the stage of early infancy.

## REFERENCES

Achenbach, T. M. (1991). *Manual for the youth self-report and 1991 profile*. Burnton, VT: University of Vermont, Department of Psychiatry. (Also: Integrative guide for the 1991 C.B.C.L./4-18, YSR, and T.R.F. profiles)

Andrus, J. K., Fleming, D. W., Heumann, M. A., Wassell, J. T., Hopkins, D. D., & Gordon, J. (1991). Surveillance of attempted suicide among adolescents in Oregon. *American Journal of Public Health, 81*, 1067-1069.

Asgard, U., Nordström, P., & Rabäck, G. (1987). Birth cohort analysis of changing suicide risk by sex and age in Sweden 1952 to 1981. *Acta Psychiatrica Scandinavica, 76*, 456-463.

Bachman, J. G., Johnston, L. D., & O'Malley, P. M. (1986). *Monitoring the future. Questionnaire responses from the nation's high-school seniors*. Ann Arbor, MI: Institute for Social Research, University of Michigan.

Barnes, R. A., Ennis, J., & Schober, R. (1986). Cohort analysis of Ontario suicide 1877-1976. *Canadian Journal of Psychiatry, 31*, 208-213.

Beck, A. T. (1976). *Cognitive therapy and the emotional disorders*. New York: International Universities Press.

Buda, M., & Tsuang, M. T. (1990). In S. Blumental & D. Kupfer (Eds.), *Suicide over the life cycle* (pp. 17-38). Washington, DC: APA Press.

Canino, G. J., Bird, H. R., Shrout, P. E., Rubio-Stipec, M., Bravo, M., Martinez, R., Sesman, M., & Guevara, L. M. (1987). The prevalence of specific psychiatric disorders in Puerto Rico. *Archives of General Psychiatry, 44*, 727-735.

Carlson, G. A., Rich, C. L., Grayson, P., & Fowler, R. C. (1991). Secular trends in psychiatric diagnoses of suicide victims. *Journal of Affective Disorders, 21*, 127-132.

Cavan, R. S. (1926). *Suicide*. Chicago: Chicago University Press.

CDC–Centers of Disease Control. (1991). Attempted suicide among high school students–United States 1990, leads from the *Morbidity and Mortality Weekly Report. Journal of the American Medical Association, 266*(14), 911.

Coleman, E. A., & Husen, T. (1985). *Becoming an adult in a changing society*. Paris: OECD.

De Wilde, E. J., Kienhorst, C. W. M., Diekstra, R. F. W., & Wolters, W. H. G. (1992). The relationship between adolescent suicidal behavior and life events in childhood and adolescence. *American Journal of Psychiatry, 149*, 45-51.

Diekstra, R. F. W. (1982). Epidemiology of attempted suicide in the EEC. In J. Wilmotte & J. Mendlewicz (Eds.), *New trends in suicide prevention* (pp. 1-16). New York: Karger (Bibliotheca Psychiatrica).

Diekstra, R. F. W. (1989a). Suicidal behavior and depressive disorders in adolescents and young adults. *Neuropsychobiology, 22*, 194-207.

Diekstra, R. F. W. (1989b). Suicidal behavior in adolescents and young adults: The international picture. *Crisis, 10*(1), 16-35.

Diekstra, R. F. W., De Heus, P., Garnefski, N., de Zwart, R., & Van Praag, B. M. S. (1991). *Monitoring the future: Behavior and health among high school students*. The Hague: NIBUD.

Diekstra, R. F. W., & Kerkhof, A. J. F. M. (1989). Attitudes towards suicide: The development of a suicide attitude questionnaire (SUIATT). In R. F. W. Diekstra, R. Maris, S. Platt, A. Schmidtke, & G. Sonnick (Eds.), *Suicide and its prevention: The role of attitude and imitation*, (pp. 91-107). World Health Organization copublication. Canberra: Leiden.

Diekstra, R. F. W., Kienhorst, C., & De Wilde, E. (in press). Suicide and parasuicide. In M. Rutter (Ed.), *Psychosocial problems of youth in a changing Europe*. Cambridge: Cambridge University Press. (prepared for the Academia Europea Study Group on Youth Problems)

Dubow, E. F., Kausch, D. F., Blum, M. C., Reed, J., & Bush, E. (1989). Correlates of suicidal ideation and attempts in a community sample of junior high and high school students. *Journal of Clinical Child Psychology, 18*, 158-166.

Farberow, N. L. (Ed.). (1980). *The many faces of suicide: Indirect self-destructive behaviour*. New York: McGraw-Hill.

Fombonne, E. (in press). Secular trends in depressive disorders. In M. Rutter (Ed.), *Psychosocial problems of youth in a changing Europe*. Cambridge: Cambridge University Press. (prepared for the Academia Study Group on Youth Problems)

Fremouw, W. J., De Perczel, M., & Ellis, T. E. (1990). *Suicide risk: Assessment and response guidelines*. New York: Pergamon Press.

Goldney, R. D., & Katsikitis, M. (1983). Cohort analysis of suicide rates in Australia. *Archives of General Psychiatry, 40*, 71-74.

Goldney, R. D., Winefield, A. H., Tiggemann, M., Winefield, H. R., & Smith, S. (1989). Suicidal ideation in a young adult population. *Acta Psychiatrica Scandinavica, 79*, 481-489.

Gould, M. S., Shaffer, D., & Davies, M. (1991). Truncated pathways from childhood into adulthood: Attrition in follow-up studies due to death. In L. Robins & M. Rutter (Eds.), *Straight and devious pathways from childhood into adulthood*. (pp. 3-9). New York: Cambridge University Press.

Häfner, H., & Schmidtke, A. (1985). Do cohort effects influence suicide rates? *Archives of General Psychiatry, 42*, 926-927.

Hagnell, O., Lanke, J., Rorsman, B., & Ojesjö, L. (1982). Are we entering an age of melancholy? Depressive illnesses in a prospective epidemiological study over 25 years: The Lundby study, Sweden. *Psychological Medicine, 12*, 279-289.

Hamburg, D. (1989). Preparing for life: The critical transition of adolescence. In R. W. F. Diekstra (Ed.), *Preventive interventions in adolescence* (pp. 4-15). Toronto/Bern, Hogrefe & Huber.

Harkavy Friedman, J. M., Asnis, G. M., Boeck, M.,

& DiFiore, J. (1987). Prevalence of specific suicidal behaviors in a high school sample. *American Journal of Psychiatry, 144*, 1203-1206.

Hawton, K., O'Grady, J., Osborn, M., & Cole, D. (1982). Adolescents who take overdoses: Their characteristics, problems, and contacts with helping agencies. *British Journal of Psychiatry, 140*, 118-123.

Holinger, P. C., Offer, D., & Zola, M. (1988). A prediction model of suicide among youth. *Journal of Nervous and Mental Disease, 176*, 275-279.

Irwin, C. E., & Vaughan, E. (1988). Psychosocial context of adolescent development: Study group report. *Journal of Adolescent Health Care, 9*(6), 11-19.

Joyce, P. R., Oakley-Browne, M. A., Wells, J. E., Bushnell, J. A., & Hornblow, A. R. (1990). Birth cohort trends in major depression: increasing rates and earlier onset in New Zealand. *Journal of Affective Disorders, 18*, 83-89.

Kaplan, S. L., Hong, G. K. & Weinhold, C. (1984). Epidemiology of depressive symptomatology in adolescents. *Journal of the American Academy of Child and Adolescent Psychiatry, 23*, 91-98.

Karno, M., Hough, R. L., Burnam, M. A., Escobar, J. I., Timbers, D. M., Santana, F., & Boyd, J. H. (1987). Lifetime prevalence of specific psychiatric disorders among Mexican Americans and non-Hispanic whites in Los Angeles. *Archives of General Psychiatry, 44*, 695-701.

Kienhorst, C. W. M., De Wilde, E. J., Van den Bout, J., Diekstra, R. F. W., & Wolters, W. H. G. (1990a). Self-reported suicidal behavior in Dutch secondary education students. *Suicide and Life-Threatening Behavior, 20*, 101-112.

Klerman, G. L. (1985). Birth cohort trends in rates in major depressive disorders among relatives of patients with affective disorders. *Archives of General Psychiatry, 42*, 689-699.

Kreitman, N. S. (1977). *Parasuicide*. Chichester: Wiley.

Lester, D. (1972). Why people kill themselves: A summary of research findings on suicidal behavior. Springfield, IL: C. C. Thomas.

Lester, D. (1984). Suicide risk by birth cohort. *Suicide and Life-Threatening Behavior, 14*, 132-136.

Maris, R. W. (1981). *Pathways to suicide. A survey of self-destructive behavior*. Baltimore: John Hopkins University Press.

Maris, R. W. (1991). Suicide. In *Encyclopedia of Human Biology* (Vol. 7, pp. 372-385). New York: Academic Press.

Mehr, M., Zeltzer, L. K., & Robinson, R. (1981). Continued self-destructive behaviors in adolescent suicide attempters: Part I. *Journal of Adolescent Health, 1*, 269-274.

Mehr, M., Zeltzer, L. K., & Robinson, R. (1982). Continued self-destructive behaviors in adolescent suicide attempters: Part II. *Journal of Adolescent Health Care, 2*, 182-187.

Miles, C. P. (1977). Conditions predisposing to suicide: a review. *Journal of Nervous and Mental Diseases, 16*, 231-246.

Moens, G. F. G. (1990). *Aspects of the epidemiology and prevention of suicide*. Leuven: Leuven University Press.

Mościcki, E. K., O'Caroll, P. W., Rae, D. S., Roy, A. G., Locke, B. Z., & Reigier, D. A. (1989). Suicidal ideation and attempts: The epidemiological catchment area study. In *Report of the Secretary's Task Force on Youth Suicide*. (DHHS Publ. (ADM) 89-1264, pp. 4-115/4-128). Rockville, MD: Department of Health and Human Services.

Murphy, E., Lindesay, J., & Grundy, E. (1986). 60 years of suicide in England and Wales. A cohort study. *Archives of General Psychiatry, 43*, 969-976.

Murphy, G. E., & Wetzel, R. D. (1980). Suicide risk by birth cohort in the United States, 1949 to 1974. *Archives of General Psychiatry, 37*, 519-523.

Nagy, S., & Adcock, A. (1990). *The Alabama adolescent health survey: Health knowledge and behaviors*. Summary Report II. University of Alabama and Troy State University.

Perry, C. L. (1989). Teacher vs. peer-led intervention. *Crisis, 10*(1), 52-61.

Petersen, A. C., Compas, B., & Brooks-Gunn, J. (1993). *Depression in adolescence: Current knowledge, research directions and implications for programs and policy*. Washington, DC: Carnegie Council on Adolescent Development.

Platt, S. (1984). Unemployment and suicidal behaviour: A review of the literature. *Social Science and Medicine, 19*(2), 93-115.

Platt, S. (1988). Data from the Royal Infirmary, Edingburgh, Scotland.

Platt, S., Bille-Brahe, U., & Kerkhof, A. J. F. M. (1992). Parasuicide in Europe: The WHO/EURO multicentre study on parasuicide. I. Introduction and preliminary analysis for 1989. *Acta Psychiatrica Scandinavica, 85*, 97-104.

Preston, S. H. (1984). Children and elderly in the U.S. *Scientific American, 251*(6), 36-41.

Pronovost, J., Cote, L., & Ross, C. (1990). Epidemiological study of suicidal behaviour among secondary-school students. *Canada's Mental Health, 38*, 9-14.

Reed, J., Camus, J., & Last, J. M. (1985). Suicide in Canada: Birth-cohort analysis. *Canadian Journal of Public Health, 76*, 43-47.

Rey, J. M., & Bird, K. D. (1991). Sex differences in suicidal behaviour of referred adolescents. *British Journal of Psychiatry, 158*, 776-781.

Robins, L. N., Locke, B. Z., & Regier, D. A. (1991). An overview of psychiatric disorders in America. In L. N. Robins & D. A. Regier (Eds.), *Psychiatric disorders in America: The epidemiologic catchment area study* (pp. 328-366). New York: Free Press.

Rose, G. (1990). Doctors and the nation's health. *Annals of Medicine, 22*, 297-302.

Rubenstein, J. L., Heeren, T., Housman, D., Rubin, C., & Stechler, G. (1989). Suicidal behavior in "normal" adolescents: Risk and protective factors. *American Journal of Orthopsychiatry, 59*, 59-71.

Rutter, M. (1980). *Changing youth in a changing society. Patterns of adolescent development and disorder*. Cambridge, MA: Harvard University Press.

Rutter, M. (1986). The developmental psychopathology of depression: issues and perspectives. In M. Rutter, C. E. Izard, & P. B. Read (Eds.), *Depression in Young People* (pp. 3-30).New York: Guilford Press.

Rutter, M., Graham, P., Chadwick, O. F. D., & Yule, W. (1976). Adolescent turmoil: Fact or fiction? *Journal of Child Psychology and Psychiatry, 17*, 35–56.

Sainsbury, P., Jenkins, J., & Baert, A. E. (1981). Suicide trends in Europe: A study of the decline in suicide in England and Wales and the increases elsewhere. WHO/EURO document ICP/MNH 036. Copenhagen: WHO.

Schoenbach, V., Kaplan, B., Wagner, E., Grimson, R. & Miller, F. (1983). Prevalence of self-reported depressive symptoms in young adolescents. *American Journal of Public Health, 73*, 1281–1287.

Smith, K., & Crawford, S. (1986). Suicidal behavior among "normal" high school students. *Suicide and Life-Threatening Behavior, 16*, 313–325.

Solomon, M. I., & Hellon, C. P. (1980). Suicide and age in Alberta, Canada: 1951 to 1977. *Archives of General Psychiatry, 37*, 511–513.

Spirito, A., Brown, L., Overholser, J., & Fritz, G. (1989). Attempted suicide in adolescence: A review and critique of the literature. *Clinical Psychology Review, 9*, 335–363.

Vaillant, G. E., & Blumenthal, S. J. (1990). Suicide over the life cycle: Risk factors and life span development. In S. J. Blumenthal, D. J. Kupfer (Eds.), *Suicide over the Life Cycle* (pp. 1–16). Washington, American Psychiatric Press.

Vecchia, C. I. Bollini, P., & Imazio, C. (1986). Age, period of death and birth cohort effects on suicide mortality in Italy, 1955–1979. *Acta Psychiatrica Scandinavica, 74*, 137–143.

Watanabe, N., Ninomiya, M., Shukutani, K., Aizawa, S., & Hasegawa, K. (1988). Structural analysis of behavioural patterns of junior high school students. *Japanese Journal of Child and Adolescent Psychiatry, 29*(3), 160–172.

Weinstein, S. R., Noam, G. G., Grines, K., Stone, K., & Schwab-Stone, N. (1990). Convergence of DSM-III diagnoses and self-reported symptoms in child and adolescence in-patients. *Journal of the American Academy of Child and Adolescent Psychiatry, 29*, 627–634.

Weissman, M. M. (1974). The epidemiology of suicide attempts, 1960–1971. *Archives of General Psychiatry, 30*, 737–746.

Weissman, M., Livingston Bruce, M., Leaf, P. J., Florio, L. P., & Hozer III, C. (1991). Affective disorders. In L. N. Robins & D. A. Regier (Eds.), *Psychiatric disorders in America: The epidemiologic catchment area study*. (pp. 53–80). New York: Free Press.

WHO. (1982). *Changing patterns in suicide behaviour*. WHO/EURO Reports and Studies 74. Copenhagen: WHO.

WHO. (1987, 1988, 1989, 1992). *World health statistics annual*. Geneva: Author.

WHO. (1989). *The health of youth*. Geneva: Author.

# 4

# Gender and the Primary Prevention of Suicide Mortality

Silvia Sara Canetto, PhD, and David Lester, PhD

Primary prevention aims at reducing the incidence of a disorder. The first step in primary prevention involves documenting the magnitude of the problem and identifying risk factors. Consistent with primary prevention practices, we review the national and international epidemiological data on suicide mortality and then discuss the implications these data hold for primary prevention. Our approach is novel because we systematically examine the suicide epidemiology data by gender and culture. Suicide mortality appears to be highest among individuals (e.g., young adult married females in some Papua New Guinea regions; older adult, isolated, White males in the United States) for whom such behavior is culturally sanctioned. Thus, an important target for primary prevention may be local cultures of gender and suicide.

Primary prevention aims at reducing the incidence (the number of new cases) of a disorder (Albee & Canetto, in press). The first step in primary prevention involves identifying the population at risk for a particular disorder and the conditions in which the disorder is most prevalent. Knowledge about a vulnerable population and its environment is then translated into primary prevention programs aimed at strengthening the resistance of the host and/or eliminating the environmental pathogens. Consistent with primary prevention practices, in this article we review the national and international epidemiological data on suicide mortality and then discuss the implications of such data for primary prevention.

Our approach is novel because we systematically examine data on suicide mortality by gender. Gender is one of the best predictors of suicide mortality (Canetto, 1992–1993). As our review demonstrates, however, cultural factors also play an important role in whether women or men are at greater risk for suicidal mortality, and under what circumstances. Our analysis is preceded by a brief discussion of the nature and limitations of the data on suicide mortality.

## THE NATURE OF SUICIDE MORTALITY DATA

Information on rates of suicidal mortality is available through local surveys and/or official government sources. The main limitations of this information result from variations in data comprehensiveness and from variations in the criteria used for the determination of suicide mortality.

Many countries compile official mortality statistics and report them to the World Health Organization (WHO). Official suicide mortality data, however, are not available for many countries, including most African and many Middle Eastern countries (Diekstra, 1990). Furthermore, official mortality statistics do not include information about important contextual factors, such as occupation, socio-

Silvia Sara Canetto, PhD, is with Colorado State University. David Lester, PhD, is with the Center for the Study of Suicide.

Address correspondence and reprint requests to: Silvia Sara Canetto, PhD, Department of Psychology, Colorado State University, Fort Collins, CO 80523.

This article benefited from feedback by Jeremy Gersovitz, David L. MacPhee, and David B. Wohl.

economic status, or living arrangements. Local epidemiological studies typically cover a broader range of variables than official mortality statistics, but may not be generalizable beyond the community from which the sample was drawn. A problem common to national and local data is that information is not always simultaneously categorized by gender, age, and ethnicity. Therefore, important comparisons across specific gender/age/ethnic groups are not always possible.

The most serious limitation of official mortality statistics is the lack of standardized and internationally accepted criteria for the determination of suicide mortality (McIntosh, 1989; O'Carroll, 1989). As a consequence, the classification of a death as suicide is influenced by the background of coroners and medical examiners; the cultural beliefs about, and social consequences of, death by suicide (e.g., burial practices and attitudes toward surviving members); and the circumstances of death (e.g., the method employed) (McIntosh, 1989; O'Carroll, 1989; Taylor, 1982). For example, according to an Irish study (Walsh, Walsh, & Whelan, 1975), coroners are more likely to miss a true suicide if the method of suicide is drowning, jumping, or ingesting poison.

While it is generally accepted that official mortality rates underestimate "true" prevalence, it is less well recognized that underreporting biases affect women's suicide rates more than men's. There is evidence indicating that women's suicidal deaths are particularly susceptible to underreporting because they tend to use methods (e.g., poison) that are more likely to lead to misclassification (Phillips & Ruth, 1993). Cultural beliefs about gender and suicide may also play a role in the underreporting of women's suicides. It has been suggested that in Western countries, coroners may be reluctant to recognize suicidal clues in a woman's death (Douglas, 1967; Kushner, 1985, 1993) because killing oneself is perceived as masculine (Canetto, 1992–1993; Kushner, 1985, 1993). It has also been speculated that in Western countries, family members may

be more likely to hide a woman's suicide than a man's (Douglas, 1967) because women's suicidal behavior is assumed to be precipitated by domestic unhappiness. Interestingly, one study of factors influencing coroners' verdicts (Walsh et al., 1975) found that living alone was more likely to lead to a verdict of suicide than living with family.

## THE EPIDEMIOLOGY OF SUICIDE MORTALITY

### Gender and Culture/Nationality

According to available data (WHO, 1969–1991), women are less likely to kill themselves than men in *almost all* countries that report their mortality statistics to the WHO. The female-to-male ratio is usually on the order of 1:2, and frequently is smaller (see Table 1).

The female:male suicide mortality ratio, however, varies considerably from country to country (WHO, 1969–1991). In general, the ratio is higher in Asian countries. For example, the female:male ratio ranges from 0.00 in Malta and Egypt to 0.86 for Singapore and 0.92 in Thailand for the latest years with data available. Lester (1982) examined international data on suicide mortality rates for females and males for 1975. He concluded that Asian countries had proportionately more female deaths from suicide than non-Asian countries. In 1975, the female:male ratio was significantly higher in Asia ($M = 0.74$) than in Europe (0.45), as well as in South America and Central America/Caribbean countries (0.34).

The countries with the highest rates of suicide mortality for men are Hungary (58.0 per 100,000 in 1991), Finland (48.9 in 1991), and Sri Lanka (46.9 in 1986). Even though women's rates of suicide mortality are generally lower than men's, in some countries women's absolute rates of suicide mortality are quite high. The countries with the highest rates of suicide mortality for women include Hungary (20.7 per 100,000 in 1991), Sri Lanka (18.9

Table 1
Female and Male Suicide Mortality Rates (per 100,000)
and Ratios for Countries of the World
(latest available year from the World Health Organization)

| | Suicide Rates | | | |
| --- | --- | --- | --- | --- |
| | Female | Male | Ratio | Year |
| Argentina | 3.8 | 10.5 | 0.36 | 1989 |
| Australia | 5.6 | 21.0 | 0.27 | 1988 |
| Austria | 11.6 | 34.6 | 0.34 | 1991 |
| Belgium | 13.8 | 32.0 | 0.43 | 1987 |
| Brazil | 2.0 | 4.6 | 0.43 | 1980 |
| Bulgaria | 8.6 | 22.6 | 0.38 | 1991 |
| Canada | 5.2 | 20.4 | 0.25 | 1990 |
| Chile | 1.5 | 9.8 | 0.15 | 1989 |
| China | 20.4 | 14.9 | 1.37 | 1987 |
| Colombia | 1.6 | 6.0 | 0.27 | 1984 |
| Costa Rica | 2.1 | 9.3 | 0.23 | 1989 |
| Cuba | 16.1 | 19.1 | 0.84 | 1977 |
| Czechoslovakia | 8.9 | 27.3 | 0.33 | 1990 |
| Denmark | 15.1 | 30.0 | 0.50 | 1991 |
| Dominican Republic | 0.9 | 3.7 | 0.24 | 1982 |
| Ecuador | 2.8 | 6.3 | 0.44 | 1988 |
| Egypt | 0.0 | 0.1 | 0.00 | 1987 |
| El Salvador | 6.1 | 14.8 | 0.41 | 1984 |
| Finland | 11.7 | 48.9 | 0.24 | 1991 |
| France | 11.1 | 29.6 | 0.38 | 1990 |
| Germany, East | 14.8 | 34.8 | 0.43 | 1990 |
| Germany, West | 9.6 | 22.4 | 0.43 | 1990 |
| Greece | 1.5 | 5.5 | 0.27 | 1990 |
| Guatemala | 0.1 | 0.9 | 0.11 | 1984 |
| Hong Kong | 9.1 | 11.8 | 0.77 | 1989 |
| Hungary | 20.7 | 58.0 | 0.37 | 1991 |
| Iceland | 3.9 | 27.4 | 0.14 | 1990 |
| Ireland | 4.7 | 14.4 | 0.33 | 1990 |
| Israel | 4.6 | 11.0 | 0.42 | 1989 |
| Italy | 4.1 | 11.2 | 0.37 | 1989 |
| Jamaica | 0.2 | 0.5 | 0.40 | 1985 |
| Japan | 11.8 | 20.6 | 0.57 | 1991 |
| Jordan | 0.0 | 0.1 | 0.00 | 1978 |
| Korea | 4.4 | 11.5 | 0.38 | 1987 |
| Kuwait | 0.6 | 1.0 | 0.60 | 1987 |
| Luxembourg | 9.8 | 30.0 | 0.33 | 1989 |
| Malta | 0.0 | 4.6 | 0.00 | 1990 |
| Martinique | 3.0 | 4.4 | 0.68 | 1985 |
| Mauritius | 8.3 | 18.2 | 0.47 | 1991 |
| Mexico | 0.7 | 3.6 | 0.18 | 1986 |
| Netherlands | 5.5 | 22.5 | 0.59 | 1990 |
| New Zealand | 5.5 | 22.5 | 0.24 | 1989 |
| Nicaragua | 0.1 | 0.4 | 0.25 | 1978 |
| Norway | 8.0 | 23.3 | 0.34 | 1990 |
| Panama | 1.9 | 5.6 | 0.34 | 1987 |
| Papua New Guinea | 0.2 | 0.1 | 2.00 | 1980 |
| Paraguay | 2.0 | 3.0 | 0.67 | 1986 |
| Peru | 0.3 | 0.7 | 0.43 | 1985 |
| Philippines | 0.5 | 0.7 | 0.71 | 1977 |

(*continued*)

Table 1
Continued

| | Suicide Rates | | | |
| | Female | Male | Ratio | Year |
|---|---|---|---|---|
| Poland | 4.4 | 23.9 | 0.18 | 1991 |
| Portugal | 4.6 | 14.9 | 0.31 | 1991 |
| Puerto Rico | 2.1 | 19.4 | 0.11 | 1990 |
| Romania | 4.5 | 14.3 | 0.31 | 1991 |
| Singapore | 11.5 | 14.7 | 0.78 | 1990 |
| Spain | 3.9 | 11.6 | 0.37 | 1989 |
| Sri Lanka | 18.9 | 46.9 | 0.40 | 1986 |
| Surinam | 11.6 | 31.8 | 0.36 | 1985 |
| Sweden | 10.6 | 26.8 | 0.40 | 1989 |
| Switzerland | 11.6 | 34.3 | 0.34 | 1991 |
| Syria | 0.1 | 0.5 | 0.20 | 1981 |
| Taiwan | 10.5 | 15.6 | 0.67 | 1969 |
| Thailand | 7.0 | 7.6 | 0.92 | 1981 |
| Trinidad and Tobago | 6.7 | 21.8 | 0.31 | 1989 |
| Turkey | 0.2 | 0.3 | 0.67 | 1979 |
| United Kingdom | 3.6 | 12.4 | 0.29 | 1991 |
| USA | 4.8 | 19.9 | 0.24 | 1989 |
| USSR | 9.1 | 34.4 | 0.26 | 1990 |
| Uruguay | 4.2 | 16.6 | 0.25 | 1990 |
| Venezuela | 1.5 | 6.6 | 0.23 | 1987 |
| Yugoslavia | 9.2 | 21.6 | 0.43 | 1990 |

in 1986), and Cuba (16.1 in 1977) (see Table 1).

One exception to the male predominance in suicide mortality is the People's Republic of China, which now reports on about 10% of its population. In 1987 the People's Republic of China had higher suicide mortality rates for women than for men, 20.4 per 100,000 per year for women and 14.9 for men in 1987 (Lester, 1990). In rural areas these rates were 32.3 and 23.2, respectively, and in urban areas 11.4 and 8.7. Another exception is Papua New Guinea, which in 1980 reported a rate of 0.2 per 100,000 for women and 0.1 for men.

Regional studies reveal more exceptions. According to Healey (1979), only women kill themselves among the Maring of Papua New Guinea. Also, in England and Wales, mortality by suicide among immigrants of Indian origin is higher among women than among men (Raleigh, Bulusu, & Balarajan, 1990). Brown (1986)

has reported that death from suicide among the Aguaruna of the Peruvian Amazon region is especially common in women and in young men. Finally, in the Deganga region of India, women constituted 79% of the deaths by suicide in 1979 (Banerjee, Nandi, Nandi, Sarkar, Boral, & Ghosh, 1990).

In the United States, death by suicide is less common in women than in men, independent of time of data collection, age, ethnic origin, and relationship status (Lester, 1988). In 1980, the female:male ratio was similar for Whites (0.21) and non-Whites (0.19) (Lester, 1989). Rates of suicide mortality, however, vary considerably across time. Nationwide data show that the female-to-male suicide mortality ratio peaked in the early 1970s; the ratio was 0.27 in 1933, 0.31 in 1940, 0.28 in 1950, 0.29 in 1960, 0.39 in 1970, 0.30 in 1980, and 0.24 in 1990 (National Center for Health Statistics, 1933–1990). There are also regional variations in suicide mortality. In 1980 the female:male ratio ranged from 0.17 in South Dakota to 0.51 in Nevada (Lester, 1988, 1991a).

## Gender and Age

The data reviewed so far indicate, with some exceptions, that women are less likely to kill themselves than men. However, when mortality data are examined by age, one finds more exceptions to the usual preponderance of men among the casualties of suicide. For example, Barraclough (1988) examined women's and men's suicide mortality rates for those aged 15 to 24. He found that in several Asian, Caribbean, and South American countries – including Brazil, Cuba, the Dominican Republic, Ecuador, Hong Kong, Paraguay, the Philippines, Singapore, and Thailand – females' suicide mortality rates exceeded those of males. Similarly, studies of police and medical records in a province of Fiji (Haynes, 1984) and in the Highlands of Malaysia (Maniam, 1988) showed that young women had higher suicide mortality rates than young men.

In 1980 the nations with high rates of suicide mortality for women aged 15–24 included Thailand (19.6 per 100,000 per year) and Switzerland (12.3); for women aged 44–54, Denmark (42.8) and Hungary (36.2); and for women aged 75 and older, Hungary (90.6) and Hong Kong (64.6) (Lester, 1991b). In the same year, the nations with high rates of suicide mortality for men aged 15–24 included Finland (37.5) and Switzerland (34.2); for men aged 44–54, Hungary (106.4) and Denmark (70.7); and for men aged 75 and older, Hungary (202.2) and Bulgaria (108.7) (Lester, 1991b).

No consistent relation was found between gender, age, culture, and suicide mortality (Lester, 1991b). In the United States, suicide mortality rates peak at midlife for women and in late life for men. In other countries, this gender pattern is reversed (e.g., Scotland) or, more commonly, the rates increase with age for both

women and men (e.g., Italy). Because in the United States female rates decrease after midlife and male rates reach their highest levels in late life, the gender differential in rates is least at midlife and greatest during late life (McIntosh, 1992). It should be noted, however, that rates for middle-aged women are less than half those for middle-aged men (McIntosh, 1991).

Lester (1982) looked at the distribution of suicide mortality rates by age for women and men in different countries as a function of the level of national economic development (defined as the gross national product per capita). For females, the peak age for death by suicide rose from 55–64 to 75 and older as the level of economic development of the nations increased, with the exception of the least-developed group of nations, where the peak was for those aged 15 to 24. For males, suicide mortality rates rose with age at all levels of economic development.

## Gender and Social Class

The relation between gender, social class, and suicide mortality is difficult to assess because of the tendency to assign social class to married women on the basis of the social class of their husbands. Furthermore, there are few sound studies of the relation between social class and suicide mortality in general, let alone studies focusing on gender.

Available studies have yielded variable findings. On the one hand, in England suicide mortality was found to be more common among the upper classes (Stengel, 1964). Similarly, Nayha (1977) reported that in Finland adult women who killed themselves were from a higher social class than men who killed themselves. On the other hand, a Finnish study (Marttunen, Hillevi, Henriksson, & Lönnqvist, 1991) found that among 13- to 19-year-olds, suicide mortality was more common among individuals (mostly males) from lower social classes (70% of cases were from manual worker families). Furthermore, a study of suicide mortality in Sacramento, California, found that the women were from lower social classes than the men (Bourque, Cosand, & Kraus, 1983).

Several studies have also noted that female suicide mortality rates are high in societies where women's social status is extremely low, such as China (Shiqing, Guang, Zhenglong, & Tiensen, 1994; Wolf, 1975); India (Adityanjee, 1986); Japan (Iga, Yamamoto, & Noguchi, 1975); the Kaliai, Gainj, and Maring people of Papua New Guinea (Counts, 1980, 1987; Healey, 1979; Johnson, 1981); and the Aguaruna of Peru (Brown, 1986). In these societies, women's social, education, vocational, and economic opportunities are severely restricted. Yet, in many societies, suicide mortality is highest among the socially privileged. For example, in the United States, suicide mortality is highest among white males, not among blacks or females (Canetto, 1992). Thus, killing oneself is not simply a function of social disadvantage; rather, cultural meanings of gender and suicide have to be taken into account.

## Gender and Employment

Available studies suggest that in most industrialized nations unemployment is associated with higher rates of suicide mortality for both women and men (Pritchard, 1988, 1990). Employed women have lower suicide mortality rates than women who are not employed, regardless of age and marital status (Cumming, Lazer, & Chisholm, 1975).

Although in the United States suicide mortality rates are lower in women than in men, professional women have suicide mortality rates as high as, and sometimes higher than, those of professional men; this is especially well documented for physicians (Lester, 1992; Yang & Lester, 1995). The reasons for the high rates of suicide mortality of professional women are not clear. A recent study of gender and suicide among chemists suggested that female chemists who killed themselves had experienced an isolating and hostile work

environment (Seiden & Gleiser, 1990). Among men, the risk for suicide mortality was found to be especially high among farmers both in the upper Midwest of the United States (Gunderson, Donner, & Nashold, 1993) and in Italy (Crepet, 1992).

## Gender and Personal Relationships

Suicide mortality rates are higher among the widowed and divorced, and lower in the married and single for both females and males. Smith, Mercy, and Conn (1988) reported these patterns for both whites and blacks in the United States.

Several studies, however, indicate that being married provides significantly better protection from suicide mortality for men than for women. For example, Gove (1972, 1979) explored the relationship between gender, marital status, and suicide in the United States. He observed that, since World War II, married women have had higher rates of mental disorder than married men, while never-married women have had lower rates of mental disorder than never-married men. Consequently, he hypothesized that marriage may be a better protector from mental disorder and suicide for men than for women. To verify this hypothesis, he compared the suicide mortality rate for the never-married with that of the married and found that, for 1959–1961, the ratio for females aged 26–64 years was 1.5, and for males, 2.0. Single females were 47% more likely to kill themselves than married females, while single males were 97% more likely to kill themselves than married males. Divorce and widowhood also seemed to be more disadvantageous for males than for females. He concluded that, in fact, marriage is more advantageous to men than to women. These findings have been replicated by Cumming and Lazer (1981) in Canada.

Bock and Webber (1972) have noted the extremely high suicide rates of elderly widowers, as compared with elderly widows. Based on a survey of the elderly in a Florida county, they attributed this pattern to greater social isolation among the widowers, as compared with the widows.

It has been suggested that single and widowed men's greater vulnerability to suicide, as compared with single and widowed women's, may result from men's reliance on women for social and emotional support (Canetto, 1992, 1995a). For example, while women typically name another woman as a confidant, many men view their wives as their sole confidant (Zarit, 1980). Thus, losing a spouse may not disrupt a woman's support system and emotional functioning to the degree that it might for a man (Canetto, 1992, 1995a). It has also been suggested that a person's risk of suicide may be reduced by relationship responsibilities (a sense that others count on you for care) — something many women maintain beyond widowhood — rather than by simply being the recipient of nurturance in relationships (see Canetto, 1992, 1995a, for a discussion).

Finally, several studies have noted that societies with high rates of female suicide mortality, such as China (Shiqing et al., 1994; Wolf, 1975); India (Adityanjee, 1986; Gehlot & Nathawat, 1983); Japan (Iga et al., 1975); the Kaliai, Gainj, and Maring people of Papua New Guinea (Counts, 1980, 1987; Healey, 1979, Johnson, 1981); and the Aguaruna of Peru (Brown, 1986) are also societies in which women's social and family status is extremely low. For example, according to Gehlot and Nathawat, married Hindu women are "often treated as chattel, living an existence of near slavery" (p. 274); furthermore, "the unfortunate young wife is not only a victim of the in-laws' desire for dominance, and sometimes avarice concerning dowry, but also of her own parents' indifference. . . . Cut off from any support group, the young wife takes her life" (pp. 276–277).

In these societies, women who kill themselves often have a history of being physically abused by their husbands and/or extended family (Counts, 1980, 1987). For example, according to a Chinese study, some of the women who killed themselves had been taunted by their in-laws over childlessness or failure to produce a son (Wolf, 1975). Similarly, Adityanjee (1986)

wrote that the suicides of married women in India are "understandable in the context of the prevalent problems surrounding dowries and consequent maltreatment of brides in the extended families" (p. 67).

Most importantly, societies with high rates of female suicide mortality have ideologies supporting death by suicide in women. In these societies, female suicide is a culturally recognized behavior that permits them, as Counts (1987) noted, "to affect the behavior of the more powerful members of their society, or at least allows them to revenge themselves on those who have made their lives intolerable" (p. 195). These women are not allowed "effective, more direct [non-self-destructive] means of affecting the behavior of others" (Counts, 1980, p. 336). For example, among the Kaliai and Gainj people of Papua New Guinea, killing oneself is a way for a woman "to require her survivors to demand compensation or take revenge on her abusive husband" (Counts, 1987, p. 203). Ironically, a woman's suicide is perceived as shameful by the husband because it is viewed as an act of willfulness and autonomy. "A suicide husband is an object of ridicule among the Gainj" because "he has failed completely to control his wife" (p. 332).

### Gender and Method

Availability, familiarity, and cultural acceptability play a role in the choice of suicide method (Marks & Stokes, 1976) and often vary with gender. In the United States (see Lester, 1984, for a review) women tend to use poison, and men firearms. For example, in 1988, 27% of the women who killed themselves used solid and liquid substances, as compared with 6% of the men. By contrast, 65% of the men used firearms or explosives, as compared with 40% of the women (National Center for Health Statistics, 1990). Similarly, between 1961 and 1985, firearms accounted for 8% of deaths by suicide in females and 36% of suicides in males in Australia (Cantor & Lewin, 1990). Among Indian immigrants residing in England

and Wales, burning is a method that is culturally acceptable and common among women, but not among men (Raleigh et al., 1990).

In some cultures, however, a suicide method may be similarly available, familiar, and culturally acceptable to women and men. For example, firearms are the most common method of suicide for women and men living in the American South (Marks & Abernathy, 1974); hanging for women and men living in Belgium (Moens, Loysch, Honggokoesoemo, & van de Voorde, 1989); and poisoning by weed killer or insecticide for women and men living in Malaysia (Maniam, 1988). In their study of suicide method by age, gender, and ethnicity in the United States, McIntosh and Santos (1985-1986) noted an increase in the use of firearms in most of the groups studied. They took it as an indication of easier access to firearms and of diminishing cultural distinctiveness in method acceptability.

It has been argued that gender differences in choice of suicide method account for the difference in fatal/nonfatal outcomes for women and men in the United States. However, even within each method (e.g., firearms), relatively more of the acts by women are nonfatal and more of the acts by men are fatal. Thus, choice of method for suicide cannot be the complete explanation of the gender difference in outcome. One reason for this difference may be that, in the United States, killing oneself is considered masculine, and therefore more "acceptable" for males than for females, independent of the reasons for it (see Canetto, 1992-1993, 1995 & Stillion, 1995, for reviews).

Lester (1993a) examined international suicide rates for 24 countries (mainly industrialized nations) and found that the female and male mortality rates from poisoning did not differ significantly. Women, however, had much lower rates of suicide mortality by methods other than poisoning than did men. Lester concluded that the gender differences in the use of these other methods accounted for the gender differences in suicide mortality. It

is also possible that these data simply reflect the fact that current medical technologies are more effective at rescuing victims of suicide by poisoning than victims of suicide by other means (Cantor & Lewin, 1990).

The importance of cultural acceptability was highlighted in a recent study by Fisher, Comstock, Monk, and Sencer (1993), where method was found to be significantly associated with sociodemographic characteristics (such as sex, age, ethnicity, place of birth) and occupational characteristics, even after adjustment for individual access to the method. The authors suggested that since "acceptability exerts an independent influence on method," one could focus prevention programs on restricting access to frequently used means "because there is imperfect substitutability among methods" (p. 99).

## Gender and Mental Disorder

Most studies find the highest suicide mortality rates in individuals diagnosed with a mental disorder (see Mościcki, 1994, for a review). The mental disorders most commonly associated with suicide are affective and addictive disorders.

There is evidence that in women, suicide mortality is typically associated with depression, and in men with alcohol abuse. Åsgård (1990) studied women who died from suicide in urban Sweden and reported that 59% suffered from depressive disorders at the time of death. A recent Finnish study of suicide mortality found that the prevalence of depression was higher among females (46%) than among males (26%) (Henriksson, Hillevi, Marttunen, Heikkinen, Isometsä, Kuoppasalmi, & Lönnqvist, 1993). The relative absence of alcohol abuse and/or illegal substance abuse in women who kill themselves, as compared to men, was noted in an early American urban study by Breed (1972), and then replicated in other studies conducted in the United States (Nuttall, Evenson, & Cho, 1980), in Denmark (Barner-Rasmussen, Dupont, & Bille, 1986), and in Finland (Henriksson et al., 1993;

Isometsä, Henriksson, Aro, Heikkinen, Kuoppasalmi, & Lönnqvist, 1994). However, in a study of San Diego county suicides (Rich, Ricketts, Fowler, & Young, 1988) no gender differences were found in the presence of alcoholism, drug abuse, or depression. Recent research on the association between eating disorders and suicidal behavior indicates that suicide mortality is higher in women with eating disorders than in women who do not have an eating disorder (Gardner & Rich, 1988).

## IMPLICATIONS FOR PRIMARY PREVENTION

A discussion of gender and suicide mortality needs to start with a reminder of the limitations in the available data. There are variations in the comprehensiveness and validity of suicide mortality statistics. Furthermore, there is evidence suggesting that women's suicides are more likely to be misclassified than men's (e.g., Phillips & Ruth, 1993). Thus, our recommendations for primary prevention are based on an underestimate of suicide mortality rates, especially for women.

Predominant paradigms of gender have tended to focus on differences and to de-emphasize similarities (see Hare-Mustin & Marecek, 1988, for a discussion). Therefore, in this discussion, we focus first on the similarities between women and men who kill themselves. For both women and men, work *and* relationships appear to contribute to the risk for suicide. There is consistent evidence of a significant association between unemployment and suicide mortality in both women and men. Relationships are also an important factor in the suicides of both women and men. The association between being unmarried (single, divorced, or widowed) and suicidal mortality appears to be stronger for men than for women—perhaps because being single is more likely to be associated with social isolation for men than for women. On the other hand, for women an important risk factor is being in an abusive relationship.

The most consistent gender difference in suicide epidemiology is that men predominate among those who die of suicide. The magnitude and pervasiveness of this trend makes it doubtful that the use of unbiased data would erase the difference between female and male rates. There are, however, *exceptions* to this pattern, depending on dimensions such as culture or age. In China, for example, women are more likely to kill themselves than men. Similarly, in several Asian, Caribbean, and South American countries, women's mortality by suicide exceeds men's among individuals age 15 to 24. Variations in suicide method by gender and culture have also been documented. In some countries (e.g., the United States) certain methods are used predominantly by women, and other methods by men; while in other countries (e.g., Belgium) women and men tend to use the same method. Finally, historical shifts in gender preferences for method have been reported. These national and historical variations in the gender epidemiology of suicide mortality suggest that cultural factors play an important role in influencing whether a person will engage in suicidal behaviors, which suicidal behaviors will be chosen, and under what circumstances such acts will be performed. These variations also suggest avenues for primary prevention.

Traditional suicide prevention programs have focused on providing services to suicidal ideators (Canetto, 1995). The effectiveness of such services, however, is unclear. One study (Miller, Coombs, Leeper, & Barton, 1984) found that these services reduced only young adult women's rates of suicidal behavior; another study (Lester, 1993b) did not find any gender differences in the preventive effect of suicide centers on state suicide rates. Finally, a meta-analysis of 18 studies (Dew, Bromet, Brent, & Greenhouse, 1987) did not produce evidence that suicide prevention centers affect community suicide rates. One limitation of these prevention programs is that they are set up to intervene with persons who are already suicidal. It could be argued that it is too late to prevent suicidal behavior when the person is already in crisis, and that prevention efforts would be more successful if they addressed the development of suicidal ideation prior to such crises (Canetto, 1995).

What may be legitimate targets of primary prevention programs? What are the conditions that breed suicidal behavior? What is common in the experiences of people who kill themselves in different cultures? Our review of studies suggests that suicidal behavior tends to be found among individuals (e.g., Papua New Guinea females, U.S. males) for whom such behavior is culturally acceptable. For example, death by suicide in women is common in cultures (e.g., certain Papua New Guinea ethnicities) where suicide is socially sanctioned, given particular circumstances (e.g., battering) and in order to achieve a particular goal (e.g., require her survivors to demand compensation from her abusive husband). Similarly, high rates of suicide in men, especially suicide by firearms, are found in cultures (e.g., the United States) that associate suicide and guns with masculinity, especially given certain losses (e.g., physical illness or achievement failures). Experiencing adversities does not appear to be sufficient to predict suicide mortality. People's response to stress, what they think of it, and what they do about it (whether they kill themselves, passively endure, or fight back) seems to depend on what is considered acceptable coping for them as women or men, given their social class and culture (Cloward & Piven, 1979).

Thus, an important avenue for primary prevention are these gender cultures of suicide. Suicide prevention programs ought to assess and focus on the meanings and acceptability of suicide within a particular group. For example, for women in Papua New Guinea it may mean challenging the cultural legitimization of wife battering, and of suicide as a woman's best recourse against such abuse; for men in the United States, it may mean overturning the cultural association between suicide and masculinity.

Because acceptability exerts an independent influence on method, and because there is imperfect substitutability among methods, primary prevention programs should also focus on restricting access to frequently used suicide methods. Thus, an effective means of preventing suicide in males in the United States may be to restrict access to firearms.

In a recent paper on the merits of primary prevention, Albee (1990) reminded us that "no mass disease or disorder afflicting humankind has ever been eliminated by attempts at treating affected individuals" (p. 370). Along the same lines, Hirsch, Walsh, and Draper (1982) concluded that a focus on sociocultural factors may be the most effective way to prevent suicidal behavior since there is little evidence of the efficacy of individual psychotherapies. We hope our analysis of the international epidemiology of gender and suicide mortality has stimulated new ideas on the role that culture and gender may play in primary prevention.

# REFERENCES

Adityanjee. (1986). Suicide attempts and suicides in India: Cross cultural aspects. *International Journal of Social Psychiatry, 32,* 64–73.

Albee, G. W. (1990). The futility of psychotherapy. *The Journal of Mind and Behavior, 11,* 369–384.

Albee, G. W., & Canetto, S. S. (in press). The role of the family in prevention. In C. A. Heflinger (Ed.), *Families and mental health services for children and adolescents: Policy, services, and research.* Newbury Park, CA: Sage.

Åsgård, U. (1990). A psychiatric study of suicide among urban Swedish women. *Acta Psychiatrica Scandinavica, 82,* 115–124.

Banerjee, G., Nandi, D. N., Nandi, S., Sarkar, S., Boral, G. C., & Ghosh, A. (1990). The vulnerability of Indian women to suicide: A field study. *Indian Journal of Psychiatry, 32,* 305–308.

Barner-Rasmussen, P., Dupont, A., & Bille, H. (1986). Suicide in psychiatric patients in Denmark, 1971–81. *Acta Psychiatrica Scandinavica, 73,* 441–448.

Barraclough, B. M. (1988). International variation in the suicide rate of 15–24 year olds. *Social Psychiatry and Psychiatric Epidemiology, 23,* 75–84.

Bock, E. W., & Webber, I. L. (1972). Suicide among the elderly. *Journal of Marriage and the Family, 34,* 24–31.

Bourque, L. B., Cosand, D., & Kraus, J. (1983). Comparison of male and female suicide in a defined community. *Journal of Community Health, 9,* 7-17.

Breed, W. (1972). Five components of a basic suicide syndrome. *Life-Threatening Behavior, 2,* 3-18.

Brown, M. F. (1986). Power, gender, and the social meaning of Aguaruna suicide. *Man, 21,* 311-328.

Canetto, S. S. (1991). Gender roles, suicide attempts, and substance abuse. *Journal of Psychology, 125,* 605-620.

Canetto, S. S. (1992). Gender and suicide in the elderly. *Suicide and Life-Threatening Behavior, 22,* 80-97.

Canetto, S. S. (1992-1993). She died for love and he for glory: Gender myths of suicidal behavior. *Omega, 26,* 1-17.

Canetto, S. S. (1995a). Elderly women and suicidal behavior. In S. S. Canetto & D. Lester (Eds.), *Women and suicidal behaviors* (pp. 213-231). New York: Springer.

Canetto, S. S. (1995b). Suicidal women: Prevention and intervention strategies. In S. S. Canetto & D. Lester (Eds.), *Women and suicidal behavior* (pp. 235-253). New York: Springer.

Cantor, C. H., & Lewin, T. (1990). Firearms and suicide in Australia. *Australian and New Zealand Journal of Psychiatry, 24,* 500-509.

Cloward, R. A., & Piven, F. F. (1979). Hidden protest: The channeling of female innovation and resistance. *Signs: Journal of Women in Culture and Society, 4,* 651-667.

Counts, D. A. (1980). Fighting back is not the way: Suicide and the women of Kaliai. *American Ethnologist, 7,* 332-351.

Counts, D. A. (1987). Female suicide and wife abuse: A cross-cultural perspective. *Suicide and Life-Threatening Behavior, 17,* 194-204.

Crepet, P. (1992). Suicide trends in Italy: New epidemiological findings. *European Psychiatry, 7,* 1-7.

Cumming, E., & Lazer, C. (1981). Kinship structure and suicide: A theoretical link. *Canadian Review of Sociology and Anthropology, 18,* 271-281.

Cumming, E., Lazer, C., & Chisholm, L. (1975). Suicide as an index of role strain among employed and not employed married women in British Columbia. *Canadian Review of Sociology and Anthropology, 12,* 462-470.

De Leo, D., & Diekstra, R. F. W. (1990). *Depression and suicide in late life.* Toronto: Hogrefe & Huber.

Dew, M. A., Bromet, E. J., Brent, D., & Greenhouse, J. B. (1987). A quantitative literature review of the effectiveness of suicide prevention centers. *Journal of Consulting and Clinical Psychology, 55,* 239-244.

Diekstra, R. F. W. (1990). An international perspective on the epidemiology and prevention of suicide. In S. J. Blumenthal & D. J. Kupfer (Eds.), *Suicide over the life cycle: Risk factors, assessment, and treatment of suicidal patients* (pp. 533-569). Washington, DC: American Psychiatric Press.

Douglas, J. D. (1967). *The social meanings of suicide.* Princeton: Princeton University Press.

Fisher, E. P., Comstock, G. W., Monk, M. A., & Sencer, D. J. (1993). Characteristics of completed suicides: Implications of differences among methods. *Suicide and Life-Threatening Behavior, 23,* 91-100.

Gardner, A., & Rich, C. L. (1988). Eating disorders and suicide. In D. Lester (Ed.), *Suicide '88* (pp. 171-172). Denver, CO: American Association of Suicidology.

Gehlot, P. S., & Nathawat, S. S. (1983). Suicide and family constellation in India. *American Journal of Psychotherapy, 37,* 273-278.

Gove, W. R. (1972). Sex, marital status and suicide. *Journal of Health and Social Behavior, 13,* 204-213.

Gove, W. R. (1979). Sex differences in the epidemiology of mental disorder. In E. S. Gomberg and V. Franks (Eds.), *Gender and disordered behavior* (pp. 23-68). New York: Brunner/Mazel.

Gunderson, P., Donner, D., & Nashold, R. (1993). The epidemiology of suicide among farm residents or workers in five North-Central States, 1980-1988. *American Journal of Preventive Medicine, 9,* 26-32.

Hare-Mustin, R. T., & Marecek, J. (1988). The meaning of difference: Gender theory, postmodernism, and psychology. *American Psychologist, 43,* 455-464.

Haynes, R. H. (1984). Suicide in Fiji. *British Journal of Psychiatry, 145,* 433-438.

Healey, C. (1979). Women and suicide in New Guinea. *Social Analysis, 2,* 89-107.

Henriksson, M. M., Hillevi, M. A., Marttunen, M. J., Heikkinen, M. E., Isometsä, E. T., Kuoppasalmi, K. I., & Lönnqvist, J. K. (1993). Mental disorders and comorbidity in suicide. *American Journal of Psychiatry, 150,* 935-940.

Hirsch, S. R., Walsh, C., & Draper, R. (1982). Parasuicide: A review of treatment interventions. *Journal of Affective Disorders, 4,* 299-311.

Iga, M., Yamamoto, J., & Noguchi, T. (1975). The vulnerability of young Japanese women and suicide. *Suicide, 5,* 207-222.

Isometsä, E. T., Henriksson, M. M., Aro, H. M., Heikkinen, M. E., Kuoppasalmi, K. I., & Lönnqvist, J. K. (1994). Suicide in major depression. *American Journal of Psychiatry, 151,* 530-536.

Johnson, P. L. (1981). When dying is better than living: Female suicide among the Gainj of Papua New Guinea. *Ethnology, 20,* 325-335.

Kushner, H. I. (1985). Women and suicide in historical perspective. *Signs: Journal of Women in Culture and Society, 10,* 537-552.

Kushner, H. I. (1993). Suicide, gender, and the fear of modernity in nineteenth-century medical and social thought. *Journal of Social History, 26,* 461-490.

Lester, D. (1982). The distribution of sex and age among completed suicides. *International Journal of Social Psychiatry, 28,* 256-260.

Lester, D. (1984). Suicide. In C. S. Widom (Ed.), *Sex roles and psychopathology* (pp. 145-156). New York: Plenum Press.

Lester, D. (Ed.) (1988). *Why women kill themselves.* Springfield, IL: C. C. Thomas.

Lester, D. (1989). *Questions and answers about suicide.* Philadelphia: Charles Press.

Lester, D. (1990). Suicide in Mainland China by sex, urban/rural location, and age. *Perceptual and Motor Skills, 71,* 1090.

Lester, D. (1991a). Patterns of suicide in America. *Proceedings of the Pavese Society, 4,* 118-211.

Lester, D. (1991b). Suicide across the life span: A look at international trends. In A. A. Leenaars (Ed.), *Life span perspectives of suicide* (pp. 71–80). New York: Plenum Press.

Lester, D. (1992). *Why people kill themselves* (3rd ed.). Springfield, IL: C. C. Thomas.

Lester, D. (1993a). Testosterone and suicide. *Personality and Individual Differences, 15*, 347–348.

Lester, D. (1993b). The effectiveness of suicide prevention centers. *Suicide and Life-Threatening Behavior, 23*, 263–267.

Maniam, T. (1988). Suicide and parasuicide in a hill resort in Malaysia. *British Journal of Psychiatry, 153*, 222–225.

Marks, A., & Abernathy, T. (1974). Toward a sociocultural perspective on means of self-destruction. *Suicide and Life-Threatening Behavior, 4*, 3–17.

Marks, A., & Stokes, C. S. (1976). Socialization, firearms and suicide. *Social Problems, 5*, 622–639.

Marttunen, M. J., Hillevi, M. A., Henriksson, M. M., & Lönnqvist, J. K. (1991). Mental disorders in adolescent suicide: DSM-III-R Axes I and II diagnoses in suicides among 13- to 19-year-olds in Finland. *Archives of General Psychiatry, 48*, 834–839.

McIntosh, J. L. (1989). Official United States elderly suicide data bases: Levels, availability, omissions. *Omega, 19*, 337–350.

McIntosh, J. L. (1991). Middle-age suicide: A literature review and epidemiological study. *Death Studies, 15*, 21–37.

McIntosh, J. L. (1992). Epidemiology of suicide in the elderly. *Suicide and Life-Threatening Behavior, 22*, 15–33.

McIntosh, J. L., & Santos, J. F. (1985–1986). Methods of suicide by age: Sex and race differences among the young and old. *International Journal of Aging and Human Development, 22*, 123–139.

Miller, H. L., Coombs, D. W., Leeper, J. D., & Barton, S. N. (1984). An analysis on the effects of suicide prevention facilities on suicide rates in the United States. *American Journal of Public Health, 74*, 340–343.

Moens, G. F. G., Loysch, M. J. M., Honggokoesoemo, S., & van de Voorde, H. (1989). Recent trends in methods of suicide. *Acta Psychiatrica Scandinavica, 79*, 207–215.

Mościcki, E. K. (1994). Gender differences in completed and attempted suicides. *American Journal of Epidemiology, 4*, 152–158.

National Center for Health Statistics. (1933–1990). *Vital Statistics of the United States*. Rockville, MD: Author.

Nayha, S. (1977). Social group and mortality in Finland. *British Journal of Preventive and Social Medicine, 31*, 231–237.

Nuttall, E. A., Evenson, R., & Cho, D. W. (1980). Patients of a public state mental health system who commit suicide. *Journal of Nervous and Mental Disease, 168*, 424–427.

O'Carroll, P. W. (1989). A consideration of the validity and reliability of suicide mortality data. *Suicide and Life-Threatening Behavior, 19*, 1–16.

Phillips, D., & Ruth, T. E. (1993). Adequacy of official suicide statistics for scientific research and public policy. *Suicide and Life-Threatening Behavior, 23*, 307–319.

Pritchard, C. (1988). Suicide, unemployment and gender in the British Isles and European Economic community (1974–1985) *Social Psychiatry and Psychiatric Epidemiology, 23*, 85–89.

Pritchard, C. (1990). Suicide, unemployment and gender variations in the Western world 1964–1986: Are women in Anglo-phone countries protected from suicide? *Social Psychiatry and Psychiatric Epidemiology, 25*, 73–80.

Rich, C. L., Ricketts, J. E., Fowler, R. C., & Young, D. (1988). Some differences between men and women who commit suicide. *American Journal of Psychiatry, 145*, 718–722.

Raleigh, V. S., Bulusu, L., & Balarajan, R. (1990). Suicides among immigrants from the Indian subcontinent. *British Journal of Psychiatry, 156*, 46–50.

Seiden, R. H., & Gleiser, M. (1990). Sex differences in suicide among chemists. *Omega, 21*, 177–189.

Shiqing, Z., Guang, Q., Zhenlong, P., & Tiensen, P. (1994). The sex ratio of suicide rates in China. *Crisis, 15*(1), 44–48.

Smith, J. C., Mercy, J. A., & Conn, J. M. (1988). Marital status and the risk of suicide. *American Journal of Public Health, 78*, 78–80.

Stengel, E. (1964). *Suicide and attempted suicide.* Harmondsworth, England: Penguin.

Stillion, J. (1995). Through a glass darkly: Women and attitudes toward suicidal behavior. In S. S. Canetto & D. Lester (Eds.), *Women and suicidal behavior* (pp. 70–83). New York: Springer.

Taylor, S. (1982). *Durkheim and the study of suicide.* New York: St. Martin Press.

Walsh, B., Walsh, D., & Whelan, B. (1975). Suicide in Dublin: II. The influence of some social and medical factors on coroners' verdict. *British Journal of Psychiatry, 126*, 309–312.

Wolf, M. (1975). Women and suicide in China. In M. Wolf & R. Witke (Eds.), *Women in Chinese society* (pp. 111–141). Stanford, CA: Stanford University Press.

World Health Organization. (1969–1991, annual). *Statistics annual.* Geneva, Switzerland: Author.

Yang, B., & Lester, D. (1995). Suicidal behavior and employment. In S. S. Canetto & D. Lester (Eds.), *Women and suicidal behavior* (pp. 95–106). New York: Springer.

Zarit, S. H. (1980). *Aging and mental disorders: Psychological approaches to assessment and treatment.* New York: Free Press.

# Part II. Prevention Theory and Models

## 5

# The Place of Suicide Prevention in the Spectrum of Intervention: Definitions of Critical Terms and Constructs

Morton M. Silverman, MD, and Robert D. Felner, PhD

The authors trace the evolution of prevention models and conceptual foundations for the prevention of disorders starting with the public health/medical model and concluding with the contemporary model recently proposed by the Institute of Medicine of the National Academy of Sciences. They compare and contrast the contributions of each model toward the theoretical reduction of suicide in the general population. Risk and protective factors as they relate to suicidal behaviors are identified. The paper explores conceptual frameworks used to understand population-level risk factors and moves toward a discussion of how to target individuals at risk for suicidal behaviors. First-order and second-order targets of change in prevention efforts are defined and examples provided.

The current paper seeks to assist in the further refinement of theoretical and conceptual frameworks to guide suicide prevention research and practice. One can start this consideration – and perhaps avoid a great deal of effort – with the simple question: "Can we simply review here current approaches to prevention and then, at the end, discuss briefly how they may apply specifically to suicide prevention?" Unfortunately the answer to this question is both yes and no. Yes, because there are clearly a number of elements of existing prevention models that apply to suicide. No, because suicide does not fit cleanly into any of the groupings of problems for which prevention models have been developed. Illustratively, in the new fourth edition of the *Diagnostic and Statistical Manual* of the American Psychiatric Association (DSM-IV, 1994), suicide does not appear as a "mental disorder."

Similarly, although suicide is certainly related to physical health, it is not in any traditional sense a medical illness until after an attempt has been made. Finally, although suicide is clearly a social-behavioral problem, it is typically not included with that group of problems (e.g., unmarried teen childbearing, delinquency) that most think of when this category is discussed. Instead it is clearly linked to all of these and, at the same time, is a "pure type" of none of these. Existing models of prevention have typically focused on one or another of these sets of problems and disorders or on some specific combinations. One of the tasks that we attempt in this paper is the development of a framework for suicide prevention that builds on existing approaches developed for each of the converging and contributing types of disorders and dysfunctions that may contribute to suicide, but in a way that re-

M. M. Silverman is with the University of Chicago. R. D. Felner is with the University of Illinois, Urbana–Champaign. Order of authorship does not imply relative contribution. Both authors contributed equally.

Portions of this paper were presented by Robert Felner as part of a theme address to the American Association of Suicidology Annual Convention, April 1987.

spects the unique characteristics of suicide.

Perhaps the first place that the uniqueness of suicide emerges is in the consideration of when it is prevention, and not intervention/treatment. To answer this question we first need to be clear about what we mean by prevention, and then examine the issues in applying this definition to suicide.

## DEFINITIONS OF PREVENTION: FROM THE PUBLIC HEALTH MODEL TO AN INTERVENTION CONTINUUM

The term *prevention* when defined apart from specificity about the phenomenon to which it is to be applied, may be so ambiguous and broad as to be meaningless. This point is underscored by Cowen (1983), who notes, "Although the terms 'prevention,' 'prevention in mental health,' 'primary prevention,' and 'primary prevention in mental health' are often used interchangeably they mean different things. Failure to understand or respect basic distinctions among them creates confusion that inhibits the development of primary prevention in mental health . . . " (p. 11). The recent Institute of Medicine (IOM, 1994) report on prevention also recognizes the need for greater clarity in the conceptualizations of prevention and the need for such clarity, declaring, "Confusion about terminology extends to prevention and prevention research, which means different things to different federal agencies, advocacy groups, and professionals" (p. 13).

Failure to attend to these issues by suicidologists will also inevitably lead to the development of a knowledge base for the prevention of suicide that is murky and confusing, and that ultimately impedes the development of more effective interventions. That is, when it is applied to suicide the generic term *prevention* has been employed in so inclusive a way as to be virtually meaningless. This confusion, and the source of it or at least some of the reasons for it, can be illustrated by considering that when applied to activities that

seek to reduce the incidence of suicide, it could be argued that *any intervention* to reduce suicide probability, targeted at an individual who has not yet successfully taken their own life, would qualify as prevention. Interventions ranging from those that seek to strengthen the context or competencies of individuals, to those that seek to change policy relating to lethal means, to those that involve inpatient hospitalization can all safely fit under the label of *prevention* when it is used in this way. Although collectively each of these strategies may result in the *prevention of the act of suicide*, when such broad usage of the term *prevention* is placed in the context of efforts to develop systematic and effective strategies to reduce the incidence and prevalence of suicide, it becomes clear that this overwhelming inclusiveness can only thwart any efforts to develop the necessary conceptual clarity for guiding the development of a systematic knowledge base for action.

To arrive at a more systematic framework to organize our thinking about suicide prevention, perhaps the best place to start is with four questions. These are (Felner, Adan, & Silverman, 1992):

1. What do we mean by the concept of "prevention" when applied to suicide?
2. Who are the target groups of suicide prevention versus, for example, intervention?
3. What and where is the focus of suicide intervention?
4. What are the goals of suicide prevention programs?

Let us now turn to each of these issues in turn, and follow the paths they lead us on in the search for our unifying framework and implications for the prevention of suicide.

## DEFINITIONAL AND TARGETING ISSUES IN SUICIDE PREVENTION

We (Felner, Silverman, & Felner, 1995) and others (see Coie et al., 1993) have recently argued for the development of a field of "prevention science" in which systematically derived knowledge from basic and intervention research can be cumulated to inform the continuing evolution of effective preventive interventions. The need for such a systematic knowledge base is brought into focus by the recognition that a defining characteristic of sound prevention programs is that they are *intentional* (Cowen, 1980). Intentionality implies that the prevention strategies that are employed and the conditions that they target for change follow directly from theory and research concerning "pathways" to disorder and adaptation (Felner & Felner, 1989). Hence, in the prevention of suicide the most immediate goals and foci of intervention are the modification of those *processes that lead to or maintain suicidal actions, thoughts, and tendencies.* (Felner & Lorion, 1985; Lorion, Price & Eaton, 1989). For a prevention initiative to meet the criteria of intentionality, those involved in its design must identify those specific causal processes that they seek to change and articulate the linkages between these target processes and suicidal behaviors. Intervention strategies should than be selected that will influence the levels of these processes in ways that first reduce risk or promote resilience and, ultimately, reduce the incidence of suicide and suicide attempts.

Put otherwise, good prevention is and must be good science. There really is no gap between action and theory/research when interventions are mounted appropriately. A suicide prevention initiative that meets the criteria of intentionality can be viewed as (and in fact should be) a test of clearly articulated hypotheses about causal pathways to suicide. The goal of the prevention effort will then be to modify these pathways in ways that reduce the probability that suicide will occur. If the hypotheses are correct, the desired outcomes will follow. If we accept that one defining feature of prevention is that it must meet the standards of intentionality—a standard that all interventions should be held to—we must now ask whether conceptual distinctions between prevention and other forms of intervention are necessary and warranted for sui-

cide. And, if they are warranted, we must also clarify the nature of those distinctions that need to be made.

## BLENDED AND UNIQUE PREVENTION MODELS

There are two quite different views concerning whether prevention is a unique intervention approach. One is a "blended approach" to prevention that holds that prevention is merely an extension of other types of intervention. By contrast, the "unique approach" stance holds that prevention is a distinct element of the continuum of care (Felner, Silverman, & Felner, 1995).

Blended views of prevention are best exemplified by the Public Health Model (PHM). In the PHM the term *prevention* is applied to the full range of traditional medical, mental health and human service interventions. *Tertiary prevention* focuses on individuals who are already displaying serious disorder and would most typically include treatment and rehabilitation maintenance efforts. *Secondary prevention* targets those persons showing early signs of disorder, with the goal of reducing the intensity, severity, and duration of these symptoms. Finally, *primary prevention* seeks to reduce the incidence of new cases of disorder. It is targeted to entire populations, not to particular individuals.

Proponents of the blended position (e.g., Lorion, Price & Eaton, 1989; Sameroff & Fiese, 1989) argue that the overlap among these prevention types, especially primary and secondary prevention, may be useful. Lorion et al., (1989) state, "rather than emphasizing the theoretical distinctions between primary (i.e., incidence-focused) and secondary (i.e., prevalence-focused) preventive efforts . . . their overlapping value for emotional and behavioral disorders [should] be appreciated" (p. 64).

What must be understood is that the Public Health Model reflects a linear view of the evolution of dysfunction and disorder. In such a model, disorders are seen to move sequentially from onset though clinical syndrome. A critical assumption is that the timing of the "onset" of dysfunction is something that can be readily identified. This model was developed when the primary focus of prevention efforts were medical diseases that typically had identifiable causes and specific courses.

That a specific etiology strategy for prevention may not fit the problem of the prevention of suicide can be seen quite clearly when one considers that many of the conditions that seem to predict suicide – for example, early trauma, sexual deviance, drug and alcohol problems, and negative social interactions (e.g., Maris, 1981) – both predict other predictors of lethal attempts, such as depression and nonlethal "gestures," and are themselves predicted by these latter predictors. Critically, however, we must also note that the overwhelming majority of those individuals who display these identified predictors and others like them do not kill themselves. When viewed this way it is clear that a linear approach to prevention, in which there is thought to be clear lines from specific predictors to lethal attempts, is simply not well suited to the reduction of the incidence of suicide. Rather suicidal ideation, suicide attempts, and suicide are typically the results of complex, multicausal factors in which the interaction of a number of predisposing and precipitating conditions are key to incidence, prevalence, and course. Thus, conditions that in a liner model might be used to mark "onset" (e.g., extended depressed mood) in actuality relate to the ultimate emergence of suicide and associated actions/thoughts *only in a probabilistic and nonspecific way*. It is to models of prevention that are more suited to these understandings that we now turn.

## APPROACHES THAT FOCUS ON RISK REDUCTION IN COMPLEX DEVELOPMENTAL PATHWAYS

### Prevention as a Unique Level of Intervention

Opponents of the blended position argue that such blending obscures important distinctions among intervention types and perpetuates old problems under new labels. Cowen (1983) states, "To lump such diversity under a unified banner of 'prevention' is sheer slight of hand. . . . Calling such things prevention . . . only dilutes and obscures a set of conceptually attractive alternatives to past ineffectual mental health ways. It perpetuates what we have always done, in a slightly altered technical guise" (p. 12). This is not an argument for assigning lesser importance to other forms of intervention. Rather, what is implicit is the recognition that the development of a sound knowledge basis for *both* prevention *and* these other forms of intervention will be hindered by inadequate attention to their differences.

We have recommended previously (Felner, Silverman, & Felner, 1995) that to develop the precision necessary for a science of prevention, a fundamental shift must occur in our language in which we abandon the traditional public health phraseology and employ terms that are more descriptive and conceptually suited to the approaches being implemented. Adopting this perspective, tertiary prevention becomes *treatment*, secondary prevention becomes *early intervention*, and primary prevention assumes the sole mantle of *prevention*.

### Definitions of Prevention and "Who Is Targeted?"

Beyond the greater conceptual clarity that will accrue, there are several additional bases for assigning a unique status to prevention. First, onset is not the sole distinguishing feature of "true" prevention. It is but one of a defining *set* of features that hold coequal status with prevention's "before the fact nature." A second defining feature of intervention efforts that is critical to keep in focus is the level of analysis to whom they are targeted. Prevention efforts are by definition *mass or population focused*.

This does not mean that prevention efforts always target all persons in the population at large. Gordon (1983) has proposed a framework for the organization of prevention trials that may be especially helpful here. This organization is based on how the target groups are selected. "Universal" interventions are those that are designed for all segments of a population. "Selected" interventions are targeted to subpopulations that are characterized by shared exposure to some epidemiologically established risk factor(s). By contrast to universal and selected interventions, "indicated" interventions are targeted to specific individuals who are already displaying preclinical levels of disorder and who have been identified through screening procedures.

In a reformulated model of prevention, both universal and selected interventions would continue to be included under the rubric of *prevention*. In the remainder of this paper, when we refer to *population-level interventions* we include those that would be subsumed under both of these categories. But, indicated interventions would not continue to be included under the flag of prevention. Instead, because the targeting of such interventions is based on identification of specific individuals through screening of these individuals, such efforts are now more clearly and appropriately labeled *early intervention*.

Our perspective is, in large part, congruent with the recent IOM (1994) report on preventive intervention research. That report, focused on the prevention of mental disorders, has likewise shifted from a model of prevention that is based on the public health perspective to one that incorporates Gordon's formulation. The IOM Committee states that "both [the Public Health and Gordon terminology] focused on prevention of disorders traditionally defined as medical disorders. The application of these terms to mental health disorders is not straightforward." They go on to propose that because of these difficulties and others "the [IOM] committee has chosen not to use the public health classification system of primary, secondary, and tertiary prevention. Rather it presents an alternative system in which the term prevention is reserved for only those interventions that occur be-

fore the initial onset of disorders" (pp. 22–23). To further clarify the place of prevention in the spectrum of interventions the IOM presents a classification system that encompasses prevention, treatment, and maintenance. Figure 1 presents the proposed IOM classification spectrum for prevention/intervention. To that model we have added notations of where our own proposed prevention/early intervention/ treatment elements would appear as well as where Public Health levels of prevention would fall.

## WHAT ARE THE APPROPRIATE FIRST- AND SECOND-ORDER TARGETS OF SUICIDE PREVENTION PROGRAMS?

To this point we have seen that the way in which we define prevention includes intentionality, and that it is groups or populations that are targeted. We must also remember that prevention is by definition "before the fact." In considering this issue and adapting the model we have presented in Figure 1 to suicide, we must return to our opening comments about suicide and the fact that it does not fit cleanly under the labels of *mental, social,* or *medical disorder*. Recall that a critical distinction between treatment and indicated prevention or early intervention is that the aim of treatment is immediately therapeutic and targeted directly at the reduction or reversal of the focal pathology. By contrast, in "indicated prevention/early interventions" (which although not pure prevention do represent a large proportion of the efforts of clinicians engaged in suicide prevention), the individual is still asymptomatic on the focal disorder although typically manifesting some "clinically demonstrable abnormalities" that are associated with the emergence of the focal condition (IOM, 1994). Applying these understandings to suicide, individuals who are showing suicidal ideation, have made recent attempts, or are engaging in other life-threatening behaviors would no longer be targets of prevention but would consti-

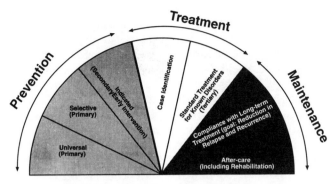

(Adapted from The Institute of Medicine, 1994)

Figure 1.   The mental health intervention spectrum. Adapted from the Institute of Medicine (1994).

tute identified cases for treatment. By contrast those individuals showing more general disorganization in coping skills, stress reactions, and depressive symptomatology, among other individual vulnerabilities for suicide, but who are not yet showing the former symptoms or suicidal behaviors, would be appropriate targets of early intervention/indicated prevention.

It must also be understood that even if one allows for indicated prevention to be included in the domain of prevention, as the IOM, one must still be careful in both the research and the intervention design to recognize and address the fact that interventions and prediction models that target population or subpopulations for change are substantively and conceptually quite different from those that focus on specific individuals. This brings us to a third defining feature of prevention that concerns the focus of change efforts. Since prevention is before the fact in its focus, it cannot have as its first-order targets of change the disorders it seeks to reduce or other individual-level pathologies. Instead, prevention activities will be applied to the enhancement, disruption, or modification, as appropriate, of the *unfolding process* (and conditions) that lead to well-being or to serious mental health or social problems. That is, "a preventive intervention involves the systematic alteration and modification of processes related to the development of adaptation and well-being or disorder, with the goals of increasing or decreasing, respectively, the rate or level

with which these occur in the [target] population" (Felner & Lorion, 1985, p. 93).

We should now raise a fourth defining feature of prevention. Integral to prevention programming are efforts to promote strengths, well-being, and positive developmental outcomes (Cowen, 1995). Promotion-focused efforts are central to prevention of suicide as they lead to significant reduction in the degree to which conditions of risk may precipitate the suicide attempts, especially that may be precipitated by the experience of acute or chronic stresses. Throughout the remainder of this paper, wherever the term *prevention* appears, it should be understood that we mean *prevention and health promotion.* Let us now turn to a more systematic consideration of the key elements of developmental and etiological pathways to disorder that are the appropriate targets of change in prevention programming.

## RISK, PROTECTIVE FACTORS, VULNERABILITIES, AND STRENGTHS: TARGETS OF CHANGE IN PREVENTION

A developmental perspective is best suited for explicating pathways to disorder that are congruent with prevention's tasks, assumptions, and defining characteristics (Felner & Felner, 1989; Lorion, et. al., 1989; Sameroff & Fiese, 1989; Seidman, 1987). Prevention efforts seek to correct those deviations in normal developmental processes, experienced by the target population, that lead to the outcomes of concern. Previous research has shown that if we are to make such corrections the major first- and second-order targets of intervention will be those conditions of risk, levels of protective conditions, and acquired vulnerabilities and competencies that are identified as impacting the rates of potential suicides in the population of concern (e.g., adolescents, young adults, middle-aged males, elderly — see other papers in this issue for more detailed discussions of the conditions that may impact specific populations). Unfortunately, too often distinctions among these concepts have been shrouded by ambiguity and a lack of precision in conceptualization. It is to a consideration of these issues that we now turn.

Perhaps the best place to start is with a brief overview of some of those conditions that have been labeled as "risk factors" for suicide.

When we examine the literature on the prediction of suicide and the construction of assessment procedures or instruments that may be helpful for such prediction, we find an almost bewildering array of conditions that have been cited as contributing to risk for suicide. Everything from the stresses and strains of everyday life to severe psychopathology and trauma have been cited. Indeed, it would be difficult to find some life experience, adaptive demand, or psychological difficulty that has not been shown to relate to suicide to one degree or another. For example, Maris (1981) notes that "under the best of conditions life is often short, periodically painful, fickle, often lonely and anxiety generating. . . . only if the human condition were dramatically altered would suicide change much" (p. 6).

Studies of life stresses, social resources, and coping skills provide further support for the common antecedents to suicide and other mental health problems (cf. Felner, Farber, & Primavera, 1983; Johnson, 1988). In this work severe, prolonged, or unmanageable stress; the experience of major life transitions; and powerlessness are but a few of the conditions that appear to be associated with increased risk for an extraordinary variety of mental and physical disorders (Felner, Farber, & Primavera, 1983; Felner, Rowlison, & Terre, 1986; Rappaport, 1987). By contrast, strong social support, a personal sense of self-efficacy, and well-developed coping skills or social competencies may all reduce the likelihood of a range of mental and physical disorders in the face of these and other conditions of risk or vulnerability (Felner, DuBois, & Adan, 1991).

Intervention research provides further evidence supportive of common early risk factors relating to a broad array of later adaptive problems. Schweinhart and Weikart (1988) report that disadvantaged youth who participated in early childhood education programs showed improvements in outcomes that ranged from life-threatening behaviors and delinquency, to school failure, to the use of welfare services and unemployment at a 15-year follow-up. Similarly, in dealing with a major stressor that may be linked to youth suicide, Felner and Adan (1988) reported that a program that reduced the stressfulness and hazardous nature of a school context during school transitions not only reduced school failure and drop-out, but also the development of psychological distress and symptomatology that may be related to suicide, delinquency, and other behavioral problems.

When we move from those experiences, resources, and capabilities that characterize daily life to less frequent, more pathological, and/or severe conditions of life, we again find a broad range of conditions that have been employed to predict to suicide. Mental illness or substance abuse of a parent (Pfeffer, 1989); a history of past or current sexual or physical abuse (Hawton, 1986); parental substance abuse, personal substance abuse, or mental health problems (cf. Berman, 1990; Christie, Burke, Regier, Rae, Boyd, & Locke, 1988; Deykin, Levy, & Wells, 1987; Regier, Farmer, Rae, Locke, Keith, Judd, & Goodwin, 1990; Schuckit & Sweeney, 1987); family disorganization and other disrupted parent child relationships (Pfeffer, 1989);

negative social interactions and feelings of helplessness or hopelessness (Huffine, 1989); and academic and other life failures (Felner & Silverman, 1989) are but a few of the many factors that have been shown to relate, at least in the majority of studies in which they have been considered, to increased risk for suicide attempts for various populations.

Silverman (1989) underscores these relationships in a review of the co-occurrence of multiple disorders. He notes that the antecedents of many problem behaviors are highly intercorrelated and that there may be a constellation of precursors or antecedents common to a broad range of clinical forms of dysfunction, including youth suicide. In a related vein, other authors (Felner & Felner, 1989; Felner, Silverman, & Adix, 1991; Sameroff & Fiese, 1989) note that data on developmental psychopathology provide additional substantiation for the existence of common antecedents to suicide and a number of the other disorders (e.g. substance abuse, depression) and also reveal that the multicausal nature of these etiological pathways in which highly similar outcomes can result from very different combinations of risk factors and very different outcomes from the same risk factors (Sameroff, Seifer, Barocas, Zax, & Greenspan, 1987).

Let us now consider the multiple levels of analysis from which conditions that are labeled as "risk conditions" have been identified. Such inclusiveness leads to important obfuscation of the actual developmental processes that are involved and, as a corollary, is debilitating to prevention efforts whose design depends on the appropriate targeting of such processes.

Current perspectives on mental disorders (e.g., DSM-IV) start with a fundamental "diathesis–stress" perspective. This model holds that individuals may have either genetically based or otherwise acquired vulnerabilities to the onset of disorder. These vulnerabilities are the diathesis side of the equation. They "set" the person's threshold of susceptibility to environmental conditions (e.g., stress) or

hazards (e.g., high levels of disorganization, restrictive opportunity structures, or danger) that may precipitate the onset of disorder. This is clearly a model that is equally applicable to suicide despite its omission from DSM-IV.

Importantly, for the purposes of prevention the concept of *risk* is defined epidemiologically *at the population level*. It is a conditional statement about the probability that any member of a given population or subpopulation will develop later disorder. Frequently overlooked in efforts to employ the concept of risk for intervention is that the designation of being a member of an "at-risk" group says little about any specific member of that group other than that they have been exposed to the condition(s) of risk under consideration. If the conditional probabilities of disorder in a population are $x$, it is not that all members of that group possess $x$ levels of predisposition or "riskness" for disorder (Felner, Adan, & Silverman, 1992; Richters & Weintraub, 1990). Many of the members of the risk group will be free of all signs of difficulties whereas others will develop significant adaptive difficulties. A risk designation is no more than an actuarial statement about the members of a selected group. Thus, assessment efforts to guide the targeting of prevention programs are based on knowledge of the probabilistic ways in which conditions of risk disrupt developmental processes in the lives of all persons in a cohort. There is no need to know the extent to which these processes have been disrupted for specific individuals (Felner, Silverman, & Felner, 1995). It is more accurate to speak of *conditions of risk* or *populations at risk* rather than *high risk individuals*. Unfortunately, the term *risk* has been frequently applied to individual characteristics and/or to imply that all individuals in a high-risk group are somehow more fragile or vulnerable than all of those in lower-risk groups.

This conceptual slippage has occurred for several reasons. Part of the problem stems from the use of individual-level variables, especially when aggregated for a population or group, as risk markers (cf.

Hawkins, Catalano, & Miller, 1992). For example, those individuals who have made prior attempts are often designated "at risk." *Actuarial statements cannot be made about particular individuals*, even those who have characteristics that, at the population level, do relate to such prediction. This loose use of terminology is simply unwise and often confusing.

To address this slippage, we have proposed several corollaries in our definition of risk (Felner, Adan, Silverman, 1992; Felner, Silverman, Felner, 1995) that are worth noting here. First, conditions of risk are primarily environmental in nature (although being part of a population group that may have some genetic risk characteristics would also qualify, so long as we remember we are talking about a population-level attribute). Second, environmental/risk conditions can have two quite distinct roles. They can act as *predisposing* conditions or as *precipitating/compensatory* conditions. When environmental conditions act in a predisposing fashion, *vulnerabilities*, which in our definition are always *person-level variables*, are *acquired* (see Figure 2). Their acquisition may stem either from problematic environmental conditions that are present or from the lack of exposure to important developmentally promoting conditions and resources (Rutter, 1981).Strengths and *personal competencies* may also be ac-

quired from positive developmental contexts and are again person-level variables. These person-level characteristics are "first-order" developmental *outcomes* (i.e., acquired vulnerabilities and competencies/strengths). It would be incorrect to label these variables as individual-level risk conditions or as early signs of "onset" of specific disorders. Although competencies and vulnerabilities will influence the probability that an individual will be resilient in the face of exposure to subsequent risk conditions, they are not markers of individual risk nor are they direct and inevitable markers of the onset of disorder. To talk about building resiliences in individuals also muddies these concepts. *Resilience* is an outcome, defined by the way in which a person or population responds to challenge and stress. Discussions of building "resiliencies" lose this essential defining element and obscure important differences between such outcomes and aspects of developmental pathways that produce them (e.g., strengths, vulnerabilities, environmental resources).

When environmental circumstances act as *precipitating conditions*, rather than predisposing ones, they interact with existing vulnerabilities and competencies to trigger the onset of more serious dysfunction. Similarly, *protective conditions* in the environment may act in a compensatory fashion, reducing the likelihood that

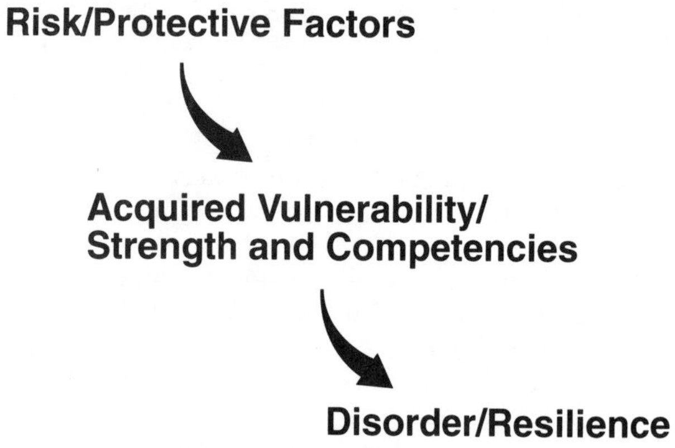

**Risk/Protective Factors**

**Acquired Vulnerability/
Strength and Competencies**

**Disorder/Resilience**

Figure 2.   Person-level variables.

existing vulnerabilities will be "activated" when the person experiences conditions of risk. Illustratively, acquired vulnerabilities may make an individual susceptible to the development of suicidal ideation in the face of experiencing major life changes. But, if these changes occur in a context in which the person receives additional support and external coping resources, such difficulties may still not be triggered, even if the person brings relatively high levels of acquired vulnerabilities to the situation.

Implicit in this view of unfolding pathways to suicide and related disorders is that exposure to conditions of risk or the acquisition of vulnerabilities is not synonymous with the onset of disorder (see Figure 2). Neither is exposure to protective factors or the acquisition of competencies synonymous with health and resilience. Rather, these are the sequential and interactive elements of developmental trajectories to dysfunction and well-being that are the appropriate direct targets for change by prevention programming. Framed this way, suicide prevention initiatives may include several strategies that target root causes and contributing factors to dysfunction, all of which would qualify as before the fact. They include: (1) attempts at reducing levels of conditions of risk or increasing levels of protective factors; (2) efforts to directly, or indirectly through the previous step, reduce the incidence rates of person-level vulnerabilities or the enhancement of personal competencies and strengths; and (3) altering levels of conditions of risk and of protective factors that have been shown to interact with acquired vulnerabilities and strengths to trigger the onset of more serious disorder or to produce resilience in the face of serious challenge.

## SUMMARY

In this model we have proposed that the first-order, direct, or "immediate" targets of change in prevention efforts will typically be non-individual-level elements of developmental trajectories to adaptation and disorder. Prevention strategies will focus on direct efforts to increase or decrease, as appropriate, the levels of conditions of risk, protective factors, and developmentally enhancing experiences to which a population is exposed. Changes in levels of these first-order elements of the developmental pathways of populations will, in turn, radiate to impact the degree to which second-order changes are accomplished. These second-order elements of developmental pathways should show changes, in desired directions, relatively soon after the attainment of the first-order changes have been obtained. These "early intermediate outcomes" provide preliminary evidence that the preventive strategy is on course for being effective in achieving its long-term goals. Second-order targets of change in developmental pathways include levels of acquired vulnerabilities as well as resilience-related strengths and competencies. Preventive initiatives will thus involve systematic actions aimed at modifying the reciprocal and interactive influences of conditions of risk, strengths, vulnerabilities, and resources, in shaping trajectories to the developmental outcomes of concern (cf. Figure 1).

Recognition of where prevention fits into the full spectrum of interventions should help to facilitate the further development and refinement of more effective strategies for preventing the occurrence of what may be called *suicidality* as well as for the treatment and rehabilitation of those individuals who have developed more specific manifestations of suicidality. Discussions of these different points on the spectrum should in no way be viewed as an argument that one or the other intervention modalities on the spectrum is more important. Rather, these elements are distinct and equally important components of a comprehensive approach to reduction of the incidence and prevalence of suicide, and of the associated disorder and disease with which it is associated. Achievement of these goals will require precision in the ways in which we "think about what we are thinking about."

Such precision can only result from the alliance of researchers and practitioners as they mutually challenge and inform each other in the pursuit of these goals.

## REFERENCES

American Psychiatric Association. (1994). *Diagnostic and statistical manual of mental disorders* (4th ed.). Washington, DC.: American Psychiatric Press, Inc.

Berman, A. L. (1990, April). *The relationship between suicide and substance abuse*. Presentation to the State of Illinois Department of Alcoholism and Substance Abuse Suicide Prevention Symposium, Springfield, IL.

Christie, K. A., Burke, J. D., Regier, D. A., Rae, D. S., Boyd, J. H., & Locke, B. Z. (1988). Epidemiologic evidence for early onset of mental disorders and higher risk of drug use in young adults. *American Journal of Psychiatry, 145*, 971–975.

Coie, J. D., Watt, N. F., West, S. G., Hawkins, J. D., Asarnow, J. G., Markham, H. J., Ramey, S. L., Shure, M. B., Long, B. (1993). The science of prevention: A conceptual framework and some directions for a national research program. *American Psychologist, 48*(10), 1013–1022.

Cowen, E. L. (1980). The wooing of primary prevention. *American Journal of Community Psychology, 8*, 258–284.

Cowen, E. L. (1983). Primary prevention in mental health: Past, present, and future. In R. D. Felner, L. A. Jason, J. N. Moritsugu, S. S. Farber (Eds.), New York: *Preventive psychology: Theory, research, and practice*. New York: Pergamon Press.

Cowen, E. L. (1995). In J. Rappaport & E. Seidman (Eds.), *Handbook of community psychology*. New York: Plenum Press.

Deykin, E. Y., Levy, J. C. Wells, V. (1987). Adolescent depression, alcohol and drug abuse. *American Journal of Public Health, 77*, 178–182.

Felner, R. D., & Adan, A. M. (1988). The school transitional environment project: An ecological intervention and evaluation. In R. H. Price, E. L. Cowen, R. P. Lorion, & J. Ramos-McKay (Eds.), *Fourteen ounces of prevention: A casebook for practitioners* (pp. 111–122). Washington, DC: American Psychological Association.

Felner, R. D. Adan, A. M., & Silverman, M. M. (1992). Risk assessment and prevention of youth suicide in schools and educational contexts. In R. W. Maris, A. L. Berman, J. T. Maltsberger, R. I. Yufit (Eds.). *Assessment and prediction of suicide* (pp. 420–447). New York: Guilford Press.

Felner, R. D., DuBois, D. L., & Adan, A. M. (1991). Community-based intervention and prevention: Conceptual underpinnings and progress toward a science of community intervention and evaluation. In C. E. Walker (Ed.), *Clinical psychology: Historical and research foundations* (pp. 459–510). New York: Plenum Press.

Felner, R. D., Farber, S. S., & Primavera, J. (1983).

Transitions and stressful life events: A model for primary prevention. In R. D. Felner, L. A. Jason, J. N. Moritsugu, & S. S. Farber (Eds.), *Preventive psychology: Theory, research, and prevention* (pp. 191–215). New York: Pergamon Press.

Felner, R. D., & Felner, T. Y. (1989): Primary prevention programs in the educational context: A transactional–ecological framework and analysis. In L. A. Bond & B. E. Compas (Eds.), *Primary prevention and promotion in the schools* (pp. 13–49). Beverly Hills, CA: Sage Publications.

Felner, R. D. & Lorion, R. P. (1985). Clinical child psychology and prevention: Toward a workable and satisfying marriage. In Proceedings: National Conference on Training Clinical Child Psychologists, pp. 41–95.

Felner, R. D., Rowlison, R. T., & Terre, L. (1986). Unraveling the Gordian Knot in life change events: A critical examination of crises, stress, and transitional frameworks for prevention. In S. W. Auerbach & A. L. Stolberg (Eds.), *Children's life crisis events: Preventive intervention strategies* (pp. 39–63). New York: Hemisphere/McGraw-Hill.

Felner, R. D., & Silverman, M. M. (1989). Primary prevention: A consideration of general principles and findings for the prevention of youth suicide. In Alcohol, Drug Abuse, and Mental Health Administration, *Report of the Secretary's Task Force on Youth Suicide, Vol. 3: Prevention and interventions in youth suicide* (DHHS Publ. No. (ADM) 89-1623, pp. 23–30). Washington, DC: U.S. Government Printing Office.

Felner, R. D., Silverman, M. M., & Adix, R. (1991). Prevention of substance abuse and related disorders in children and adolescence: A developmentally-based, comprehensive ecological approach. *Family and Community Health: The Journal of Health Promotion and Maintenance, 14*(3), 12–22.

Felner, R. D., Silverman, M. M., & Felner, T. Y. (1995). Prevention in mental health and social intervention: Conceptual and methodological issues in the evolution of the science and practice of prevention. In J. Rappaport & E. Seidman (Eds.). *Handbook of community psychology*. New York: Plenum Press.

Gordon, R. (1983). An operational classification of disease prevention. *Public Health Reports, 98*, 107–109.

Hawkins, J. D., Catalano, R. F., & Miller, J. Y. (1992). Risk and protective factors for alcohol and other drug problems in adolescence and early childhood: Implications for substance abuse prevention. *Psychological Bulletin, 112*(1), 64–105.

Hawton, K. (1986). *Suicide and attempted suicide among children and adolescents*. Beverly Hills, CA: Sage Publications.

Huffine, C. (1989). Social and cultural risk factors for youth suicide. In Alcohol, Drug Abuse, and Mental Health Administration, *Report of the Secretary's Task Force on Youth Suicide, Vol. 2: Risk Factors for youth suicide*. (DHHS Publ. No. (ADM) 89-1622, pp. 56–70). Washington, DC: U.S. Government Printing Office.

Institute of Medicine. (1994). *Reducing risk for men-

*tal disorder: Frontiers for preventive intervention research.* Washington, DC: National Academy Press.

Johnson, D. L. (1988). Primary prevention of behavior problems in young children: The Houston parent–child development center. In R. H. Price, E. L. Cowen, R. P. Lorion, & J. Ramos-McKay (Eds.), *Fourteen ounces of prevention: A casebook for practitioners* (pp. 44–52). Washington, DC: American Psychological Association.

Lorion, R. P., Price, R. H., & Eaton, W. W. (1989). The prevention of child and adolescent disorders: From theory to research. In D. Schaffer, I. Philips, N. B. Enzer, M M. Silverman, & V. Anthony (Eds.), *Prevention of mental disorders, alcohol, and other drug use in children and adolescents* (OSAP Prevention Monograph 2, DHHS Publ. No. (ADM) 89-1646, pp. 55–96). Washington, DC: U.S. Government Printing Office.

Maris, R. W. (1981). *Pathways to suicide: A survey of self-destructive behaviors.* Baltimore: Johns Hopkins University Press.

Pfeffer, C. (1989). Family characteristics and support systems as risk factors for youth suicide. In Alcohol, Drug Abuse, and Mental Health Administration, *Report of the Secretary's Task Force on Youth Suicide,* Vol. 2: (DHHS Publ. No. (ADM) 89-1622, pp. 71–87). Washington, DC: U.S. Government Printing Office.

Rappaport, J. (1987). Terms of empowerment/exemplars of prevention: Toward a theory for community psychology. *American Journal of Community Psychology, 15,* 121–148.

Regier, D. A., Farmer, M. E., Rae, D. S. Locke, B. Z., Keith, S. J., Judd, L. L., & Goodwin, F. K. (1990). Comorbidity of mental disorders with alcohol and other drug abuse: Results from the epidemiologic catchment area (ECA) study. *Journal of the American Medical Association, 264,* 2511–2518.

Richters, J., & Weintraub, S. (1990). Beyond diatheses: Toward an understanding of high-risk environments. In J. Rolf, A. S. Masten, D. Cichetti, K. H. Nuechterlein, & S. Weintraub (Eds.), *Risk and protective factors in the development of psycho-pathology* (pp. 67–96). Cambridge, England: Cambridge University Press.

Rutter, M. (1981). Stress, coping, and development: Some issues and some questions. In N. Garmezy & M. Rutter (Eds.), *Stress, coping and development in children.* New York: McGraw-Hill.

Sameroff, A. I., & Fiese, B. H. (1989). Conceptual issues in prevention. In D. Shaffer, I. Philips, N. B. Enzer, M. M. Silverman, & V. Anthony (Eds.), *Prevention of mental disorders, alcohol, and other drug use in children and adolescents.* (OSAP Prevention Monograph 2, DHHS Publ. No. (ADM) 89-1646, pp. 23–54. Washington, DC: U.S. Government Printing Office.

Sameroff, A. J., Seifer, R., Barocas, R., Zax, M., & Greenspan, S. (1987). IQ Scores of 4 year-old children: Social-environmental risk factors. *Pediatrics, 79*(3): 343–350.

Schuckit, M. A., & Sweeney, S. (1987). Substance use and mental health problems among sons of alcoholics and controls. *Journal of Studies on Alcohol 48*(6): 528–534.

Schweinhart, L. I., & Weikart, D. P. (1988). The High/Scope Perry Preschool Program. In R. H. Price, E. L. Cowen, R. P. Lorion, & J. Ramos-McKay (Eds.), *Fourteen ounces of prevention: A casebook for practitioners* (pp. 53–65). Washington DC: American Psychological Association.

Seidman, E. (1987). Toward a framework for primary prevention research. In J. A. Steinberg & M. M. Silverman (Eds.), *Preventing mental disorders: A research perspective* (DHHS Publ. No. (ADM) 87-1492). Washington, DC: U.S. Government Printing Office.

Silverman, M. M. (1989). Commentary: The integration of problem and prevention perspectives: Mental disorders associated with alcohol and drug use. In D. Schaffer, I. Philips, N. B. Enzer, M. M. Silverman, & V. Anthony (Eds.), *Prevention of mental disorders, alcohol, and other drug use in children and adolescents.* (OSAP Prevention Monograph 2, DHHS Publ. No. (ADM) 89-1646, pp. 7–22). Washington, DC: U.S. Government Printing Office.

# 6

# Suicide Prevention from a Public Health Perspective

Lloyd B. Potter, PhD, MPH, Kenneth E. Powell, MD, MPH,
and S. Patrick Kachur, MD, MPH

The public health approach to health problems provides a strong framework and rationale for developing and implementing suicide prevention programs. This approach consists of health-event surveillance to describe the problem, epidemiologic analysis to identify risk factors, the design and evaluation of interventions, and the implementation of prevention programs. The application of each of these components to suicide prevention is reviewed. Suggestions for improving surveillance include encouraging the use of appropriate coding, reviewing suicide statistics at the local level, collecting more etiologically useful information, and placing greater emphasis on analysis of morbidity data. For epidemiologic analysis, greater use could be made of observational studies, and uniform definitions and measures should be developed and adopted. Efforts to develop interventions must include evaluating both the process and the outcome. Finally, community suicide prevention programs should include more than one strategy and, where appropriate, should be strongly linked with the community's mental health resources. With adequate planning, coordination, and resources, and the public health approach can help reduce the emotional and economic costs imposed on society by suicide and suicidal behavior.

Injury from suicidal behavior is a major public health problem in the United States (Diekstra, 1989; Rosenberg, O'Carroll, & Powell, 1992; Rosenberg, Smith, Davidson, & Conn, 1987). In 1992, suicide was the ninth leading cause of death in this country. Each year suicide claims more than 30,000 lives; about 80% of those who die are males. Suicide takes its highest toll among the elderly. Suicide rates begin to increase during adolescent years and continue to increase through 25 years of age (Figure 1). The suicide rate tends to level between ages 25 and 65, and then begins to increase through the oldest age groups. Recent trends (1980 to 1990) indicate continued increasing rates among the young, level or slightly declining rates among the middle aged, and increasing rates among the elderly. In general, suicide rates are highest in western states. The percentage of suicides involving firearms has been increasing steadily for at least a decade, and in 1992 firearms were involved in more than 60% of the suicides in the United States.

Public health, with its systematic approach to preventing illness, disability, and premature death, provides a strong framework for creating an effective national plan to prevent suicide. Although early public health efforts focused on changing the environment to protect people against infectious diseases, the emphasis in public health today is on changing the behaviors that put people at risk for conditions such as injury, chronic diseases, and AIDS. With this shift in focus, the value of health promotion, which combines health education and environmental

From the National Center for Injury Prevention and Control, Centers for Disease Control and Prevention, Atlanta, Georgia 30333.

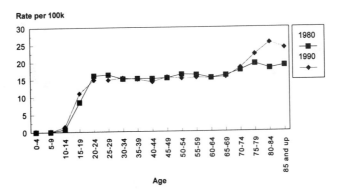

Figure 1.   Age-specific suicide rates, United States, 1980 and 1990.

support, has appreciated. The value of community influences on health has also taken on greater significance.

One of the earliest studies examining the relationship between community characteristics and suicide was conducted by Emile Durkheim (1951), who demonstrated that suicide rates in a population were related to social conditions. His work was followed by Freudian psychoanalytic psychiatry, in which neuroses and mental illness were treated with individualized therapy to correct problems that developed during the evolution of the individual psyche. The differences between the Freudian and Durkheimian approaches to suicidal behavior are similar to the distinction between "sick individuals and sick populations" made by Geoffrey Rose (1985). Rose described these two approaches as the "high-risk approach," which seeks to protect susceptible individuals, and the "population approach," which addresses the broader social and environmental factors that influence suicidal behavior. There has been little emphasis on implementing a population-based approach to suicide prevention in the United States.

Public health acknowledges the importance of both the high-risk and the population approach to prevention. Ultimately, the goal is to reduce the incidence of suicide, and this can be best accomplished using a variety of methods. In seeking the most effective prevention methods, the public health approach combines four fundamental activities: *surveillance* to identify patterns and epidemics of suicide and the differential rates of suicide, *epidemiologic research* to identify the chain of causes leading to suicide, the *design and evaluation of interventions* to interrupt this chain and prevent suicide, and the *implementation of programs* consisting of proven interventions (Figure 2). Part of the strategy in implementing programs is to transfer knowledge and skills in prevention to public health practitioners in communities.

In practice, the four components of the public health approach are interactive, and distinctions are often ambiguous. In fact, integration among these components is important. Surveillance often provides epidemiologic information; epidemiologic hypotheses are often generated and tested during evaluations of interventions; and programs frequently provide a source of data for surveillance. Though they are integrated, we discuss each component separately.

## SURVEILLANCE

Surveillance is a mechanism used to identify and characterize selected problems. It is characterized by the collection, analysis, and interpretation of health-related information that is used for planning, implementation, and evaluation of public health

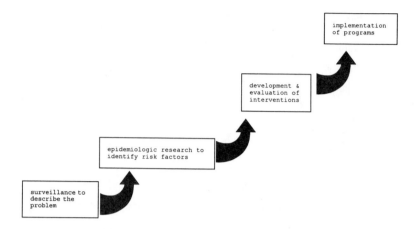

Figure 2.   The public health approach.

programs. A surveillance system includes a functional capacity for data collection, analysis, and dissemination linked to public health programs (Thacker & Berkelman, 1988). Although never perfect, our ability to count injury events improves as the physical injury associated with the event becomes more serious (Jeanneret, 1992; Lester, 1992).

For surveillance purposes, suicidal behavior is measured on a continuum of seriousness from merely thinking about self-destruction to actually completing the act. Suicide attempts resulting in no or very minor injury are almost impossible to monitor. However, most deaths from suicide are regularly documented and reported. These differences in the reporting of suicides and suicide attempts suggest that surveillance of mortality and morbidity should be considered separately.

## Mortality Surveillance

The major source of surveillance information for deaths from suicide is the United States Vital Statistics system operated by the National Center for Health Statistics (NCHS) of the Center for Disease Control and Prevention (CDC) (see Table 1). NCHS compiles and edits data from the states and territories, most of which produce computerized vital statistics mortality files from death certificates. These re-

cords usually contain data on place, cause of death, age, sex, race, marital status, residence, and, sometimes, information on occupation and education. Although the U.S. Vital Statistics system is one of the more advanced and efficient systems in the world, it is limited by underreporting of suicides, a time lag in reporting, and insufficient sociodemographic information.

The underreporting of suicide as a cause of death is a problem not only for the vital statistics system in the United States, but probably for all efforts to count suicides (O'Carroll, 1989; Rosenberg et al., 1988). Specificity of suicide is high; however, sensitivity is lower than for most other causes of death because of the need to determine the intention of the deceased. The variation in estimates of the sensitivity with which coroners and medical examiners certify true suicides suggests that suicides may be significantly undercounted (O'Carroll, 1989). The magnitude of the problem is especially underestimated for injuries that lend themselves to varying interpretations of intention, such as those from single car-crashes (Lester, 1992). A systematic means of identifying suicide deaths with greater sensitivity is needed.

The time lag between fatal injuries and their being reported in the national mortality detail files is 2 to 3 years after the event year. Although the Current Mortality Sample, produced by NCHS, is available about 4 months after a fatal injury oc-

Table 1
Surveillance Systems and Instruments by Type of Data
in the United States

|  | Mortality | Morbidity | Demographic traits | Risk factors |
|---|---|---|---|---|
| U.S. Vital Statistics | x |  | x |  |
| NMFS | x |  | x | x |
| NHDS |  | x | x |  |
| YRBS |  | x | x | x |
| NEISS |  | x | x |  |
| ICARIS |  | x | x | x |
| NHAMCS |  | x | x |  |

*Note.* NMFS, National Mortality Followback Survey (1986); NHDS, National Hospital Discharge Survey (started 1970); YRBS, Youth Risk Behavior Survey (started 1990); NEISS, National Electronic Injury Surveillance System (started monitoring firearm injuries 1993); ICARIS, Injury Control and Risk Factor Identification Survey (started 1994); NHAMCS, National Hospital Ambulatory Medical Care Survey (started 1980).

curs (Chevarley, Godfrey, Rosenberg, Kochanek, & Feinleib, 1993), the number of suicides captured in this 10% sample is insufficient for identifying anything but gross national trends. Without timely and complete reporting, prompt response to trends or epidemics is thwarted. Suicide surveillance could be more effective if data were regularly reviewed at the state or local department of health, where vital statistics are compiled before being sent to NCHS.

Finally, the vital statistics system captures little information of etiologic use from death certificates. Consequently, we are unable to identify potentially causal associations between suicide and modifiable individual characteristics. In one effort to overcome this deficiency, NCHS has initiated the periodic National Mortality Followback Survey (NMFS). This survey samples 1% of all death certificates, contacts proxies (next of kin, close friends) and attempts to obtain information on the decedent's behavior and risk characteristics. Thus, the NMFS can be used to estimate prevalence of various characteristics among persons by cause of death.

Despite these limitations, periodic reviews of national trends and patterns in suicide are useful. CDC's National Center for Injury Prevention and Control

(NCIPC) publishes this information in surveillance reports of trends in the numbers and rates of suicide by age, sex, race, and method of suicide (Centers for Disease Control and Prevention, 1985). These reports may be used to identify specific groups in need of more intensive study and intervention.

## Morbidity Surveillance

Data collection systems for suicide morbidity are much less complete and less systematic than the suicide mortality data collected by the United States Vital Statistics system (Meehan, Lamb, Salzman, & O'Carroll, 1992). Although the United States has no formal system for surveillance of suicide-related morbidity, several recently developed data collection systems may allow for some assessment. These surveillance efforts include the National Hospital Ambulatory Medical Care Survey (NHAMCS), the National Electronic Injury Surveillance System (NEISS), the National Hospital Discharge Survey (NHDS), the Youth Risk Behavior Surveillance System (YRBSS), and the Injury Control and Risk Factor Identification Survey (ICARIS) (see Table 1).

NHDS, conducted by NCHS, is a national sample survey that abstracts information on conditions diagnosed and procedures performed from the hospital records of discharged patients. Diagnosed conditions are coded using the *International Classification of Diseases*, 9th revision (ICD-9) (Health Care Financing Administration, 1991), and injury-related diagnoses are coded using the supplementary classification of external causes of injury and poisoning (E-codes). Intentional self-inflicted injuries are thus identifiable in the data. Although little etiologically useful information is collected, this survey is a potential source of data for estimating the magnitude and cost of suicide attempts that require hospital admission. To date, this source has not been adequately explored as a surveillance tool for suicide morbidity.

NHAMCS, conducted by NCHS, samples and abstracts patient records from emergency departments. This survey provides basic information, including the physician's diagnosis, on patients arriving at emergency rooms. It may provide a national estimate of the number of suicide attempts requiring emergency medical attention.

NEISS, operated by the Consumer Product Safety Commission (CPSC), collects data from 91 hospitals in an effort to monitor hazards from products other than food. This sample-based system relies on a network of emergency room physicians. Although the focus is on consumer products, firearms have recently been added in a collaborative effort between CPSC and NCIPC. Data from this system will provide information on intentional self-inflicted firearm injuries and will enable a more detailed assessment of firearms as a means of suicide and attempted suicide. Analyses of types of firearms used and related injuries should be possible.

The YRBSS involves a series of Youth Risk Behavior Surveys that are coordinated by CDC and conducted by departments of education in 23 states and 10 cities. There is also a national survey administered separately to in-school youth. Most states and the national component include questions on suicidal thoughts and behavior. These questions have been the basis for national and state estimates or suicidal thoughts and behavior among youth in school (Centers for Disease Control and Prevention, 1990). In an effort to sample all youth, the YRBS protocol was administered to a population-based sample in 1992.

ICARIS is being developed by the NCIPC as a population-based telephone survey of adults. When completed, this survey will provide data on suicidal thoughts and behavior, and selected presumptive risk factors, such as alcohol abuse and access to firearms. Preliminary results from the first round of ICARIS should be available in 1995.

Several specific activities would enhance the surveillance of suicide morbidity and mortality. Publicizing and encouraging appropriate coding of suicide deaths may reduce the undercounting of mortality. Also, local review of suicide mortality statistics would reduce the time lag between data collection and a response to local problems. In states and localities with suicide intervention programs, such reviews may enhance efforts to provide effective services. Finally, surveillance data could augment etiological research if more information were collected on the deceased. Such an effort would probably require additional special studies, such as the NMFS.

Several potential sources of morbidity surveillance data exist, but analysis of these data needs to be consolidated. Specifically, the social and economic burden of suicide-related morbidity should be estimated. This information is essential to building public awareness and support for developing research and interventions. Additionally, more specific information on the means used in suicide attempts would be useful in designing special studies.

## EPIDEMIOLOGIC RESEARCH

Understanding the etiology of suicide is essential to implementing the public health approach (O'Carroll, 1993). Designing and implementing effective interventions depends upon identifying modifiable risk factors. To identify such risk factors, hypotheses about causal relationships must be generated and tested using appropriate methodology.

In the traditional scientific model, theories evolving from observation and analysis of patterns suggest hypotheses. A theory and the hypotheses it generates are related to the types of observations used as data. Freud's psychoanalytic theory and the individualized approach to suicide prevention grew out of highly qualitative detailed interviews and case studies with patients, many of them psychologically disturbed. In his analysis of suicidal behavior, Durkheim studied population-specific suicide rates. Ecological analyses, such as Durkheim's, and qualitative research, such a Freud's, are well suited for generating hypotheses, but not for establishing causation. Effective primary prevention interventions cannot be developed on the basis of theory alone. They must be founded on scientifically sound evidence of causal factors.

The most powerful method for establishing causation is the experimental design with random allocation of subjects to various exposures. Obviously, this design is neither feasible nor ethical for studying suicide; therefore, other study designs must be used. Epidemiologists commonly use cohort and case–control methodologies to study the "natural experiments" of free-living populations. Although no single study can determine causation, scientists have established guidelines for determining whether evidence supports a cause-and-effect relationship. These criteria include strength of association, consistency of findings among studies, temporal sequence of exposure and outcome, and logical plausibility of the relationship (Rothman, 1986).

For rare events, such as suicide, case-control studies are especially useful (Rothman, 1986). Case-control methodology is also useful in studying self-reported suicidal thoughts and behavior within population-based cross-sectional survey designs. More frequent use of such quantitative methodologies will be necessary to further understand the causes of suicide.

Standardized terminology and measurements for assessing the reliability and validity of research findings are critical to advancing the understanding of suicide etiology. Development of standard definitions is difficult, however. Not only do researchers disagree about the meaning of existing terms used to describe suicide and suicidal behavior, but our relatively undeveloped understanding of suicide and suicidal behavior means that related concepts are correspondingly undeveloped and ambiguous. As further research helps to refine our understanding of suicide and suicidal behavior, it will in turn lead to more concise definitions of important concepts.

Another barrier to suicide research is the fear that asking questions about suicidal thoughts and behaviors may upset respondents. Although some respondents may become upset by such questions, there is no theoretical basis or empirical evidence to suggest or support the notion that asking questions about suicide will cause suicidal behavior. Furthermore, numerous research and intervention efforts have been completed without any reports of harm. In order to develop interventions, strong scientific research must progress while maintaining ethical standards of avoiding harm.

## INTERVENTION DEVELOPMENT AND EVALUATION

After causal relationships are established, interventions are developed and evaluated. Although the public health perspective recognizes the importance of secondary and tertiary prevention of suicide-related injuries, the ultimate goal of public health is primary prevention.

Interventions may affect the sequence of causes leading to suicide at several points (Figure 3). For example, an intervention that attempts to improve mental health may interrupt this sequence before

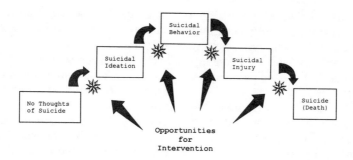

Figure 3.   Causal sequence toward suicide and potential intervention points.

a person even begins thinking about suicide. Thus, it serves as primary prevention of suicidal thoughts, suicidal behavior, suicidal injury, and suicide. Crisis intervention and referral is primary prevention for suicide, but it may be secondary and tertiary prevention for suicidal thoughts and behavior. Designing an effective intervention involves specifying how the intervention will interrupt the causal sequence. Implementation must be consistent with this specification, yet in practice, it often is not. Reasons for this deviation may include insufficient resources and inadequately trained workers.

Before interventions are broadly implemented, they should be evaluated for effectiveness using appropriately collected baseline, process, and outcome measures (Centers for Disease Control and Prevention, 1992). Identifying significant change in rare events such as suicide and suicidal injuries may be difficult in small-scale interventions. More prevalent indicators are suicidal thoughts and behavior. These indicators may serve as baseline and outcome measures in evaluations of interventions. A range of measures should include indicators of the intervention's immediate goals, such as reducing the prevalence of risk factors, should be considered. Process evaluation (assessment of service delivery) is crucial for assessing efficacy. This type of evaluation is similar to measuring dose delivered versus dose prescribed in a medical model.

Once an intervention has been designed and evaluated, it can be implemented on a larger scale. Interventions that have already been implemented should continue to be assessed regarding their ability to achieve primary prevention goals. Even though few have been evaluated, numerous prevention programs have been implemented by federal, state, and local agencies, and by community-based organizations.

## PROGRAM IMPLEMENTATION

Suicide intervention programs in North America have been described in CDC's *Youth Suicide Prevention Programs: A Resource Guide* (Centers for Disease Control and Prevention, 1992). This guide describes the rationale and evidence for the effectiveness of eight strategies to prevent youth suicide and identifies model programs that incorporate them. It is intended as an aid for communities interested in developing or augmenting programs to prevent youth suicide.

In developing the guide, CDC asked suicide prevention experts throughout the United States and Canada to identify and describe programs that in their judgment, were likely to be effective. Representatives from these programs were then asked about the number of persons exposed to their intervention, the number of years the program had been operating, the nature and intensity of the intervention, the availability of data to evaluation, and other pertinent criteria. The eight strategies described in the guide are:

- *School Gatekeeper Training.* This type of program is directed at school staff (teachers, counselors, coaches, etc.) to help them identify students at risk of suicide and refer such students for help. These programs also teach staff how to respond in cases of a tragic death or other crisis in the school.
- *Community Gatekeeper Training.* This type of gatekeeper program provides training to community members such as clergy, police, merchants, and recreation staff, as well as physicians, nurses, and other clinicians who see youthful patients. This training is designed to help these people identify youth at risk of suicide and refer them as appropriate.
- *General Suicide Education.* These programs provide students with facts about suicide, alert them to suicide warning signs, and provide information about how to seek help for themselves or for others. These programs often incorporate a variety of self-esteem or social competency development activities.
- *Screening Programs.* Screening involves the administration of an instrument to identify high-risk youth in order to provide more detailed assessment and treatment. Repeated administration of the screening instrument can be used to measure changes in attitudes or behavior over time, to test the effectiveness of an employed prevention strategy, and to obtain early warning signs of potential suicidal behavior.
- *Peer Support Programs.* These programs, which can be conducted in either school or nonschool settings, are designed to foster peer relationships, competency development, and social skills among youth at high risk of suicide or suicidal behavior.
- *Crisis Centers and Hotlines.* Among other services, these programs primarily provide telephone counseling for suicidal people. Hotlines are usually staffed by trained volunteers. Such programs may also offer a "drop-in" crisis center and referral to mental health services.
- *Means Restriction.* This prevention strategy consists of activities designed to restrict access to handguns, drugs, and other common means of suicide.
- *Intervention After a Suicide.* Strategies have been developed to cope with the crisis sometimes caused by one or more youth suicides in a community. They are designed in part to help prevent or contain suicide clusters and to help youth effectively cope with feelings of loss that come with the sudden death or suicide of a peer. Preventing further suicides is but one of several goals of interventions made with friends and relatives of a suicide victim, the so-called postvention efforts.

A review of suicide prevention efforts listed in the guide suggests that most programs embrace the high-risk model of prevention, in which the goal is case finding and referral (Rose, 1985, Centers for Disease Control and Prevention, 1992). Screening and referral and crisis centers are common examples of this approach. Interventions directed toward the general population – such as suicide awareness or education activities, media guidelines, and means restrictions – are rare. Currently neither of these approaches can be said to be more effective than the other.

Because current scientific information about the efficacy of suicide prevention strategies is insufficient, one intervention strategy cannot be recommended over another. However, the guide makes several general recommendations. First, suicide prevention programs should be linked as closely as possible with professional mental health resources in the community. Second, communities should not rely on only one prevention strategy. Certain strategies tend to predominate among prevention efforts, despite limited evidence of their effectiveness. Promising but underused strategies (e.g., means restriction) should be incorporated into current programs where possible. Third, although a large percentage of suicide prevention efforts are directed toward adolescents and teenagers in school, suicide rates are higher among other segments of the population. Suicide prevention efforts for young adults aged 20–24 years and other age groups with high suicide rates should be expanded. Fourth, it is important to incorporate evaluation into new and existing suicide prevention programs when practical. Evaluation should include measures of, or closely associated with, the incidence of suicidal behavior.

Although a knowledge base for making programmatic decisions is growing, the need to evaluate interventions is critical. There is simply insufficient scientifically based, quantitative information for making decisions about where to spend precious resources. Nonetheless, we must maintain ongoing interventions and develop new ones. Finding the balance between service delivery and evaluative research involves difficult choices. It is important to note, however, that effective service delivery requires interventions that have been well planned, well executed, and carefully evaluated.

Nationally, numerous organizations are implementing an array of promising suicide prevention interventions. However, there is a need to develop, implement, and evaluate new innovative suicide interventions. Individual interventions are the foundation of most suicide prevention programs, yet it is preferable for prevention programs to move toward multifaceted approaches that include numerous interventions and multiple segments of the community. Community organization and networking should be vital components to any suicide prevention effort. The CDC's *Recommendations for . . . Containment of Suicide Clusters* (Centers for Disease Control and Prevention, 1988) emphasizes the need for communities to get organized before they find they are in the midst of a crisis. Such preparation and implementation may reduce the likelihood of suicide clusters and may reduce endemic suicide rates.

## CONCLUSION

The public health approach to suicide prevention is being adopted by a variety of federal, state, and local agencies, and community-based organizations. While progress has been made, further development of a public health oriented suicide prevention with a public health orientation is essential. Surveillance efforts, especially of suicide-related injuries, must be further developed and refined. Research into causes of suicidal thoughts and behavior has only begun to uncover modifiable risk factors. New innovative interventions need to be developed and evaluated. Adequate resources need to be allocated for all of these activities and for broad implementation of proven interventions.

The public health perspective provides a strong framework and rationale for developing and implementing suicide prevention programs. While suicide prevention efforts have progressed, the framework suggested by the public health perspective has not been fully implemented. Suicide prevention in the United States needs more planning, coordination, and resources. With these, the public health perspective can be used to reduce the emotional and economic costs imposed on society by suicide and suicidal behavior.

## REFERENCES

Centers for Disease Control and Prevention. (1990). Attempted suicide among high school students–United States, 1990. *Morbidity and Mortality Weekly Report, 40,* 633–635.

Centers for Disease Control and Prevention. (1985). *Suicide surveillance, 1970–1980.* Atlanta: Centers for disease Control and Prevention.

Centers for Disease Control and Prevention. (1988). CDC recommendations for a community plan for the prevention and containment of suicide clusters. *Morbidity and Mortality Weekly Report, 37*(S-6) Suppl., 1–12.

Centers for Disease Control and Prevention. (1992). *Youth suicide prevention programs: A resource guide.* Atlanta: Centers for Disease Control and Prevention.

Chevarley, F. M., Godfrey, A. E., Rosenberg, H. M., Kochanek, K. D., & Feinleib, M. (1993). Mortality surveillance system: Models from the first year. *Vital Health Statistics, 20*(21).

Diekstra, R. F. (1989). Suicide and the attempted suicide: An international perspective. *Acta Psychiatrica Scandinavica, 80,* 1–24.

Durkheim, E. (1951). *Suicide: A study in sociology.* New York: The Free Press.

Health Care Financing Administration. (1991). *The international classification of diseases*, 9th revision. Washington, DC: Health Care Financing Administration.

Jeanneret, O. (1992). A tentative epidemiologic approach to suicide prevention in adolescence. *Journal of Adolescent Health, 13*, 409–414.

Lester, D. (1992). Miscounting suicides. *Acta Psychiatrica Scandinavica, 85*, 15–16.

Meehan, P. J., Lamb, J. A., Saltzman, L. E., & O'Carroll, P. W. (1992). Attempted suicide among young adults: Progress toward a meaningful estimate of prevalence. *American Journal of Psychiatry 149*(1), 41–44.

O'Carroll, P. W. (1993). Suicide causation: Pies, paths, and pointless polemics. *Suicide & Life-Threatening Behavior, 23*(1), 27–36.

O'Carroll, P. W. (1989). A consideration of the validity and reliability of suicide mortality data. *Suicide & Life-Threatening Behavior, 19*,1–16.

Rose, G. (1985). Sick individuals and sick populations. *International Journal of Epidemiology, 14*(1), 32–38.

Rosenberg, M. L., O'Carroll, P. W., Powell, K. E. (1992).Let's be clear: Violence is a public health problem. *Journal of the American Medical Association, 267*(22), 3071–3072.

Rosenberg, M. L., Davidson, L. E., Smith, J. C., et al. (1988). Operational criteria for the determination of suicide. *Journal of Forensic Science, 33*(6), 1445–1456.

Rosenberg, M. L., Smith, J. C., Davidson, L. E., & Conn, J. M. (1987). The emergence of youth suicide: An epidemiologic analysis and public health perspective. *Annual Review of Public Health, 8*, 417–440.

Rothman, K. J. (1986). *Modern epidemiology*. Boston: Little, Brown.

Thacker, S. B., & Berkelman, R. L. (1988). Public health surveillance in the United States. *Epidemiology Review, 10*, 164–182.

# 7

# Suicide Prevention Programs: Issues of Design, Implementation, Feasibility, and Developmental Appropriateness

Morton M. Silverman, MD, and Robert D. Felner, PhD

Emerging models of prevention focus on population-level risk reduction through enumerating antecedent conditions that are linked to subsequent expressions of disorder and dysfunction. The authors discuss the essential ingredients for successful prevention programs – comprehensiveness, fidelity, and intensity. The authors describe how to mount prevention programs to increase feasibility, access, and effectiveness. Suicide is an epidemic of low frequency in the general population and therefore does not receive appropriate attention in public health prevention campaigns. They argue for nesting suicide prevention programs within existing public health preventive intervention programs and provide some examples of how to reduce vulnerabilities and risk conditions for subsequent suicidal behaviors.

Prevention has become a central goal among those concerned with a wide array of human conditions (Cowen, 1985; Felner, Jason, Moritsugu, & Farber, 1983). The Secretary of Health and Human Services has labeled prevention as the nation's number one health priority for the 1990s (Department of Health and Human Services – DHHS, 1990). The reasons for prevention's becoming a central priority on the national health agenda are quite clear. Simply put, after-the-fact treatment approaches have proven to be inadequate to the task of reducing the ever-rising levels of social and health problems confronting the nation.

Suicide is no exception to these patterns and needs. Over the past three decades the numbers of those who have died or who have suffered serious injury and health problems resulting from a suicide attempt has reached epidemic proportions. Illustratively, documented cases alone make youth suicide the second leading killer of all youth aged 15–24 in the United States (Silverman, Lalley, Rosenberg, et al., 1988). The startling rise in these rates has brought with it a national call for more intensive and effective actions to reduce the terrible human and economic toll. With this understanding has come a major emphasis on the development of effective risk assessment, prediction, and prevention strategies for suicide.

In this paper we consider a number of the issues that need to be addressed in the pursuit of more effective means for preventing suicide. As we consider these issues we attempt to pay particular attention to the interplay, and potential complementarity, of practical concerns and what we know from research and theory about best practices. With this frame in mind let us start with a consideration of conditions and issues in the nation, communities, and host settings that define the

M. M. Silverman is with the University of Chicago. R. D. Felner is with the University of Illinois, Urbana–Champaign. Both authors contributed equally and order of authorship does not imply relative contribution.

Portions of this paper were presented by Robert Felner as part of his invited theme address to the Annual Convention of the American Association of Suicidology, April 1987.

implementation context and that must be understood and addressed if any initiative is to be successfully mounted.

## FEASIBILITY, COMORBIDITY, AND BUILDING ACCEPTANCE AND SUPPORT FOR SUICIDE PREVENTION PROGRAMS

When a serious suicide attempt, or completion, occurs in a family, school, or community, there is often a dramatic increase in urgency about and openness to the development and implementation of prevention measures and programming. Unfortunately, these windows of receptivity and commitment often fade rapidly. Even worse, as should be clear, the initial "spike" in interest is often dependent on a tragic event. These are clearly less than desirable circumstances in which to build support for mounting a program.

There are many reasons for these patterns of waxing and waning enthusiasm for suicide prevention programs. Discussion of suicide is often met with anxiety and fear by community members. In our own research, for example, whenever we have attempted to ask youth in schools about suicide or suicidal ideation, parents and other community members often voice concern about whether asking the questions will lead students to think about suicide or to make attempts. Suicide prevention programs, when labeled as such, are often met with similar concerns and responses. Hence, the affective negativity that often surrounds direct efforts to confront the problem of suicide, except in the face of immediate requirements for action, may seriously impede efforts to mount necessary programming.

A second major barrier to obtaining necessary support and resources for suicide prevention programming lies in the relationship of its epidemiology to that of other pressing health and social concerns in society. Although when considered at the national level, rates of suicide are alarming, at the level of local communities suicide is a relatively low-frequency event.

Further, even when a suicide does occur there are often concerted efforts to either reduce the visibility of the event or to relabel what has taken place so that the community is typically unaware of actual levels of attempted or completed suicide. Indeed, as we have noted above, communities often actively resist collecting direct data on suicidal actions and thoughts due to fears about the impact of such work.

Those attempting to develop support for suicide prevention efforts must recognize that the relatively low rates and frequencies of reported suicide in local communities, and at broader state and national levels, interact with the constellation of relatively more visible, pervasive, and thus to local communities more pressing, social and health problems that are vying for attention, resources (both human and economic), and access to settings that may host prevention programming (e.g., schools, workplaces). These latter problems may have absolute rates that are staggering compared to those of reported suicides. Illustratively, most estimates are that 15–20% of all children and families, or approximately 35–50 million people in the United States, are in need of intensive mental health services (Joint Commission on Mental Health and Mental Disabilities, 1961; President's Commission on Mental Health, 1978). Social ills are also at epidemic levels. Current levels of AIDS, "crack babies," births to unmarried teenaged mothers, substance abuse, children living in poverty, and homicide levels are but a few of the social problems whose rates are at historic levels. The "good news" about these rates for those concerned with suicide prevention, if such a phrase can be used in relation to these epidemic and tragic problems, is that they make the case for prevention quite clearly. There will never be adequate levels of human or economic resources to address these dramatic levels of need if we rely on reconstructive and individually focused models of intervention (see Albee, 1959; Sarason, 1981). To have a realistic hope of combating these problems, strategies are necessary that include efforts to reduce the incidence of new cases of dysfunction. As Albee (1982) reminds us, no epidemic was ever successfully brought under control or eliminated by treating those already affected.

Of course, the "bad news" for those who wish to mount suicide prevention programs, especially programs targeted to individuals for whom potentially lethal or health-endangering attempts have not yet occurred, is that the competition for time, resources, and access to the settings in which prevention programs are typically mounted (e.g., schools, workplaces, media) is often so overwhelming that suicide prevention programs—both because of the natural fear and resistance to them and because the problem is typically one that is not immediately apparent—are often pushed to the side (McGinnis, 1985).

A final barrier to the successful mounting of suicide prevention programs relates to squabbles and misperceptions among professionals themselves (Broskowski & Baker, 1974). The scarce resource context of human services has led to issues of "turf." Treatment and prevention have often been set up, however inappropriately, as competitors. What is not understood is that if prevention efforts succeed there will be a decrease in demand for treatment such that extant levels of treatment resources may be more effective. Thus, prevention is not a competitor to treatment but an important ally. This is a critical issue to remember while reading this paper. That is, we are not arguing that prevention is somehow "better" than treatment when we argue for clarity and differentiation from treatment in the spectrum of intervention. Rather, we are simply arguing that such clarity will facilitate the creation of more systematic and useful knowledge bases and action strategies that will enhance both.

Given the barriers to the mounting of suicide prevention programming, the question is: What can be done about it? Clearly, rates of suicide, hidden and otherwise, are at levels that make clear to those who are aware of them and concerned with the area that successful prevention programming must be developed and implemented. Fortunately, the answers to the question of what can be done to address the barriers to the mounting of suicide prevention programs are ones that are also consistent with the best available evidence for the ways in which suicide prevention programs should evolve in order to be maximally successful. That is, designers of suicide prevention programs must move from a focus that is uniquely and specifically on suicide to the development of programming that seeks to impact more broadly focused risk and protective factors. When successfully mounted these programs will not only reduce risk and incidence levels of suicide and suicide attempts, but should also address and successfully impact the reduction of other social, behavioral, and health problems confronting the target community. At this point let us briefly turn to the conceptual and empirical support for this contention before returning to the application of these lessons to actual program design and evaluation. In our discussion we highlight some of the reasons that may have led to misunderstandings and inappropriate conclusions. We also discuss relevant data on the causes and prevention of suicide that can serve as the basis for increased efficacy in both current and future prevention strategies. Let us start with a brief discussion of a clear definition of what we mean by prevention and what is necessary for an adequate prevention program.

## THE SPECTRUM OF INTERVENTION AND THE PLACE OF PREVENTION

A first issue to understand is that although there are a wide variety of interventions that may reduce the actual occurrence of suicide, and thus in the most general sense are "preventive," not all of these efforts are appropriately labeled as *prevention*. Elsewhere in this issue (Silverman & Felner, "The Place of Suicide Prevention in the Spectrum of Intervention") we discuss in far more detail the issues of the definition of suicide prevention programs as contrasted to other forms of intervention. This discussion moves away from the Public Health Model of primary, secondary, and tertiary prevention to one where these levels of intervention are relabeled to reflect their quite distinct targeting, goals, approaches, and timing. Prevention is accorded its own unique status, and secondary prevention is given the more descriptive and appropriate label of *early intervention*. Similarly, treatment is also accorded the separate and unique status it requires, rather than simply being lumped as merely another form of prevention.

The unique and defining features of prevention are in its timing, the level of analysis that is targeted, and the conditions that are the first- and second-order (most direct) targets of change. Although using just one of these criteria to define whether an initiative is *prevention* may, as we will see, prove confusing, the combination of all three should make clear the distinctions among prevention programs and other elements of the intervention spectrum. Let us consider these issues briefly as they relate to suicide.

The question of when it is *prevention* — especially employing the criterion of an intervention focused on suicide reduction "before the fact" — is one that, if not attended to more explicitly by the suicide literature, could become a source of unintended conceptual confusion and dead-end efforts. Given the "before-the-fact" nature of primary prevention, it could be argued that *any intervention* to reduce suicide probability, targeted at an individual who has not yet successfully taken his or her own life, would qualify as prevention. Here the reasoning is that because they have not yet committed suicide, they do not yet have the disorder. Although there is often difficulty identifying the specific point of "onset" for many socio-emotional and health-related disorders, clearly the issue is even more difficult for suicide than for most, because to wait for anything up to the point of clear "onset" as the appropriate criterion for the timing of prevention efforts is to court tragedy. Fortunately, the other two elements of our definition of prevention clarify this issue.

A second critical feature of prevention programs is the level of analysis to which they are subjected. Prevention initiatives are targeted to populations or subpopulations, and the individuals who are the recipients of the intervention are selected based on their membership in the target group rather than through a process of screening and selection based on individually specific characteristics. Once interventions move to such screening and identification of conditions that are specific to discrete individuals, they have moved to early intervention and/or treatment. The targeting of populations is based on their exposure to conditions of risk (which are always population- or subpopulation-level, never individual-level conditions) or the lack of exposure to important protective and developmentally enhancing conditions. In each local community these conditions may be quite different, and careful analysis of the local community conditions is necessary for effective prevention program design. Although conditions that are stressful, that fail to promote the acquisition of important competencies, or that fail to provide necessary support are all ones that may predispose to or precipitate a lethal attempt, their specific manifestation in a local community requires attention and appropriate adaptation of "one-size-fits-all programming."

The third defining feature for prevention efforts is what is targeted. In early intervention or treatment there are clearly identifiable, highly individually specific conditions that need to be reversed or strengthened. These conditions are the direct targets of change and the evaluation of programming can follow from them, in that changes in these focal conditions will be apparent.

In prevention, the first- and second-order targets of change are those conditions that lead to the focal conditions (i.e., suicide and suicide ideation/attempts).

First-order targets of change, or those conditions that are most directly targeted for change by the intervention, are the conditions of risk or protective factors to which all members of the population or subpopulation are exposed that have been identified as etiologically significant. Second-order targets of change are the levels of those vulnerabilities and competencies that result from exposure to the risk and protective factors of concern. Finally, through the modification of these critical elements of the etiological pathway, the incidence and prevalence of suicide will be impacted. Let us now turn to a discussion of what may be the most appropriate ways in which to define these first- and second-order target conditions as they relate to suicide as well as the implications of this resolution for the receptivity to mounting such programs.

## Suicide Prevention Efforts and Developmental Pathways to Disorder

A major dimension on which we can sort prevention programs is the *degree of outcome specificity* that underlies their targeting. Some suicide prevention programs focus very specifically on suicide per se. By contrast, other emerging efforts seek to build general competencies, reduce stressors, and otherwise influence that set of root cause, predisposing, and precipitating conditions that may relate both to a broad set of problematic developmental outcomes and to an enhancement of resilience and existing, adequate functioning. In designing prevention programs we need to be clear about how what is done is guided by implicit or explicit models or "pathways" to the focal problem. We must ask what are our assumptions about what "causes" suicide and how the activities of our prevention program will modify the levels of those conditions we think must be changed. The assumptions that are inherent in the specific disorder approach versus a broad-based multicausal pathway antecedent condition/risk reduction approach, which we (Felner & Silverman,

1989) and others (e.g., Institute of Medicine, 1994) have argued for, reflect two quite different perspectives on pathways to disorder. The former is based in a *specific disease prevention* model that rests heavily on public health paradigms. These perspectives hold that suicide (and other dysfunctions) is caused by specific conditions that interact with individual vulnerabilities, which are again specifiable. By contrast, the *risk reduction/protective factor or antecedent condition* perspective is based on the assumption that, at least for a wide range of disorders and developmental outcomes, the specific etiology model is neither appropriate nor supported by data.

By contrast, the risk/antecedent condition approach holds that there is a need for a comprehensive, multicausal, nonspecific developmental pathway perspective (Felner & Felner, 1989; Felner & Silverman, 1989). This model recognizes that: (1) most of the disorders we seek to prevent have a large number of common risk factors; (2) conditions that protect against one disorder generally also protect against others; and (3) there are nonspecific, personal vulnerabilities that increase an individual's susceptibility to the onset of a wide array of dysfunctions. The pathways to most of the social, emotional, and adaptive difficulties with which we are concerned are generally complex and shared by more than one disorder. Hence, for a wide range of developmental outcomes and pathologies, it appears that efforts to identify specific and unique etiological "causal agents" are not appropriate (Felner, Silverman, & Felner, 1995; Goldstein, 1985).

As Shaffer and Bacon (1989) pointed out, we do not know how to prevent the initial appearance of any psychiatric disorder, with the exception of certain disorders of childhood. There is also a developing consensus that most disorders cannot be explained solely as the result of stresses imposed on normal developmental processes. This model was essentially based on the belief that all individuals have a universal potential for disturbance, and it de-emphasizes the observation that some people are at substantially greater risk for specific disorders than are other people.

The American Psychiatric Association (APA) Task Force on Prevention Research (1990) has clearly supported the broader view. They state:

[N]on-specific predisposing factors and precipitating conditions may be responsible for the expression of many disorders, moving away from the focus on specific risk factors to the possibility of a more universal potential for disturbance in various populations. (p. 1702)

The complex etiology and pathogenesis of most behavioral disorders has several important implications. No single solution will prevent the expression of a particular disorder at all developmental stages. Those who seek to identify the one "real" cause of a particular type of disorder (in order to design the one, comprehensively effective preventive intervention) will inevitably be disappointed because no single factor is a necessary component in the etiology of all symptoms or signs of a major psychiatric disorder, emotional disturbance, or behavioral dysfunction (DHHS, 1992).

In a Position Paper entitled "Prevention of Violence and Injuries Due to Violence," submitted to the Third National Injury Control Conference (DHHS, 1992), the following paragraph highlights the opportunities for creative thinking applied to the development and implementation of preventive interventions for a wide range of behavioral disorders, not just those related to suicidal behaviors, violence and injury:

Having recognized that no single type of intervention is likely to be universally effective, we can turn our attention to a much more appropriate question: Which combination of the many potential interventions is likely to be most effective (as well as feasible) in preventing violent injuries? This question can be broken down into a series of more specific questions: Which points in the causal chain are particularly vulnerable to interruption? Which interventions are likely to contribute to the prevention of a large proportion of a given type of violent injury? Which are

likely to be effective across different types of violent injuries? What sorts of interventions will result in immediate reductions in such injuries? In long-term reductions? Which of the potential interventions are feasible and most readily adopted? Finally, what are the costs of the various promising interventions, relative to their effectiveness? (p. 169)

To address these questions requires that we first recognize that prevention as employed in our reformulated model applies to the unfolding of a diagnosable mental health or social problem. Thus, in prevention the most immediate goal for any intervention strategy is to change those processes that lead to disorder. The corollary of this view is that prediction efforts are now based on and concerned with the identification of these processes. That is, such efforts seem to predict not only the incidence of end-stage disorder (i.e., an actual serious suicide attempt) but also when pathogenic processes that may lead to this outcome will emerge or be present. By contrast, when we are dealing with early intervention and treatment we are concerned about factors related to prognosis, not incidence. A critical concept in helping us bridge between these levels of intervention focus is that of developmental trajectories to suicide. In its most simple terms the developmental trajectory of a disorder is the evolutionary history of that disorder (Felner & Felner, 1989).

To clarify what we mean by developmental trajectories and their implications for intervention, a useful starting point may be a medical analogy. If we were to consider that any action that reduces the occurrence of youth suicide, including the specific treatment of existing disorder, would qualify as "prevention," we can see that this stance is akin to saying that heart bypass surgery can be considered as primary prevention of death from heart disease. Clearly, although the specific "final form" manifestation of the target disorder has not occurred, the processes leading to it (whether youth suicide or heart disease) may have been unfolding for some time. If we are targeting these unfolding processes at the population level, we are engaged in prevention. But if we identify pathogenic processes that are specific to identifiable individuals, we are engaged in early intervention/secondary prevention. Implicit then in our categorization scheme for intervention and prediction levels is a developmental model of disorder in which the conditions targeted not only become progressively more severe but also progressively more specific, first to the individual, and then to the disorder, as we move closer to full clinical manifestation.

We must next understand that most current perspectives on the evolution and emergence of disorder start with a fundamental "diathesis–stress" perspective. Diathesis-stress models hold that individuals may have either genetically based or otherwise acquired trait-like, individual-level vulnerabilities to the onset of disorder. These vulnerabilities are the diathesis side of the equation and set the person's threshold of susceptibility to developmentally hazardous environmental conditions. Here, environmental conditions have two quite distinct roles. First, they may be sources from which vulnerabilities may be acquired. That is, acting as *predisposing* factors, environmental conditions may increase the probability that those within a given population will develop first-order outcome problems or "vulnerabilities" that create susceptibility to later disorder. Environmental stresses or conditions of risk may also impact developmental trajectories to disorder in a second fashion. Depending on the levels of vulnerabilities that have been previously acquired, these environmental factors may act as *precipitants* to the onset of more serious dysfunction.

In considering developmental trajectories from lessor to greater specificity of disorder, environmental and other population risk factors are more developmentally distant or "distal" from the onset of diagnosable conditions and predispose to a vulnerability to the broadest level of difficulties. By contrast, once individuals "acquire" vulnerabilities, the specific manifestation(s) of disorder that emerges (in our case suicide) will depend on or be triggered by identifiable, quite specific "risk" conditions that describe the person's recent, proximal life experiences (Felner, Jason, Moritsugu, & Farber, 1983; Felner, Silverman, & Adix, 1991). Without this understanding of developmental trajectories to disorder, these late-stage conditions are often mistaken for specific *causal* factors. With this formulation one can now see that both the early "broadband," antecedent "predisposing" conditions (both early risk factors and acquired vulnerabilities), and the later, quite specific, manifestation-"shaping" and -precipitating conditions are each necessary; but neither set alone is sufficient to cause the disorder to emerge.

There is one more set of key points that derives from this model. That is, it should now be clear that person-level vulnerabilities, that in the past have been mislabeled as "risk factors," are themselves: (1) early problematic developmental outcomes that can be targets of and reduced by prevention; (2) that these vulnerabilities result from risk conditions; (3) that the acquisition of vulnerabilities is not synonymous with the onset of disorder; and (4) programs that target not only the reduction of risk factors but the reduction of these vulnerabilities, or that seek to develop and provide compensatory "innoculatory" strengths, can reduce the incidence of our focal problem, that is suicide.

Before continuing, a very brief and by no means comprehensive example of how this approach can be combined with our notions of predisposing and precipitating conditions to understand youth suicide may be helpful here. One of the issues with which suicidologists have been very concerned is the issue of cluster suicides among youth in the same school or town (Davidson & Gould, 1989). The predisposing conditions for the youths that follow the first suicide may be existing levels of depression or other psychiatric problems, and/or a low level of family support, and/or a high level of alienation from friends and family. The latter two may both contribute to and be contributed to by the emotional problems present.

To this may be added feelings of a lack of belonging in school or a sense of restricted future from doing less well in school then they might like. These latter conditions might result from the social climate of the school, its structure, or recent school transitions that the system has required. Thus, individual, family system, and broader social system (e.g., peer/school) factors all contribute. Nonetheless the children we are talking about have not yet generally considered seriously suicide or attempted suicide as a solution. Indeed, although the "predisposing conditions" of a heightened level of vulnerability may have been created, the students may have attained relative stability in their adaptation to it.

It is not until we throw key destabilizing "precipitating" conditions into this pot that the necessary, but not sufficient, conditions of existing vulnerabilities may be activated. The occurrence and awareness of the first suicide may demonstrate to the vulnerable youth that suicide may be an alternative coping strategy, one they had not considered and one that might produce what they see as a desirable reaction from the social system, whatever the immediate cost. For a lonely, highly stressed adolescent, with the particularly strong needs for identity and acceptance, the overwhelming attention and grief that the system and many of those around them may pay to the event may be highly attractive and seem to satisfy many of their immediate needs. Also, if access to [necessary] lethal means is relatively easy (e.g., guns and ammunition are available in the home), the probability that a momentary, impulsive act may occur increases.

What we see here is the very complex interplay of developmental and environmental circumstances and the individual's own truncated range of coping efficacy. Perhaps even more ironic is that such children may be more "at risk" in systems in which we might assume lower risk, that is, small, cohesive ones. Similar examples may be developed for the high rate of suicides among children who seem to be doing very well academically or socially

(Maris, 1981) as well as those who are more obvious risks for the full array of psychological and self-injurious difficulties that plague adolescents. But, what must be understood is that: (1) both predisposing and/or precipitating conditions may be necessary for many instances of youth or other suicides to occur, and (2) even when both sets of conditions are present, in most instances suicide does not occur.

The above may make it seem that prevention programs targeted to suicide will have little payoff, and that broad-scope programs may actually influence the actions of only a small group of individuals. What we would like to argue at this point is that such views are short-sighted but, given base rates, perhaps natural conclusions that will result from specific etiology or specific outcome targeted prevention programs. What we mean here is, if we develop broad-based prevention programs for the prevention of suicide, with our only goal being the reduction of actual cases of suicide, the very limited resources we have available for medical and mental health programs may force us to conclude that what little funding is directed toward prevention of suicide may be better spent elsewhere. What is particularly ironic here is that although other federal agencies, such as the Department of Defense and NASA take pains to try to convince us that we get far more for our dollar, especially our R&D dollar, than the targeted "product," we in human services are going the other way. There is little to apologize for in reducing the incidence of school failure, increasing attachment and adaptive behaviors in school, and reducing depression and the range of associated health problems, while also attempting to reduce the suicide rate. Indeed, given the model we have advanced above, if we follow it, such multiple-outcome effects seem necessary and, if the programs are effective, unavoidable.

Critically, we can now see that the design of such programs is scientifically preferable and that there is also a practical benefit to such an approach that relates to being able to attract resources and acceptance for such efforts. That is, the receptivity that schools and other host systems (e.g., workplaces, parent groups, etc.) may have to an approach that avoids the "fragmentary," multiple, "disease of the month" specific approach strategies that they are bombarded with these days, may be greatly enhanced and more likely to fit with the needs, abilities, and ecologies of the settings we are attempting to work with—many of whom have multiple other non–mental health-oriented demands. Clearly such an approach affords a far greater likelihood that what have been the competing demands of the multiple agendas that may face a host setting (e.g., productivity, substance abuse, absenteeism, health benefit costs and insurance, etc.) can be met within the purview of a suicide prevention program. Important to recognize here is that we do not need to do anything we would not want to do to develop an effective suicide prevention program other than mention its additional benefits and play down, at least somewhat, its suicide focus. Such a general prevention/wellness strategy is both good science and good practice.

## Suicide Prevention Efforts: Toward Comprehensive Programming

Collectively these understandings provide an important context in which to evaluate the adequacy of both past and future suicide prevention efforts. First, it should be clear that suicide prevention programs that attempt to deal with suicide as if it were a unique disorder may be far too narrow in their focus. This may be particularly the case when we are dealing with populations in which there are either significantly heightened levels of other disorders and/or heightened exposure to high levels of multiple risk conditions for such disorders. Illustratively, we might posit that peer resistance training and/or coping skill enhancement models may be most effective with youth who are *not* failing in school, exposed to the harsh environmental conditions associated with pov-

erty, or otherwise showing adaptive difficulties in other domains. This speculation is, in fact, consistent with the data. That is, for those youth who are not at particularly high risk, interventions of this sort do seem to be relatively effective. But, for youth with multiple problems and vulnerabilities, or who are exposed to high levels of environmental risk conditions, the results from such programs are more disappointing.

One outgrowth of this view is the understanding that to ask "Does $X$ suicide prevention program work?" is far too simplistic. Rather, much as has become the standard in the psychotherapy research literature, we need to ask, "which suicide prevention programs, for which youth, under what conditions?" Although this would seem to lead to the need for an impossibly high level of tailoring, there are several interrelated strategies for addressing this concern in an effective and efficient fashion.

Given a developmental perspective on prevention and the preceding discussions about the complex pathways to suicide, we can examine each stage of the individual's life for the presence of conditions that will predispose to heightened risk for suicide, the acquisition of vulnerabilities for suicide, and/or factors that may serve "innoculatory" functions, increasing resiliency in the face of risk conditions. The prevention of suicide does not only take place at that point in development just prior to onset of the targeted behavior. It involves building a developmental ladder for individuals that helps them to avoid developmentally hazardous conditions while at the same time acquiring those abilities and resources necessary to cope adaptively and in a prosocial fashion with life's challenges at later stages and ages.

If we adopt such a perspective we can then apply it to an evaluation of the lives of populations and the assessment of key points for intervention. Here, we need not know the particular circumstances of each member of the population with which we are concerned but, rather, the circumstances that define the more general experience of the entire focal population. In prevention it is not the case that we assume that all members of our target group are equally vulnerable or "at risk." Rather, we simply know that the entire population with which we are concerned has been exposed to conditions that heighten the probability that each member may have acquired certain vulnerabilities or been exposed to certain environmental risks.

A particularly striking example of how this may occur can be seen if we consider youth from different socioeconomic conditions. A broad array of risk conditions may be present across all groups, for example, lack of parental supervision, history of family addiction, high levels of family conflict, negative peer pressures, and pro–substance use norms in the community. But some risk factors may be far more prevalent and/or take quite different forms in different socioeconomic conditions. For example, low income status is associated with a significantly heightened probability of occurrence of such "risk chains" as low birth weight, which, in combination with low levels of preschool educational stimulation, may result in poor school readiness, school failure, poor self-esteem, alcohol and other drug abuse, and consequently, significantly increased risk for suicide and suicide attempts (Berman & Schwartz, 1990).

By contrast, consider an upper-income group in a suburb where there are great academic pressures. The risk conditions for suicide in this population may be quite different. Pressure to succeed in school and achieve may overtax the coping abilities of many youth. So too may many of the social pressures that may be present. Pro-use norms for alcohol use during recreational functions may also be high. A youth in this population that is "average" may have expectations and self-esteem levels that are far worse than would be predicted if he or she were in a less high achieving group. Each of these conditions may, individually and collectively, result in heightened risk and vulnerability for suicide.

The central point of the two examples above is that a transactional and ecological analysis (Felner, Adan, & Silverman, 1992) of the prevailing risk and protective factors that the target population is exposed to is essential for developing prevention programs that have high levels of efficacy. Such a model attends to *both* the characteristics of the persons in the settings and the key conditions in their environments. These latter conditions may result in the acquisition of vulnerabilities, create developmentally hazardous situations, and/or provide adaptively negative meanings to interactions that would not otherwise be there.

We can now consider assertions that prevention programs for suicide are not effective and/or that we know little about what works. Again, we will use youth suicide as our exemplar but the issues apply to most suicide prevention efforts. Given our multicausal, multi-outcome antecedent model above, we see that the first-order or immediate program outcome objectives of prevention efforts for the reduction of suicide would be to: (1) reduce the number of antecedent conditions of risk present, (2) reduce the acquisition of vulnerabilities, and (3) increase the number of protective factors – all after a careful ecological analysis of the characteristics of the conditions in the community and other primary developmental settings (e.g., the schools, peer groups, family, and worksites) in which our target population is functioning.

What should now be clear is that the lack of efficacy or at least lack of demonstrated efficacy of programs that focus specifically on suicide – a condition we have noted ignores the multicausal factors that may contribute to suicide – is not surprising. Such programs do not meet the most basic standards required for an adequately designed prevention program. They are also targeted at a point in the developmental trajectory that is very close to the emergence of conditions of concern. There is little attention to factors that may have been developed previously that may influence an individual's vulnerability to suicide. What is equally as unfortunate about these efforts as their lack of efficacy is the fact that, all too often, researchers and program planners alike have mistaken them for adequate tests of the efficacy of prevention approaches more generally. Not only are they not adequate for this task but they are, in fact, exactly what one would not do, except for a small proportion of the population, if one were to engage in conceptually well-grounded suicide prevention programming and planning. Let us now close with a brief consideration of what some of the most basic elements of a well-designed suicide prevention initiative would, at minimum, include.

## NECESSARY FEATURES OF EFFECTIVE PREVENTION PROGRAMMING

One issue that is emerging in all prevention efforts is the need to consider integrative and comprehensive approaches. That is, both practically and as would follow from the multicausal models detailed above, it has been increasingly recognized that each area of potential risk and resiliency that may be relevant in a particular population group needs to be carefully addressed. This has resulted in models such as those that are family focused and that, for example, may involve comprehensive family resource centers and programming. Such programs explicitly recognize that the needs of the child or adolescent cannot be fully or maximally addressed independent of the needs and resources of the family.

Supportive of this view and the more generally ecologically focused developmental ladder approach we have proposed, Felner, Silverman, and Adix (1991) and others (cf. Dryfoos, 1990) recently summarized several assumptions and approaches common to prevention programs that have been found to be effective:

1. There is no one solution to a problem.
2. High-risk behaviors are interrelated.
3. An integrative package of services and programs is required in each community.
4. Preventive interventions should be aimed at changing institutions (e.g., schools, welfare systems, community settings) rather than individuals.
5. The timing of interventions is critical and should start early, long before the anticipated emergence of the focal difficulties.
6. Continuity of efforts must be maintained. "One-shot" efforts and short-term programming that lacks intensity and fidelity does not work. Continuing, follow-up, and booster sessions are necessary.

Further, as a prevention program is developed, its authors need to be able to specifically address the following questions:

1. Is there a well-defined population at risk for a disorder?
2. Are the program developers starting from a well-defined theory/hypothesis about the critical etiological and contributing conditions to suicide in that population?
3. Does the intervention as designed conceptually take into account and follow logically from the above two points and meet the six conditions for successful prevention efforts?

Before closing, there is one additional set of issues that we have alluded to, but that is deserving of additional attention given their role in the potential failure of what may be appropriately targeted programming. In particular we need to deal with the issues of program dosage, intensity, duration, and fidelity. These conditions are important to consider in both the design of adequate intervention programs and in assessing the results of studies of the efficacy of such programs. That is, it is not enough to ask whether a program has all of the pieces necessary to address the conditions targeted for change. We must also ask whether they are delivered in sufficient dosage (e.g., number/length of exposures/sessions), intensity (the ratio of frequency of exposure to duration—e.g., five sessions in one week versus one session each week for five weeks), and over a long enough period of time. Finally, fidelity relates to the quality of implementation of the program or, put otherwise, the degree to which the program takes place as intended.

## EVALUATION OF PREVENTION PROGRAMMING

The conceptualization of developmental pathways as the primary focus of preventive interventions that we have offered here has direct implications for the evaluation of prevention programs. Now, initial and ongoing assessments of the efficacy of suicide prevention efforts can and should be built, at least in part, on the degree to which they are successful in reducing those risk factors and vulnerabilities and/or increasing those protective factors and competencies that they identify as primary targets. Such an approach may be especially useful when prevention programs are targeting conditions such as suicide that may have relatively low rates of emergence, and/or where the group targeted may be several years younger than the ages at which significant onset may be expected.

Hence, by adopting a perspective based on the above understandings of developmental pathways, it is possible to obtain relatively rapid assessments of the degrees to which the program and its effects are "on course" and show potential for having the desired long-term effects. This can be done by assessing the degree to which the initiative has produced changes in the desired directions in key conditions that are earlier in the developmental pathway, even when they are far distant from the time when we might expect the onset of dysfunction.

For example, our first assessments of program impact would focus on the degree to which levels of risk have been reduced and levels of enhancing conditions increased. Next, we would assess the degree to which the incidence and prevalence of vulnerabilities and competencies in the population have been changed. Finally, as population members experience identifiable conditions that have been shown to have a high likelihood to act as precipitants (e.g., school transitions), and/or moves through developmental periods when maximum onset is expected, we would examine differential rates of the occurrence of adaptive difficulties. To the degree to which desired differences emerge between those receiving the prevention trial and nonparticipating comparison groups, at each of these points in the developmental course, we can, with some assurance, argue that the intervention has shown evidence of being on course for attaining its longer-term, central goals. In this way, throughout the period from program involvement until the population reaches the age when they are most likely to experience the onset of the focal problems, or are in the age group that our program was designed to impact, we can continuously evaluate the success of the efforts.

To summarize, comprehensive developmentally based efforts to prevent suicide appear to have far greater potential for success than do more narrow, suicide-specific approaches. As prevention efforts move to a new generation of sophistication, building on what we know about factors that enhance development for all children and youth and targeting the reduction of conditions that impede optimal development, it is clear that both the cost efficacy and outcome efficacy of our efforts should increase markedly.

## REFERENCES

Albee, G. W. (1959). *Mental health manpower trends*. New York: Basic Books.

Albee, G. W. (1982). Preventing psychopathology and promoting human potential. *American Psychologist, 32*, 150–161.

American Psychiatric Task Force on Prevention Research. (1990). Report of the APA task force on prevention research. *American Journal of Psychiatry, 147*, 1701–1704.

Berman, A. L., & Schwartz, R. H. (1990). Suicide attempts among adolescent drug users. *American Journal of Diseases of Children, 144*, 310–314.

Broskowski, A., & Baker, F. (1974). Professional, organizational, and social barriers to primary prevention. *American Journal of Orthopsychiatry, 44*(5), 707–719.

Cowen, E. L. (1985). Person-centered approaches to primary prevention in mental health: Situation-focused and competence-enhancement. *American Journal of Community Psychology, 13*, 31–48.

Davidson, L., & Gould, M. S. (1989). Contagion as a risk factor for youth suicide. In Alcohol, Drug Abuse, and Mental Health Administration, *Report of the Secretary's Task Force on Youth Suicide*, Vol. 2: *Risk factors for youth suicide* (DHHS Publ. No. (ADM) 89-1623, pp. 88–109). Washington, DC: U.S. Government Printing Office.

Department of Health and Human Services. (1990). *Healthy people 2000: National health promotion and disease prevention objectives* (DHHS Publ. No. (PHS) 91-50212). Washington, DC: U.S. Government Printing Office.

Department of Health and Human Services. (1992). *The Third National Injury Control Conference* (DHHS Publ. No. 1992-634-666). Washington, DC: U.S. Government Printing Office.

Dryfoos, J. G. (1990). *Adolescents at Risk: Prevalence and prevention*. New York: Oxford University Press.

Felner, R. D., Adan, A. M., & Silverman, M. M. (1992). Risk assessment and prevention of youth suicide in schools and educational contexts. In R. Maris, A. Berman, J. Maltsberger, & R. Yufit (Eds.), *Assessment and prediction of suicide* (pp. 420–447). New York: Guilford Press.

Felner, R. D., & Felner, T. Y. (1989). Primary prevention programs in the educational context: A trans-actional–ecological framework and analysis. In L. A. Bond & B. E. Compas (Eds.), *Primary prevention and promotion in the schools* (pp. 13–49). Beverly Hills, CA: Sage Publications.

Felner, R. D., Jason, L. A., Moritsugu, J. N., & Farber, S. S. (1983). *Preventive psychology: theory, research, and practice*. New York: Pergamon Press.

Felner, R. D., & Silverman, M. M. (1989). Primary Prevention: A consideration of general principles and findings for the prevention of youth suicide. In Alcohol, Drug Abuse, and Mental Health Administration, *Report of the Secretary's Task Force on Youth Suicide*, Vol. 3: *Prevention and interventions in youth suicide* (DHHS Publ. No. (ADM) 89-1623, pp. 23–30). Washington, DC: U.S. Government Printing Office.

Felner, R. D., Silverman, M. M., & Adix, R. (1991). Prevention of substance abuse and related disorders in children and adolescence: A developmentally-based, comprehensive ecological approach. *Family and Community Health: The Journal of Health Promotion and Maintenance, 14*(3), 12–22.

Felner, R. D., Silverman, M. M., & Felner, T. Y. (1995). Prevention in mental health and social intervention: Conceptual and methodological issues in the evolution of the science and practice of prevention. In J. Rappaport and E. Seidman (Eds.), *Handbook of community psychology*. New York: Plenum Press.

Goldstein, M. (1985). Comments on the possibility of primary prevention in mental health. In R. L. Hough, P. A. Gongla, V. B. Brown, & S. E. Goldston (Eds.), Psychiatric epidemiology and prevention: The possibilities (pp. 65–70). Rockville, MD: National Institute of Mental Health.

Institute of Medicine. (1994). *Reducing risk for mental disorders: Frontiers for preventive intervention research*. Washington, DC: National Academy Press.

Joint Commission on Mental Health and Mental Disabilities. (1961). *Action for mental health*. New York: Basic Books.

Maris, R. W. (1981). *Pathways to suicide: A survey of self-destructive behaviors*. Baltimore: Johns Hopkins University Press.

McGinnis, J. M. (1985). The limits of prevention. *Public Health Reports, 100*(3), 255–260.

President's Commission on Mental Health. (1978). *Report to the President*, Vol. 1 (Stock No. 040-000-0390-8). Washington, DC: U.S. Government Printing Office.

Sarason, S. B. (1981). *Psychology misdirected*. New York: Free Press.

Shaffer, D., & Bacon, K. (1989). A critical review of preventive intervention efforts in suicide, with particular reference to youth suicide. In Alcohol, Drug Abuse, and Mental Health Administration, *Report of the Secretary's Task Force on Youth Suicide*, Vol. 3: *Prevention and interventions in youth suicide* (DHHS Publ. No. (ADM) 89-1623, pp. 31–61). Washington, DC: U.S. Government Printing Office.

Silverman, M. M., Lalley, T., Rosenberg, M. A., Parron, D. L., et al. (1988). Control of stress and violent behavior: Midcourse review of the 1990 health objectives for the nation. *Public Health Reports, 103*(1), 38–49.

# III. A Settings Perspective

# 8

# Suicide Prevention in Canada: A National Perspective Highlighting Progress and Problems

## Bryan Tanney, MD

Responses to suicidal behavior have been organized at levels from the local community to an awareness by the World Health Organization (WHO, 1982) and the United Nations of the global prevalence of this often preventable behavior. Beyond the request by the editors of this special issue, a focus on suicide prevention activities at the level of the nation state deserves some justification. Although initiatives at other levels of community are encouraged, activities at the national level are most likely to impact the largest number of citizens. There are opportunities for leadership and agenda setting, mandates for protecting the lives of citizens may be a legislated responsibility, appropriate financial support can be generated through taxation and levies, and prevention activities can be implemented within a large enough system to permit economies of scale.

Although Finland today presents the most orderly and measured example (National Research and Development Center for Welfare and Health) of a model for preventing suicidal behaviors on a national scale (1993), it is not the only nation embarked on a large-scale effort to address this enduring medical–social–psychological issue. Norway is another Scandinavian nation with a documented strategy, and Australia is in the process of finalizing their Task Force's recommendations for suicide prevention (Baume, 1994). Canada lays some claim for recognition in the general field of prevention beginning in 1974 with a federal document focusing on health promotion and lifestyle change (Lalonde, 1974). Interest in suicide prevention has been ongoing and vigorous at various levels of government for over two decades. Although focusing on Canada affords the opportunity to partially catalogue the quality and quantity of activities in suicide prevention ongoing in late 1994, this is not the major goal. The Canadian experiences are also not theoretically unique although there are some innovations in program implementation. Reviewing and commenting on the Canadian scene from a personal, academic, and critical perspective shares our progress and problems in preventing suicide. With an emphasis on lessons learned, others may use our experience to monitor their own progress, to diagnose obstacles, or to aid them in navigating new solutions. A Canadian perspective may be of particular interest to American readers considering the many similarities in the social and political forces and institutions operating in these neighboring nations.

## CONTEXTS

A brief backgrounder on Canada socially, politically, and culturally appropriately sets the stage upon which suicide preven-

Bryan Tanney is Professor of Psychiatry, Faculty of Medicine, University of Calgary, Calgary, AB, Canada.

tion is being addressed. The added necessity to clarify and offer operational definitions of both prevention and suicide forewarns the reader that this topic is not without controversy and competitive viewpoints.

## Canada

Canada is a large nation with a small population that has increasingly urbanized over the past several decades. There are large urban agglomerations and vast stretches of land dotted with isolated rural settlements. The country is painfully struggling with a bilingual heritage and a more recent emphasis on multiculturalism through immigration. The predominant culture is Euro-American with an increasing influence from the United States across the longest undefended border in the world. Like other colonially settled nations (Australia, South Africa, United States), the native or aboriginal population and their relationship to the larger culture remains problematic.

Canada is a relatively wealthy nation, with membership in the G-9 economic council of industrialized nations. Development of a significant social safety net in the areas of health and welfare over the past decades has generated significant debt at all levels of government, with a particular focus in the past several years on cost cutting or reorganizing these programs.

The political organization is federal and democratic with a constitutional division of powers between central and provincial governments. The importance of this division of powers for suicide prevention is considerable. Suicide prevention activities largely fall in the area of human services [health, education, justice, and welfare (human resources)], and both levels of government have accepted some level of responsibility in these areas (Table 1). For the agency advocating suicide prevention, there are many "players" with some measure of jurisdiction, responsibility, and interests. Often, activities in suicide prevention must be negotiated through numerous departments at multiple levels.

There are clearly defined mechanisms for such interdepartmental and cross-level agreements (Table 1). It is critically important to be fully aware of the specific areas of responsibility allocated to each government, and of the agreed-upon processes by which some government services are negotiated and shared between jurisdictions.

Specific to suicide prevention, several points warrant special note. There are a few areas of direct federal responsibility for the provision of human services. Constrained from direct program delivery in areas of provincial jurisdiction, there are legislated agreements — for example, transfer payments for financial support of certain programs — through which the federal government does direct and influence human services activities. The national government does provide support for suicide research and for the collection of national data concerning mortality.

## Suicidal Behaviors and Persons at Risk

The mandate of suicide prevention must be extended to include not only reducing the mortality of completed suicide, but also the morbidity associated with nonfatal suicidal behaviors. Without entering the controversy of whether suicidal behaviors are one population or two (Linehan, 1987), there is agreement: (1) about a substantial (?) overlap between these two classes of self-harming behavior and (2) that prior suicidal behavior is the best established single predictor of eventual completed suicide. From this consensus, even those who adopt the most rigorous and restricted definitions — that suicide requires a death outcome — usually accept that measures intended to prevent any suicidal behavior are appropriately considered as suicide prevention. The term *suicidal behaviors* seems appropriate to describe the problem being addressed for prevention (Beck et al., 1973). This is an area of ongoing controversy with at least four independent groups presently considering opera-

Table 1
Government in Canada: The Constitutional Division of Powers
As It Affects Some Human Resource/Service Activities

| Issue | Government jurisdiction | Interface procedures |
|---|---|---|
| Aboriginals (Native Canadians) | Federal | Consensus conference, Confrontation |
| Education | Provincial | Duplication |
| Justice | Federal/provincial | Purchase services |
| Health | Provincial | Provinces accept federal regulation; e.g., universality, if federal funds are transferred for support |
| Welfare (human services) | Provincial | Provinces accept federal regulation, if federal funds are transferred for support |

tional definitions for the classification of self-harm behaviors.

Although the Operational Criteria for the Certification of Suicide (Jobes & Josselson, 1987) are not fully applied, reliable medical examiner certifications of death at the provincial and territorial levels are collectd and reported annually. For study and comparison, basic demographic data for completed suicides are also available. Due to an early closure date for inclusion in the national data set, there exists an ongoing underestimate of the actual magnitude of the problem of completed suicides in Canada. This system "glitch" has been remarked for more than a decade, but no distinction between preliminary and final completed suicide numbers is available. Canadian researchers have reported some of the only data estimating the magnitude of the problem of nonfatal suicidal behaviors (Dyck, Bland, Newman, & Om, 1988; Johnson, Frankel, Ferrence, Jarvis, & Whitehead, 1975; Ramsay & Bagley, 1985).

Both absolute numbers and rates have increased over the past several decades, with some recent stabilization (Figure 1). Other trends are similar to those noted internationally: a major increase notable among 15- to 29-year-old males and a significant decrease in female suicides (Huchcroft & Tanney, 1988) over the past two decades. Suicide in rural areas remains a major problem likely related to methods availability and limited resource supports. Canada has a significant proportion of suicides due to carbon monoxide poisoning, probably attributable to the northerly climate where enclosed garages for vehicles provide a suitable "gas chamber." Among minorities, correctional system inmates and aboriginals show increased rates of suicide relative to the general population, but the absolute numbers of such deaths are very small. Significant resources directed toward suicide prevention in these two populations reflect the federal mandate of service responsibility, and a vocal social-democratic, civil libertarian lobby speaking out on their behalf. In total, suicidal behaviors are much more prominently a behavior of females (despite notable increases in male "parasuicide" behavior over the past decade). With women's health issues a recognized priority on the national agenda, there is a window of opportunity to include suicide prevention activities within programs to maintain women's mental and emotional health.

## Prevention/prevention

In the broadest approach, activities or interventions to prevent suicide may occur

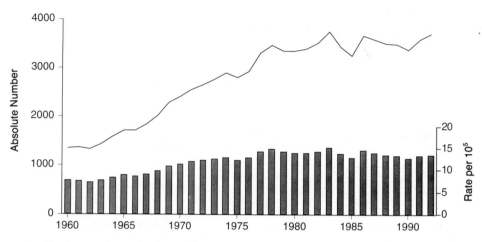

Figure 1.    Absolute number and rate per $10^5$ of completed suicides in Canada, 1960–1992. (Source: Statistics Canada and Living Works Education, Inc.).

anywhere along the "river of prevention" prior to the "waterfall" that represents the self-harm event. Among numerous reworkings of the terminology, the distinctions offered by Seidman (1987) and by Felner and Felner (1988) form the basis for the discussion of Prevention within this text. Prevention addresses the sum of all activities aimed at reducing mortality and morbidity associated with suicidal behaviors. The aim of *prevention* is to reduce the incidence of new suicidal behaviors, either in the overall population or in a specific subpopulation, by undertaking interventions at some macrolevel directed at conditions of risk and not at the level of the individual person at risk. A related series of activities usually focused specifically upon the individual person at risk and aiming to prevent occurrences, or to reduce their intensity, duration and severity are framed as *early interventions*. There are undoubtedly numerous points at which intervention might make a difference in suicidal behaviors. This emphasis on activities before the self-harm event does not diminish the impact of *treatment* (clinical) interventions in ultimately reducing the magnitude of this problem. They are simply excluded from the present discussion, which thus focuses on *prevention/early intervention* and not Pre-

vention. Purists would suggest that including *early intervention* within the realm of *prevention* is inappropriate, but excluding these activities would leave this author with virtually nothing to report about progress toward suicide Prevention in Canada. In the following text, Prevention should be understood to encompass both Prevention and *early intervention* activities.

## SUICIDE PREVENTION IN CANADA: A PROGRESS REPORT

In general, Canada has a positive experience with prevention activities directed toward "lifestyle" disorders and diseases. A Commission of Enquiry into the Nonmedical Use of Drugs (LeDain, 1973), active health promotion efforts to encourage physical activity through "Participation," and partnerships between nongovernment organizations and industry to encourage the use of child bicycle helmets and to specifically target accidental injuries in children have all been successfully implemented.

Prevention of suicidal behaviors may prove more obstinate as a focus because Canadian society seems ambivalent at this time with respect to a permissive or restrictive stance toward suicidal behaviors. Completed suicide was decriminalized in 1971 to remove one source of stigma, but it remains illegal to attempt, to counsel, or to assist suicide. There is evidence of an intergenerational increase in tolerance toward suicidal behavior (Boldt, 1983). With the introduction of the term *physician-assisted suicide*, suicide has been embroiled in the ongoing debate about euthanasia. In late 1994 one chamber of the federal government held hearings to develop national policy and the other proposes a "free vote" (independent of party affiliations) within the next year with respect to legalizing physician-assisted suicide. The pendulum has moved toward permissiveness and it may be difficult to motivate either suicide Prevention or *prevention* in such an atmosphere.

## Models

Preventive interventions should be undertaken within the framework of a model. The model of choice derives from reasoned and reasonable theory. In turn, theory derives from ordered observations and other research that have generated a body of information about the subject. Even a brief review of notable Canadian research (Bagley & Ramsey, 1985) is beyond the present mandate, although an overview is offered. [For a complete bibliography concerning research activities pertaining to suicide in Canada, consult the computerized database of the Suicide Information and Education Centre (SIEC) in Calgary Alberta.] There is breadth and diversity with activity in the areas of basic, applied, clinical, and action research. Centers of interest have been established, although these are usually driven by the interest of individual researchers. There is no organized research unit activity entitled *Centres of Excellence* in Canada, that might be likened to the Medical Research Council Units in the United Kingdom. With the exception of deCatanzaro (1981) and his interest in sociobiology Canada has no prominent theorist concerning the origins of suicide. In theorizing about suicide pre-

vention, several centers and authors deserve recognition. As an important internal protective factor, A. H. Thompson has focused on the importance of developing a sense of internal competency through success experiences in childhood. Queen's University in Kingston, Ontario, has shown an interest in the general area of risk factors for harmful behaviors in adolescence. D. R. Offord has recently included suicidal behavior as an outcome that might be prevented through the manipulation of the social and family environments of children identified at risk for a spectrum of deviant behaviors, including depression, substance abuse, truancy, and suicide. An approach to coordinating services and resources at all levels of Prevention has been ongoing in the province of Alberta over the past several decades, with activities directed toward prevention occurring as early interventions (Boldt, 1976, 1982, 1985; Boldt et al., 1983; Tanney 1983). In large part, the underlying theory reiterates the American document, *Suicide Prevention in the Seventies* (Resnik & Hathorne, 1973).

In Canada at present, there is no dominant or widely accepted prevention model Efforts at a *grand unifying theory* of suicidal behaviors are clearly not within our present grasp. This seems appropriate in addressing a behavior that has been regarded as heterogeneous or encompassing a spectrum, and whose origins arise in numerous factors operating along a large number of overlapping and interconnected pathways (multifactorial and multidetermined).

Within this mix of environment, there must be recognition and opportunity for collaboration between the perspectives of different theories and models. The assumptions of the UN/WHO Guidelines for the Development of a National Strategy for the Prevention of Suicide (Appendix A) (Ramsay & Tanney, 1993) developed in Alberta Canada during 1993 are clearly influenced by and congruent with this generalist and all-encompassing approach to Prevention.

There are numerous models being used

in the Canadian context to guide suicide prevention and early intervention activities. Their relative merits are described and debated elsewhere in this issue. Implementation is largely at the demonstration, pilot, and field trial levels with only the education and training component of the Alberta approach having achieved widespread, though incomplete, national dissemination.

Significant prevention activities include the Brighter Futures program of Health Canada. This program addresses the social and cultural circumstances of young Native Canadians and proposes broad-based activities with this subpopulation. Suicide prevention would be an indirect measurable outcome of the effectiveness of these socially directed preventive interventions. D. R. Offord in Ontario is directing a large-scale environmental intervention directed at children believed to be at risk of adult socially deviant behaviors, including suicidal behaviors. This long-term project is itself the outgrowth of over 15 years of preliminary investigation.

With respect to early interventions, the Correctional Service of Canada has been offering caregiver training in "suicide first-aid" to both employees and inmates within its system for over a decade. There are a large number of local, action–research projects directed toward adolescents at risk. Most often they involve the school and other socializing systems in a program of sensitization and awareness education around the issues of suicidal behavior. Curriculum in Laval (Raymond, 1988) and a resource text for teachers in Hamilton (Martin, 1987) were important first-generation efforts in this regard. Many programs are presently into a second or third generation of development, often including community networking and resource components. At present, these activities are not supported at a large-scale national level and few provinces have included them in curriculum objectives.

The province of Alberta is in the forefront both nationally and internationally in the organized implementation of a

model for Preventing suicide. The approach or strategy has been evolving since 1973. It proposes a number of well-defined, coordinating objectives embracing all aspects of Preventing suicide, including policy making, consumer input, and supporting infrastructure. The system is a knowledge-based framework driven by technology transfer or the "development" aspect of research and development activity (Tanney & Ramsay, 1984). Current knowledge is rapidly disseminated as a tool for guiding decision making. Separate agencies have been developed with responsibility for the various objectives (Table 2). The flow of information encourages interventions and other activities that are effective, responsive to and current with recent developments, and integrated with other agencies in the model. Within the more limited context of prevention, the main component is an early intervention focused on the environment and dedicated to ensuring coordination and networking among the available external supports for persons at risk of suicide. This is integrated with an education and training component aiming to establish capable and competent caregiving resources for persons at risk of suicide within all communities. With funding over C$1,000,000 annually, this project has now been in place for over a decade. The strategy was significantly compromised soon after the outset when the research component was deleted from receiving active financial support in the project funding. This incomplete implementation makes full evaluation of the strategy impossible. After a decade of operations, there was a reworking and reformulation of objectives by a diverse group of stakeholders in 1993. Significantly, this group endorsed and renewed the model and strategy (White, 1993).

## Prevention Activities

Contributions by governments, by diverse nongovernment organizations (NGOs), and by industry should be noted. Progress can be gauged using the summary chart for developing and implementing Na-

Table 2
Alberta's Model for Suicide Prevention

| Objective | Agency |
|-----------|--------|
| Research | Alberta Institute for Suicide Research (AISR) |
| Education/training | Suicide Information and Education Centre (SIEC) |
|  | Suicide Prevention Training Programs (SPTP) |
| Clinical services coordination | Community Interagency Suicide Prevention Program (CISPP) |
| Policy | Suicide Prevention Provincial Advisory Committee (SPPAC) |
| Infrastructure | Provincial suicidologist |

tional Strategy (Table 3) from the Draft Guidelines of the Interregional Expert Meeting for the Formulation and Implementation of a Comprehensive National Strategy for the Prevention of Suicidal Behaviors (Ramsay & Tanney, 1993).

*Federal.* Commissioned in 1980, and finally available in 1987, the Report of the National Task Force on Suicide in Canada (Syer-Solursh, 1987) provides a review and a summary, and makes 40 diverse recommendations for Preventing suicide. There are 12 that could be categorized as prevention (7) or preventive/early (5) interventions (Appendix B). There is only one recommendation addressing the potential impact of mental disorders on suicidal behaviors. Three years after publication, a review of progress suggested some activity

Table 3
Guidelines for Developing a National Strategy for Suicide Prevention

| Actor(s) | Action |
|----------|--------|
| Leading private sector or government agency | 1. Organize initial review |
|  |   a. Determine what must be addressed |
|  |   b. Include effectiveness of current measures |
|   + content specialists |     i. Convene expert meeting |
|  |     ii. Compile policy-oriented report |
|  |     iii. Review report |
|  |     iv. Formal presentation to government |
| Leading stakeholder groups | 2. Establish coordination and collaboration |
|   Ad hoc committee |   a. Consultation (ongoing) |
|  |   b. Lobbying (ongoing) |
| Responsible government agency | 3. Formal preparation of strategy |
|  |   a. Identify need |
|  |   b. Determine what elements already in place |
|  |   c. Establish working-group with secretariat |
| Working group: focal or lead agency | 4. Review strategy |
|   + interdepartmental |   a. Request input |
|   + private sector |   b. Provide guidelines & specifications |
|  |   c. Ensure compliance |
|  |   d. Coordinate and harmonize input |
|  |   e. Redraft strategy |
| Stakeholders |   f. review |
| Working group |   g. revise strategy |
| Ad hoc committee | 5. Mobilize societal support |
| Government | 6. Propose legislation |

*Source.* Adapted from UN/WHO Interregional Expert Meeting (Ramsay & Tanney, 1993).

Table 4
Progress on Recommendations of the
National Task Force (1987) by 1990

| Strategies | Recommendations | | Implementation activity | |
|---|---|---|---|---|
| | Subcategory | Total | Subcategory | Total |
| Prevention | | 12 | | 7 |
| Prevention | 7 | | 3 | |
| Prevention – intervention | 5 | | 4 | |
| Intervention | | 12 | | 4 |
| Mental health | 6 | | 2 | |
| Community | 4 | | 1 | |
| General | 2 | | 1 | |
| Postvention | | 2 | | 1 |
| Research | | 16 | | 6 |
| Basic | 5 | | | |
| Applied | 5 | | | |
| Clinical | 3 | | | |
| Infrastructure | 3 | | | |

*Source.* Tanney in Leenaars, Mishara, Tanney & Sakinousky, 1990.

in implementing 7 of the 12 prevention recommendations (Leenaars, Mishara, Tanney, & Sakinousky, 1990) (Table 4).

At the direct service level, the federal
government is limited by its mandate to
provide services only for aboriginal (Native Canadian) persons and for federal
prison inmates. Prevention initiatives are
underway for both of these groups. A
Health Services branch is responsible for
data collection and collation concerning
suicide morbidity and mortality, (e.g.,
H&W Canada, 1982), and has significant
opportunities to promote and to fund research in this area. At present, suicidal behaviors do not appear among the priority
topics for research funding in any federal
policy initiative.

In the jargon of medicine, suicide *Prevention* has a heartbeat, but only just. In
an attempt at resuscitation, an update of
the 1987 Task Force Report has been in
progress over the past 3 years.

*Provincial.* Alberta, Saskatchewan and
New Brunswick fund significant initiatives in suicide Prevention. Using the
measure of financial commitment to prov-

incewide prevention programs, activity in
other provinces can be summarized (Table
5). Lamentably, Manitoba's involvement
is now declining. Awaiting review of a formally prepared strategy, British Columbia remains in anticipation. Support by responsible government departments and
some leading stakeholders is ensured. The
(apparently) complete lack of interest by
the governments of the two largest provinces, largely urbanized and with over half
the country's population, is a massive obstacle to suicide Prevention activities at
the national level.

Most provincial activity is in the area of
education and training in early intervention. There are few prevention initiatives.
In different provinces, activities might involve departments of health, education,
social welfare, or justice. There is little indication of any coordination of efforts between or at the interdepartmental level. It
is noteworthy and positive that several
other provinces and territories have
adopted or adapted components of the Alberta strategic approach, without "reinventing the wheel" within their own jurisdictions.

Table 5
Level of Activity in Suicide Prevention in the Provinces/Territories of Canada, 1994

| Major | Some | Planning | Considering | None |
|---|---|---|---|---|
| Alberta | Manitoba | British Columbia | Ontario | Prince Edward Island |
| Saskatchewan | NW Territories | Yukon | Quebec | Nova Scotia |
| New Brunswick | | | | |

*Nongovernmental Organizations.* The Canadian Mental Health Association has been in the forefront of suicide prevention and Prevention activities in Alberta, New Brunswick, the Northwest Territories, and also in Ontario. Their activities clearly stimulated several provincial governments to commit funds for suicide prevention. A large and very supportive association of persons interested in suicide prevention (Quebec Association of Suicidology – QAS) is active in the province of Quebec. Individual members have undertaken many local initiatives, mainly directed toward clinical intervention. Thus far, they appear to have had little success in lobbying for a provincewide, governmentally supported effort. The potential for survivors of suicides to form an effective lobby and pressure group is barely underway in Canada. The Canadian Association for Suicide Prevention (CASP) was organized in conjunction with the effort by interested stakeholders to produce *Suicide in Canada*, the National Task Force Report. A useful rallying point and a major contributor to networking among those interested in suicide prevention and intervention across the nation, it remains a small organization struggling with its mission and with its remarkably diverse constituency.

There has been minimal success in garnering the support of the private sector for prevention activities. Acquiring such support in the area of suicidal behaviors is difficult as there is no obvious constituency to be targeted (Tanney & Ramsay, 1993). Pharmaceutical houses specializing in psychotropic drugs seem an obvious source of support because of the association of mental disorders with suicidal behaviors (Tanney, 1992), but their commit-

ment has not been extracted. The relatively low level of support is usually in the form of humanitarian or public relations donations. The QAS has had some success in establishing partnerships with the pharmaceutical industry. The Canadian Mental Health Association in Sasketchewan has recently negotiated support for province-wide, rural-focused Prevention activities from a major utility industry. These are significant accomplishments.

In the process of implementing large-scale Prevention activities through a national strategy, the Canadian effort appears to be stalled at step 5 (Table 3), the mobilization of significant societal support. Among many explanations, the following discussion addresses obstacles and some solutions. There is hope that the Canadian experiences, positive and negative, might be generalized to aid those at earlier stages of national strategy development.

## PROBLEMS IN SUICIDE PREVENTION

### The Issues of Suicide

*Attitudes.* There are large barriers to surmount in motivating and justifying large-scale efforts at preventing suicide. Canadian society is ambivalent about suicide. On the one hand is the permissive stance toward self-death underlying the renewed discussion of euthanasia and physician-assisted suicide. This attitude suggests that some suicidal behavior is to be tolerated and expressly condoned. Proponents are unlikely to be vigorous in supporting suicide Prevention activities. Likely of greater concern is the ongoing stigmatization by society of suicidal behavior and of those associated with it. Although portrayed and overdramatized in the popular media, suicide educators regularly confront resistance to the presentation of learning activities aimed at sensitization to and awareness about suicidal behaviors. This response is identical to that arising around the open discussion of other lifestyle choice issues such as sexual activity/preference and substance use.

The beliefs surrounding this restrictive approach often are misinformed or lacking in supportive evidence. The argument for a *Werther effect* (Philips, 1974) of such informed learning activities is only very weakly supported and ignores the high-dose exposure already present in the popular media. Clinical experience contradicts the notion that suicide can be suggested by exposing a person at risk through direct enquiry about suicidal ideation. Epidemiological data on the prevalence of suicidal behaviors and suicidal ideation confirm that it is disturbingly common. Despite this evidence, the barriers to talking openly about suicide remain firmly in place.

The restriction of information about suicide seems motivated by some taboo originating in emotions. Perhaps the pain of survivorship and the destructive denial that can accompany it is more common than we can imagine. Perhaps the siren song of the death instinct is louder today and must similarly be denied and suppressed. Whatever the reason, the restrictive approach to suicide will not support any prevention program in which the subject is broached. This has led to the support of indirect prevention models (see below) and also to the presentation of early interventions for suicidal behavior in which the entire subject is avoided. It is hard to imagine that these later activities lessen their audience's anxiety about this stigmatized topic. The difficulty in mobilizing concern about suicide in either the public or the private sector may largely reflect the astonishing lack of or even misinformation about even the most basic facts about suicide (Tanney & Ramsay, 1993).

The recent effort to link suicidal behaviors to mental disorders, based largely on psychological autopsy findings, offers no solution to this problem. In fact, it may further jeopardize suicide *Prevention* activities by allocating persons at risk to the doubly stigmatized category of both being suicidal *and* being mentally disordered.

*Controversy.* Limited government resources are allocated in the face of severe and stiff lobbying competition for the relief of a multitude of other societal and human problems. In particular, the highly successful campaign to achieve significant funding for interventions in AIDS is out of proportion to the numerical reality and the financial burden associated with the disorder. Proponents of suicide Prevention activities have seen suicide disappear from the national agenda of most health and welfare agencies in the past decade. It has also been suggested that the complexity of suicide itself as a multifactorial and multidetermined human behavior has contributed to this failure to maintain or move it up the national agenda. With a behavior of such heterogeneity, there is no particular constituency that "owns" the problem and that can generate a champion to represent and speak effectively for it. (Tanney, 1991). The situation might in fact be even worse. Not only is there no unified view or strong voice to move government action, there is dissonance and disarray among the proponents of suicide Prevention. Such discord particularly concerning the role of mental disorders and suicidal behavior delayed the proceedings and conclusions of the Canadian National Task Force for several years. More recently, two negative reports concerning the impact of community awareness and education about suicide (Gould & Shaffer, 1986; Shaffer et al., 1990) resulted in delays and cancellations of broad-based, community wide early interventions addressing attitudes and knowledge about suicide in both general and at-risk populations in Canada and the United States.

The impact of these two studies is especially notable not only because of the intense controversy surrounding their results, but even more from the realization that the data questioning the safety of community wide preventive education activities were reported by a research group strongly committed to an equally worthy but alternative approach to suicide *Prevention* (identification and treatment of at-risk individuals, using screening instruments largely reflecting individual psychopathology).

Although significant direct, indirect, and opportunity costs can be allocated to the mortality and morbidity of suicidal behaviors, legislators remain unimpressed of the need for action. Motivating a committment to suicide prevention/Prevention may not be an entirely rational process. Suicide lobbyist are particularly warned to be aware of the widespread impact of unrecognized or unresolved survivorship in both politicians and policy makers.

## The Issue of (Self) Interest

Enumerating the multitude of stakeholders with an interest in suicidal behaviors is beyond the scope of this text. From consumers and survivors to nongovernment and government agencies at all levels involved in human services, each group has a particular investment. There is a theoretical basis in genetics and sociobiology for building strength in diversity, and the Canadian social experiment in promoting multiculturalism over the past quarter century reflects this approach. Unfortunately, there are now serious questions about this approach with the disintegration of Czechoslovakia and the recent political events in Rwanda and the former Yugoslavia epitomizing the violent breakdown of these enforced alliances. Stakeholders in suicide Prevention have not solved this difficulty of integrating or resolving diverse interests. The Alberta approach offers several examples of this failure in diversity. 1) The internationally known clearinghouse for information about suicidal behaviors (Suicide Information and Education Centre) offers worldwide computer access. Almost 40% of those using the database are from outside Alberta. Although there have been numerous efforts, Alberta has shouldered the financial burden of supporting this valued national and international resource with no support from any other level of government. 2) With a topic as heterogeneous as suicide, there is also a need to bring together a "critical mass" of researchers and practititioners from different disciplines to allow the evolution and testing of effective models for suicide prevention. Surprisingly, the fatal flaw perceived in the Alberta Institute for Suicide Research, the proposed research component of the Alberta strategy, was its committment to support such a cadre of involved researchers at all levels and discipline. One might suppose that not all reviewers were aware of the contributions to suicide Prevention that could derive from such collaboration.

The fragility of the national voice for suicide Prevention (CASP) as an extended organization with low membership and few areas of strength further highlights this issue. The majority of its membership are involved in direct services (treatment) using locally developed expertise. Whatever the membership in terms of professional orientation or discipline, the voice of CASP, and most organizations devoted to doing something about suicidal behaviors, is largely determined by these caregivers with their focus on issues of direct helping. With no strong prevention theory and no exceptional defenders of the prevention or early intervention approach, there seems little impetus at present for a strong, prevention-based initiative in Canada. One assumes that a charismatic leadership, similar to that of the National Task Force chairperson who was also instrumental in founding CASP, might draw together the diverse interests of those involved with suicidal behavior. It is questionable whether a prevention project would be enough of a common purpose even for such a dynamic individual.

## The Issue of Prevention

Consumers, clinical practitioners, and funders are confused about the application of prevention concepts and models to suicide prevention.

There is a realistic concern about models and theories which suggest that major and complex societal changes may be required in order to influence or effect any behavioral outcome, including suicide. Although Platt cautions against the "ecological fallacy," it is not uncommon for his work on unemployment and suicide (Platt, 1986) to be used in arguments that societal wealth must be redistributed for an effective resolution of unemployment and (thus) suicide.

A current and knowledgeable text diagrams some 43 variables believed to contribute to the origins of suicidal behaviors and distributes them among 4 phases in the evolution of the behavior (Maris, Berman, Maltsberger & Yufit, 1992). It cannot manage or explain the interactions between these variables, either within or between phases. If most preventive interventions have the objective of modifying some variable(s) in one of the many sequences or pathways that can lead to a self-harm outcome, this model implies that there are multiple sites of activity with a potential for preventive effect. (It is important to recognize that other theories for justifying particular interventions are available.) Organizing these intervention possibilities has led to the elaboration of a number of prevention hierarchies. The interventions themselves are variously described as modifying or targeting initial or mediating conditions, predisposing and precipitating conditions, or antecedent and distal conditions. These terms are close to synonymous, but there is no standard nomenclature at present. If a particular intervention addresses a site more "upstream" on some figurative "river of Prevention," the proposed outcomes may only exert an indirect effect on suicidal behaviors. In order to account for and hold constant both the intervening and the other contributory variables so that the effect of influencing some single variable

at a particular site can be estimated, prevention theories and models must use statistical techniques well beyond the scope of understanding of most stakeholders with an interest in preventing suicide. One effort at simplifying the chain of causation has involved the hypothesizing of clusters of deviant behavior that are themselves either associated (comorbid) with or are necessary antecedents to suicidal behaviors. The most popular cluster linked to youthful suicide involves depression, substance abuse, truancy, and other legal involvements. There are numerous others (Yang and Clum, 1994). There is an inference that prevention of suicidal behavior results when some or all of the cluster of antecedent deviant conditions is prevented. This is again an indirect approach. It assumes that interventions that modify the deviant behavior cluster are surrogates of effective prevention activity for suicidal behaviors. Though it directs the largest amount of prevention modeling, this is entirely a theoretical assumption. Suggestions for preventive interventions based on models are speculative at best.

Such complex models are needed only because the outcome to be prevented is the relatively rare event of completed suicide. If prevention activities might be directed toward the morbidity associated with suicidal behaviors as well as the mortality of completed suicide, it is likely that simpler models targeted at this much more common outcome could be developed. Another solution would involve opportunistic experiments such as the impact of natural gas detoxification on suicides in the United Kingdom (Kreitman, 1976) or the impact of newspaper strikes on the frequency of suicidal behaviors (Motto, 1967).

Concisely, the available models for suicide prevention are complex, competing, and difficult to discriminate. With increasing sophistication, they become increasingly hard to apply with any expectation of significant effect. They have not attracted the interest or support of advocates for suicide Prevention.

Table 6
Suicide Prevention: Suggested Priorities for Action

| Priority | Possible activity |
| --- | --- |
| Mental disorders, including substance abuse | Enough and informed helpers |
| | Increase price of alcohol |
| | Increase cost of alcohol over use |
| Males | Social and coping skill development |
| | Help-using behavior |
| | Competency (success) experiences |
| | Affect expression/regulation |
| Methods | Restriction |
| Marriage | Premarital counselling |
| | Alter media focus |
| | License child-bearing |
| Maintaining caregiver competencies | Education/training |
| | "Suicide first-aid" |
| Minorities | Culturally oriented approaches |

There is also very little here to attract the support of politicians. Such projects are time consuming over many years, involve considerable expense devoted to maintaining personnel on the project, and might generate only partial or incomplete answers about the effectiveness of the prevention activities that are initially hypothesized. The interventions most likely to be supported are those which offer direct answers, justify a staged approach, or aid in reaching specific and prioritized objectives. It may be possible to develop a list or menu of such activities. The activities on one such list (Table 6) have been accepted and endorsed in presentations to both community-based and professional stakeholders. Six factors are targeted along with some suggested activities for each that it is generally agreed would have noticeable impact on the magnitude and severity of the problem of suicidal behavior. It is important to note that five of the six areas clearly involve prevention/early intervention activities. The approach is simplistic. If adopted by opinion leaders in the field, it may also be effective in mobilizing a broad base of support for prevention activities.

Changes could be made in public policy that would likely decrease the incidence of suicidal behaviors. Legislation respecting firearms control (via methods restriction) or substance abuse prevention (through decreased violence and comorbid mental disorders) are obvious examples. For each of these action interventions, there is a well-organized opposition lobbying against the changes. In assessing the priority to be assigned to public policy change as a prevention strategy, or to decide on which activities are to be targeted for legislative lobbying, the strength of these opposing forces must be realistically considered. In the United States it required a decade of lobbying by a coalition of antiviolence organizations (including the American Association of Suicidology) to overcome highly organized and well-funded opposition to the mild firearm restrictions of the Brady bill.

There is little coordination between levels of government or within departments and agencies at any particular level. This is especially difficult for suicide Prevention as so many government departments have a legitimate claim of interest or mandate. Numerous examples of reinventing the same program or duplicating the research required for its development are well known in Canada. This has been particularly true for early intervention awareness programs. Between nations, there are often replications of the basic epidemiology of suicide despite little evidence suggesting that substantial or meaningful differences will be found. Funding is limited and the practical need for such information should be questioned.

The trend devolving control over health care resources to an autonomous, local level with significant input from consumers will make the establishment of any large-scale, non-treatment-focused program even more difficult. History informs that prevention activities received limited if any attention during an era when available resources for all human services are drastically shrinking.

A commitment to prevention activities is lengthy not only for those funding the project and its outcome, but also for the involved personnel. In some cases, carrying out and evaluating a preventive intervention might require the investment of an entire career. The recent proposal for establishing an endowed chair in suicidal studies at the University of Toronto is a significant positive move to allow such a career commitment.

## The Issue of Implementation

As in Finland, the initial decade of the Alberta approach was to be spent in research, in developing infrastructure and policy, and in establishing the agencies and mechanisms for disseminating information about suicidal behaviors into prevention, early intervention, and treatment activities. The status of funding allocated among the various components is far removed from that proposal (Table 7). Treat-

ment activities receive the majority of available funds. From the foregoing discussion of issues surrounding suicide, prevention itself and the (self) interests of various stakeholders, such an outcome is neither unusual nor unexpected. There are also barriers to prevention directly tied to action and not to these other issues.

## CONCLUSIONS

1. Social attitudes, political agendas, and governments forced to shrink human services activities as the primary means of controlling expenditures all augur a declining interest in prevention and early intervention activities in the area of suicidal behaviors.

2. Simplified models with clear specification of mechanisms, outcomes and priorities are needed to give prevention activities any realistic opportunity for funding. A "prevention of suicide consensus conference" might generate a limited agenda of action priorities that could then be echoed, in a unified voice, by all suicide Prevention stakeholders.

3. Tolerance among the multiple stakeholders with an investment in suicidal behaviors is essential. In an environment with such diversity of interests and approaches, mechanisms for accommodating and welcoming differences must be in place. This particularly involves collaboration, communication, and coordination between nongovernmental organizations and government agencies at and within both the federal and provincial governments.

Table 7
Alberta's Model for Suicide Prevention: Program Implementation at 10 Years

| Program agency | Established | Operating | Evaluated | % of project funding |
|---|---|---|---|---|
| AISR | No | – | – | 0 |
| SPPAC | Yes | – | + | 0 |
| SIEC/SPTP | Yes | + | + | 17 |
| CISSP | Yes | + | + | 70 |
| Provincial suicidologist | Yes | + | – | 13 |

4. Action research initiatives and pilot or demonstration projects utilizing naturalistic opportunities for evaluating prevention activities are strategies deserving of significant support. *Beta* site activities or multicenter consortias patterned after the European study of parasuicidal behaviors are implementation approaches meriting serious consideration.

Although the Canadian experience with suicide prevention activities continues to evolve, this review of progress and obstacles highlights common problem areas for any large-scale suicide Prevention initiative at a national level. It suggests that a major reorganization of both the models and strategies for accomplishing preventive interventions directed at suicidal behaviors may be required. The critical need may not be for a paradigm shift as much as for a realistic appraisal and reorientation of our existing and potentially effective resources.

## APPENDIX A: GUIDELINES FOR A NATIONAL STRATEGY FOR THE PREVENTION OF SUICIDE: ORGANIZING PRINCIPLES

1. Suicidal behaviors and the conditions antecedent to them are the appropriate focus for prevention activities. This expansion of the field of interest includes completed suicide, attempted suicide, or parasuicide, and those conditions, states, and disorders which proximally herald or predispose self-destructive behavior.

2. Employing a bio-psycho-social framework, the contexts of suicide are viewed from a broad perspective of human development. Suicidal behaviors are understood to be multifactorial, multidetermined, and transactional in their origins, and to develop cumulatively through identifiable but complex pathways or trajectories.

3. No single discipline or level of social organization is solely responsible for suicide or for suicide prevention. As a consequence, the issues and solutions of suicidal behavior are appropriately acted on by everyone in the community. Both individuals and agencies are, within their areas of competence and capacities, empowered to action as part of a network of community-wide resources.

4. Individuals in many roles and at all levels of community/society possess the expertise to make a unique and productive contribution to the prevention of suicidal behaviors.

5. The mosaic of community resources for suicide prevention operates most effectively when their activities are coordinated and integrated. Collaboration at an intersectorial and interregional level, between government and NGOs, and involving public and private sector contributions is also of fundamental importance.

6. A conceptual framework for understanding suicidal behaviors is needed to generate systematic and goal-oriented research and prevention activities.

7. Equipping individuals, families, and communities with the knowledge, skills, and values to foster and maintain the general health and social well-being of themselves and their communities is essential. These universal activities directed toward all members of the society should complement the continuing availability of specific interventions for known problem or at-risk groups.

8. A convergence of experience and wisdom in many nations supports the belief that some, perhaps many, suicidal behaviors can be prevented.

## APPENDIX B. PREVENTION/EARLY INTERVENTION—SELECTED RECOMMENDATIONS OF THE REPORT OF THE NATIONAL TASK FORCE ON SUICIDE ON CANADA (1987)

### Prevention

2. Mental health professionals knowledgeable about suicide should consult with media representatives in an attempt

to mitigate the negative effects of media coverage of suicides.

3. Public education programs should be developed by recognized mental or public health authorities in collaboration with media agencies (e.g., The Press Council), with a view to reducing the stigma attached to seeking treatment for states of depression; informing the public about the warning signs of suicide; and familiarizing society with various coping skills to use in times of distress.

4. Measures should be taken to reduce the lethality and availability of instruments of suicide (e.g., more stringent enforcement of gun control legislation, more stringent control of the distribution of medications, and wherever possible, limitations on the accessibility of attractive hazards).

17. Efforts to reduce the incidence of alcoholism should be strongly encouraged.

19. Provincial Ministers of Education should consider the feasibility of developing provincewide mental health programs for adolescent students; focusing on factors crucial to the development of self-confidence and self-esteem, strategies in problem solving and decision making, and interpersonal skills.

24. The development and implementation of suicide prevention strategies for Canadian Native peoples should be based on a comprehensive and culturally oriented approach.

40. Priority should be given to multicentre and multidisciplinary research with particular focus on the various factors (i.e., social integration, isolation, mental disorder, alcoholism, drug abuse, family and education difficulties) influencing young people who are suicidal.

## Early Intervention

5. Governmental assistance should be provided (e.g., to universities and community colleges) for education and training programs, to be provided on an interdisciplinary basis for the various service disciplines (e.g., health care professionals and gatekeepers) in order to improve their expertise in dealing with suicidal individuals.

6. In recognition of the unique set of problems inherent in the custodial and correctional services, workshops for suicide prevention training should be implemented for all custodial officers and for the police who are employed in presentencing custodial facilities in all jurisdictions.

7. Discipline, or group-specific issues and concerns related to suicide, should be addressed through additional training materials developed at the initiative of the group involved (e.g., physicians, clergy, teachers).

8. Teachers should be informed, either through initial training or professional development, of techniques in the detection and assessment of suicidal risk in students, and of the available counselling services in the community.

38. Formal research into the effectiveness of training methods should be encouraged on an interdisciplinary basis for those involved with suicide and suicidal individuals.

## REFERENCES

Bagley, D., & Ramsay, R. (1985). Problems and priorities in research on suicidal behaviours: An overview with Canadian implications. *Canadian Journal of Community Health, 4*(1), 15–49.

Baume, P. R. (1994). Personal communication. Chairperson, National Health Medical Research Council, Committee on Suicide Prevention.

Beck, A. T., et al. (1973). Classification and nomenclature. In *Suicide Prevention in the Seventies* (pp. 7–12). National Institute of Mental Health.

Boldt, M. (Chairman) (1976). *Report of the Alberta Task Force on Suicide to the Minister of Social Services and Community Health, The Honorable Helen Hunley*. Alberta, Canada.

Boldt, M. (1982). A Model for suicide prevention, intervention and postvention: The Alberta Task Force proposals. *Canada's Mental Health, 30*(1), 12–15.

Boldt, M. (1983). Normative evaluations of suicide and death: A cross-generational study. *Omega, 13*(2), 145–157.

Boldt, M., Ramsay, R., James, S. T., Tanney, B. L. (1983). *The first year: A multi-thrust approach to the prevention of suicidal behaviors*. Paper presented at the Annual Meeting, American Association of Suicidology, Dallas.

Boldt, M. (1985). Toward the development of a systematic approach to suicide prevention: The Alberta model. *Canada's Mental Health, 33*(2), 2–4.

deCatanzaro, D. (1981). *Suicide and Self-damaging Behavior.* New York: Academic Press.

Department of Health and Human Services. (1989). *Report of the Secretary's Task Force on Youth Suicide.* Washington, DC: U.S. Department of Health and Human Services, Alcohol, Drug Abuse and Mental Health Administration.

Dyck, R. J., Bland, R. C., Newman, S. C., & Orn, H. (1988). Suicide attempts and psychiatric disorders in Edmonton. *Acta Psychiatrica Scandinavica, 77*(Suppl. 338), 64–71.

Felner, R. D., & Felner, T. Y. (1988). Prevention programs in the educational context: A transactional-ecological framework for program models. In L. Bonds & B. Campas (Eds.), *Primary Prevention in the Schools.* Beverly Hills, CA: Sage.

Gould, M. D., Shaffer, D. (1986). The impact of suicide in television movies: Evidence of imitation. *New England Journal of Medicine, 315*(11), 690–694.

Health and Welfare Canada. (1982, March). *Suicide among the aged in Canada.*

Health and Welfare, Canada. *Brighter Futures.*

Huchcroft, S. A., & Tanney, B. L. (1988). Sex-specific suicide trends in Canada, 1971–1985. *International Journal of Epidemology, 17*(4), 839–843.

Jobes, D. A., & Jossellson, A. R. (1987). Improving the validity and reliability of medical-legal certifications of suicide. *Suicide and Life-Threatening Behavior, 17*(4), 310–325.

Johnson, F., Frankel, B., Ferrence, R., Jarvis, G., & Whitehead, P. (1975). Self-injury in London, Canada – Perspective study. *Canadian Journal of Public Health, 66*, 307–316.

Kreitman, N. (1976). The coal gas story. *British Journal of Preventive Social Medicine, 30*, 86–93.

Kreitman, N., & Platt, S. (1984). Suicide, unemployment, and domestic gas detoxification in Britain. *Journal of Epidemiology and Community Health, 39*(1), 1–6.

Lalonde, M. (1974). *A new perspective on the health of Canadians. A working document.* Ottawa: Government of Canada.

LeDain, G. M. (1972). A Report of the Commission of Enquiry into the Non-Medical Use of Drugs. Information Canada, Ottawa.

Leenaars, A., Mishara, B. M., Tanney, B. L., & Sakinovsky, I. S. (1990). *Suicide in Canada* (Plenary). Paper presented at the First National Conference of the Canadian Association for Suicide Prevention. Vancouver, B.C.

Linehan, M. M. (1986). Suicidal people: One population or two? In J. J. Mann & M. Stanley (Eds.), *Annals of the New York Academy of Sciences: Vol 487. Psychobiology of suicidal behavior* (pp. 16–33). New York: The New York Academy of Sciences.

Maris, R. M., Berman, A. L., Maltsberger, J. T., & Yufit, R. I. (1992). *Assessment and Prediction of Suicide.* New York: Guilford, p. 668.

Martin, D. (1987). *A handbook for the caregiver on suicide prevention.* Board of Education for the City of Hamilton, Hamilton, Ontario.

Motto, J. A. (1967). Suicide and suggestibility: The role of the press. *American Journal of Psychiatry, 124*(2), 252–256.

National Research and Developmental Center for Welfare and Health. (1993). *Suicide can be prevented: A target and action strategy for suicide prevention.* Helsinki.

Offord, D. R. Centre for Studies of Children At Risk. Chedoke-McMaster Hospitals/McMaster University. Hamilton, Ontario.

Philips, D. D. (1974). The influence of suggestion on suicide: Substantive and theoretical implications of the Werther effect. *American Sociological Review, 39*, 340–354.

Platt, S., & Kreitman, N. (1984). Trends in parasuicide and unemployment among men in Edinburgh, 1968–82. *British Medical Journal, 289*, 1029–1032.

Platt, S. (1983). Unemployment and suicidal behaviour. In M. Colledge et al. (Eds.), *Unemployment, health and social policy.* Leeds: Nuffield Centre for Health Services Studies, University of Leeds.

Platt, S. (1986a) Parasuicide and unemployment. *British Journal of Psychiatry, 149*, 401–405.

Platt, S. (1986b). Clinical and social characteristics of male parasuicides: Variation by employment and duration of unemployment. *Acta Psychiatrica Scandinavica, 74*(1), 24–31.

Ramsay, R., & Bagley, C. (1985). The prevalence of suicidal behaviors, attitudes and associated experiences in an urban population. *Suicide and Life-Threatening Behavior, 15*, 151–167.

Raymond, S. (1988). *L'effet d'une intervention preventive du suicide aupres d'une populaton adolescente en milieu scolaire.* Thesis (MA), L'Universite du Quebec a Montreal, p. 173.

Resnik, H. L. P., & Hawthorne, B. C. (1973). *Suicide prevention in the seventies.* Washington, DC: National Institute of Mental Health.

Rothman, J. (1980). *Social R&D: Research and development in the human services.* Englewood Cliffs, NJ: Prentice-Hall.

Seidman E. (1987). Toward a framework for primary prevention research. In J. A. Steinberg & M. M. Silverman (Eds.), *Preventing mental disorders: A research perspective* (pp. 2–19) (DHHS Publication No. ADM87-1492). Washington, DC: U.S. Government Printing Office.

Shaffer, D., et al. (1990). Adolescent suicide attempters: Response to suicide-prevention programs. *Journal of the American Medical Association, 264*(24), 3151–3155.

Syer-Solursh, D. (1987). *Suicide in Canada: Report of the National Task Force on Suicide.* Ottawa: Health and Welfare Canada.

Tanney, B. L. (1983). *Preventing suicide: New technologies recycle an older model.* Paper presented at the XII Conference, International Association for Suicide Prevention, Caracas, Venezuela.

Tanney, B. L. (1985). *Accurate, adequate, and available information: A foundation for effective suicide prevention.* Paper presented at the National Conference on Youth Suicide, Washington, DC.

Tanney, B. L. (1989). Preventing suicide by improving the competencies of caregivers. In *Report of the Secretary's Task Force on Youth Suicide. Vol. 3: Preventions and Interventions in Youth Suicide* (pp. 213–223) DHHS Publ. No. (ADM)89-1623). Washington, DC: U.S. Government Printing Office.

Tanney, B. L. (1991). Suicide prevention needs a good publicist. *Newsline, 17*(4), 12–13.

Tanney, B. L. (1992). Mental disorders, psychiatric patients and suicide. In R. Maris, A. L. Berman, J. T. Maltsberger, & R. I. Yufit (Eds.), *Assessment and Prediction of Suicide* (pp. 277–320) New York: Guilford.

Tanney, B. L. (1993, May). *Progress toward a national strategy for suicide prevention in Canada.* United Nations and WHO Interregional Expert Meeting on National Strategies for Suicide Prevention, Calgary, AB.

Tanney, B. L., & Ramsay, R. (1984). *The components of a knowledge-based strategy to decrease the frequency of suicidal behaviours.* In *Proceedings, Third International Conference on System Science in Health Care*, Munich, FDR.

Tanney, B. L., & Ramsay, R. (1993). *The cost of suicide: Will business support large-scale suicide prevention activity?* Paper presented at the Second World Congress on Injury Control, Atlanta, GA.

White, J. (1993). *Suicide prevention in Alberta: Working towards results.* Alberta Mental Health Services, Alberta Health, Edmonton, Alberta.

World Health Organization (1982). *Prevention of Suicide* (Public Health Papers No. 35). Geneva: WHO.

Yang, B., & Clum, G. A. (1994). Life stress, social support, and problem-solving skills predictive of depressive symptoms, hopelessness, and suicide ideation in Asian student population. A test model, *Suicide and Life Threatening Behavior 24*(2), 127–39.

# 9

# Suicide Prevention in an Educational Context: Broad and Narrow Foci

## John Kalafat, PhD, and Maurice J. Elias, PhD

This paper reviews the needs and conceptual bases of school-based youth suicide prevention programs, summarizes their current status, and recommends objectives, processes, and evaluation strategies for focused educational programs in this area. In addition, a broad systemic approach is called for that reorganizes the school context to increase students' contributions to and involvement with the educational process. Such approaches appear to have been effective with a variety of youth deviant behaviors such as dropout and delinquency, and seem to be particularly appropriate to suicidal behavior that is characterized by alienation and withdrawal from social supports. A combination of these broad and narrow foci may be necessary to address suicidal behavior in the educational context.

Since their initiation 15 years ago, school-based youth suicide prevention programs have become ubiquitous. School-based programs remain the centerpiece of youth suicide prevention efforts, because, at least until some begin to drop out in the higher grades, this is where the youths are (Dryfoos, 1993). This is not to say that youths who have dropped out and youths in the 20–24 age group are not important, and neglected, targets for prevention efforts (Centers for Disease Control – CDC, 1992). While suicide rates are higher in the 20–24 age group than among 15- to 19-year-olds, the rate of increase among the younger group continues at a greater pace than in the older group (National Center for Health Statistics, 1992). Thus, prevention in educational settings remains important.

As the title of this paper suggests, both broad and narrow foci are proposed for prevention in educational settings. A narrow focus is called for in regard to the educational components targeted to educators and students because of the limited amount of time and resources that schools can allot to the specific issue of suicide. Such time frames are likely not sufficient to reduce the suicidality of at-risk youths. The appropriate goal, then, of these programs is to ensure effective responses (i.e., identification and referral) to at-risk youths. Instructional objectives, and associated content and media, must each be specifically targeted to this goal.

At the same time, a broad focus (if this is not an oxymoron) is called for because the *context* of these programs cannot be ignored. This is because, as Felner and Felner (1989) point out in their call for ecological programs, students are affected by their (school) setting more than almost any other group, and because the school context is undergoing a dramatic change since educators initially requested assistance in dealing with rising suicide rates. Initial prevention efforts were categorical programs based on community education and crisis intervention principles (Kalafat, 1990). Currently, many schools are de-emphasizing (though not eliminating) categorical programs (e.g., substance abuse, pregnancy, suicide) as the interrelatedness of these phenomena is acknowledged, and are accepting the need for comprehensive school-based health and mental health services based on the recognition of

---

John Kalafat is with Spalding University. Maurice J. Elias is with Rutgers University.

linkages between adolescent health status and educational achievement (Dryfoos, 1993).

In the remainder of this paper we review the needs and conceptual bases for both the broad and narrow foci of prevention programs in educational contexts, suggest what specific needs these programs can best address, propose appropriate objectives and cost effective strategies for achieving these objectives, and briefly review formative and summative evaluations that can assess their impact.

## FACTS ABOUT YOUTH SUICIDE

Suicide is the second leading cause of death among White, and the third leading cause among Black adolescents (National Center for Health Statistics, 1992). This is the only age group that has a higher mortality rate than 20 years ago. While suicide completions remain a cause for concern, suicide attempts also present a serious public health problem.

In a variety of surveys throughout the U.S., an average of 10% of adolescent respondents report having made a suicide attempt (Harkavay-Friedman, Asnis, Boeck, & DiFiore, 1987; Ritter, 1990; Smith & Crawford, 1986). The prevalence of such suicidal behaviors is such that every school and community must be prepared to deal with them (Davis & Sandoval, 1991). Other relevant characteristics of youth suicide attempters include:

- Aside from gender (about 8 times more females attempt; 4 times more males compete), we cannot clinically or demographically distinguish attempters from completers, (Harkavay-Friedman et al., 1987; Kosky, Silburn, & Zubith, 1990; Shaffer, Bacon, Fisher, & Garland, 1987). We must therefore conservatively consider attempts as possibly presaging completion. In fact, among youths who have been hospitalized for suicide attempts, the completion rate for males is about 1 in 12; and for females, 1 in 300.
- Suicide attempts can produce serious in-

juries such as brain damage or paralysis (a fact often forgotten by both adults and attempters) (Kleiner, 1981).
- The seriousness of the attempt does not reliably distinguish those who subsequently complete suicide. All attempts may increase the likelihood of subsequent attempts or completions.
- Suicidal adolescents most often reveal their thoughts and feelings to peers. (Brent, Perper, Kolko, & Goldstein, 1988; Shafii, Whittinghill, Dolen, Parson, Derrick, & Carrington, 1984; Spirito, Overholser, Ashworth, Morgan, & Benedict-Drew, 1988). About one half of adolescent females and about one third of males report knowing someone who had attempted or completed suicide – about the same percentages report having talked to someone who was definitely or potentially suicidal. Perhaps only 25% of these peer confidants tell an adult about their suicidal peers (Kalafat & Elias, 1992). This may be due to adolescents' growing autonomy from adults; the importance of keeping confidants of peers (Cause & Srebnik, 1989); and, misgivings about adult helpers, as evidenced by surveys of adolescents' preferred supports and adolescent lack of follow-up of referrals to, and dropouts from, treatment (Aaronson, Underwood, Gaffney & Rotheram-Borus, 1989).

These facts about youth suicide provide the needs rationale for school suicide prevention programs. Comprehensive programs designed to address these specific needs are described after a review of the conceptual bases for such programs.

## CONCEPTUAL BASES FOR SCHOOL-BASED PREVENTION PROGRAMS

Following a medical model, some have recommended schoolwide screening to identify suicidal youth based on known risk factors. However, current risk factors cannot reliably predict suicidal behavior (ADAMHA, 1989) and are poor candidates for intervention because they are not on a linear trajectory to a low incidence event (Felner & Felner, 1989). They have been described as "sensitive, but not specific" (Shaffer, Garland, & Bacon, 1987, p. 1) and thus yield many false positives that would render such screening initiatives counterproductive in a supportive school environment. Also, while some students may self-identify as suicidal on self-report instruments, such reports are not reliable as given students may respond affirmatively to questions about suicidality at one administration and negatively at a second administration a few weeks later, and vice versa (Shaffer, Vieland, Garland, Rojas, Underwood, & Busner, 1990). While currently identified risk factors are not yet appropriate for general screening, they can provide early indications of troubled youth whom school officials can monitor. Informed school personnel can combine such information with other data to identify possibly suicidal youths for further assessment. These other data include warning signs that a youth is troubled, such as significant behavioral changes, drop in school performance, or withdrawal from activities and social contacts. Another piece of important information are precipitating events identified in psychological autopsy studies (Shaffer & Gould, 1984) as often occurring prior to a suicide attempt or completion (e.g., getting into trouble, break up with girlfriend/boyfriend, or other humiliating event).

Focusing on the latter factors in an effort to identify imminent suicidal behavior rather than make general predictions represents a paradigm shift in primary prevention from long-standing predisposing factors to more recent precipitating factors (Bloom, 1979). This is the basis for school-based intervention programs that emphasize education of all school personnel (administration, faculty, staff, and students) to enhance their ability to identify and respond to at-risk youth. This approach in fact represents a classic prevention strategy proposed by Caplan (1964), who indicated that "[i]n the absence of a knowledge of the causes of mental disorders, primary prevention must be directed toward improving nonspecific helping resources in the community" (1964, p. 30). The goal of these educational efforts is to build what Iscoe (1974) referred to as a competent community and to move toward the supportive environment entailed in the growing call for "full service schools" (Dryfoos, 1994).

The necessary competencies for assisting at-risk youth include not only knowledge (e.g., information about identifying factors and helping resources), but also specific skills for responding to and referring such youth. In addition, effective response also includes appropriate attitudes concerning active intervention, breaking confidences, and seeking help. Research on help seeking in particular has explored the attributions one makes about help seeking and the related "costs" of this activity (DePaulo, Nadler, & Fisher, 1983). The emphasis on attitudes as important components is based on social learning (Rotter, 1954) and social cognitive (Bandura, 1977) theories that posit that behavior is a function of both expectancies and attitudes as well as reinforcement value or consequences.

In fact, the more established substance abuse prevention programs have demonstrated the importance of both specific skills (i.e., refusal skills) and attitudes (i.e., misperception of the prevalence of drug use) as targets of prevention efforts (Johnson, Pentz, Weber, Baer, MacKinnon, & Hansen, 1990). Similar misperceptions of norms (students will not take peers' threats seriously) have been found to be associated with nonintervention with suicidal peers (Kalafat, Elias, & Gara, 1993).

The focus on the consequences of the behavior (in this case active intervention and help seeking) implies that the provision of knowledge and skills to all school personnel is only half the battle. Those involved in school-based prevention programs have called for ecological or transactional programs (Felner & Felner, 1989) that address the nature of the environment confronted by individuals. In this case, the relevant characteristics of the school environment are barriers to effective response following identification of at-risk youth (e.g., clear policies and procedures and established community linkages); or barriers to help seeking, particularly by students (e.g., lack of culturally, temporally, or psychologically accessible adults). Thus, comprehensive school-based programs must not only inculcate particular knowledge, skills, and attitudes, but must also reduce the cost of active intervention and help seeking, and ensure effective and efficient responses to suicidal behavior ranging from at-risk youths, attempts, completions (postventions), and students returning to school after hospitalization.

Of course, those school consultants calling for "ecological" programs are belatedly discovering what organizational consultants have known for some time. That is, trainers in organizations have recognized that they must ensure not only knowledge or skills gains in their trainees or consultees, but must ensure transfer of those skills into performance on the job (outside the classroom) and must demonstrate that such performance impacts the quality of the production or services (Lee, 1989; Rummler & Brache, 1988). For example, Kirkpatrick (1975) has constructed a four-step hierarchy of evaluation of training programs:

1. Reaction: what participants did or did not like about a learning experience.
2. Learning: how much participants learned by the end of the program; can include knowledge and skills assessed by questionnaires (tests) and simulations.
3. Behavior (performance): changes in job behavior produced by instruction; depends on environmental resources and contingencies.
4. Results: the tangible consequences of the performance taught by the program.

This evaluation framework can be applied to school-based preventions programs as follows:

1. In order for the program to be well received (and thus institutionalized) by all school personnel, it must have a practical, educational (rather than "clinical") focus that conforms to the educational and protective mission of schools (Kalafat, 1990), the student component must fit into, rather than add on to, current health curricula, and the program must employ regular school personnel as instructors (Kalafat & Underwood, 1989). Many programs report positive feedback from participants (CDC, 1992; Kalafat & Elias, 1994; Shaffer, Garland & Whittle, 1988) and long-term retention in school systems (Ryerson, 1993).

2. The material must be problem versus content centered (Knowles, 1973), which emphasizes its application to the specific preventive roles of the faculty, staff, students, and parents. Specific skills, self-expectancies, and knowledge relevant to effective intervention must be learned. For example, the student classes must prepare students for their encounters with suicidal peers—they are aimed at students as helpers, not victims (Cause & Srebnik, 1989; Kalafat & Elias, 1992; Ross, 1985). Such training must include elements that teach skills, not just knowledge, such as practice and feedback (Gagne, 1985; Kalafat & Neigher, 1983). A variety of programs have demonstrated knowledge gains on the part of educators and students (Kalafat & Elias, 1994; Overholser, Hemstreet, Sprito & Vyse, 1989; Shaffer, Garland & Whittle, 1988), improved student attitudes toward help seeking and intervention with peers (Ciffone, 1993; Kalafat & Elias, 1994), and improved educators' attitudes toward taking responsibility for referring at risk youth (Shaffer, Garland & Whittle, 1988). Skill gains, which can be demonstrated in simulations or analogs, have yet to be demonstrated.

3. In order to ensure performance (i.e., obtaining help for a troubled student or peer), the school must be organized to respond appropriately. For example, interviews with students have indicated that school faculty and staff are perceived as responsive (approachable) based on how

much time they spend with students outside their formal roles. School schedules often prevent such informal contacts and thus must be arranged to promote them in order to encourage student help seeking. This illustrates the contention based on systems principles that lack of organizational responsiveness is more often due to the characteristics of organizational processes than personnel (Deming, 1986). Referrals and help-seeking contacts can be logged in school systems as a measure of this performance. A number of programs have reported increases in referrals following implementation (CDC, 1992).

4. The first three levels of evaluation are proximal outcomes, while this level is a distal outcome. In this case, the distal outcome would be a reduction in suicidal behavior (attempts and completions). As in all training programs and in psychotherapy outcome studies, such distal outcomes are difficult to assess because it is difficult to tie them to program (or treatment) proximal outcomes, and because they are influenced by a variety of other variables. That is, the degree to which the school-based program can achieve its primary goal of getting at-risk youth to professional helpers can be assessed through tracking referrals. The inclusion of the reduction of suicidal behavior would necessitate an evaluation of the efficacy of the professional helpers or mental health system, and as noted by the Centers for Disease Control, "there is surprisingly little objective evidence that treating persons with mental disorders actually reduces the overall rate of death from suicide" (1992, p. 3). In spite of this, CDC notes that no one doubts that identification and treatment must be part of any effort to prevent suicide. Suicide rates can be monitored for the communities in which the programs are implemented. For example, some programs have documented reductions in suicide rates in the county in which the program was widely disseminated (CDC, 1992; Ryerson, 1994). While this reduction cannot be causally linked to the program, it does demonstrate that no increases in suicidal behavior were associated with the program, thus refuting an objection that has been raised against widespread training on this topic.

In sum, a number of evaluations have provided evidence for knowledge gains, positive attitude changes, and increased referrals following school-based suicide awareness and response education for students and educators. Large-scale evaluations are still needed that include careful implementation evaluation and can include sufficiently large follow-up samples of program participants and comparison groups who can report actual experiences with suicidal youths.

## OVERVIEW OF PROGRAMS

Comprehensive, conceptually grounded programs have been developed to address the specific suicidal phenomena reviewed earlier. Detailed descriptions of these programs are beyond the scope of this paper and can be found elsewhere (CDC, 1992; Kalafat & Underwood, 1989). In general, these programs include the following components covering prevention, intervention, and postvention:

1. Administrative policies and procedures for responding to at-risk students, attempts, completions, and students returning to school after attempts. This component may include the development and training of school-based crisis response teams that can respond to a variety of crises.
2. Educational presentations to all adults in the school system—administration, faculty, staff, and parents—that address warning signs, initial response and referral, and resources.
3. Classroom lessons for students that address warning signs, initial response and referral, and resources, with an emphasis on giving up confidences in this area and the consequences of not acting.
4. Ensuring linkages between the school and community caregivers to provide coordinated responses to these situa-

tions. This component may include caregiver or gatekeeper training and/or the development of community-based crisis response teams that coordinate with school resources. Another strongly recommended school–community component is the development of procedures for ensuring the coordinated, supportive return of students to schools after hospitalization for suicidal threats or behavior. Such procedures include, among other things, the provision of information relevant to the management and coordinated support of the student to school personnel immediately prior to discharge of the youth (Kalafat & Mackey, 1994).

Table 1 provides an overview of the components, objectives, and suggested ways of evaluating the achievement of objectives of school-based preventive programs. These programs, then, are designed to cover the spectrum of *prevention* (early identification and referral), *intervention* (rapid, coordinated response), and *postvention* (school/community recovery after a suicide completion or serious attempt; ensuring coordinated return of youth discharged from the hospital). Of course, the postvention activities are also aimed at preventing subsequent suicides. The overall goal of such school-based response procedures is to interrupt the pathway to suicide at the earliest possible point along the continuum from individual vulnerability through suicidal feelings (which may be shared or inferred from behavior) to suicidal behavior. The specific goals of the programs are to ensure:

1. That persons who may come into contact with potentially suicidal adolescents can more readily identify them, know how to respond to them initially, know how to obtain help for them rapidly, and are consistently inclined to take such action.
2. That troubled adolescents are aware of and have immediate access to helping resources and may be more inclined to seek such help as an alternative to suicidal behavior.

*Note.* A small cadre of individuals has raised persistent objections to such school-based programs. The first objection focuses on the student curriculum and maintains that discussion of suicide may stimulate suicidal behavior in vulnerable individuals. First, there is absolutely no evidence for this effect (Centers for Disease Control, 1992; Ryerson, 1994). This finding is not surprising, given the specious connection made between structured lessons focusing on help seeking and coping, and media depictions of readily modeled youth engaged in suicidal behavior (Orbach & Bar-Joseph, 1993). Second, as the studies reviewed earlier demonstrate, such classes do not represent the students' first or only exposure to the topic any more than is the case for sex or drug education classes, for which similar objections have been raised. The point made by the studies of students' experience with suicidal phenomena is that contacts with suicidal peers are common, and students must be prepared to appropriately deal with these encounters. The second objection is that such programs place an unnecessary burden of identification and response on school systems. Such responsibility is not only acknowledged by many school officials (Davis & Sandoval, 1991) but is included in education statutes and codes (Kalafat, 1990). Moreover, this objection flies in the face of the growing trend for school-based health and mental health initiatives that clearly demonstrate the role and responsibility of schools in this area (Bond & Compas, 1989; Carnegie Council on Adolescent Development, 1988; Christopher, Kurtz & Howing, 1989; Dryfoos, 1994). This trend sets the stage for the broad focus for addressing youth suicide in educational contexts.

## THE BROAD FOCUS: ORGANIZATIONAL INTERVENTIONS

Up to this point, we have noted that the application of knowledge and skills gained

Table 1
Program Overview

| Program component | Objective | Measure[a] |
|---|---|---|
| 1. Administrative policies and procedures | 1. Faculty and staff will know school procedure for responding to at-risk, attempt, completion, students returning after hospitalization (including appropriate school contact persons). | 1. Faculty/staff written evaluation of policies and procedures.<br>2. Knowledge assessed by written response to vignettes. |
| 2. Faculty/staff education | 1. Faculty and staff will know relevant suicide facts, indicators of at-risk students, and response guidelines, including referral procedure.<br>2. Faculty and staff will accept role in identification and referral. | 1. Faculty/staff evaluation of training.<br>2. Knowledge and attitudes assessed through response to vignettes and questionnaires.<br>3. Performance monitored through referral records and follow-up question as to any responses to at-risk students. |
| 3. Student curriculum | 1. Students will recognize the threat of suicidal thoughts and behavior and take troubled peers seriously.<br>2. Students will demonstrate positive attitudes about intervention and help seeking.<br>3. Students will know relevant facts about suicide, including warning signs.<br>4. Students will know how to respond to troubled peers.<br>5. Students will know resources: be able to name one adult and know how resources will respond. | 1. Student evaluation of classes.<br>2. Knowledge, attitudes, and skills assessed by questionnaire and response to vignettes.<br>3. Referral records and follow-up questionnaire as to any response to suicidal peers.<br>4. County adolescent suicide rates 1 year prior to program implementation through 2 years after initial implementation. |
| 4. Community connections | 1. School officials (administrators and other school personnel designated to respond to at-risk referrals, attempts, completions, return after hospitalization) will be able to identify appropriate community referral sources. | 1. Knowledge assessed through questionnaire.<br>2. Referrals tracked and assessed for appropriateness. |

*Number = Kirkpatrick (1975) level

in programs requires attention to systemic or ecological variables, and that a classic prevention strategy involves the enhancement of the support system in which the program occurs. This concurs with the consensus that the school context must be taken into account when considering the efficacy of interventions directed at the problems of youths (Jessor, 1993; Linney & Seidman, 1989; Purkey & Smith, 1993; Sarason, 1982).

This growing consensus is forcefully captured by Dryfoos (1990, 1994) in her reviews of programs that appear to be effectively addressing what she calls the "new morbidities" (1994, p. 2) of adolescence— unprotected sex, drugs, violence, and depression (in contrast to such "old morbidities" as chronic diseases). In addition to her own national investigations, Dryfoos (1994) reviews findings and recommendations from an impressive array of sources, including the American Medical Association and National Board of Education, the Carnegie Council Task Force on the Education of Young Adolescents, the Ford Foundation School Reform Initiative, the Office of Technical Assessment, and the Panel on High Risk Youth of the National Academy of Sciences. These recommendations represent a clear call for multiagency school–community initiatives that direct attention, in addition to the individuals affected, to the institutional settings of home, family, and school in which the risk status arises; and that create what the president of the Carnegie Corporation calls "an authentic community program in the schools [that] could provide a universal, integrating experience" (Hamburg, 1994).

A review of prevention programs aimed at the interrelated behaviors of low achievement, dropout, delinquency, and substance abuse reveals that this call has been answered by the development of programs aimed at creating a sense of community (Purkey & Smith, 1983). Specifically, these programs involve a variety of strategies for engaging youth in the operations of their schools and thus promoting bonding with the school (Hawkins & Weiss, 1985). Strategies have included providing students opportunities for increased decision making about rules, skills to make such contributions, and praise and recognition for their contributions (Natriello, Pallas, McDill, McPartland, & Royster, 1988). Also, schools have been reorganized to provide students with enhanced interactions with teachers (Felner & Adan, 1988); and, large schools have been organized as schools-within-schools that reduced "overmanning" and limited niches that had led to alienation and limited participation, and had attenuated a sense of responsibility on the part of students (Linney & Seidman, 1989). These organizational plans have been shown to enhance achievement and reduce a variety of forms of deviancy. As with specific suicide prevention curricula, most of these programs feature strong peer involvement in buddy/tutoring programs

to increase involvement and reduce alienation (Cauce, Comer, & Schwartz, 1987; Cowen, Hightower, Pedro-Corrall, & Work, 1989; Jason & Rhodes, 1989; Supir, 1991).

These strategies for involvement and bonding seem particularly suited to the suicidal process that is characterized by social isolation, alienation, withdrawal, and low social supports (Berman & Jobes, 1991; Gammon, John, & Weissman, 1984; Motto, 1984; Trout, 1980). They have been included in at least one school-based suicide prevention program that has been funded by the National Institute of Mental Health (Eggert, Thompson, Herting, & Nicholas, 1994). These successful strategies from prevention programs aimed at related adolescent deviant behaviors can be combined with current promising school-based suicide prevention efforts. The goal of enhancing student engagement in the educational context provides a bridge to new intervention possibilities that can inspire both educators and students in ways that may not occur when the goal of preventing students from killing themselves — thankfully, a relatively low-frequency occurrence — is paramount. Indeed, it is too narrow to ignore the pain of students who may not be thinking of suicide but who are nevertheless damaging themselves through high-risk behaviors, or by allowing severe emotional states to compromise their academic and social growth. Suicide prevention will be well served by efforts to create educational investment for all students, particularly those whose behavior or learning patterns render them in need of services beyond what the mainstream ordinarily provides.

While a curriculum may serve as the anchor of a program, it is not itself sufficient to accomplish the goals of suicide prevention. Simple solutions (and simple interventions) are unlikely to serve preventive purposes (Price, Cowen, Lorion, & Ramos-McKay, 1988). Many skills are needed, some of which require complex programs with periodic boosters over long periods of time. Interventions that combine teaching of skills in a classroom-based curricu-

Table 2
Essential Elements in Successful Suicide Prevention and Related School-Based Programs

Curriculum and instructional design factors
- Focus on delivering specific skills at the appropriate developmental points
- Teach specific skills for resisting negative social infleunces
- Include both promotion of life skills and specific skills related to prevention of particular problem or condition (include a promotion and prevention strategy)
- Include a peer leadership component at the upper grades
- Have clear articulation with other existing subject areas, including some basic academic subject areas and health or family life education.
- Contain materials that are clear, up to date, and "user friendly"
- Ensure active student engagement through learning methods including modeling, role plays, performance feedback, dialoguing, and positive reinforcement

School and systemwide factors
- Evaluate the nature of norms for responding to misbehavior, victimization, and related violations of school rules; the degree to which these are shared among school staff and parents; and the extent to which they are consonant with the philosophy and approaches of a program
- Determine the state of organizational readiness or health—indicated by such variables as teacher morale, school planning, decision making, and reward structures, articulated and shared school goals, willingness to adapt programs, and staff health—to see if the school is capable of implementing the program with fidelity and subsequently integrate it into other factors of the schooling experience
- Include programming of sufficient duration and intensity, and in a coordinated manner
- Involve well-trained teachers or program deliverers who have an ongoing role in the host system
- Design programs in a way that is acceptable to and reaches populations at risk and is coordinated with and linked to a continuum of services, including the school resource committee and special services/child study team services
- Assess effects through a method of monitoring that includes indicators of the integrity of implementation and of goal-focused impact

lum, organizational modifications that permit specific and regular opportunities to use those skills, and activities that foster positive bonding among students and with the school can be expected to have a synergistic impact on student social competence and proclivity for deviance. Such an approach also combines peer models to provide social support as a buffer against stress (Albee, 1982; Gilchrest, Schinke, Snow, Schilling, & Senechal, 1988) with skills to make those supportive relationships most effective in providing instrumental and problem-focused coping assistance. Table 2 summarizes some of the essential elements of the proposed educational-context prevention programs. As these efforts move forward, they create the climate in which individual suicide prevention programs can operate and a climate in which suicide itself is less likely to be contemplated by reason of default, apa-

thy, or isolation. In this way, both broad- and narrow-focus efforts may combine to interrupt the pathway toward youth self-destructive behavior.

# REFERENCES

Aaronson, S. L., Underwood, M., Gaffney, D., & Rotheram-Borus, M. J. (1989, April). *Reluctance to help-seeking by adolescents*. Paper presented at the Annual Conference of the American Association of Suicidology, San Diego, CA.

Albee, G. W. (1982). Preventing psychotherapy and promoting human potential. *American Psychologist, 37*, 1043–1050.

Alcohol, Drug Abuse and Mental Health Administration. (1989). *Report of the secretary's task force on youth suicide. Vol. 1: Overview and recommendations* (DHHS Pub. No. (ADM) 89-1621). Washington, DC: U.S. Government Printing Office.

Bandura, A. (1977). Self efficacy: Toward a unifying theory of behavior change. *Psychological Bulletin, 84*, 191–215.

Berman, A. L., & Jobes, D. A. (1991). *Adolescent sui-*

*cide: Assessment and intervention.* Washington, DC: American Psychological Association.

Bloom, B. L. (1979). Prevention of mental disorders: Recent advances in theory and practice. *Community Mental Health Journal, 15,* 179–191.

Bond, L. A., & Compas, B. E. (1989). *Primary prevention and promotion in the schools.* Newbury Park, CA: Sage.

Brent, D. A., Perper, J. A., Kolko, D. J., & Goldstein, C. E. (1988). Risk factors for adolescent suicide: A comparison of adolescent suicide victims with suicidal inpatients. *Archives of General Psychiatry, 45,* 581–588.

Caplan, G. (1964). *Principles of preventative psychiatry.* New York: Basic Books.

Carnegie Council on Adolescent Development. (1988). *Review of school-based health services.* New York: Carnegie Foundation.

Cause, A. M., Comer, J., & Schwartz, D. (1987). Long term effects of a systems-oriented school prevention program. *American Journal of Orthopsychiatry, 57,* 127–131.

Cauce, A. M., & Srebnik, D. S. (1989). Peer networks and social support: A focus for preventive efforts with youths. In L. A. Bond & B. E. Compas (Eds.), *Primary prevention and promotion in the schools* (pp. 235–254). Newbury Park, CA: Sage.

Centers for Disease Control. (1992). *Youth suicide prevention programs: A resource guide.* Atlanta: Centers for Disease Control.

Christopher, G. M., Kurtz, P. D., & Howing, P. T. (1989). The status of mental health services for youth in the school and community. *Children and Youth Services Review, 11,* 159–174.

Ciffone, J. (1993). Suicide prevention: A classroom presentation to adolescents. *Social Work, 38,* 196–203.

Cowen, E. L., Hightower, A. D., Pedro-Carroll, J. A., & Work, W. C. (1989). School-based models for primary prevention programming with children. *Prevention in Human Services, 7,* 133–160.

Davis, J. M., & Sandoval, J. (1991). *Suicidal youth: School-based intervention and prevention.* San Francisco, CA: Jossey-Bass.

Deming, W. E. (1986). *Out of crisis.* Cambridge, MA: MIT Center for Advanced Engineering Study.

DePaulo, B. M., Nadler, A., & Fisher, J. D. (1983). *New directions in helping,* Vol. 2: *Help-seeking.* New York: Academic Press.

Dryfoos, J. G. (1990). *Adolescents at risk: Prevalence and prevention.* New York: Oxford University Press.

Dryfoos, J. G., (1993). Schools as places for health, mental health, and social services. *Teachers College Record, 94,* 540–567.

Dryfoos, J. G. (1994). *Full service schools.* San Francisco: Jossey-Bass.

Eggert, L. L., Thompson, E. A., Herting, J. R., & Nichols, L. J. (1994). A prevention research program: Reconnecting at-risk youth. *Issues in Mental Health Nursing, 15,* 107–135.

Felner, R. D., & Adan, A. M. (1988). The school transitional project: An ecological intervention and evaluation. In R. H. Price, E. L. Cowen, R. P. Lorion, & J. Ramos-McKay (Eds.), *14 ounces of prevention* (pp. 111–122). Washington, DC: American Psychological Association.

Felner, R. D., & Felner, T. Y. (1989). Primary prevention programs in the educational context: A transactional-ecological framework and analysis. In L. A. Bond & B. E. Compas (Eds.), *Primary prevention and promotion in the schools* (pp. 13–49). Newbury Park, CA: Sage.

Gagne, R. M. (1985). *The conditions of learning.* New York: Holt, Rinehart & Winston.

Gammon, G. D., John, K., & Weissman, M. M. (1984). Structured assessment of psychiatric diagnosis and of psychological function and supports in adolescence: A role in the secondary prevention of suicide. In H. S. Sudak, A. B. Ford, & N. B. Rushforth (Eds.), *Suicide in the young* (pp. 183–208). Littleton, MA: John Wright · PSG.

Gilchrist, L., Schinke, S., Snow, W., Schilling, R., & Senechal, V. (1988). The transition to junior high school: Opportunities for primary prevention. *Journal of Primary Prevention, 8,* 99–107.

Hamburg, D. A. (1994). Forward. In J. G. Dryfoos, *Full service schools.* San Francisco: Jossey-Bass.

Harkavay-Friedman, J. M., Asnis, G. M., Boeck, M., & DiFiore, J. (1987). Prevalence of specific suicidal behaviors in a high school samples. *American Journal of Psychiatry, 144,* 1203–1206.

Hawkins, J., & Weis, J. (1985). The sociodevelopmental model: An integrated approach to delinquency prevention. *Journal of Primary Prevention, 6,* 73–97.

Iscoe, I. (1974). Community psychology and the competent community. *American Psychologist, 29,* 179–188.

Jason, L., & Rhodes, J. (1989). Children helping children: Implications for prevention. *Journal of Primary Prevention, 9,* 203–212.

Jessor, R. (1993). Successful adolescent development among youths in high-risk settings. *American Psychologist, 48,* 117–126.

Johnson, C. A., Pentz, M. A., Weber, M. D., Dwyer, J. H., Baer, N., MacKinnon, D. P., & Hansen, W. B. (1990). Relative effectiveness of comprehensive community programming for drug abuse prevention with high-risk and low-risk adolescents. *Journal of Consulting and Clinical Psychology, 58,* 447–456.

Kalafat, J. (1990). Suicide intervention in the schools. In A. R. Roberts (Ed.), *Contemporary perspectives on crisis intervention and prevention* (pp. 447–474). Englewood Cliffs, NJ: Prentice-Hall.

Kalafat, J., & Elias, M. (1992). Adolescents' experience with and response to suicidal peers. *Suicide and Life-Threatening Behavior, 22,* 315–321.

Kalafat, J., & Elias, M. (1994). An evaluation of a school-based suicide awareness intervention. *Suicide and Life-Threatening Behavior 24,* 233–244.

Kalafat, J., Elias, M., & Gara, J. (1993). The relationship of bystander intervention variables to adolescents' responses to suicidal peers. *Journal of Primary Prevention, 13,* 231–244.

Kalafat, J., & Mackey, K. (1994, April). *School return of hospitalized suicidal youth.* Paper presented at the Annual Conference of American Association of Suicidology, New York.

Kalafat, J., & Neigher, W. D. (1983). Can quality survive in public mental health programs? The challenge for training. *Professional Psychology: Research and Practice, 1,* 90–104.

Kalafat, J., & Underwood, M. (1989). *Lifelines: A school-based adolescent suicide response program.* Dubuque, IA: Kendall/Hunt.

Kirkpatrick, D. (1975). *Evaluating training programs.* Madison, WI: American Society for Training and Development.

Kleiner, A. (1981, Summer). How not to commit suicide. *CoEvolution Quarterly,* pp. 89–111.

Knowles, M. (1973). *The adult learner: A neglected species.* Houston: Gulf Publishing.

Kosky, R., Silburn, S., & Zubrick, S. R. (1990). Are children and adolescents who have suicidal thoughts different from those who attempt suicide? *Journal of Nervous and Mental Disease, 178,* 38–43.

Lee, C. (Ed.). (1989). *Performance technology.* Minneapolis, MN: Lakewood Books.

Linney, J. A., & Seidman, E. (1989). The future of schooling. *American Psychologist, 44,* 336–340.

Motto, J. A., (1984). Suicide in male adolescents. In H. S. Sudak, A. B. Ford, & N. B. Rushforth (Eds.), *Suicide in the young* (pp. 227–244). Littleton, MA: John Wright · PSG.

National Center for Health Statistics. (1992). *Advance report of final mortality statistics.* NCHS monthly vital statistics report, *40*(8, Suppl. 2).

Natriello, G., Pallas, A., McDill, E., McPartland, J., & Royster, D. (1988). *An examination of the assumptions and evidence of alternative drop-out prevention programs in high school* (Report 365). Baltimore: Johns Hopkins University, Center for Research on Elementary and Middle Schools. (ERIC Documentation Reproduction No. ED-299374)

Orbach, I., & Bar-Joseph, H. (1993). The impact of a suicide prevention program for adolescents on suicidal tendencies, hopelessness, ego identity, and coping. *Suicide and Life-Threatening Behavior, 23,* 120–129.

Overholser, J. C., Hemstreet, A. H., Spirito, A., & Vyse, S. (1989). Suicide awareness programs in the schools: Effects of gender and personal experience. *Journal of the American Academy of Child and Adolescent Psychiatry, 28,* 925–930.

Price, R. H., Cowen, E., Lorion, R. P., & Ramos-McKay, J. (Eds.). (1988). *Fourteen ounces of prevention: A casebook for practicioners.* Washington, DC: American Psychological Association.

Purkey, S. C., & Smith, M. S. (1983). Effective schools: A review. *Elementary School Journal, 83,* 427–452.

Ritter, D. (1990). Adolescent suicide: Social competence and problem behavior of youth at high risk and low risk for suicide. *School Psychology Review, 19,* 8395.

Ross, C. P. (1985). Teaching children the facts of life and death: Suicide prevention in the schools. In M. L. Peck, N. L. Farberow, & R. E. Litman (Eds.), *Youth suicide.* (pp. 147–169). New York: Springer.

Rotter, J. (1954). *Social learning and clinical psychology.* Englewood Cliffs, NJ: Prentice-Hall.

Rummler, G. A., & Brache, A. P. (1988, September). The systems view of human performance. *Training, 25,* 45–53.

Ryerson, D. (1993, April). *A ten-year follow up of a multi-site school program.* Paper presented at the Annual Conference of the American Association of Suicidology, San Francisco, CA.

Ryerson, D. (1994, May). *Report on a survey of school-based suicide prevention programs in three northern New Jersey counties.* For the Turrell Fund, West Orange, NJ.

Sarason, S. B. (1982). *The culture of the school and the problem of change.* Boston: Allyn and Bacon.

Shaffer, D., Bacon, K., Fisher, P., & Garland, A. (1987). *Review of youth suicide prevention programs.* New York: New York State Psychiatric Institute.

Shaffer, D., Garland, A., & Bacon, K. (1987, July). *Prevention issues in youth suicide.* Paper prepared for Project Prevention, American Acedemy of Child and Adolescent Psychiatry, New York.

Shaffer, D., Garland, A., Vieland, V., Underwood, M., & Busner, C. (1991). The impact of curriculum-based suicide prevention programs for teenagers. *Journal of the American Academy of Child and Adolescent Psychiatry, 30,* 588–596.

Shaffer, D., Garland, A., & Whittle, B. (1988). *An evaluation of youth suicide prevention programs.* New Jersey adolescent suicide prevention project: Final project report. Trenton, NJ: New Jersey Division of Mental Health and Hospitals.

Shaffer, D., & Gould, M. (1984). *A study of completed and attempted suicide in adolescents* (Progress Report, Grant No. MH 38198). Rockville, MD: National Institute of Mental Health.

Shaffer, D., Vieland, V., Garland, R., Rojas, M., Underwood, M., & Busnor, C. (1990) Adolescent suicide attempters: Response to suicide prevention programs. *Journal of the American Medical Association, 264,* 3151–3155.

Shafii, M., Whittinghill, J. R., Dolen, D. C., Pearson, V. D., Derrick, A., & Carrington, S. (1984). Psychological reconstruction of completed suicide in childhood and adolescence. In H. S. Sudak, A. B. Ford, & N. B. Rushforth (Eds.), *Suicide in the young* (pp. 271–294). Littleton, MA: John Wright · PSG.

Smith, K., & Crawford, S. (1986). Suicidal behavior among "normal" high school students. *Suicide and Life-Threatening Behavior, 3,* 313–325.

Spirito, A., Overholser, J., Ashworth, S., Morgan, J., & Benedict-Drew, C. (1988). Evaluation of a suicide awareness curriculum for high school students. *Journal of the American Academy of Child and Adolescent Psychiatry, 6,* 705–711.

Supir, J. (1991). Partners for valued youth: The final report. *International Development Research Association (INDRA) Newsletter, 18,* 1–4.

Trout, D. L. (1980). The role of social isolation in suicide. *Suicide and Life-Threatening Behavior, 10,* 10–23.

# 10

# Suicide Prevention in a Treatment Setting

## Robert E. Litman, MD, PhD

Reducing the suicide rate through treatment depends on the development of new knowledge and new technology with emphasis on early intervention and continuing low-intensity contact for many troubled suicidal people, rather than the current preoccupation with detecting and hospitalizing the "highest risk." I anticipate that sophisticated interactive computer programs will be effective in improving screening and case finding, thus bringing many more suicidal persons into contact with primary care physicians and outpatient mental health services for the purpose of relieving psychological pain. Computer programs will be invaluable in improving training for both primary care providers and outpatient mental health workers. Improved communication networks will prove to be useful resources for maintaining continuity of care and consultation, which is important in long-term treatment. Other technical developments include simplifying and making explicit various treatment approaches, in both psychotherapy and drug therapy, so that research can proceed to clarify what type of treatment helps which type of suicidal patient.

It is our impression that the only generally effective means of reducing the suicide rate is to hospitalize in a closed ward the potentially suicidal person. (Robins, Murphy, Wilkinson, Gassner, & Kayes, 1959)

Based on their classic psychological autopsy study of 134 completed suicides in St. Louis in the mid 1950s, Robins and his colleagues reported that 98% of the suicides were clinically ill, 94% of them psychiatrically ill. Two thirds of the suicides were suffering from one or the other, or both of two diseases, manic–depressive depression or chronic alcoholism. These decedents had been suicidal for a considerable period of time, and a majority of them had communicated their suicidal intentions. The authors stressed the importance of diagnosing these patients and hospitalizing them for treatment, and the authors felt that it would be helpful to educate primary care physicians and the general public on the symptoms of these two diseases and the necessity of treatment so that the patients and their families would be more cooperative.

This was solid research, confirmed over the years by similar studies, for example, in Seattle (Dorpat & Ripley, 1960) and San Diego (Rich, Young, & Fowler, 1986), with clear clinical recommendations. Yet, clinical practice (along with everything else) has been ineffective in reducing the suicide rate in the United States and elsewhere. Where suicide rates have fallen — for example, in Great Britain and in California — explanations other than improved clinical practice have been proposed. The 30% drop in suicide rates in Great Britain in the 1960s was mainly associated with detoxification of household gas, although some effect was claimed for the community work of the Samaritan Crisis Centers (Cutter, 1979). To account for the dramatic decline in California suicide rates between 1970 and 1990, Males (1994) suggests changes in population composition and also complex changes in collective psychosocial currents. In this chapter I examine the major difficulties that impede successful suicide prevention by health care providers, and I make some recommendations for improvement, looking toward the year 2000.

## THE CLINICAL DILEMMAS

1. The basic clinical problem in my opinion is our ignorance of the fundamental

psychopathophysiologies of suicides, and of the processes by which prevention could occur. For example, some evidence has been offered to show that electroconvulsive treatment and/or lithium carbonate treatment for manic–depressive patients reduces their suicide rates, but there is no accepted explanation for why these particular treatments should be effective.

2. Each suicidal patient is different, and what is helpful for one may be harmful for another. For example, Teicher, Glod, and Cole (1993) point out that antidepressant drugs help many persons recover from suicidal depressions but make a few patients become more suicidal. In Teicher et al.'s opinion the result from antidepressant drugs for suicide prevention is a wash – no difference in the total number of suicides of depressed persons. A similar situation may exist for psychiatric hospitalization. I agree with Brent, Dupfer, Bromet, and Dew (1988), who state that it would be difficult to provide evidence that inpatient hospitalization is a necessary, or even always helpful, therapeutic intervention for acutely suicidal patients.

3. At present it is impossible to predict accurately any person's suicide. Sophisticated statistical models (Goldstein, Black, Nasrallah, & Winokur, 1991; Pokorny, 1993) and experienced clinical judgments are equally unsuccessful. When I am asked why one depressed and suicidal patient commits suicide while nine other equally depressed and equally suicidal patients do not, I answer, "I don't know." We try with some success to evaluate suicide risk. However, most patients evaluated as "high risk" do not commit suicide, and many patients correctly evaluated as "low risks" do commit suicide. After an assessment consultation, I might well have evaluated each of 10 patients as extremely suicidal and estimated for each a 10% risk for committing suicide within a year. But I could not have predicted accurately which one would commit suicide or when.

In their classic paper, Robins and colleagues (1959) argued that all high-risk persons are mentally ill and deserve to be treated in psychiatric hospitals. But then the question becomes for how long, and at what cost? And finally, will the hospital treatment be effective in preventing suicide in the hospital and later after the patient leaves the hospital?

4. In fact, hospitals are not always safe. Suicides of psychiatric patients while they are hospitalized seem to be increasing, and currently account for about 5% of the total suicides (Busch, Clark, Fawcett, & Kravitz, 1993). Six of the 134 St. Louis cases committed suicide in hospitals. Often hospital treatment is unable to prevent suicides of patients after they are discharged. For discharged hospital patients there is a fairly consistent suicide rate of 3–7 suicides per 1000 patients for each year of follow-up, which is similar to the suicide rate reported in follow-up studies of outpatients treated for depression in such excellent studies as the National Institute of Mental Health collaborative study of depression (Fawcett, Scheftner, Clark, et al., 1987).

5. The magnitude of the problem is enormous. Surveys indicate that in any 1 year about 10% of the population becomes clinically depressed, 4% with major depression (Regier, Narrow, Rae, et al., 1993). Those data suggest that at any one time there are about 10 million depressed people, many of whom are having thoughts of suicide (Regier, Myers, Kramer, et al., 1984). In addition, there are large numbers of suicidal alcoholics and suicidal schizophrenics, and a passionate and dramatic host of personality-disordered people who make suicide attempts and sometimes die. From data collected in urgent-care centers and emergency rooms, I estimate there are approximately 500,000 suicide attempts yearly in the United States serious enough to call for medical attention. Many of these suicide attemptors are hospitalized in psychiatric units and form a sizable proportion of the approximately 1,700,000 psychiatric admissions yearly. I estimate that during any year in the United States, approximately 3 million people find themselves seriously considering suicide, and yet only 1 in 100

actually completes the act. Most of the suicidal people have contacts with the health system. The problem is, what can the health system do to help these people? At what cost? And with what effectiveness in preventing suicide?

## HOSPITALIZATION AS SUICIDE PREVENTION

History repeats itself. Here is a quote from a group of highly respected leaders in suicidology research and practice (Fawcett, Clark, & Busch 1993): "The most appropriate place to treat a patient in imminent danger of suicide is a psychiatric inpatient unit, with a staff trained to care for such patients." This seems reasonable although it is difficult and often impossible to tell which patients are in imminent danger of suicide, as compared to other patients who are in less imminent danger. The same team of Fawcett, Clark, and Busch, (1993) report that about 5% of U.S. suicides occur in hospitalized psychiatric patients, 1% within the walls of the ward itself, 2% when patients elope out of hospitals without leave, and another 2% of suicides by patients who are out on pass or trial visit. European authors (Crammer, 1984) report about the same percentage of suicides in their psychiatric hospitals and observe that the numbers of suicides in hospitals are increasing. Various reasons are offered for this increase. Hospital stays are shorter, so there is an increased turnover of patients (Geller, 1992). Suicides tend to occur in the first few days or around discharge of hospitalized patients. Secondly, there has been an increased emphasis on the rights and dignity of psychiatric patients, with increased freedom and autonomy as part of their therapeutic milieau. There is more separation between the providers of outpatient service and the inpatient hospital staff, so that often the patient has to adjust to a new doctor and a totally new environment.

A newly emerging problem in hospital care is the increasing emphasis on cost control and management by administration. Managed care may require discharge from the hospital prematurely for some patients, which may lead to additional problems in the aftercare of these patients. All this makes some authorities pessimistic about the prospect of improving suicide prevention through hospital care. For example, Alexander Gralnick (1991), another highly respected senior psychiatrist with great experience in hospital administration, has observed suicides in his own hospital and in every other psychiatric hospital. He states that some suicides in hospitals are unavoidable, they often occur when patients seem to be improving and the patients have denied suicidal plans or ideation.

Other suicidologists are more optimistic. Fawcett and colleagues (1993) emphasize the importance of anxiety-reducing drugs for anxious and panicky patients. In their opinion, hospitals should be ready to make a judgment of imminent danger of suicide, and management should include constant one-on-one observation, even in the bathroom. This, of course, is drastic treatment and expensive, and may evoke a sharply negative reaction from some patients, as pointed out by Pauker and Cooper (1990). At present there is no research to tell us whether a more liberal use of constant observation would actually save more lives.

Another controversial issue is the use of involuntary commitment (Parrish, 1993), forcing patients into a locked ward when they are unwilling to enter voluntarily. It is argued that this sometimes saves the life of a patient who is temporarily despondent, hopeless, and suicidal. On the other hand, involuntary commitment often alienates the patient and leaves the person with a permanent grudge against the whole health service system and unwilling to seek help even though he or she may still be suicidal. In California, as indications for involuntary hospitalization have been limited and the legislature has made the process more difficult to carry out, there has been no increase in suicides. I doubt there will be any reduction in the suicide rate in the future through the use of involuntary commitment. More broadly, it is hard to imagine how any future change in the number or practices of psychiatric hospitals can reduce the suicide rate.

## SUICIDE PREVENTION THROUGH TREATMENT: ANOTHER STRATEGY

Perhaps it is time for a drastic change in strategy.

If we have the goal of making a substantial reduction in suicide rates through therapeutic interventions, we will in my opinion have to renounce the dependency on psychiatric hospitals for suicide prevention, although hospitals have an important role in the treatment of some individuals. We will focus then on screening and case finding in the general population (note the early success of "National depression screening day"—NIH, 1994), and aim to bring several million more "suicidal" persons into treatment contacts that recognize suicidality as one component of the need for help. We will have to improve the sensitivity and the therapeutic resources of primary care/family doctors and their assistants, and also we must be prepared to treat effectively more persons with suicidal ideation as ambulatory patients in outpatient practice.

Progress in computer technology will provide tremendous assistance in bringing in the new patients and be helpful both in training and in treatment. The major change in strategy is that we give up our reliance on psychiatric hospitals as the major resource for suicide prevention and accept the inevitability of risk. (See Keeney, 1994, on making such decisions.) Using consultation and the team approach we try to share the risk. But the risk concept means there will be some suicides. Our goal is to reduce the number and rate.

## WHAT'S NEW IN TREATMENT?

An overview of the epidemiology of suicide as provided by the San Diego suicide study (Rich, et al., 1986) emphasizes the need for improved screening and case finding. About 50% of the suicides have had no contact with the mental health system although half of those persons had a re-

cent contact with their family doctor within a few months before committing suicide. Of the 50% of the suicides that had contact with the mental health system, 25% were out of treatment when they committed suicide, and 25% were in treatment, often receiving inadequate care (Isometsa, Henriksson, Aro et al., 1994). This suggests the need for more continuity of care and improvement in treatment success.

What we are looking for are new treatment modalities that can be adapted to give service to large numbers of suicidal people, that will be acceptable to them and are flexible enough to meet the needs of a variety of different people.

It is obvious that in the future there will be a vastly increased use of computer technology in diagnosis and treatment (Berner, Webster, Sugerman, et al., 1994; Glowniak and Bushway, 1994) and increased use of communication networks in follow-up. There will be interactive computer programs for taking the patients' histories, including asking questions about suicidal ideation, suicide attempts, and attitudes, all of which amount to a suicide assessment. At present (and much more so in the future) it is feasible to give the Minnesota Multiphasic Personality Inventory by interactive computer presentation and get an immediate printout and immediate report (Greene, 1991). Already I see in many hospital charts a prepared questionnaire that the patients fill out in their own time. Often the problem is that the clinicians don't have time to read what the patient has written. Computer programs will highlight the unusual answers of patients for the staff, thus indicating those patients at increased suicide risk. Of course, some patients will respond well to the interaction with computer programs and others may not. In summary, new computer programs will yield a much more complete and rapid history and suicide assessment, "red flag" special situations that need to be investigated by the clinician, and offer suggestions for treatment. Computer networks will improve staff communication, consultation, and follow-up for aftercare.

In the future our methods of educating staff can be greatly improved by the use of video programs and role-playing techniques. I am always surprised to learn how many staff persons at all levels of nursing care have had no training in suicidology or suicide awareness, even though they are working in hospitals and clinics where almost half of their patients and clients are potentially suicidal.

Reviewing primary prevention in psychiatry, Sharfstein (1986) foresees the discovery of biological markers that identify individuals at high risk for alcohol problems, and possibly a vaccine against alcoholism and other substance abuse problems. Stanley and Stanley (1988) state: "Data from numerous investigators indicate that suicidal behavior may be associated with abnormality of the serotonergic system." One important implication of this is that suicidal behavior may be viewed as a distinct disorder, not invariably tied to a primary psychiatric disorder such as depression or schizophrenia. This may explain why the treatment of associated psychiatric diagnoses may not be sufficient to deter suicide. At times the suicidal behaviors may be targeted independently for treatment.

Nordstrom, Samuelsson, Asberg, et al. (1994) found that in a large group of suicide attemptors, those patients whose cerebrospinal fluid (CSF) 5-HIAA was below the median had a considerably higher suicide rate than patients who had a higher level of CSF 5-HIAA. There was a 20% mortality among suicide attemptors who have a low CSF 5-HIAA level. These researchers echo my plea (Litman, 1991) that there is a great need for intervention–research programs in the area of suicidal behaviors.

## RESEARCH ON TREATMENT AS SUICIDE PREVENTION

There has not been a great deal of intervention research using suicide (compared to survival) as the outcome criterion. Motto (1976) reported a follow-up study of a large number of high-risk-for-suicide psychiatric patients in San Francisco. The therapeutic intervention for one group of patients consisted of follow-up letters at intervals, expressing interest on the part of Dr. Motto's team. There were fewer suicides in this "treatment" group than in two control groups that did not receive the letters. As a whole this was a moderate risk for suicide group, with 63 known suicides (2.35%) out of 2675 patients followed up for the first year. Forty percent of the suicides were within the first 90 posthospital days. Motto emphasized the importance of persisting in expressions of concern, without indicating any expectation of some form of response. The question is: Can such an influence be built into the health care system even to a small degree? Motto has faith that the health care system has something to offer suicidal persons and believes his letter writing helped to encourage the ex-hospitalized patients to continue searching for help within the health care system.

Litman and colleagues (Litman, 1989; Litman & Wold, 1976) provided "relationship maintenance" for high-risk-for-suicide patients from the Suicide Prevention Center in Los Angeles. The intervention consisted of a volunteer worker calling on the telephone and talking with the client at least once a week, as a befriender. The outcome of these interventions was paradoxical. Clients who had been depressed and suicidal liked the program and seemed to profit from it. However, some suicidal alcoholics came to resent what they regarded as an intrusion. There were more suicides of alcoholic clients in the intervention group than in the control group. The results of this study emphasize that interventions have to be designed uniquely for each patient, since what was helpful for suicidal depressives was harmful for suicidal alcoholics.

Although it is popular now to conceptualize suicide as the outcome of a relatively time-limited crisis (hence the emphasis on short-term safety in hospitals), more than half of all suicides represent the outcome of chronic disorders that require continuing treatment. Coppen and colleagues (Coppen, 1994; Coppen, Standish-Barry, Bailey et al., 1991) have conducted a prospective controlled study of lithium carbonate for recurrently suicidal manic–depressive patients. They report a suicide rate of 0.7 suicides per 1000 patient years on long-term lithium therapy. Comparison groups of manic–depressive patients in treatment without long-term lithium showed considerably higher suicide rates, from 5.1 to 11.6 suicides per 1000 patient years in various studies. Coppen (1991) states: "It is clear that recurrent mood disorders are lethal disorders with a poor outcome if not treated long-term." In a similar vein Frank, Cupfer, Perel, and colleagues (1990) have reported favorable results in treatment of depressed patients who were given maintenance antidepressant drug therapy over a period of 3 years or more.

## SUICIDE PREVENTION AT THE LEVEL OF PRIMARY CARE

It is a fact of life that the great majority of depressed and anxious "suicidal" people are being seen by primary care doctors, with great potential for relieving suffering and reducing the devastating social costs of this illness (Bowman & Schwenk, 1994). But they have inadequate training and experience (Barrett, Barrett, Oxman, & Gerber, 1988; Eisenberg, 1992) for the task of appropriate intervention. I believe it will be helpful to bring their attention to the suicide problem repeatedly and dramatically. When I did research on suicide and accidental deaths due to poisoning with prescription narcotics, such as codeine and propoxyphene (Litman, Diller, & Nelson, 1983), the primary care doctors who were prescribing these drugs had little or no information concerning the mental state of their patients. Therefore the doctors were shocked and surprised to learn about the deaths from overdoses of the very medicines they had prescribed.

Primary care doctors need to be told that if they are serving a patient group comprising 2000 adults (see, for example, Kindig, 1994), they can expect a suicide in their group every 2 years on the average, plus 10 suicide attempts a year serious enough to need medical attention; and that at any one time approximately 50 of the 2000 persons will be thinking seriously about committing suicide. However, primary care/family physicians are well aware of the high prevalence of anxiety and depression in the patients they are treating, and the doctors prescribe large amounts of sedatives, tranquilizers, and antidepressants.

Researchers and educators in Sweden (Rutz, Von Knorring, & Wilinder, 1992) report that a special effort at education for primary care doctors in one region of Sweden resulted in a sizable reduction in suicide in that area. The educators focused on recognition and treatment.

In England, Michel and Valach (1992) compared the results of training general practitioners in suicidology by the use of written materials to training in seminars/workshops. They report that handing out written materials was ineffective training. However, seminars and workshops were quite helpful in changing attitudes and behaviors, and made the practitioners more sensitive in suicide assessment and more self-confident in their interventions. These efforts have precipitated ongoing discussions in the medical journals of Great Britain (McCabe, 1993; Morgan, 1992; Morgan & Hawton, 1994) about the expectations for suicide prevention that suicidologists wish to place on the primary care doctors. These doctors are extremely important in the British health care system as the gatekeepers for health care, for all the persons in a particular "panel".

We can look forward to improvements in screening through the use of computer programs that eventually will be in every doctors' office. Through these programs and by taking some extra time to talk with patients, doctors will be able to identify many more of the high-risk patients. Then what can they do? They can give antidepressant drugs and monitor the results through follow-up by telephone calls and repeat visits. This takes time that may not be paid sufficiently by managed care. The doctors need to have trained psychological assistants who are less expensive, and who can stay in communication with the patients. The doctors can try to get patients in touch with the network of helping groups, such as the befrienders who are in Samaritan-type organizations, and the great variety of support and recovery groups. For specific problems doctors could make referrals to specific resources; for example, for problems of divorce and unwillingness to accept divorce, problems of unemployment, and especially problems of illness. For severely suicidal people it is a good idea to try contracting with patients, that is, asking them to guarantee they will not commit suicide for a given short period of time (Drye, Goulding, & Goulding, 1973) while the doctor is making a psychiatric referral.

Primary care doctors could modify the technique that Motto used and send letters to patients found to be at risk, reminding the patients of the interest of the doctor. If high-risk-for-suicide people in a general practice situation were asked to come in every 3 months for health review and a mental health checkup, and remained at suicide risk, what else could the doctor's office do? This question brings us to the domain of outpatient therapy and outpatient treatment by people more specialized in mental health care than family doctors.

## OUTPATIENT TREATMENT

At present, research and practice in suicidology focuses on the assessment of acute or imminent suicide risk and treatment in hospitals of such high-risk patients. I recommend that we focus research and practice on the large number of low to moderate risk-for-suicide patients, with the goal of preventing them from becoming high-risk patients. What do I mean by "high risk" or "low to moderate risk"? We assess a certain level of risk to patients based on "risk factors," which are symptoms, traits, or circumstances that

they have in common with people who have committed suicide. More accurately, "high-risk" patients resemble or fit into a population of previous patients who had a high suicide rate, for example, 5% to 10% over the next year (Litman, 1974). "Low to moderate risk" patients resemble patients in a population where the suicide rate was 0.5% to 3% over the next year. On the average, suicide attemptors are in the low-moderate risk range. So are depressed persons hospitalized with suicidal ideation, during the first year of their posthospital aftercare.

There are relatively few high risk-for-suicide patients. But there are several million low to moderate risk-for-suicide persons, and it is in treating these persons that we have the potential for making significant reductions in the suicide rates. In my experience with psychological autopsies, the majority of persons who committed suicide would have been evaluated at low to moderate risk if they had been assessed 24 hours before death.

The statistics on outpatient treatment from the epidemiological catchment area studies (Regier, Narrow, Rae, et al., 1993) are impressive. The total number of persons treated in the mental health system was almost 23 million in a sample year; the number of visits, 325 million. Adding 1 or 2 million more low to moderate risk-for-suicide patients would not be an intolerable extra burden. Already about half the patients treated in outpatient clinics have a history of suicidal ideation or suicide attempts (Asnis, Friedman, Sanderson, et al., 1993). With increased screening of the general population and increased case finding, we may expect many more persons with suicidal ideation and with various degrees of suicide risk being treated as outpatients by mental health services. The referrals will come directly from the general public, from primary care facilities, and from hospitals for aftercare. Of course, all of these "suicidal" patients will have other problems that demand treatment, problems of anxiety, insomnia, low self-confidence, excessive personal demands made upon themselves, depression, schizophrenia, alcoholism and drug abuse, etc. Every sort of problem can be associated with suicidal ideation. In my opinion, one of the keys to successful outpatient treatment is to accept the risk of suicide and not let it interfere with the ongoing treatment, but for this most therapists need the confidence of the team concept, with ready consultation for sharing the responsibility when taking risks (Litman, 1989).

A helpful development, which will aid in research on treatment in practice, is the increasing focus on specific therapeutic approaches. In the interpersonal therapy of Klerman, Weissman, Rounsaville, and Chevron (1984): "Exploration of the meaning of suicide to the patient is in order, beginning with the assumption that suicide represents an attempt at interpersonal communication or problem solving." The cognitive therapists (Beck, Brown, Berchick, Stewart, & Steer, 1990 & Linehan, Armstrong, Suarez, Allman, & Heard, 1991) explore dysfunctional thinking, especially hopelessness. Shneidman (1993) focuses on psychache resulting from the frustration of needs. He asks, "Where do you hurt?" Each of these approaches leads to a somewhat different and researchable treatment modality. A similar process is going on in drug therapeutics, with extensive efforts to find in theory and in practice models for fitting the medication to the patient and the patient to the medication.

At present the mental health services delivery system is so disorganized that it appears chaotic to the potentially suicidal person. When patients shift from doctor to doctor, therapist to therapist, or from hospital to aftercare there is little or no possibility for continuity, even of records. A patient will often be getting medication at one clinic, and a different medication at another clinic, and going to a third clinic for management or psychotherapy. Many therapeutic options—such as recovery groups, drop-in groups, and assistance in counseling, employment, and housing—are not widely known even within the system. For want of tracking, patients often feel unwanted or rejected, or they just drop out.

In the future we can expect that there will be greatly improved techniques for tracking patients from one part of the health care system to another, with easy transmission of records. Then each new clinic involved with a patient will know quickly which patients have been suicidal in the past, what has been tried unsuccessfully, and which treatment in the past has helped. Continuity of care will join crisis therapy as a second major concept in suicide prevention through treatment.

## REFERENCES

Asnis, T. M., Friedman, R. A., Sanderson, W. C., et al. (1993). Suicidal behaviors in adult psychiatric outpatients. *American Journal of Psychiatry, 150*, 108–112.

Barrett, J. E., Barrett, J. A., Oxman, T. E., and Gerber, P. D. (1988). The prevalence of psychiatric disorders in a primary care practice. *Archives of General Psychiatry, 45*, 1100–1106.

Beck, A. T., Brown, G., Berchick, R. J., Stewart, B. L., and Steer, R. A., (1990). Relationship between hopelessness and ultimate suicide. *American Journal of Psychiatry, 147*, 190–195.

Berner, E. S., Webster, G. D., Sugerman, A. A., et al. (1994). Performance of four computer based diagnostic systems. *New England Journal of Medicine, 330*, 1792–1796.

Bowman, M. A., and Schwenk, T. L., (1994). Family medicine. *Journal of the American Medical Association, 271*(21) 1670–1671.

Brent, D. A., Dupfer, D. J., Bromet, E. J., and Dew, M. A. (1988). The assessment and treatment of patients at risk for suicide. In A. J. Frances & R. E. Hales (Eds.), *Review of psychiatry* (Vol. 7, pp. 366–367). Washington, DC: American Psychiatric Press.

Busch, K. A., Clark, D. C., Fawcett, J., and Kravitz, H. M. (1993). Clinical features of inpatient suicide. *Psychiatric Annals, 23*(5), 256–262.

Coppen, A. (1994). Depression as a lethal disease: prevention strategies. *Journal of Clinical Psychiatry, 55*(4), Suppl., 37–45.

Coppen, A., Standish-Barry, H., Bailey, J., et al. (1991). Does lithium reduce the mortality of recurrent mood disorders? *Journal of Affective Disorder, 23*, 1–7.

Crammer, J. L. (1984). Symposium on suicides in hospital. *British Journal Psychiatry, 145*, 459–476.

Cutter, F. (1979). The relationship of new Samaritan clients and volunteers to high risk people in England and Wales. *Suicide and Life-Threatening Behavior, 9*(4), 245–250.

Dorpat, T. L. and Ripley, H. S. (1960). A study of suicide in the Seattle area. *Comprehensive Psychiatry, 1*, 349–359.

Drye, R. C., Goulding, R. L., & Goulding, M. E. (1973). No-suicide decision: Patient monitoring of suicidal risk. *American Journal of Psychiatry, 130*, 171–174.

Eisenberg, L. (1992). Treating depression and anxiety in primary care. *New England Journal of Medicine, 326*(16), 1080–1084.

Fawcett, J., Clark, D. C., & Busch, K. A. (1993). Assessing and treating the patient at risk for suicide. *Psychiatric Annals, 23*(5), 244–254.

Fawcett, J., Scheftner, W., Clark, D., et al. (1987). Clinical predictors of suicide in patients with major affective disorders. *American Journal of Psychiatry, 144*, 35–40.

Frank, E., Cupfer, D. J., Perel, J. M., et al. (1990). Three year outcomes for maintenance therapies in recurrent depression. *Archives of General Psychiatry, 47*, 1093–1099.

Geller, J. L. (1992). A historical perspective on the role of state hospitals viewed from the era of the revolving door. *American Journal of Psychiatry, 149*, 1526–1533.

Glowniak, J. V. and Bushway, M. K. (1994). Computer networks as a medical resource. *Journal of the American Medical Association, 271*(24), 1934–1939.

Goldstein, R. B., Black, D. W., Nasrallah, A., & Winokur, G. (May 1991). The prediction of suicide. *Archives of General Psychiatry, 48*, 418–422.

Gralnick, A. (April 1991). *Suicide in the psychiatric hospital.* Lecture to the American Association of Suicidology, Annual Conference, Boston.

Greene, R. L. (1991). *The MMPI-II-MMPI: An Interpretive Manual.* Needham Heights, MA: Allyn & Bacon.

Isometsa, E. T., Henriksson, M. M., Aro, H. M., et al. (1994). Suicide and major depression. *American Journal of Psychiatry, 151*, 530–536.

Keeney, R. L. (1994). Decisions about life-threatening risks. *New England Journal of Medicine, 331*(3), 193–196.

Kindig, D. A., (1994). Counting Generalist physicians. *Journal of the American Medical Association, 271*(19), 1505–1507.

Klerman, G. L., Weissman, M. N., Rounsaville, B. J., & Chevron, E. S. (1984). *Interpersonal psychotherapy of depression* (p. 208). New York: Basic Books.

Linehan, M. M., Armstrong, H. E., Suarez, A., Allman, D., & Heard, H. L. (1991). Cognitive behavioral treatment of chronically parasuicidal borderline patients. *Archives of General Psychiatry, 48*, 1060–1064.

Litman, R. E. (1974). Models for predicting suicide risk. In Charles Neuringer (Ed.), *Psychological assessment of suicidal risk.* Springfield, IL: C. C. Thomas.

Litman, R. E. (1989). Long-term treatment of chronically suicidal patients. *Bulletin of The Menninger Clinic, 53*, 215–228.

Litman, R. E. (1991, Spring). Predicting and preventing hospital and clinic suicides. *Suicide and Life-Threatening Behavior, 21*(1), 56–73.

Litman, R. E., Diller, J., & Nelson, F. (1983). Deaths related to propoxyphene or codeine or both. *Journal of Forensic Sciences, 28*(1), 128–138.

Litman, R. E., & Wold, C. I. (1976). Beyond crisis. In E. S. Shneidman (Ed.), *Suicidology: Contemporary developments.* Grune and Stratton.

Males, M. (1994). California's suicide decline, 1970–1990. *Suicide and Life-Threatening Behavior, 24*(1), 24–37.

McCabe, E. (1993). The "myth" of suicide prevention. *British Journal of Psychiatry, 161*, pp. 162–270.

Michel, K., & Valach, L. (1992). Suicide prevention: Spreading the gospel to general practitioners. *British Journal of Psychiatry, 160*, 757–760.

Michels, R., & Marzuk, P. M. (1993). Progress in psychiatry. *New England Journal of Medicine, 329*, 628–637.

Morgan, H. G. (1992). Suicide prevention: Hazards on the fast lane to community care. *British Journal Psychiatry, 160*, 149–153.

Morgan, H. G., & Hawton, K. (1994). Suicide prevention. *British Journal Psychiatry, 164*, 126–127.

Motto, J. A. (1976). Suicide prevention for high risk persons who refuse treatment. *Suicide and Life-Threatening Behavior, 6*(4), 223–230.

NIH. (1994). Editorial. Screening proves effective in reaching individuals with untreated depression. *National Institute of Health Observer, 1*, 1–7.

Nordstrom, P., Samuelsson, M., Asberg, M., et al. (1994). CSF 5-HIAA predicts suicide risk. *Suicide and Life-Threatening Behavior, 24*, 1–9.

Pauker, S. L., and Cooper, A. M. (1990). Paradoxical patient reactions to psychiatric life support. *American Journal of Psychiatry, 147*, 480–491.

Parrish, J. (1993). Involuntary use of intervention: Pros and cons. *Innovations and Research, 2*, 15–22.

Pokorny, A. D. (1993). Suicide prediction revisited. *Suicide and Life-Threatening Behavior, 23*, 1–10.

Regier, E. A., Myers, J. K., Kramer, M., et al. (1984). The NIMH Epidemiologic Catchment Area Program. *Archives of General Psychiatry, 41*, 934–941.

Regier, E. A., Narrow, W. E., Rae, E. S., et al. (1993). The defacto US mental and addictive disorders service system. *Archives of General Psychiatry, 50*, 85–94.

Rich, C. L., Young, D., and Fowler, R. C. (1986). San Diego suicide study. *Archives of General Psychiatry, 43*, 577–582.

Robins, E., Murphy, G. E., Wilkinson, R. H., Gassner, S. and Kayes, J. (1959). Some clinical considerations in the prevention of suicide based on a study of 134 successful suicides. *American Journal of Public Health, 49*, 888–899.

Rutz, W., Von Knorring, L. And Wilinder, J. (1992). Long-term effects of an educational program for a practitioner. Given by the Swedish Committee for the Prevention and Treatment of Depression. *Acta Psychiatrica Scandinavia, 85*(1), 83–88.

Sharfstein, S. (1986). Issues to consider in primary prevention in psychiatry. In J. Barter & S. Talbott (Eds.), *Primary prevention in psychiatry.* Washington, DC: American Psychiatric Press.

Shneidman, E. S. (1993). *Suicide as psychache.* Hillsdale, NU: Aronson.

Stanley, M., and Stanley, B. (1988). Reconceptualizing suicide: A biological approach. *Psychiatric Annals, 18*, 646–651.

Teicher, M. H., Glod, C. A., and Cole, J. O. (1993). Antidepressant drugs and the emergence of suicidal tendencies. *Drug Safety, 8*(3), 186–212.

# IV. A Population Perspective

## 11
## Suicide Prevention in Adolescents (Age 12–18)

### Alan L. Berman, PhD, and David A. Jobes, PhD

The epidemiology of adolescent suicide is summarized with particular emphasis on temporal trends by age and gender. "First-generation" prevention programs, as reviewed and critiqued by the Centers for Disease Control and Prevention, are then examined. In the absence of compelling empirically based behavioral outcome data, selective targeted "second-generation" prevention efforts are then described across the primary–secondary–tertiary continuum. These efforts are focused toward targets of individual predisposition, the social milieu, or proximal agents associated with high risk for suicidal behaviors. Finally, with an eye toward the future, current obstacles and unanswered questions are explored as they relate to opportunities and hopes for change in effecting reduced rates of these behaviors.

Adolescence, defined as a transitional developmental period between childhood and adulthood, is initiated by puberty. The physiological changes attendant to pubescence are precursors to a host of psychosocial demands and personality changes common to the years bridging toward maturity. It is a period of significant development – for example, a sense of personal identity (Erikson, 1950/1963) and of morality (Kohlberg, 1981).

The end of adolescence is less well defined. Typically it is thought to coincide with sociocultural life transitions, for example, movement away from the shelter of family and mastery of the practical demands of independent living. However, this definition is not clear-cut and is defined differentially by self and others coinciding with no one particular age. In Western societies, adulthood is thought to begin in one's early 20s (Levinson, Darrow, Klein, Levinson, & McKee, 1978). In more primitive societies, adulthood may *begin* with puberty!

The definition of adolescence is important to our epidemiologic understanding of suicidal behaviors during this period. Epidemiologic data in the United States are reported by 5-year (e.g., 15–19) and 10-

year (e.g., 15–24) age groups (National Center for Health Statistics – NCHS, various years). The distinction is relevant in appreciating that suicide is either the second (15- to 19-year-olds) or third (15- to 24-year-olds) leading cause of death among adolescents. Moreover, as will be noted below, trends in recent years have been different for these two age groups.

The rate of suicide among 15- to 24-year-olds in the United States in 1950 was 4.5 per 100,000. In 1990 the rate among youth in this age group had almost tripled to 13.2 per 100,000. For 15- to 19-year-olds, the rate of suicide in 1950 was only 2.7 per 100,000. Two generations later, in 1990, the rate had climbed to 11.1, and increase of better than 300%!

Whereas the ratio of male to female suicide among 15- to 24-year-olds in 1950 was 2.5 : 1, by 1990 the ratio had grown to 5.3 : 1. In 1990, 73% of suicides among 15- to 24-year-olds were by white males. In 1950 the white-to-black ratio of suicide rates was 1.8 : 1; in 1990 the ratio was 2.3 : 1.

Table 1 shows the 1990 rates of completed suicide for 15- to 19-year-olds and 20- to 24-year-olds by race and sex in the United States. As can be seen, rates are

Alan L. Berman is with the American Association of Suicidology. David A. Jobes is with the Catholic University of America.

Table 1
Suicide Rates by Race and Sex for 15- to 19-
and 20- to 24-year-olds, United States, 1990

|  | Age group[a] | |
| --- | --- | --- |
|  | 15–19 | 20–24 |
| Total | 11.1 | 15.1 |
| Male | 18.1 | 25.7 |
| Female | 3.7 | 4.1 |
| White male | 19.3 | 26.8 |
| Non-White male | 13.0 | 20.6 |
| White female | 4.0 | 4.4 |
| Non-White female | 2.5 | 3.0 |

*Source*: National Center for Health Statistics, unpublished data, 1993.
[a]Rates per 100,000 population.

considerably higher in the older age group. This trend holds, also, for both the white-male-to-white-female and the non-white-male-to-non-white-female ratios of suicide rates.

Epidemiologic alarms regarding dramatic increases in adolescent suicide have been sounding since the late 1970s, when rates peaked. These dramatic and frightening rates of adolescent suicide signaled the need to develop effective preventive and interventive models to reduce this tragic waste of both life and human potential. The resulting call to action produced a flurry of preventive programs in North America, mostly through the secondary school system. At best, these programs can be credited with stemming any further increases in rates. However, to date, no research has been presented to clearly and causatively link any of these planned preventive interventions with a reduction in observed rates (see below).

## WHY HAVE ADOLESCENT SUICIDE RATES INCREASED?

We might better conceptualize successful intervention approaches by first establishing causal connections to these observed increases. If we were to better define risk factors associated with adolescent suicide and, particularly, that which

caused observed changes in adolescent suicide rates, we could better design the necessary antidotes. Our answers to the question of why adolescent suicide rates have increased remain partial and more correlational (or covariant) than causative. Some hypotheses, however, have both sufficient empirical support and intuitive appeal to guide preventive programming.

For example, suicide risk is clearly and intimately tied to psychopathology, with only a small subset of completed suicides giving no evidence of psychopathology (Brent, Perper, Moritz, Baugher, & Allman, 1993). More specifically, affective disorder is generally acknowledged to be a key risk factor for completed suicide in youth (Brent, Perper, Moritz, Allman, Friend, Roth, Schweers, Balach, & Baugher, 1993). The relative risk of major depressive disorder has increased significantly for both period and age since the 1920s (Leon, Klerman, & Wickramaratne, 1993). Leon et al. documented the relative risk in the period 1941–1959 as 0.27 compared to a relative risk of 1.38 in the period from 1971 on. Moreover, the relative risk of a first major depressive episode occurring between the ages of 16 and 25 was greater than between 26 and 35, and 2.75 times greater than the risk for 6- to 15-year-olds.

Often co-occurring with depression is substance abuse (Greenbaum, Prange, Friedman, & Silver, 1991; Kaminer, 1991), and the comorbidity of active substance abuse and depression has been established as a significant risk factor for adolescent suicide (Bukstein, Brent, Perper, Moritz, Baugher, Schweers, Roth, & Balach, 1993; Shafii, Carrigan, Whittinghill, & Derrick, 1985). By 1991 the prevalence of alcohol use among high school students was 82% (Centers for Disease Control, 1992a).

Substance abuse in adolescence also has a high incidence of comorbidity with conduct disorders (Bukstein, Glancy, & Kaminer, 1992; Hovens, Cantwell, & Kiriakos, 1984), with the latter, moreover, being an independent risk factor for adolescent suicide (Berman & Jobes, 1991).

Almost one in four adolescents with a history of both substance abuse and suicide attempt live with families who still maintain a firearm in the home (Berman & Schwartz, 1990). Greater availability of firearms in American homes has been one of the most often cited findings related to both the observed increased incidence of youth suicide and the increased use of firearms by adolescents who suicide (Boyd & Moscicki, 1986; Brent, Perper, Allman, Moritz, Wartella, & Zelenak, 1991). In 1990, 65% of U.S. 15- to 24-year-olds used firearms to complete suicide, a prevalence 40% greater than that observed in 1970.

Another significant area of risk that has undergone dramatic change in the past few decades is within the nuclear family. There is now sufficient evidence that family factors are an important correlate of suicidal behavior among youth (Asarnow, Carlson, & Guthrie, 1987; Hawton, 1986). For example, separation from and/or rejection by parents, poor family communication and problem-solving, and parental psychopathology have all been identified as major issues implicated in youth suicidal behaviors (Brent et al., 1988; Spirito, Brown, Overholser, & Fritz, 1989).

## WHY IS MALE SUICIDE INCREASING?

Females are almost twice as likely to experience a major depressive episode as are males (relative risk: 1.82 : 1.00), with rates most elevated between the ages of 16 and 25 (Leon et al., 1993). Females also attempt suicide more than males. Given that both depression and prior nonfatal attempt are known risk factors for completed suicide (Berman & Jobes, 1991), it may appear paradoxical that the 1990 male suicide rate (ages 15–24) has mushroomed to more than five times that of females.

However, when we examine those risk factors noted above, the answers to this paradox become readily apparent. Males, in contrast to females, have a higher prevalence and severity of conduct disorder

and alcohol dependence (Hovens et al., 1984). Comorbidity between affective disorder and substance abuse has also been found to be more frequent among males (Rich, Ricketts, Fowler, & Young, 1988). Males are more likely to use a firearm (NCHS, various years) and to be intoxicated at the time of their suicide (Brent, Perper, & Allman, 1987). In a recently reported study of completed suicides among 13- to 19-year-olds (Marttunen, Aro, Henriksson, & Lonnqvist, 1994), there was a higher frequency of interpersonal loss among alcohol-abusing male suicides than among those with depressive disorders. Marttunen and colleagues (Marttunen, Aro, Henriksson, & Lonqvist, 1991) have also hypothesized that males have a lower threshold of reactivity to stress. Lastly, when most vulnerable to suicide, males may be less likely than females to seek help or communicate to potential help-givers (Shaffer, Vieland, Garland, Rojas, Underwood, & Busner, 1990).

## FIRST-GENERATION PREVENTION PROGRAM

The Centers for Disease Control (1992b) has reviewed and recommended a range of "exemplary" youth suicide prevention programs. Eight different prevention strategies were delineated. Among the significant findings reported in this review, these eight strategies were considered to represent just two conceptual strategies: (1) recognition and referral, and (2) risk factor counteraction. This first generation of prevention programs was critically evaluated further as inadequate in: (1) linkages to both other community resources (e.g., mental health services) and risk prevention programs (e.g., drug abuse treatment programs), (2) focusing means restriction and/or other promising preventive efforts, and (3) evaluation research, particularly focusing on preventive outcomes and iatrogenic effects. It might be noted, also, that there is very little attention to primary prevention models focused on the high-risk individual. Each of these first-generation suicide prevention strategies is now briefly reviewed and summarized.

## School Gatekeeper Training

These school training programs help school personnel (e.g., counselors, coaches, cafeteria workers) identify and refer at-risk students to professional mental health services. These are typically school/knowledge-based educational models of training. Usually, content topics include warning signs for suicide, referral sources and procedures, and school crisis policies. Initial evaluations have documented both satisfaction and learning gains; however, behavioral outcomes have yet to be documented.

## Community Gatekeeper Training

Similarly, these community training programs focus on comparable training goals for members of the nonschool community who may have frequent contact with youth (e.g., clergy, doctors, police, etc.). Core objectives of these models include increasing knowledge of warning signs, referral sources, referral behaviors, and increasing confidence/competence in helping skills. Again, initial evaluation studies have yet to focus on changes in desired behaviors among those given this form of training.

## √ General Suicide Education

These school-based programs are classroom-centered, knowledge-based models predicated on the assumption that the more students know about suicide warning signs and sources of help, the more likely they will ask for help or refer others for help. Typical content topics include discussion of relevant facts, statistics, myths, warning signs, available community resources (and how to use them), help-seeking and problem-solving skills, and skill development in the areas of stress management, communications, social

and/or coping. Measures of the success of this model might include increased utilization of local hotlines and increased frequencies of intake at mental health services. However, evaluations have only demonstrated short-term gains in knowledge and increased recognition of referral sources. Attitudes toward seeking help generally have not been affected by these programs, and changes in behavior have not been formally evaluated to date.

## Screening Programs

Early detection and referral (secondary prevention) has long been a mainstay of prevention programming. It also has the advantage of appealing most to clinicians, generally inadequately trained in public health prevention models. The typical school screening program administers a questionnaire or screening instrument regarding psychological problems related to suicide (e.g., symptoms of depression) to all students. Those with scores above a cutoff point might then be referred to a school guidance counselor who would interview the student for further signs of risk. Referral to a third-stage intervention (treatment) would then be made for those students identified as at risk.

As noted by the CDC, "most screening protocols are in a developmental stage" (p. 101), with significant problems in scale construction (e.g., psychometric specificity and sensitivity) compromising the effectiveness and accuracy of these instruments. Other problems with this model of triage have yet to be resolved. For example, as suicide risk heightens and ebbs with the tide of precipitating events (Berman & Jobes, 1991), screenings need to occur frequently in order to minimize "false negatives." On the other hand, the likelihood of large numbers of "false positives" (youth incorrectly identified as at risk) potentially poses serious and "adverse consequences" (e.g., stigmatization).

## √ Peer Support Programs

These school or community-based peer support programs aim to foster social and coping competencies and peer relationships and networking among at-risk youth. Evaluations suggest that peer support programs may be able to reduce high-risk behaviors (e.g., drug use); however, the link to preventing suicide has yet to be empirically established.

## Crisis Centers and Hotlines

Volunteer paraprofessionally staffed telephone crisis services have an inherent appeal to youth. They are typically open late at night when traditional services are not, the caller can maintain anonymity (and control), support is often nondirective (thus, nonjudgmental), and contact is by telephone—a particularly favorite tool among adolescents. Evidence of hotlines' effectiveness in preventing suicide is inconsistent (CDC, 1992b, p. 128), although Miller, Coombs, Leeper, and Barton (1984) did demonstrate a small but statistically significant difference in suicide rates among young white women in communities with versus those without hotlines. These demographics suggest that the more at-risk young males may not be socialized to seek help or to communicate to a hotline their suicidality in a cry for help, making these services less effective in reducing overall suicide rates.

## Means Restriction

Public health officials strongly advocate means restriction as an especially valuable prevention tactic. The argument for this approach is that thoughts or impulses to attempt suicide cannot translate into self-harmful behaviors without an available means that can be used to put a destructive intent into action. As nearly two thirds of all youth suicides are by firearms, the thrust of this preventive effort has been geared toward reducing access to firearms, thus introducing delay and the opportunity for redirection. At worst, limiting available lethal agents of self-destruction might lead to the use of other, less immediately lethal agents. If success-

ful, one consequence of this approach, therefore, could be an increase in less lethal attempts.

There are already some naturalistic data in support of the means restriction approach. Studies comparing suicide rates in Vancouver, British Columbia (restrictive handgun regulations) versus Seattle, Washington (Sloan, Rivara, Reay, Ferris, Path, & Kellerman, 1990), and before versus after a 1976 restrictive handgun licensing law was passed in Washington, D.C. (Loftin, McDowall, Wiersema, & Cottey, 1991) have demonstrated compelling evidence in support of the effectiveness of handgun restrictions. Yet, this approach awaits more widespread and purposeful implementation in a carefully designed and well-evaluated program to prevent youth suicides.

## Postvention and Cluster Prevention

The potential of one or more imitative ("copycat") suicides after a completed suicide requires a ready crisis intervention response to prevent potential suicide clusters. The CDC (1988) has issued recommended guidelines for schools and communities to follow in such events. To date, the implementation of such planned interventions appears to be relatively common in most senior high schools as part of an overall crisis response team approach to a variety of potential school and community traumata.

## A SECOND GENERATION

In the absence of convincing empirically based behavioral outcomes, the apparent failure of these early prevention efforts should not be discouraging. Indeed, as Gelles has observed:

The smallpox vaccine was discovered in 1780 and it took 200 years to wipe out the illness. That problem had one cause and one cure and it took 200 years. Imagine the difficulty [we] face with a multifactored problem and multiple solutions. (Lipsitt, 1994, p. 56)

In the wake of initial efforts, and as we approach the next century, model development in youth suicide prevention must now be appropriately considered second generation. This next generation of prevention efforts must seek to refine and extend earlier efforts, must focus more selectively on targeted ("indicated") groups of higher-risk youth, and must define and measure behavioral outcomes to either establish effectiveness or prepare for third-generation programs.

Furthermore, these new efforts should be targeted toward *primary prevention* when the model is population focused. Thus, prevention efforts that focus on reducing the likelihood of antecedent conditions (e.g., mental disorders, comorbidity) and, alternatively, to strengthening protective factors (e.g., attachments, family cohesion, help seeking, etc.) would appear to have the greatest promise. The next wave of prevention programs needs to better focus change efforts on *secondary prevention* – early detection and treatment of those empirically based risk factors (as delineated above) known to predispose youth to completed suicide. Finally, further efforts are needed in the area of *tertiary prevention* to reduce long-term psychiatric disability, provide thorough and effective rehabilitation programming, and provide community support needed for the chronically suicidal as well as suicide survivors. As shown in Table 2, these prevention strategies may take many forms dependent upon whether the focus is the individual, the social milieu, or proximal agents. The following is brief description of these models and some examples that are known to us.

## Primary Prevention

Illustrative of this approach are programs developed at the level of secondary prevention but adaptable and deliverable to both children and adolescents at the primary prevention level.

*Individual Predisposition.* Many of these primary prevention skill-based training models that focus on the individual can be adapted for elementary-age children and taught over the grade school years with "booster shots" and follow-up practice to help decrease a child's predisposition to suicidal behaviors. These models include the following:

1. *Depression Management Skills Training.* Various authors (Lewinsohn, Antonnuccio, Steinmetz, & Teri, 1984; Rehm, 1987; Reynolds & Coats, 1986) have noted the effectiveness of behavioral and cognitive-behavioral approaches to control depression and teach substantive skills that may serve as antidotes (e.g., self-reinforcement, assertiveness, etc.).
2. *Anger and Aggression Management Skills.* These models target anger and rageful affects, and teach techniques of anger control and emotional regulation (Feindler & Ecton, 1986; Lochman & Curry, 1986; Novaco, 1979).
3. *Loneliness Prevention.* Young's (1982) work recognizes the salience of early childhood loneliness as a precursor to later drug use and suicidal behavior (see Berman & Schwartz, 1990) and specifically focuses on both cognitions and behaviors that maintain loneliness.
4. *Interpersonal Problem-Solving Skills.* Training in this area challenges impulsivity by teaching thinking and cognitive problem-solving skills (e.g., cause–effect reasoning) to children as young as 4 years of age (Shure & Spivack, 1988).
5. *Competency Enhancement Skills.* As discussed by Botvin and Tortu (1988), this approach teaches decision making, self-directed behavior change, anxiety management, and social skills (see also Hansen, Watson-Perczel, & Christopher, 1989).
6. *Critical Viewing Skills.* This training recognizes that violence potential is enhanced by overattention to popular media, especially television, and that youth can be taught to resolve conflict and deal with stress in productive ways (cf., Charren, 1994).

Table 2
A Conceptual Model of Prevention Strategies

|  | Individual predisposition | Social milieu | Proximal agents |
|---|---|---|---|
| Primary prevention | Depression management Anger management Loneliness prevention Problem-solving training Competency enhancement Critical viewing skills Help-seeking training | Dropout prevention Early detection/referral of parental pathology Surrogate role models Media guidance | Gun safety training for parents and pediatricians Suicide awareness among health care providers Federal firearms prevention education |
| Secondary prevention | Triage programs Volunteerism Outpatient treatment | Gatekeeper training Peer counseling Parental pathology Case finding Caregiver training | Medication emetics Environmental safety Decrease access to guns |
| Tertiary prevention | Psychiatric treatment Substance abuse treatment | Community mental health treatment Juvenile justice programs Case management follow-up | SSRI treatment Psychotherapy for depression Neuroleptics for psychosis |

7. *Help-Seeking Behavior Skills*. Training in this area encourages youth to serve as consumer advocates to identify "user-friendly" community resources, serve as peer referral sources, and learn skills in seeking help for themselves.

*Social Milieu.* These primary preventive approaches are specifically targeted as community-based interventions that may affect the larger social milieu providing for health education, promotion, and protection. Models in this area include:

1. *School Dropout Prevention/School Enhancement Programs*. These programs work to minimize failure experiences, increase vocational skill development, and foster educational growth.
2. *Early Detection and Referral of Parental Pathology*. As discussed by Brent (1994), the role of parental dysfunction and psychopathology is significant in the lives of suicidal youth. Programs in this area would therefore facilitate iden-

tification and effective treatment of parental dysfunction and its effect on family members.
3. *Surrogate Role Model Programs*. Various community-based models such as Big Brother, Big Sister, Concerned Black Men, or mentor-oriented programs serve to replace absent or neglectful parents with nurturing and supportive role models.
4. *Media Guidelines for Reporting Suicide Stories*. As discussed by the CDC (1992b), media guidelines, if adopted, have the potential to minimize the negative and potential contagious impact of publicity about suicide and can help in the facilitation of referrals further assessment of suicide risk.

*Proximal Agents.* These include primary prevention efforts to educate and train responsible parties and potential gatekeepers about the hazards of potentially lethal methods of suicide. For example, these might include the following:

1. *Gun Safety Training for Parents.* Programs in this area would encourage parents to create effective barriers to access of firearms by youth, as well as the proper use and storage of guns.
2. *Pediatrician Gun Education.* This training would encourage primary caregivers to ask parents about gun ownership and to provide safety information where a child is at questionable risk.
3. *Suicide Awareness Among Health Care Providers.* Broad-based educational programming for all health care providers in adolescent suicide might facilitate the detection of youth at risk and help effect appropriate referrals for treatment.
4. *Long-Term Federal Firearms Prevention Education.* Akin to the surgeon general's warnings about the risks of smoking, long-term firearm prevention education holds the promise of raising a national level of awareness about the danger and risks of accessible firearms in the home environment.

## Secondary Prevention

These models target early identification, assessment, and referral to outpatient treatment for at risk adolescents (and their families).

*Individual Predisposition.* To reduce the prevalence of suicidal behaviors among adolescents, a range of outpatient screening and intervention programs are needed to appropriately identify and refer at-risk youth.

1. *Population-Based Triage Programs.* As discussed by Rotherman-Borus and Bradley (1991), triage programs can be targeted for high-risk groups (e.g., runaway youth successively screened from distal to proximal risk and referred for treatment accordingly). Ideally, triage-based programs should be conducted through annual health screenings within school settings.
2. *Volunteerism/Tutoring Programs.* These programs place at-risk youth into positions of caregiving and helping others,

giving them a sense of purpose and meaning.
3. *Outpatient Treatment for Suicidal Youth.* As discussed by Gutstein and Rudd (1990), models for safe and effective outpatient treatment are available. Outpatient individual, family, and group psychotherapies represent important intervention modalities within the secondary prevention movement.

*Social Milieu.* Within communities there are a range of services that could effectively provide secondary prevention in terms of early detection, intervention, and treatment referral.

1. *Gatekeeper Referral Training.* As noted above, such training would educate adults and peers in referral skills for helping when risk factors are observed in a troubled youth.
2. *Peer Counseling Programs/Hotlines.* These programs continue to provide a valuable service to those they reach. Further efforts need to be made to find similar models that are more attractive to young high-risk males.
3. *Case Finding–Parental Pathology.* Interventions in this area would allow for early identification of mental health problems of children of dysfunctional parents. Home service delivery might be designed to increase compliance with treatment.
4. *Mental Health Caregiver Training.* Given that most mental health professionals receive little, if any, formalized training in clinical suicidology (Bongar, 1991), there is a clear need for further training in suicide risk assessment and treatment approaches to help maximize effective prevention efforts.

*Proximal Agents.* Some secondary prevention/intervention efforts related to proximal agents may include the following:

1. *Medication Emetics.* As discussed by Cantor (1989), immediately available antidotes for potentially lethal medications may help decrease the proximal risk posed by lethal substances. Sold

along with prescription medications, with the capacity to nullify the effects of an overdose, emetics provide an immediate antidote to an impulsive lethal overdose.

2. *Assuring Environmental Safety.* Various physical barriers such as fences or nets and can be installed on bridges used for suicide jumps (refer to Berman, O'Carroll, & Silverman, 1994). In addition, the installation of suicide hotline telephones on bridges has also been used in an effort to provide an available intervention resource for those considering a jump from a bridge. Similarly, guard rails installed on precarious roads at dangerous turns provide yet another form of physical environmental protection from vehicular suicide attempts.

3. *Limiting the Accessibility of Firearms.* As discussed by Brent (1994), the removal of firearms and ammunition from the home is probably the single most protective secondary-level intervention possible. In the absence of complete removal, it would seem that securing (locking away) firearms and/or separating weapon and ammunition would provide some measure of decreasing the immediate risk that guns create within the home environment.

## Tertiary Prevention

To reduce psychiatric disability and institutional dependency, a range of tertiary prevention programs are needed. To decrease the overall incidence of adolescent suicide, tertiary treatment and rehabilitative programs should be specifically targeted to address those empirical risk factors (e.g., depression, substance abuse, and comorbid psychiatric disorders) and populations (psychiatrically disturbed adolescent boys) who account for the bulk of our completed suicides (Brent, 1994).

*Individual Predisposition.* At a basic level, resources must be available to psychiatrically treat disturbed youth—especially young males with mood and/or substance abuse disorders. Brent (1994)

advocates an integrative psychoeducation and cognitive-behavioral treatment approach for the youth at risk as well as his/her family.

*Social Milieu.* Community-based mental health resources (that can provide family-oriented treatment) are necessary to effectively treat at-risk youths and prevent chronic psychiatric disability. A range of affordable psychiatric treatment settings must be made available to provide inpatient, residential, and day treatment services to psychiatrically disturbed youth. In addition, adequate resources and care must be available for at-risk youth in juvenile justice systems. For all treatment and rehabilitation programming, active (proactive) case management as well as frequent and consistent contact and follow-up with health care professionals can provide valuable support and prophylaxis.

*Proximal Agents.* Again, there is a strong need to limit those proximal agents that directly or indirectly facilitate suicidal behaviors. For example, initial empirical data show the clear potential risks of using traditional tricyclic medications to treat depression (Brent, 1994). Since tricyclics can be used in lethal overdoses, there is strong support for the use of serotinergic-specific antidepressant medications (e.g., fluoxetine), which are not lethal if taken in an overdose. For schizophrenic spectrum disorders, depot agents that are injected intramuscularly offer the prospect of better treatment compliance since the patient is not required to take oral medication on a daily basis. Whether taken orally or by injection, the overall risk of suicide in this population can be significantly decreased by the appropriate use of well-monitored neuroleptic management of psychotic symptomatology.

## OBSTACLES, LIMITATION, AND OPPORTUNITIES

The primary obstacles to effective prevention of adolescent suicide in the future are largely cultural, political, and financial. Despite the media attention given to youth suicide since the 1970s, suicide is generally still not widely regarded as a major public health problem. As discussed by Potter (1994), suicide receives far less media, political, and fiscal attention than does homicide, even though it is a more prevalent manner of death. As discussed by Berman and Jobes (1991), cultural avoidance and denial may exist regarding youthful suicidal behaviors, thus limiting appropriate responses. Large-scale preventive efforts simply cannot be mounted where there is insufficient concern.

√ While it is politically compelling to voice the need to prevent youth suicide, legislative concerns have not translated into suicide prevention dollars. Similarly, federal spending cutbacks have limited available research monies for further basic and applied empirical investigation. From yet another perspective, the political minefield surrounding the most obvious and potentially beneficial intervention — controlling access to guns — raises constitutional and/or emotional issues that make prospects for change neither proximal nor hopeful.

As we eye the future, pending health care reform and the potential for broad-based managed care create a measure of uncertainty as to what insurance-based supports will exist for mental health resources to our youth at risk. Will integrated outpatient treatment of the child and family, rehabilitative programs, and general community-based psychiatric treatment (e.g., for depression and substance abuse) be judged to be important enough and sufficiently cost-effective to receive parity with physical health care needs? From the research perspective, particularly in the "decade of the brain," will there be sufficient grant monies available to fund psychosocial and public health prevention research? In the face of dwindling financial resources, powerful lobbies, and professional encampments, how will health care providers, public health officials, and health care adminis-

trators be able to mount a unified effort to prevent suicide among our youth?

√ While formidable, these potential obstacles, limitations, and unanswered questions should not diminish our hope for change. As we approach the next millennium, we believe there are genuine opportunities and reasons to be hopeful about the next wave, the second generation, of adolescent suicide prevention efforts. There are at least three basic reasons for hope. First, in a general sense, suicidology (in the course of its relatively brief history) has virtually exploded as a multidisciplinary subspeciality field of study. Professional suicidologic organizations have developed nationally and internationally, centers for the study and prevention of suicide have formed, new suicide- and crisis-oriented journals have been founded, and the general effort to undertake empirical suicide research has increased dramatically over the last three decades. Second, the initial returns from the first wave of groundbreaking empirical studies are providing important and useful data upon which we can build our future prevention efforts. Indeed, in just two decades, we have developed a basic understanding of who is at risk for completed suicide, and we are just beginning to know how we might best go about helping these at-risk youth. Although health care reform creates uncertainty, unique opportunities exist for the development of new and effective treatments and intervention-based programs (especially if they prove to be cost-effective). Third, and perhaps most importantly, a certain undeniable momentum has built in the area of adolescent suicide since the late 1970s. In spite of the above-mentioned societal avoidance, there exists a counterbalancing and ever-increasing level of awareness about the issue. The inherent virtue of finding new and better ways to identify and help young people standing at the precipice of death continues to be a profoundly compelling and rewarding undertaking.

Perhaps the greatest hope for future advances in adolescent suicide prevention lies in what we have already learned from the first generation of prevention efforts. We now know that most adolescent suicides share their suicidal feelings with others, have diagnosable and treatable mental disorders, and do not necessarily want the finality of death that suicide inherently offers. Given this knowledge, we stand poised at the threshold of a second generation of preventive work that may help provide available and responsive listening ears, potentially life-saving assessment and treatment for diagnosable mental disorders, and viable life-sustaining alternatives to suicide.

# REFERENCES

Asarnow, J. R., Carlson, G. A., & Guthrie, D. (1987). Coping strategies, self-perceptions, hopelessness, and perceived family environments in depressed and suicidal children. *Journal of Consulting and Clinical Psychology, 55*, 361–366.

Berman, A. L., & Jobes, D. A. (1991). *Adolescent suicide: Assessment and intervention*. Washington, DC: American Psychological Association.

Berman, A. L., O'Carroll, P. W., & Silverman, M. M. (1994). Case consultation: Community suicide prevention: The effectiveness of bridge barriers. *Suicide and Life-Threatening Behavior, 24*, 88–99.

Berman, A. L., & Schwartz, R. (1990). Suicide attempts among adolescent drug users. *American Journal of Diseases of Children, 144*, 310–314.

Bongar, B. (1991). *The Suicidal Patient: Clinical and Legal Standards of Care*. Washington: American Psychological Association.

Botvin, G. J., Tortu, S. (1988). Preventing adolescent substance abuse through life skills training. In R. H. Price, E. L. Cowen, R. P. Lorian, & J. Ramos-McKay (Eds.) *Fourteen ounces of prevention: A casebook for practitioners* (pp. 98–110). Washington, DC: American Psychological Association.

Boyd, J. H., & Moscicki, E. K. (1986). Firearms and youth *American Journal of Public Health, 76*, 1240–1242.

Brent, D. A. (1994, April). *Risk factors for youth suicide*. Paper presented at the Annual Meeting of the American Association of Suicidology, New York.

Brent, D. A., Perper, J. A., & Allman, C. J. (1987). Alcohol, firearms, and suicide among youth: Temporal trends in Allegheny County, Pennsylvania, 1960–1983. *Journal of the American Medical Association, 257*, 3369–3372.

Brent, D. A., Perper, J. A., Goldstein, C. E., Kolko, D. J., Allan, M. J., Allman, C. J., & Zelenek, J. P. (1988). Risk factors for adolescent suicide: A comparison: Adolescent suicide victims with suicidal inpatients. *Archives of General Psychiatry, 45*, 581–588.

Brent, D. A., Perper, J. A., Allman, C. J. Moritz, G. M., Wartella, M. E., & Zellenak, J. P. (1991). The presence and accessibility of firearms in the homes of adolescent suicides: A case–control study. *Journal of the American Medical Association, 266*, 2989–2995.

Brent, D. A., Perper, J. A., Moritz, G., Allman, C., Friend, A., Roth, C., Schweers, J., Balach, L., & Baugher, M. (1993). Psychiatric risk factors for adolescent suicide: A case-controlled study. *Journal of the American Academy of Child and Adolescent Psychiatry, 32*, 521–529.

Brent, D. A., Perper, J. A., Moritz, G., Baugher, M., & Allman, C. (1993). Suicide in adolescents with no apparent psychopathology. *Journal of the American Academy of Child and Adolescent Psychiatry, 32*, 494–500.

Bukstein, O. G., Glancy, L. J., & Kaminer, Y. (1992). Patterns of affective comorbidity in a clinical population of dually diagnosed adolescent substance abusers. *Journal of the American Academy of Child and Adolescent Psychiatry, 31*, 1041–1045.

Bukstein, O. G., Brent, D. A., Perper, J. A., Moritz, G., Baugher, M., Schweers, J., Roth, C., & Balach, L. (1993). Risk factors for completed suicide among adolescents with a lifetime history of substance abuse: A case–control study. *Acta Psychiatrica Scandanavia, 88*, 403–408.

Cantor, P. (1989). Intervention strategies: Environmental risk reduction for youth suicide. In *Report of the Secretary's Task Force on Youth Suicide: Volume 3. Preventions and Interventions in Youth Suicide* (pp. 285–293) (DHHS Publication No. ADM 89-623). Washington, DC: U.S. Government Printing Office.

Centers for Disease Control, (1988, August 19). CDC recommendations for a plan for the prevention and containment of community clusters. *Monthly Morbidity and Mortality Weekly Report: Supplement, 37*(Suppl. S-6), 1–12.

Centers for Disease Control. (1991). Attempted suicide among high school students – United States, 1990. *Mortality and Morbidity Weekly Report, 40*, 633–635.

Centers for Disease Control. (1992a). Tobacco, alcohol, and other drug use among high school students – United States, 1991. *Mortality and Morbidity Weekly Report, 41*, 698–703.

Centers for Disease Control. (1992b). *Youth suicide prevention programs: A resource guide*, Atlanta: Centers for Disease Control.

Charren, P. (1994). Improve children's television choices. In L. Lipsitt (Ed.), *Violence: Its causes and cures* (pp. xx). Providence, RI: Manisses Communications Group.

Erikson, E. (1950/1963). *Childhood and society*. New York: Norton.

Feindler, E. L., & Ecton, R. B. (1986). *Adolescent anger control: Cognitive-behavioral techniques*. New York: Pergamon Press.

Greenbaum, P. E., Prange, M. E., Friedman, R. M., & Silver, S. E. (1991). Substance abuse prevalence and comorbidity with other psychiatric disorders among adolescents with severe emotional disturbances. *Journal of the American Academy of Child and Adolescent Psychiatry, 30*, 575–583.

Gutstein, S. E., & Rudd, M. D. (1990). An outpatient

treatment alternative for suicidal youth. *Journal of Adolescence, 13*, 265–277.

Hall, G. S. (1904). *Adolescence*, New York: Appleton.

Hansen, D. J., Watson-Perczel, M., & Christopher, J. S. (1989). Clinical issues in social-skills training with adolescents. *Clinical Psychology Review, 9*, 365–391.

Hawton, K. (1986). Suicide in adolescents. In A. Roy (Ed.), *Suicide* (pp. 135–150). Baltimore: Williams & Wilkins.

Hovens, J. G. F. M., Cantwell, D. P., & Kiriakos, R. (1984). Psychiatric comorbidity in hospitalized adolescent substance abusers. *Journal of the American Academy of Child and Adolescent Psychiatry, 33*, 476–483.

Kaminer, Y. (1991). The magnitude of current psychiatric disorders in hospitalized substance abusing adolescents. *Child Pschiatry and Human Development, 22*, 89–95.

Kohlberg, L. (1981). *Essays on moral development*, Vol. 1. New York: Harper & Row.

Leon, A. C., Klerman, G. L., & Wickamaratne, P. (1993). Continuing female predominance in depressive illness. *American Journal of Public Health, 83*, 754–757.

Levinson, D. J., Darrow, C. W., Klein, E. B., Levinson, M. H., & McKee, B. (1978). *The seasons of a man's life*. New York: Knopf.

Lewinsohn, P. M., Antonuccio, D., Steinmetz, J., & Teri, L. (1984). *The coping with depression course: A psychoeducational intervention for unipolar depression*. Eugene, OR: Castalia.

Lipsitt, L. (Ed.). (1994). *Violence: Its causes and cures*. Providence, RI: Manisses Communications Groups.

Lochman, J. E., & Curry, J. F. (1986). Effects of social problem-solving training and self-instruction training with aggressive boys. *Journal of Clinical Psychology, 15*, 159–164.

Loftin, C., McDowall, D., Wiersema, B., & Cottey, T. J. (1991). Effects of restrictive licensing of handguns on homicide and suicide in the District of Columbia. *New England Journal of Medicine, 325*, 1615–1619.

Marttunen, M. J., Aro, H. M., Henriksson, M. M., & Lonqvist, J. K. (1991). Mental disorders in adolescent suicide: DSM III-R Axes I and II diagnoses in suicides among 13 to 19 year olds in Finland. *Archives of General Psychiatry, 48*, 834–839.

Marttunen, M. J., Aro, H. M., Henriksson, M. M., & Lonqvist, J. K. (1994). Psychosocial stressors more common in adolescent suicides with alcohol abuse compared with depressive adolescent suicides. *Journal of the American Academy of Child and Adolescent Psychiatry, 33*, 490–497.

Miller, H. L., Coombs, D. W., Leeper, J. D., & Barton, S. N. (1984). An analysis of the effects of suicide prevention facilities on suicide rates in the United States. *Journal of Public Health, 74*, 340–343.

National Center for Health Statistics. (various years). *Vital statistics of the United States*. Washington, DC: U.S. Government Printing Office.

Novaco, R. (1979). The cognitive-behavioral regulation of anger. In P. C. Kendall & S. D. Hollon (Eds.), *Cognitive-behavioral interventions: Theory, research, and procedures* (pp. 241–286). New York: Academic Press.

Potter, L. (1994, April). *Reducing the toll: Means to an end*. Paper presented at the annual conference of the American Association of Suicidology, New York.

Rehm, L. (1987). Approaches to prevention of depression with children: A self-management perspective. In R. F. Munoz (Ed.), *Depression prevention: Research directions* (pp. 79–91). Washington, DC: Hemisphere Publishing.

Reynolds, W. M., & Coats, K. I. (1986). A comparison of cognitive-behavioral therapy and relaxation training for the treatment of depression. *Journal of Consulting and Clinical Psychology, 54*, 653–660.

Rich, C., Ricketts, J., Fowler, R. C., & Young, D. (1988). Some differences between men and women who commit suicide. *American Journal of Psychiatry, 145*, 718–722.

Rotheram-Borus, M. J., & Bradley, J. (1991). Triage model for suicidal runaways. *American Journal of Orthopsychiatry, 61*, 122–127.

Shaffer, D., Vieland, V., Garland, A., Rojas, M., Underwood, M., & Busner, C. (1990). Adolescent suicide attempters, response to suicide prevention programs. *Journal of the American Medical Association, 264*, 3151–3155.

Shafii, M., Carrigan, S., Whittinghill, J. R., & Derrick, A. M. (1985). Psychological autopsy of completed suicide in children and adolescents. *American Journal of Psychiatry, 142*, 1061–1064.

Shure, M. B., & Spivack, G. (1988). Interpersonal cognitive problem solving. In R. H. Price, E. L. Cowen, R. P. Lorian, & J. Ramos-McKay (Eds.), *Fourteen ounces of prevention: A casebook for practitioners* (pp. 69–82). Washington, DC: American Psychological Association.

Sloan, J. H., Rivara, F. P., Reay, D. T., Ferris, J. A. J., Path, M. R. C., & Kellerman, A. L. (1990). Firearms regulations and rates of suicide. *The New England Journal of Medicine, 322*, 369–373.

Spirito, A., Brown, L., Overholser, J., & Fritz, G. (1989). Attempted suicide in adolescence: Review and critique of the literature. *Clinical Psychology Review, 9*, 335–363.

Young, J. E. (1982). Loneliness, depression, and cognitive therapy: Theory and application. In L. A. Peplau and D. Perlman (Eds.), *Loneliness: A sourcebook of current theory, research, and therapy* (pp. 379–405). New York: Wiley.

# 12

# Suicide Prevention in Young Adults (Age 18–30)

## Alan Lipschitz, MD

The rate of suicide in young adults has more than doubled since 1950. This paper presents some explanations for this rise and analyzes the diagnoses and population groups whose high rates of suicide contribute most of this increase. The factors leading to suicide are presented for each group, and preventative interventions are developed from the analyses. Groups that can be readily affected by suicide reduction measures are discussed, and methods for reducing their suicide rates are proposed.

Data collected over the last 40 years show that in persons 18 to 30 years old there has been a marked increase in the percentage of deaths due to suicide—even though in the older age groups, where suicide was formerly more prevalent, there has been a drop in the percentage of suicide deaths (U.S. Department of Health and Human Services—USDHHS, 1993). Figure 1 illustrates the age shift that is making suicide a young man's disease: by 1970 the suicide rate for the cohort aged 25–34 exceeded the suicide rate for the overall United States population (USDHHS, 1993). Men's suicides account for a growing fraction of the deaths in this cohort, and it is the young men's suicides that have especially increased during this period: Figures 2 and Figure 3 illustrate the steady disparity between the suicide rates of men and women.

There has been a marked shift in the methods of suicide used by each gender. While in the past men chose violent means—firearms, explosives, hanging—and women more frequently overdosed on prescription medications, this pattern changed as more women utilized firearms for their suicides, so that by 1990 guns accounted for 65% of the male suicides and 53% of the female suicides committed by 20- to 24-year-olds in the United States (Hollinger, Offer, Barter, & Bell, 1994).

Suicide is more frequent in people who are single, childless, separated, divorced, or widowed. Marriage does not exercise this protective effect in adolescents, however, probably because marriages in this age group are often markers of impulsivity or a need to escape from an especially difficult parental relationship. Losing a wife raises the suicide risk across all ages, but this effect is most pronounced in young men less than 34 years old. In this cohort the suicide rate in divorced men is 2 to 4 times, and in young widowers 12 to 15 times, the rate found in single men (Buda & Tsuang, 1990).

Groups that have a high suicide risk occupy the most visible pole of the prevention spectrum. Characterizing these groups is important for clarifying the factors that increase suicide, as well as for suggesting ways of locating high-risk individuals. However, intervention characteristics as well as risk define the groups that prevention efforts can reach most efficiently. Preventive programs have been developed for reducing suicide in the highly structured milieus of military, penal, and academic institutions. The suicide rates in these institutions may be greater (jail) or

Alan Lipschitz, MD, is Associate Director for Research at the American Suicide Foundation, Assistant Professor in the Department of Psychiatry at New York Medical College, and Medical Director at Value Behavioral Health.

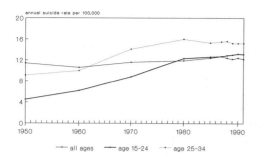

Figure 1. U.S. Suicide, 1950–1991. *Source:* USD-HHS, 1993.

less (schools, military) than in the general population, but their high degree of organization and regimentation simplifies the task of installing defined systems for monitoring and preventing suicide.

Mental illness and substance abuse are often cited as suicide risk factors; most reports estimate that up to 95% of those who commit suicide have such a psychiatric disturbance (Buda & Tsuang, 1990; Robins et al., 1959). Each psychiatric condition has its own characteristic presentation in this age group, and in each condition it is a different scenario that eventuates in suicide. Each offers special opportunities for suicide prevention interventions.

## MOOD DISORDER

Nearly 20% of the men and women with unipolar depression or bipolar disorder die by suicide, and patients with major mood disorders account for half of all suicides (Goodwin & Jamison, 1990; Hyman & Arana, 1989). In both sexes 20 is the median agent of onset; suicide claims an equal number of men and women with this illness, but marked sex differences characterize the age distribution. The suicide attempts and completions by women with mood disorders all occur within the first 15 years of its onset, while men's suicide attempts are bimodally distributed, with 60% occurring in the first 2 years of the illness, and the other 40% after 23 or more years (Goodwin & Jamison, 1990).

Earlier onset of depression is associated with a higher frequency of psychosis, and some investigators have found the presence of psychotic delusions to be a major additive risk factor for suicide (Roose et al., 1983), although other investigators have not (Black, Winokur, & Nasrallah, 1988; Coryell & Tsuang, 1982).

While most studies find that the suicide rate in bipolar I disorder equals the rate in unipolar depression, two out of three studies have found higher suicide rates in patients with bipolar II disorder (Goodwin & Jamison, 1990). Suicide rarely occurs during a manic episode (Robins et al., 1959), but mixed states of mania and depression are periods of high suicide risk, when the patient exhibits the dangerous combination of dysphoric mood, depressed cognitions, increased energy, and heightened impulsivity. This combination of factors may account for the many suicides observed in rapidly cycling patients and in those whose depressions have begun to improve (Goodwin & Jamison, 1990).

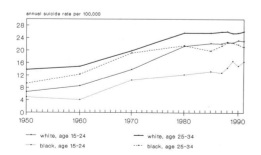

Figure 2. U.S. Suicide, males. *Source:* USDHHS, 1993.

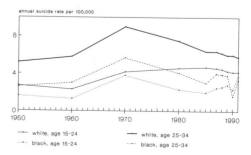

Figure 3. U.S. suicide, females. *Source:* USDHHS, 1993.

As in other psychiatric disorders, a history of a previous suicide attempt, unemployment, living alone, being unmarried – all elevate the suicide risk in depressed patients (Roy, 1982, 1983). Social isolation, bereavement, moving to a new home, losing a job, and other psychosocial stresses that precipitate depression have also been shown to precipitate suicide (Sainsbury, 1986).

Many investigators have noted the additive effect of comorbid alcoholism and substance abuse in raising the suicide risk in depressed patients (Fawcett et al., 1990; Fowler, Fogarty, & Young, Rich, 1988). Just as chronic substance abuse may foster suicide by increasing impulsivity or aggressiveness, environmental factors that facilitate enactment of impulsive behaviors can similarly foster suicide. Ready access to firearms has this facilitating effect – Brent's group (Brent et al., 1988) found that four risk factors accounted for 82% of the adolescent suicide they studied: bipolar diagnosis, comorbid substance abuse, lack of treatment, and the availability of firearms.

√ The presence of other comorbid conditions can markedly elevate the risk of suicide. Fawcett et al. (1990) prospectively found that the factors elevating the risk that a depressed subject would commit suicide within the first year after assessment were panic attacks, severe anxiety, diminished concentration, insomnia, alcohol abuse, and anhedonia; while after the first year three distinct factors were associated with suicide – hopelessness, suicidal ideation, and previous suicide attempts. It is likely that the acute pain of panic and anxiety propel the depressed patient to terminate what has evolved into an acutely unbearable state of desperation.

√ Medication is demonstrably effective for the acute treatment of depression and for preventing recurrences, but it is not clear if antidepressant treatment has reduced the suicide rate (Hyman & Arana, 1989). Demonstrations of the suicide-preventing effects of antidepressant treatment are confounded when primary care physicians prescribe lethal quantities in doses adequate to relieve anxiety or insomnia but insufficient to produce an antidepressant effect; this may account for the greater success rates reported from clinics that specialize in treating affective disorders. While more evidence supports the efficacy of lithium in lowering the suicide rate in treated patients (Goodwin & Jamison, 1990), a definitive prospective study to address this question has not been executed.

The proliferation of newer, safer, antidepressant agents – the selective serotonin reuptake inhibitors – now makes it simple to give patients adequate antidepressant doses without risking lethal ingestion of the drug. Yet the dangerous potential of mixed affective states should temper enthusiasm for these new agents and should spur caution in the diagnosis and treatment of bipolar patients. Physicians must consider the exchange of safety for efficacy when treating depression in the bipolar patient: While lithium or carbamazepine are less often effective than antidepressant drugs in treating depressed bipolar patients, these mood-stabilizing drugs are far less likely to induce dangerous mixed or rapid-cycling states.

These observations suggest a number of loci for preventative interventions, yet studies continue to confirm the finding that half the suicides consult a physician during the month prior to death, presenting complaints related to their psychiatric illness (Robins et al., 1959). Clinicians must be educated to recognize the additive risks conferred by comorbid anxiety, alcoholism, substance abuse, psychosis, and gun ownership. The primary care doctors who see these patients must learn to recognize depression, to inquire about psychosocial stressors, to ask about suicidal thoughts and plans, and to mobilize the patient and family to ensure prompt psychiatric consultation or hospitalization.

## SCHIZOPHRENIA

Schizophrenic persons have a significant risk for premature death by suicide and accident; this shortens their lives by an average of 9 to 10 years (Roy, 1986). Ten to thirteen percent of schizophrenic patients die by suicide; this is 10 to 15 times the rate found in the general population (Bleuler, 1978; Buda & Tsuang, 1990). While the suicide risk for male schizophrenics is greater than for females, schizophrenia may increase the suicide risk more in women (Black, Winokur, & Warrack, 1985; Caldwell & Gottesman, 1990) or in men (Roy, 1986).

The suicides in both men and women schizophrenics generally occur 5 to 10 years after the illness is diagnosed (Roy, 1982). Suicide among schizophrenics predominantly affects the young, peaking in men before age 30 and in women before age 40; the later age for the women's suicides reflecting the women's later age of onset for this disease (Black, et al., 1985; Black & Winokur 1988; Loranger, 1984). A severe relapsing course often characterizes the illness prior to the suicide, with one or two hospital readmissions occurring annually and the periods between hospitalizations growing progressively shorter (Roy, 1982).

Schizophrenia is the most frequent diagnosis in hospitalized patients who commit suicide. The suicide risk for psychiatric inpatients is highest in the first month of hospitalization, and half the inpatient suicides occur in the first 6 months. Most of these suicides occur while the patient is off the ward, elsewhere on the hospital grounds, or on a pass outside the hospital (Caldwell & Gottesman, 1990; Roy, 1986). The immediate postdischarge period is also a vulnerable time; Roy (1982) found that 30% of the suicides among discharged inpatient schizophrenics occurred in the first month, and 50% within the first 3 months after discharge. As always, previous suicide attempts are an indicator of increased risk.

Studies have found no treatment factor that distinguished the suicides, with no significant differences appearing in the frequency of outpatient visits, duration of the last hospital stay, administration of vocational rehabilitation and social work follow-up, or enrollment in day care treatment. Many studies find a high degree of social isolation among schizophrenics who commit suicide; most are unemployed, unmarried, and live alone, with little familial support. Many schizophrenic suicides occur under the stress of family conflict or interpersonal tension; the stressor that most often precipitates schizophrenic suicide is ejection by the family (Brier & Astrachan, 1984). Other stressors implicated in the suicides of schizophrenic patients are predominantly losses, real or imagined, of spouse, children, home, or job (Bolin, Wright, Wilkinson, & Lindner, 1968; Drake, Gates, Cotton and Whitaker, 1984; Roy, 1982, 1986).

Treatment with neuroleptic medication offers no assurance of safety, as a number of studies have found that schizophrenics received adequate doses of neuroleptic medication at the time of their suicides, and well-controlled studies have retired the supposition that schizophrenics kill themselves during psychotic exacerbations or in response to command hallucinations (Cohen, Leonard, Farberow, & Shneidman, 1964; Drake, Gates, Cotton, & Whitaker, 1984; Hogan & Awad, 1983; Roy, 1982). Most schizophrenic suicides occur during periods of relative remission of the psychosis, when the patients become crushingly aware of their impairment and fear more extensive mental disintegration. This may be especially true of the large subgroup of schizophrenic suicides who are white, college educated males with good premorbid social functioning, gradual onset of the illness, and high pre-morbid achievement expectations who grow frustrated by the disease and commit suicide when in their 30's (Drake, et al., 1984). Many patients in this formerly high-functioning group carry diagnoses of schizophreniform, schizoaffective, and atypical psychoses (Buda, Tsuang, & Fleming, 1988). Farberow et al. noted a similar phenomena in the excess of higher military ranks among the suicides that occurred in hospitalized soldiers (Farberow, Shneidman, & Neuringer, 1966).

The lower-functioning subgroup is characterized by severe illness with early psychosocial impairment, poor premorbid function, and chronic course with many exacerbations and remissions. These patients typically commit suicide when in their 20's (Drake, Gates, Whitaker, & Cotton, 1989).

The characteristics of those schizophrenics who commit suicide have been reviewed in a number of recent papers (Caldwell & Gottesman, 1990, 1992; Haas & Mente, 1994). While some studies did not find that depression distinguished suicidal schizophrenics from controls (Roy, 1986), others have found depression to be a robust risk factor (Caldwell & Gottesman, 1990; Drake & Cotton, 1986; Drake, et al., 1989; Roy 1982). have suggested that schizophrenics may experience feelings of hopelessness rather than typical depressive symptoms, and many investigators have confirmed the high frequency of hopelessness in suicidal schizophrenics (Beck, Kovacs, & Weissman, 1975; Drake & Cotton, 1986).

Farberow (e.g., Farberow, Shneidman, & Leonard, 1961) and others have suggested that our intensive hospital-centered treatment of schizophrenics may reduce their anxiety and depression in that context, without improving their capacity to adapt to the stresses they confront on facing the outside world. Their passes and leaves would then evoke feelings of anxiety and hopelessness about successfully meeting the demands of life outside the hospital. The patient, chastened by failure and painfully aware of his deficiencies, would harbor the conviction that life outside the hospital can hold only frustration and further defeat. The expectations of staff and family that the patient function independently would inhibit the patient's confessing his or her need for continued guidance and concrete support. Cultural barriers that prevent men from communicating a need for help may account for their higher suicide rate in this group, as in the general population. Interpersonal losses would strengthen the patient's conviction of the impossibility of finding help in the world.

These factors would explain the paradox of the elevated rates of suicide found both among schizophrenics who hold negative attitudes toward treatment and toward medication, and among those who fear hospital discharge, expressing excesses of dependency and neediness (Cohen et al., 1964; Farberow, et al., 1961). Both groups feel that the treatment they have received leaves them unable to contend with the demands of the world.

The quality and quantity of the exchanges that take place between schizophrenics and their families has a strong connection to their relapse risk, perhaps because the social sphere of the schizophrenic often constricts down to a small circle of concerned relatives. Methods for improving the family interaction of schizophrenics and reducing their suicide risk have emerged from studies designed to reduce critical "expressed emotion" in their families (Haas & Mente, 1994). Psychoeducational efforts directed toward family members could reduce patient suicide by improving the family's communication, fostering their understanding of schizophrenia, ensuring their continued acceptance of the patient, and alerting them to recognize the signs of acute suicide risk.

Measures to prevent hopelessness, isolation, and depression in schizophrenic patients should reduce their risk of suicide. Inpatients could benefit by the reassurance that after discharge they will continue to receive support, perhaps through their registration in day-hospital treatment prior to discharge. The provision of successful role models who share the diagnosis may dispel some of the sense of doom held by schizophrenic patients for whom the diagnosis is synonymous with the decompensated states of their inpatient peers; self-help groups and patient advocacy organizations may be good sources for such role models.

In recent years the biological treatment of schizophrenia has undergone a sea change with the recognition that some schizophrenic suicides can be prevented by aggressive treatment of akathisia (Drake & Ehrlich, 1985), by antidepressant therapy (Siris et al., 1994), and by electroconvulsive therapy of schizoaffective patients (Tsuang, Dempsey, & Fleming, 1979). The last few years have also seen a flurry of investigations of the abnormal serotoninergic mechanisms found in the brains of schizophrenic patients, offering the hope that the mechanism provoking their depressions might be found. A major advance has been the dissemination in the United States of the atypical antipsychotic drug clozapine; it has brought improvement to more than one third of formerly refractory schizophrenics, and it is clear that clozapine has marked antidepressant and antisuicide properties as well (Meltzer & Okayli, 1994). New classes of antipsychotic medication soon to be marketed in the United States extend the hope of better treatment for still-refractory schizophrenics.

## PERSONALITY DISORDERS

Suicide is the cause of death for 10% of the patients diagnosed with borderline personality disorder, and longitudinal studies find that suicide annually claims 500 to 600 per 100,000 with this diagnosis, a rate comparable to schizophrenics' (McGlashan, 1987; Stone, 1990). Most borderline patients who commit suicide are white, single, unemployed, 20 to 29 years old, and from the middle or upper socioeconomic classes. The borderline diagnosis especially raises the women's suicide risk, with the suicide rate of borderline women approximating the men's rate.

The most important comorbid risk factor is alcohol abuse, which doubles (McGlasha, 1987) or triples (Stone, 1990) the suicide rate. Suicide rates of nearly 40% were found in borderline women with alcoholism and major depression, and in patients who met all of the eight core DSM-III criteria for the diagnosis (Paris, 1990; Stone, 1990). Stone (1990) has recommended that clinicians remember the "four As" in treating borderline patients: to help them feel less *alone* and less *angry*, and to help them overcome *alcohol* and *antisocial* trends. He found that their antisocial behaviors lessened spontaneously

with advancing age, or with their acceptance of religious observations that fostered obedience to a strict behavioral code.

Patients with this disorder often engage in manipulative gestures, parasuicidal acts, and self-mutilation. While longitudinal studies do show that suicide is a rare event in patients who never perform these acts, such acts are not inevitably followed by suicide; among hospitalized borderlines, those "frequent" self-mutilators who made five or more self-mutilation attempts were more likely to report suicidal ideation, suicide attempts, and were more likely to report comorbid diagnoses of major depression, bulimia nervosa, and anorexia nervosa (Dulit, Fyer, Leon, Brodsky, & Frances, 1994). In borderline patients who have been hospitalized, the suicide risk is greatest during the 5 years after discharge, but even well after that time they continue to carry an elevated suicide risk.

One hopeful development in treating these difficult patients has been the construction of dialectical behavior therapy, a manual-driven cognitive-behavioral program of individual and group psychotherapy elaborated by Linehan's group (Linehan, Heard, & Armstrong, 1993). A randomized trial of dialectical behavior therapy administered for one year to parasuicidal patients with borderline personality disorder found it successfully reduced parasuicidal behaviors and hospital stays, both during treatment and during the 1-year follow-up period. Administration of dialectical behavior therapy to larger samples and continued follow-up will determine if this treatment does indeed serve to prevent suicides in this high-risk group.

Suicide claims 5% of patients with antisocial personality, which characteristically occurs in those who have comorbid substance abuse (Paris, 1990; Robins et al., 1959). Sobriety is the most effective tool for preventing their suicides. The fenfluramine challenge test, currently emerging from the laboratory into the clinic, may prove especially useful in identifying which of these patients have the highest suicide risk and are most in need of therapeutic intervention (Mann et al., 1992).

## ALCOHOLISM, COCAINE ABUSE, AND FIREARMS

While some authors have reported that suicide claims 15% of all alcoholics, others find as few as 0.2% dying of this cause, and Murphy has argued convincingly for a rate around 3% (Hirshfeld & Davidson, 1988; Murphy, 1992). Nonetheless, alcoholism is so prevalent that it commonly afflicts around about one third of all suicides, with the typical alcoholic suicide a depressed, elderly, married man whose suicide is precipitated by some interpersonal loss, job loss, legal difficulties, or financial trouble (Murphy, 1992; Rich, 1988).

Suicide is a late outcome of alcoholism, with an average of 20 years of drinking preceding the suicide, and few suicides reported in alcoholics less than 40 years old (Black & Winokur, 1990; Murphy, 1992; Robins et al., 1959). Years of drinking may be necessary to develop the symptoms diagnostic of alcoholism, but the epidemic use of alcohol, cocaine, and firearms by young people could account for most of the suicide increase in this cohort. The more recent studies have implicated the conjunction of these factors in the suicides of younger people: Brent's postmortem toxicology study of adolescent suicides found that from 1960 to 1983 the frequency positive for alcohol rose from 13% to 46%, and that suicide victims who used firearms were five times more likely to have been drinking than were those who used other methods (Brent, Perper, & Allman, 1987).

Similarly, Marzuk's autopsy study of all suicides in New York in 1985 (Marzuk, Tardiff, Leon, Stajic, Morgan, & Mann, 1992) found that 29% of those age 21 to 30 tested positive for cocaine, and 15% were positive for both cocaine and alcohol. Those suicides who used firearms were twice as likely to be positive for cocaine metabolites as those who used another

method. Cocaine was an especially potent social toxin among Puerto Ricans: The highest prevalence of cocaine metabolites detected at autopsy – 46% – occurred in Puerto Rican suicides age 18 to 30 (Marzuk et al., 1992).

These studies suggest that alcohol and cocaine could promote suicide in this cohort by fostering the use of impulsive methods, especially firearms. This disinhibitory effect appeared as well in Murphy's older alcoholic suicides; all were actively drinking up to the time of death – no suicides occurred in alcoholics who were in recovery.

The implications of these findings for suicide prevention are clear. Treatment of alcoholism or cocaine abuse, resulting in sustained sobriety, is likely to be a substantial protective measure. Interpersonal losses and major environmental misfortunes should occasion close scrutiny and close monitoring, with family members and concerned friends mobilized at these junctures to reduce the impact of social and financial losses. Patient's efforts at rehabilitation, sobriety, and attendance at Alcoholics Anonymous should be emphasized. The cognitive retraining promoted in Alcoholics Anonymous, its relapse prevention focus, and its ready provision of emergency support all counter disinhibited impulsivity, while the interpersonal contacts fostered there may help mitigate otherwise fatal interpersonal losses.

The exclusion of firearms from the home is a vitally important protective measure. Boyd and Moscicki (1986) found that in the cohort aged 20 to 24, firearm suicides increased ten times faster than other methods in the years between 1933 and 1982. While the issue continues to be fought tooth and nail, the evidence is compelling that the presence of firearms in the home increases the suicide rate of young people by fostering the enactment of aggressive impulses. Clinicians have long understood the importance of removing guns from the homes of depressed patients; this now seems equally vital for alcoholics and cocaine users.

New research techniques offer the possibility of distinguishing the suicides caused by chronic deteriorating effects of these drugs from those due to their acute disinhibition of impulsive behaviors. Newly discovered biochemical markers such as carbohydrate-deficient transferrin hold the promise of assessing even cryptic chronic alcohol use, while psychological autopsy studies can help characterize the early warning signs and terminal stressors in these patients.

## MEDICAL ILLNESS

A number of medical conditions have been associated with high suicide rates: Huntington's chorea, brain trauma, seizure disorders, multiple sclerosis, cancer, and active peptic ulcer (Black & Winokur, 1990). Major physical illness also raises the suicide risk in depressed patients (Robins et al., 1959). In the recent past few young people were afflicted with major physical illnesses, but this has changed with the epidemic spread of HIV infection (Beckett & Shenson, 1993).

AIDS is a novel illness that afflicts many people in this cohort. Marzuk's group (Marzuk et al., 1988) found that 12 patients from the AIDS registry of the New York City Health Department appeared in the 1985 suicide roster of the city's Medical Examiner, giving an extraordinary suicide rate of 681 per 100,000 for New York men who have AIDS – 36 times the rate of New York men aged 29 to 59 who do not have the disease. Most of the patients were profoundly depressed during the month prior to suicide. Most of the suicides occurred within the first 9 months after the diagnosis, and nearly a quarter occurred on medical wards. Subsequent studies of patients with AIDS have found age-adjusted relative risks of suicide of 17 for California men and 7.4 for U.S. men nationwide, with medication overdose the most frequently used suicide method (Beckett & Shenson, 1993). It is not yet clear if the high frequency of suicide in AIDS patients is due to depres-

sion, demoralization induced by illness-related stressors, or to direct brain effects of the neurotropic HIV virus.

## NATIVE AMERICANS

The 15 per 100,000 annual suicide rate reported for Native Americans in reservation states does not capture the dramatically higher rates seen in certain tribes, and in Native American male adolescents and young adults (USDHHS, 1991). These have extraordinarily high annual suicide rates: 44 per 100,000 for in the 15- to 24-years-old cohort, and 29 per 100,000 in the 25- to 34-year-olds, while the same-age Native American women's rates were 8 and 5 per 100,000, respectively. By way of comparison, during this period the annual rates for the same-age white male cohorts were 23 and 26 per 100,000, and 4 and 7 per 100,000 for white females (USDHHS, 1993).

The Native American tribes are a diverse collection of cultures occupying disparate geographic habitats, speaking a variety of languages, and varying widely in their values, social structure, wealth, access to care, and in their integration into the dominant culture. Suicide rates in this diverse population vary widely, ranging from 6 per 100,000 among the Chippewa to 130 per 100,000 among the Blackfeet (Group for the Advancement of Psychiatry, 1989). Traditional tribal attitudes toward suicide are equally diverse, and the circumstances under which it is sanctioned, if any, defy generalization.

Seventy percent of Native Americans live in rural settings, where more than half are nonfarmers who hunt, trap, and fish for a major part of their subsistence. Increasing numbers of young Native Americans are migrating into the large cities of the western and southwestern states, impelled by rural poverty, unemployment, and federal training incentives (Group for the Advancement of Psychiatry – GAP, 1989).

Until 1970, most rural Native Americans who attended high school were required to attend boarding schools run by the Bureau of Indian Affairs, where they were separated from home and family, and subjected to curricula that deprecated traditional Native American values and cultural norms. Separation, divorce, and family violence generated a high number of broken homes and led to the placement of many Native American children in foster care with non-Native American families. The social disruption they sustained was exacerbated by the stresses of poverty: defective housing, dietary deficiencies, faulty sanitation, inadequate medical care, and epidemics of tuberculosis, measles, and enteric diseases.

Alcoholism is endemic in many tribes and is fatal even in adolescents and young adults: In Native Americans aged 15 to 34 a death certificate diagnosis of cirrhosis of the liver occurs 10 to 14 times more frequently than in the population at large.

Explanations of the high suicide rate in certain Native American groups have focused on the stress they experience in relating to the dominant United States culture. Lower suicide rates are found to prevail in tribes like the Navajo, who have succeeded in maintaining a separatist cultural identity, and in those like the Cree, who have evolved a cultural, economic, and political integration with the dominant society over the course of their long period of contact. Both forms of adaptation allow these tribes to provide a supportive milieu that sustains identity consolidation in their young people. In other groups the separatist and integrationist paths have failed to prevent the disruption of cultural values. Concurrently, members of these marginalized groups have not been able to adopt values from the prevailing American culture in ways that preserve their social pride and personal self-esteem. The social alienation, identity confusion, and self-hate that they experience are reflected in their high rates of alcoholism and suicide (GAP, 1989).

This model suggests that a strong effect in preventing Native American suicides could be gained by fostering positive self-identities in their young people. Primary prevention measures that accomplish this objective include environmental improvements that allow for safe childhoods in families that are not disrupted by poverty, separation, illness, or alcoholism; the dissemination of positive role models; and the promotion of positive images of self and Native American culture, in the service of either integration or separatism. These trends are already well underway and are likely to continue.

## GHETTO YOUTH

A number of studies have found that elevated suicide rates are present in young, urban, African-American, and Hispanic men. Suicide among young African-American men has occasioned much debate since Hendin published his classic study of African-American suicide in 1969, but subsequent studies find similarly high suicide rates in other urban ghetto ethnic groups.

Among African-American overall, the suicide rate has been consistently lower than the rate for white Americans since at least 1920; in 1991 their rate was 13 per 100,000 versus the white rate of 20 per 100,000. Among African-American women, suicide is even less common: their rate is less than half the suicide rate of white women (Hollinger et al., 1994; USD-HHS, 1993).

However, Hendin (1969) noted that urban residence and young adulthood distinguish an especially high-risk African-American population, where a much different situation prevails. Across the United States, there were 3 white suicides for every African-American suicide that occurred between 1920 and 1960, but over this same period in New York City the ratio was 1.75 to 1.

Black male suicide peaks in the young adult cohorts: from 1989 to 1991, the annual rate was 16 per 100,000 in the group 15–24 years old, and 20 per 100,000 in those 25–34, versus white male rates of 23 and 25, respectively. These cohorts also have the highest African-American homicide rates: 137 and 103 per 100,000 respectively (USDHHS, 1993). This has led some authors to propose that these homicides include miscounted "victim-precipitated suicides," where unconscious guilt leads urban African-American men to commit suicide by provoking their murderers (GAP, 1989). Hendin's interviews of suicidal young African-American men, however, found them all too imminently aware of their aggressive wishes (Hendin, 1991). Suicide, for these men, was "usually the outgrowth of a devastating struggle to deal with conscious rage and conscious murderous impulses. . . . Suicide can be a form of control exercised by people who feel torn apart by rage and violence." He proposed that these intense affects originate from "early personal exposure to violence . . . in a violent family situation that produced identification with a parent or parental surrogate who was violent, self-destructive, or both." He suggested that these early affects grow especially malignant under the impact of white society's rejection of African-American people in the ghetto, which reinforces the young African-American man's sense of rage and worthlessness.

A similarly elevated suicide rate has been found among Puerto Rican men over age 17 living in East Harlem: 45 per 100,000 per year, 40% greater than the rate for white men in East Harlem and nearly three times the rate for men living in Puerto Rico. The median age for these suicides was 27; most were born in Puerto Rico and raised in New York (Group for the Advancement of Psychiatry, 1989). Other studies have found similarly elevated rates for Cubans in Miami, but not for Mexican Americans living in the southwestern United States (Copeland, 1989; Shai & Rosenwaike, 1988; Smith, Mercy, & Warren, 1986).

These observations suggest that the suicidal young African-American, Puerto Rican, and Cuban men in their ghettos share multiple risk factors with their Native American counterparts: they endure childhoods disrupted by the chaos of poverty, separations, and object losses; they

are threatened by the lure of endemic substance abuse; and they then face further demeaning, enraging, and demoralizing experiences as their ethnic identities, manners, and cultures draw scorn from white society. As in the Native American population, this oppression weighs most heavily on the young men, burdened by the mandate to succeed in mastering a hostile world. The 1989 GAP report captures their frustration: "If it is right that hopelessness is the key concept in understanding suicidal behavior, it is unfortunate that this hopelessness is being borne by the young, those who would seem to merit most the chance to achieve their dreams."

In the face of these pressures, no satisfactory explanation has emerged to explain why the suicide rate is not higher in the African-American men and women who labor against these impediments. Measures to reduce their deaths should focus on stabilizing their families, reducing their substance abuse, reducing the multiple childhood trauma that leave them unsettled, and on providing more experiences that affirm the worthiness of their culture and their value as individuals. As in the case of the Native Americans, our data cannot decide the question of whether these changes can best be effected through sequestration in separatist cultural institutions or through better integration into the mainstream of American life.

A fertile area for further study is the disparity in the suicide rates among Hispanic Americans of different origin. Certainly it would be important to understand the factors that protect Mexican-Americans and other Hispanic immigrants from the higher suicide rates of their Puerto Rican and Cuban-American peers.

## PRISONS

Suicide is the most frequent cause of death in U.S. jails, although it may soon yield this distinction to AIDS. Jail suicides occur at annual rates from 90 to 230 per 100,000, with the rate in county jails and police lockups up to 16 times that of the population at large (Haycock, 1993; USDHHS, 1991).

Inmates who die by suicide are most commonly young adult white males. Three quarters of the inmate suicides are arrested for nonviolent offenses; one quarter of the jailed suicide victims are arrested for charges related to alcohol or drugs, and half the victims are intoxicated at the time of death. Two thirds of the victims die in isolation. Over 90% of the victims die by hanging; half use bedding for this purpose. High-risk periods are the times when the inmate undergoes a major change in his status, when he returns to the facility from a court adjudication, when he receives bad news regarding his family or himself, and when he suffers some major rejection or humiliation. Psychosis, depression, antisocial personality, and substance abuse are frequent risk factors in this population.

Although effective programs for the prevention of prison suicides have been developed, these have not been widely implemented (National Standards, 1989). Adoption of these programs has been especially slow in the smaller holding facilities and detention pens that keep inmates for shorter periods. Many facilities, particularly those located in rural areas, fail to provide court-mandated routine mental health evaluations and treatment for mental disorders. Only 36 of the 50 states have promulgated voluntary or mandatory jail standards for suicide prevention. Only 12 of these state standards specify suicide prevention procedures; 8 include a suicide inquiry in their intake screening, 6 train staff in suicide prevention, and only 2 specify the characteristics of inmates who warrant continuous observation.

The growing size of the prison inmate population ensures that increasing numbers of young people will be exposed to this risk factor. The suicide incidence in jails approaches that found in psychiatric hospitals, and both institutions draw their inmates from overlapping population groups. Jails should be designed with the same suicide-preventing physical features that have become standard in psychiatric facilities: Inmates should not have access to bedding, fixtures, bars, and other architectural elements that can support the load of a hanging. Reducing the number of prisoners who die by suicide requires that each state implement programs that provide inmate screening and psychiatric evaluation, continuous monitoring of high-risk prisoners and those in isolation cells, and suicide awareness training for correctional officers.

## THE MILITARY

After accidents and homicide, suicide is the third leading cause of death among active-duty personnel in the peacetime U.S. armed forces. Studies find the prevalence of suicide in the U.S. Army, Navy, and Air Force to be 60–70% that in the same-age general population, after adjusting for differences in age, sex, and race (Kawahara and Palinkas, 1991; McDowell, 1994; Rothberg, Bartone, Holloway, & Marlowe, 1990). As in the civilian population, interpersonal loss, depression, substance abuse, and work problems are the major risk factors.

There are large variations in the suicide rates in different administrative departments; for example, from 1980 to 1989 the Air Force Logistic Command recorded an annual suicide rate of 32 per 100,000, while the rate in the Air Force Communication Command was 14 per 100,000, with lower rates obtaining overseas. No attempt to analyze these variations in risk has appeared – at least not in the published literature.

While the service branches have identified suicide prevention as an essential command function, each branch applies widely different procedures for training staff, screening individuals at risk, and responding to suicidal acts. There is no consistency in the postvention procedures they deploy to prevent contagion – a major concern in the highly enmeshed environment of a military installation.

Prevention efforts here should focus on implementing in all military commands uniform, state-of-the-art procedures for identifying troubled servicemen and women and referring them for treatment; the Army's detailed directive *Suicide Prevention and Psychological Autopsy* is a useful starting point that deserves to be emulated and updated (Department of the Army, 1988). Each installation should implement a consistent postvention program that includes a psychological autopsy and measures to limit suicide contagion. Commands whose suicide rates are exceptionally low or high should be subjected to special scrutiny to elicit the risk factors and protective factors that account for these discrepant rates, and this analysis should be used to direct remedial services to those who are most at risk.

## COLLEGE STUDENTS

Although suicide is the second leading cause of death on college campuses, it has been studied so inconsistently that its incidence can only be estimated very roughly (Silverman, 1993). Most studies find the overall campus suicide rate to be lower than the age-adjusted rate in the general population, and alarmist warnings of an epidemic have been effectively critiqued and dispelled (Schwartz & Whitaker, 1990). Nonetheless, there are disturbing reports of elevated rates in certain student groups and at some of the elite schools in the U.S., England, and Japan (Lipschitz, 1990).

Certainly the most striking finding is the elevated suicide rates of foreign nationals enrolled in American and British schools. This has not been studied since the 1950s, when foreign students were found to have annual rates of 76–86 per 100,000, roughly five times the suicide rate for their nonforeign peers.

Among nonstudents in this age group, most suicides occur in those with impul-

sive, high-risk-taking personalities, often with concurrent substance abuse. The college suicides present a contrasting picture; they are largely depressed, socially isolated students who do not abuse alcohol or drugs. These students draw little attention to themselves, but their lengthy residence in the monitored college environment offers the possibility that a sufficiently determined effort could detect the suicidal students and press them into treatment. Teachers, coaches, and dormitory counselors need to direct their concern not only at the disruptive students, but also at the quietly withdrawn ones, whose intellectual investigations of suicide may disclose their hopelessness and suicidal interest. Once suicidal students are detected, schools hold considerable ability to assure their compliance with treatment. The students are not well served by policies that impose automatic medical leaves and send them home, sometimes returning the now-stigmatized student into a chaotically disorganized family.

Postvention in this environment focuses on outreach to survivors and management of the information that is presented to the press and public about the suicide. Good postvention plans have been constructed for managing the acute disruption in campus life following a suicide, but few schools have such plans in place. Few suicides occur on each campus; any better understanding of this phenomena can only come from multicampus collaborative studies.

## PREVENTING SUICIDE

Of all the institutions that serve the young adult population, only psychiatric hospitals have consistently accepted the responsibility for suicide prevention. If prisons, colleges, and military bases were to adopt the comprehensive suicide prevention programs that have been tailored for these facilities, many deaths could be prevented. These institutional programs have four elements in common:

- The promotion of a facilitywide awareness of suicide as a real and preventable hazard, so that all staff members recognize a personal responsibility for detecting and referring suicidal prisoners, students, soldiers, sailors, and airmen and women
- The identification of high-risk groups who are given special monitoring and prevention services
- The provision of intensive interventions at times of special risk, with psychiatric evaluation and hospitalization readily available
- The preparation of postvention plans that are actuated after a suicide occurs, in order to prevent contagion

Impulsivity is a strong suicide risk factor in many conditions, and a major impact could be produced by interventions that reduce impulsivity and that render impulsive acts less lethal. In this young adult cohort, notorious for its impetuosity, measures to foster sobriety by reducing the abuse of alcohol and drugs would be especially effective in preventing hasty acts. Another layer of protection could be obtained by restricting access to firearms; this would be an effective tool for reducing the lethality of the suicide attempts that occur.

Improving access to psychiatric care and reducing its stigma would help reduce the suicide rate among the mentally ill. A still greater impact would be effected by educating all physicians to identify the suicide risks in patients whom they treat for depression or medical problems.

The treatments we dispense for depression and schizophrenia have demonstrated their efficacy in providing acute symptomatic relief in these conditions. Novel treatments for these high-risk illnesses should only be accepted when adequate long-term clinical trials prove them as efficacious in preventing suicide as are the reference treatments currently in use. Extended studies of large numbers of patients may be necessary if we are to discriminate which treatments are truly effective in preventing suicide, but the need for large-scale trials has not daunted evaluations of cancer chemotherapies, hypertension treatments, and other medical interventions.

Reducing suicide in minority ethnic groups presents a more difficult social engineering task, since poverty fosters so many of the factors that promote suicide in these groups—family disruption, early object loss, and ethnic self-hate. The legacy of chaotic childhoods haunts these young men when they leave home to seek their fortunes and to define themselves in a hostile world. Their suicide rates could be reduced by interventions that stabilize family structures; that reduce object losses caused by disease, drugs, homicide and unemployment; and that foster employability, self-esteem, and positive role model identifications. Improved access to health care, psychiatric treatment, and drug rehabilitation programs could directly reduce their major suicide risk factors. Here there is a clear need for research: both investigations of protective ethnic factors and outcome studies of service projects to determine which interventions are most effective in each ethnic group.

Medicine expends exertions massive and hopeful in our quest to prolong life and reduce disease, we embrace vast civil engineering projects that promise to enrich the material quality of our lives, and our society gratefully undertakes large-scale scientific investigations whose utility is a matter of faith. Measured on this scale, we do not lack the resources to execute the research studies and social engineering projects that can reduce suicide; we simply have failed to recognize the worthiness of this task.

There is little hope of preventing suicide so long as we avert our gaze from drug abuse, mental illness, and its other stigmatized antecedents. When we overcome this disdain, society can begin to mobilize an attack on suicide that deploys re-

sources commensurate to its great social
cost.

# REFERENCES

Achte, K., Stenback, A., & Teravainen, H. (1966). On
suicides committed during treatment in psychiatric hospitals. *Acta Psychiatrica Scandinavia, 42,*
272–284.

Beck, A. T., Kovacs, M., & Weissman, M. (1975).
Hopelessness and suicidal behavior: An overview.
*Journal of the American Medical Association, 234,*
1146–1149.

Beckett, A., & Shenson, D. (1993). Suicide risk in patients with human immunodeficiency virus infection and acquired immunodeficiency syndrome.
*Harvard Review of Psychiatry, 1,* 27–35.

Black, D. W., & Winokur, G. (1988). Age, mortality
and chronic schizophrenia. *Schizophrenia Research, 1,* 267–272.

Black, D. W., & Winokur, G. (1990). Suicide and psychiatric diagnosis. In S. J. Blumenthal & D. J.
Kupfer (Eds.) *Suicide over the life cycle: Risk factors, assessment, and treatment of suicidal patients* (pp. 135–153). Washington, DC: American
Psychiatric Press.

Black, D. W., Winokur, G., & Nasrallah, A. (1988).
Effect of psychosis on suicide risk in 1593 patients
with unipolar and bipolar affective disorders.
*American Journal of Psychiatry, 145,* 849–852.

Black, D. W., Winokur, G., & Warrack, G. (1985).
Suicide in schizophrenia: The Iowa Linkage Study.
*Journal of Clinical Psychiatry, 46,* 14–17.

Bleuler, M. (1978). *The schizophrenia disorders:
Long-term and family studies.* New Haven, CT:
Yale University Press.

Bolin, R. K., Wright, R. E., Wilkinson, M. N., and
Lindner, C. K. (1968). Survey of suicide among patients on home-leave from a mental hospital. *Psychiatric Quarterly, 42,* 881–889.

Boyd, J. H., & Moscicki, E. K. (1986). Firearms and
youth suicide. *American Journal of Public Health,
76,* 1240–1242.

Brent, D. A., Perper, J. A., & Allman, C. J. (1987). Alcohol, firearms, and suicide among youth: Temporal trends in Allegheny County, Pennsylvania,
1960 to 1983. *Journal of the American Medical Association, 257,* 3369–3372.

Brent, D. A., Perper, J. A., Goldstein, C. F., Kolko,
C. J., Allan, M. J., Allman, C. J., & Zelenak, J. P.
(1988). Risk factors for adolescent suicide: A comparison of adolescent suicide victims with suicidal
inpatients. *Archives of General Psychiatry, 45,*
581–588.

Brier, A., & Astrachan, B. M. (1984). Characteriza-
tion of schizophrenic patients who commit suicide.
*American Journal of Psychiatry, 141,* 206–209.

Buda, M., & Tsuang, M. T. (1990). The epidemiology
of suicide: Implications for clinical practice. In S.
J. Blumenthal & D. J. Kupfer (Eds.), *Suicide over
the life cycle: Risk factors, assessment, and treatment of suicidal patients* (pp. 17–37). Washington,
DC: American Psychiatric Press.

Buda, M., Tsuang, M. T., & Fleming, J. A. (1988).
Causes of death in DSM-III schizophrenics and
other psychotics (atypical group). *Archives of
General Psychiatry, 45,* 283–285.

Caldwell, C. B., & Gottesman, H. (1990). Schizophrenics kill themselves too: A review of risk factors for suicide. *Schizophrenia Bulletin, 16,* 571–
589.

Caldwell, C. B., & Gottesman, H. (1992). Schizophrenia – A high-risk factor for suicide: Clues to risk reduction. *Suicide and Life Threatening Behavior,
22,* 479–493.

Cohen, S., Leonard, C. V., Farberow, N. L., & Shneidman, F. S. (1964). Tranquilizers and suicide in the
schizophrenic patient. *Archives of General Psychiatry, 42,* 312–321.

Copeland, A. R. (1989). Suicide among nonwhites.
The Metro Dade County experience, 1982–1986.
*American Journal of Forensic Medical Pathology,
10,* 10–13.

Coryell, W., & Tsuang, M. T. (1982). Primary unipolar depression and the prognostic importance of
delusions. *Archives of General Psychiatry, 39,*
1181–1184.

Department of the Army. (1988). Suicide prevention
and psychological autopsy. Pamphlet 600-24. In
M. Moldeven (Ed.), *Military–civilian teamwork in
suicide prevention* (pp. 1-7 to 1-21). Del Mar, CA:
Moldeven Publishing.

Drake, R. E., & Cotton, P. G. (1986). Depression,
hopelessness, and suicide in chronic schizophrenia.
*British Journal of Psychiatry, 148,* 554–559.

Drake, R. E., & Ehrlich, J. (1985). Suicide attempts
associated with akathisia. *American Journal of
Psychiatry, 142,* 499–501.

Drake, R. E., Gates, C., Cotton, P. G., & Whitaker,
A. (1984). Suicide among schizophrenics: Who is at
risk? *Journal of Nervous and Mental Disorders,
172,* 613–617.

Drake, R. E., Gates, C., Whitaker, A., & Cotton, P.
G. (1989). The suicidal schizophrenic. In D. J. Jacobs and H. N. Brown (Eds.), *Suicide: Understanding and responding: Harvard Medical School perspectives on suicide* (pp. 183–199). Madison, CT:
International Universities Press.

Dulit, R. A., Fyer, M. R., Leon, A. C., Brodsky, B. S.,
& Frances, A. J. (1994). Clinical correlates of self-
multilation in borderline personality disorder.
*American Journal of Psychiatry, 151,* 1305–1311.

Farberow, N. L., Shneidman, E. S., & Leonard, C. V.
(1961). Suicide among psychiatric hospital patients. In N. J. Farberow & E. S. Shneidman
(Eds.), *The cry for help.* New York: McGraw-Hill.

Farberow, N. L., Shneidman, E. S., & Neuringer, C.
(1966). Case history and hospitalization factors in
suicides of neuropsychiatric hospital patients.
*Journal of Nervous and Mental Diseases, 142,* 32–
44.

Fawcett, J., Scheftner, W. A., Fogg, I., Clark, D. C.,
Young, M. A., Hedeker, D., & Gibbons, R. (1990).
Time-related predictors of suicide in major affective disorder. *American Journal of Psychiatry,
147,* 1189–1194.

Goodwin, F. K., & Jamison, K. R. (1990). *Manic depressive illness.* New York: Oxford University.

Group for the Advancement of Psychiatry. (1989). *Suicide and ethnicity in the United States* (Report No. 128). New York: Brunner/Mazel Publishers.

Haas, G. L., & Mente, D. L. (1994). Family factors in the assessment and management of suicide risk in schizophrenia. In D. C. Clark, J. Fawcett, & S. Hollon (Eds.), *Therapies for suicidal behavior*. Washington, DC: American Psychiatric Press.

Haycock, J. (1993). Suicide rates in forensic hospitals. *Suicide and Life-Threatening Behavior, 23,* 130–138.

Hendin, H. (1969). *Black suicide.* New York: Basic Books.

Hendin, H. (1991). Psychodynamics of suicide, with particular reference to the young. *American Journal of Psychiatry, 148,* 1150–1158.

Hirschfeld, R. M. A., & Davidson, L. (1988). Risk factors for suicide. In A. J. Francis & R. E. Hales (Eds.), *Review of psychiatry* (Vol. 7, pp. 307–331). Washington, DC: American Psychiatric Press.

Hogan, T., & Awad, G. (1983). Pharmacotherapy and suicide risk in schizophrenia. *Canadian Journal of Psychiatry, 28,* 277–281.

Hollinger, P. C., Offer, D., Barter, J. T., & Bell, C. C. (1994). *Suicide and homicide among adolescents.* New York: Guilford Press.

Hyman, S., & Arana, G. W. (1989). In D. J. Jacobs & H. N. Brown (Eds.), *Suicide: Understanding and responding: Harvard Medical School perspectives on suicide* (pp. 171–181). Madison, CT: International Universities Press.

Kawahara, Y., & Palinkas, L. A. (1991). Suicides in active-duty enlisted Navy personnel. *Suicide and Life-Threatening Behavior, 21,* 479–493.

Linehan, M. M., Heard, H. I., & Armstrong, H. E. (1993). Naturalistic follow-up of a behavioral treatment for chronically parasuicidal borderline patients. *Archives of General Psychiatry, 50,* 971–974.

chitz, A. (1990). *College suicide: A review monoaph.* New York: American Suicide Foundation.

nger, A. W. (1984). Sex differences in age at onset of schizophrenia. *Archives of General Psychiatry, 41,* 157–161.

n, J. J., McBride, P. A., Brown, R. P., Linnoila, ., Leon, A. C., DeMeo, M., Mieczkowski, T., My-s, J. E., & Stanley, M. (1992). Relationship between central and peripheral serotonin indexes in pressed and suicidal psychiatric inpatients. *Arives of General Psychiatry, 49,* 442–446.

uk, P. M., Tierney, H., Tardiff, K., Gross, E. M., rgan, E. R. & Hsu, M. A. (1988). Increased risk suicide in persons with AIDS. *Journal of the erican Medical Association, 259,* 1333–1337.

uk, P. M., Tardiff, K., Leon, A. C., Stajic, M., rgan, E. B., & Mann, J. J. (1992). Prevalence of aine use among residents of New York City o committed suicide during a one-year period. erican Journal of Psychiatry, 149,* 371–375.

owell, C. P. (1994). Suicide among active duty AF members 1980–1989. In M. Moldeven l.), *Military–civilian teamwork in suicide pretion* (pp. 3-4 to 3-71). Del Mar, CA: Moldeven blishing.

ashan, T. H. (1987). Borderline personality disorder and unipolar affective disorder. *Journal of Nervous and Mental Diseases, 175,* 467–473.

Meltzer, H. Y., & Okayli, G. (1994, in press). The reduction of suicidality during Clozapine treatment in neuroleptic-resistant schizophrenics.

Murphy, G. E. (1992). *Suicide in alcoholism.* New York: Oxford University Press.

National standards of jail suicide prevention. (1989). *Jail Suicide Update, 2*(2), 1–6.

Paris, J. (1990). Completed suicide in borderline personality disorder. *Psychiatric Annals, 20,* 19–21.

Rich, C. L., Fowler, R. C., Fogarty, L. A., & Young, D. (1988). San Diego suicide study. III. Relationships between diagnoses and stressors. *Archives of General Psychiatry, 45,* 589–562.

Robins, E., Murphy, G. E., Wilkinson, R. H., Gassner, S., & Kayes, J. (1959). Some clinical considerations in the prevention of suicide based on a study of 134 successful suicides. *American Journal of Public Health, 49,* 888–898.

Roose, S. P., Glassman, A. H., Walsh, B. T., et al. (1983). Depression, delusions, and suicide. *American Journal of Psychiatry, 140,* 1159–1162.

Rothberg, J. M., Bartone, P. T., Holloway, H. C., & Marlowe, D. H. (1990). Life and death in the US Army. In corpore sano. *Journal of the American Medical Association, 264,* 2241–2244.

Roy, A. (1982). Suicide in chronic schizophrenia. *British Journal of Psychiatry, 141,* 171–177.

Roy, A. (1983). Suicide in depressives. *Comprehensive Psychiatry, 24,* 487–491.

Roy, A. (1986). Suicide in schizophrenia. In A. Roy (Ed.), *Suicide* (pp. 97–112). Baltimore: Williams & Wilkins.

Sainsbury, P. (1986). Depression, suicide, and suicide prevention. In A. Roy (Ed.), *Suicide* (pp. 73–88). Baltimore: Williams & Wilkins.

Schwartz, A. J., & Whitaker, L. C. (1990). Suicide among college students: Assessment, treatment, and intervention. In S. J. Blumenthal & D. J. Kupfer (Eds.), *Suicide over the life cycle: Risk factors, assessment, and treatment of suicidal patients* (pp. 303–340). Washington, DC: American Psychiatric Press.

Shai, D. and Rosenwaike, I. (1988). Violent deaths among Mexican-, Puerto Rican- and Cuban-born migrants in the United States. *Social Science and Medicine, 26,* 269–276.

Silverman, M. M. (1993). Campus student suicide rates: Fact or artifact? *Suicide and Life Threatening Behavior, 23,* 329–342.

Siris, S. G., Bermanzohn, P. C., Mason, S. E., & Shurwall, M. A. (1994). Maintenance imipramine therapy for secondary depression in schizophrenia. A controlled trial. *Archives of General Psychiatry, 51,* 109–115.

Smith, J. C., Mercy, J. A., & Warren, C. W. (1986). Comparison of suicides among Anglos and Hispanics in five southwestern states. *Suicide and Life Threatening Behavior, 15,* 14–26.

Stone, M. H. (1990). *The fate of borderline patients.* New York: Guilford Press.

Tsuang, M. T., Dempsey, G. M., & Fleming, J. A. (1979). Can ECT prevent premature death and suicide in "schizoaffective" patients? *Journal of Affective Disorders, 1*, 167–171.

U.S. Department of Health and Human Services. Public Health Service. (1991). *Healthy people 2000: National health promotion and disease prevention objectives*. Washington, DC: U.S. Government Printing Office.

U.S. Department of Health and Human Services. Public Health Service. (1993). *Health, US, 1993*. Washington, DC: U.S. Government Printing Office.

# 13

# Suicide Prevention in Adults (Age 30–65)

Ronald W. Maris, PhD

Relatively little is known about midlife suicides, compared to adolescent and elderly suicides. A life-span model of suicidal behaviors is suggested as a heuristic conceptual tool. General midlife tasks and crises, as outlined by Levinson and Erikson, are reviewed. However, more than routine midlife developmental problems occur in most suicides. Some of the possible distinctive traits of midlife suicides (versus younger and older suicides) include: loss of spouse, years of heavy drinking, reaching the age of high depression risk, and occupational problems (including unemployment, inability to work, and retirement). Midlife suicide rates tend to be highest among white males, although female suicide rates peak in midlife. The paper concludes with a review of assessment and treatment issues related to a half-dozen high-risk midlife suicide types.

We have a problem right away. No one really knows very much about midlife suicides. Almost all of the empirical studies of suicide prevention have focused on adolescent and, to a lesser extent, elderly suicides. So, by default the comments that follow will tend to be theoretical or about midlife development in general.

Some of the basic issues that need to be considered in this paper are as follows:

- What are the various stages in the life span of the "suicidal career" (cf. Maris, 1981).
- Can one differentiate age-specific factors (here, midlife factors) in suicide and separate them from more diffuse, common suicidogenic factors?
- What are the major types of midlife suicides and how would interventions be tailored for these specific types?
- What is the optimum midlife suicide rate? (Note: *Healthy People, 2000*, 1991: p. 210, does not even have a target suicide rate for the year 2000 for people ages 35–65!)
- Do we really prevent suicide per se or is not suicide more like gradual, Darwinian life incompetencies that leave suicide as the only residual alternative?

A helpful conceptual tool for resolving the midlife suicide prevention issues just listed is to frame our inquiry in the context of a more general life-span model of suicidal behaviors – such as that depicted in Figure 1. First, this figure suggests that any suicidal outcome is a complex, multidomain, interactive effect of many biopsychosocial factors evolving over a fairly long time (usually 40 to 60 years). Second, there is a mix of predisposing, predictor or risk, protective, and "triggering" or precipitating factors in suicide. Third, there is an acute "suicide zone" that acts as a bridge to a threshold for suicide, but 98 to 99 out of 100 people in this suicide zone never complete suicide. In fact, most people who fit the general suicide model will not suicide at all; that is, they are false positives. People in high-risk suicide zones tend to get treatment and support (protective factors).

Fourth, there are feedback loops in the typical suicidal career. Most suicides cycle through the suicide zone to protective factors and/or further risk factors many times before they complete suicide. People in the suicide zone can also exit by way of accidental, homicidal, and natural deaths (with the latter being the most common

---

R. W. Maris is with the University of South Carolina.

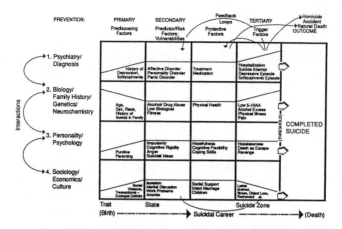

Figure 1.   A general model of suicidal behaviors. Not all possible interactions are depicted here. Relative height of line in each domain indicates approximate importance of those factors at the different stages of the suicidal career.

outcome). Fifth, the relative importance of risk factors for suicidal outcomes varies over the life cycle. Sixth, stages of suicidal careers are related to primary, secondary, and tertiary interventions and preventions. Finally, precipitating factors in suicide are more likely to be a gradual, nondramatic accumulation of many interactive risks; usually not the sole result of an intense, single negative life event or stressor.

The remainder of this paper is organized into sections on midlife development (general and suicide specific), data and empirical results on midlife suicides, midlife suicide assessment, and specific midlife suicide interventions.

## MIDLIFE DEVELOPMENT

Midlife is usually a time when power peaks. By age 40 most of us are pretty much what we are ever going to be (with a few notable exceptions). Erikson claimed (1950) that there are eight ages or stages of life (see Figure 2). In this model midlife occurred between ages 31 and 50. The main problem of middle age for Erikson was to be creative ("generate") or to stagnate. When early skills were not mastered, developmental debits tended to accrue, making later life-stage transitions more

difficult. Since Erikson's time the stages of the life cycle obviously have changed, especially since people now live longer and are on the whole healthier. Many critics question whether there are clear life stages, even with attendant developmental tasks, all progressing toward some ideal goal.

Most developmental social-psychologists have focused upon early childhood, not on midlife development. A notable exception is the work of Daniel Levinson (1978). Levinson claims that there are four life structure periods and three major life transitions in adulthood (see Figure 3). The midlife transition (a major problem for about 80% of all of Levinson's males) begins at about age 40 and ends at about age 60. At roughly ages 40 to 45 we need to make changes in our life dreams that will modify existing early adult life structure, to appraise the past and rid ourselves of our illusions, accommodate to other given

| 1. Infancy | (Ages 0–2) |
| 2. Toddlerhood | (2–4) |
| 3. Early childhood | (5–7) |
| 4. Middle childhood | (8–12) |
| 5. Adolescence | |
|    a.  Early adolescence | (13–17) |
|    b.  Later adolescence | (18–22) |
| 6. Early adulthood | (23–30) |
| 7. Middle adulthood | (31–50) |
| 8. Later adulthood | (51+) |

Figure 2.   Life stages suggested by Erikson's Eight Ages of Man.

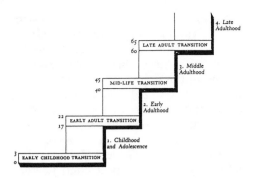

Figure 3.   Levinson's era's in the male life cycle.

life changes (such as divorce, job plateau-ing, children leaving home, diminished life energies, and job shifts), turn more inward and be less concerned with mastery or the external environment, and resolve four basic polarities (viz., young–old, creation–destruction, masculine–feminine, and attachment–separation). At midlife we need to modify our Dream and realize that success does not necessarily entail happiness.

Farrell and Rosenberg (1981) counter Levinson by arguing that midlife is a true crisis for only a few males (perhaps only 25% of all middle-aged men; Cf., Ciernia, 1985). Farrell and Rosenberg's work, *Men at Midlife*, is much more statistically and empirically sophisticated than that of Levinson. Looking at a representative sample of 300 midlife males (and comparing them to 150 young males in their 20s), Farrell and Rosenberg claim that there are four basic types of midlife males (differentiated by whether they deny or accept stress and are satisfied or dissatisfied with their lives): (1) antiheroes (an alienated group), (2) transcendent generatives (a healthy group in which family is important), (3) the pseudodeveloped (who are depressed and denying), and (4) authoritarians (who are dissatisfied and rigid).

Vaillant (1977) differs from Levinson, Farrell, and Rosenberg by doing a longitudinal analysis, in this case of 1942–1944 Harvard graduates. Looking at the mental health of the best and worst outcomes of these Harvard graduates at midlife, Vaillant contends that adaptive styles

(not especially stress levels) are critical to midlife well-being. The most mature psychological defenses (says Vaillant) are: suppression, altruism, sublimation, anticipation, and humor. Those Harvard graduates who did well in midlife had (1) married by age 30, (2) had more good friendship patterns by age 50, (3) were not dominated by their mothers in adult life, (4) had strong career identification with their fathers, (5) were not pessimistic, (6) had little self-doubt, and (7) did not fear sexuality at age 50.

In contrast to life-cycle theories, Baltes et al. (Baltes & Brim, 1979–1987; Baltes, Featherman, & Lerner, 1988) have edited a series of life-span monographs with important theoretical differences. For example, life-span theory is critical of the lasting effects of childhood experiences, tends not to study discrete age periods isolation from one another, considers historical factors in development, and allows for discontinuous developmental factors.

Of course, more than routine midlife developmental problems occur in the histories of most suicides. Suicide can be thought of as the ultimate in developmental stagnation. Some midlifers simply cannot negotiate the midlife transition. That is, they cannot survive their divorce(s), can no longer take pleasure in work, cannot give up the tyranny of youth – especially if they have nagging physical illnesses, recurring affective disorders, alcohol dependence problems, and low economic, emotional, or spiritual resources. Midlife often means that one must continue to live without the help of alcohol, work advances, or sexual acting out. Other midlife individuals kill themselves in part because they simply do not believe it is possible to change their young adult lifestyles and become viable middle-aged people. If you will, their "middlescence" does them in.

Almost none of the leading middle developmental literature has addressed the subject of suicide. Maris (1981) originated the concept of "suicidal careers." He argued that all suicides have relevant biographies or life histories. Every suicide is chronic in the sense that the etiologies develops over about 40 to 50 years. For example, repeated depressive illnesses and developmental failures tend eventually to lead to suicidal hopelessness. Maris (1991) contended that complex interactive multidisciplinary models with adequate samples and controls are required to understand midlife suicides. Robins (1981) concentrated on 134 midlife male suicide completers in St Louis. He claimed that the distinctive traits of midlife suicidal males were loss of spouse, years of heavy drinking, reaching the age of high depression risk, personal experience with other suicides, and facing debilitating old age without psychological compensations. The primary problems with the Robins, Murphy et al. studies are that the data were gathered in 1956 and 1957, were without adequate control groups, and were not empirically or statistically sophisticated.

Sainsbury also did early investigations (1962) of midlife males, finding a preponderance of occupational loss, drug and alcohol problems, depressive illness, and other mental illness in this age group. More recent studies of midlife suicides (e.g., Barraclough, 1987) have concentrated on simple, descriptive demographic traits (such as crude rates of mental disorder or economic factors). Alburg and Shapiro (1984) believe that a large cohort of young adult males (the baby boom generation) competing in the labor force tend to create stress for established middle-aged males and that the baby boomers will carry over their own earlier high suicide rates into middle age (Easterlin, 1980; cf., McIntosh, 1994, baby boomers and 13ers).

## DATA ON MIDLIFE SUICIDES

As with the entire life span, suicide in midlife occurs at the highest rates among white males (see Table 1). For example, white male suicide rates (ages 55–64, 1990) exceed those of black males by a ratio of 2.5, white females by 3.4, and black females by 10.8. Generally each additional decade from ages 25 to 65 reveals an increase in the white male suicide rate (especially in the 1970 data). Interestingly, the reverse is true for black males and females, with the highest suicide rates occurring in the youngest age groups (especially ages 25 to 34). White female suicide rates tend to peak in the 45 to 54 age group, then decline slightly thereafter. Indeed, midlife is the age of greatest suicide risk for white females (cf., Humphrey and Palmer, 1987; cf., Canetto and Lester in Part I of this issue). Kaplan and Klein (1989, Chap. 14) claim that female suicides do not fit developmental schemata like those of Erikson and Levinson, because those schemata are "phallocentric" or male biased. Kaplan and Klein believe that the key to understanding midlife female suicides is part sociobiological and part sociological. That is, female suicides have more to do with interpersonal disconnectedness and especially with mothering and nurturing disconnections (cf., Gilligan, 1982).

Figure 4 shows data similar to Table 1 except for longer time spans and for other age groups. Notice again that female suicide rates are at their highest in midlife and that male middle-age suicide rates are exceeded only by those of elderly males 65 and older. Also, note the largely silent increase in the suicide rates of both men and women ages 25 to 44 from about 1950 to the late 1970s (See Lipschitz in Part IV of this issue).

Unfortunately the empirical age group comparisons needed are not available, since for the most part specific risk and protective factors have not been delineated for midlife suicides. Maris (1981: Chap. 3, 1985) did apply Levinson's developmental concepts to a sample of midlife suicides in Chicago (mean age = 51) and concluded that a salient trait of midlife suicides is that their major life transitions tend to be abortive, and thus their development stagnates (Maris, 1981: 59). Midlife suicide is the product of accumulated developmental debits in the absence of live, work, and, in a few instances, of essential physical functions.

Table 2 reveals an interesting finding: Older (30 years plus) suicides were not differentiated from suicides under age 30 by

Table 1
Midlife Suicide Rates by Sex, Race, and Age:
United States, 1970 versus 1990

|  | Male | | | | Female | | | |
|  | White | | Black | | White | | Black | |
| Age | 1970 | 1990 | 1970 | 1990 | 1970 | 1990 | 1970 | 1990 |
|---|---|---|---|---|---|---|---|---|
| 25–34 | 19.9 | 25.6 | 19.2 | 21.9 | 9.0 | 7.5 | 5.7 | 3.7 |
| 35–44 | 23.3 | 25.3 | 12.6 | 16.9 | 13.0 | 9.1 | 3.7 | 4.0 |
| 45–54 | 29.5 | 24.8 | 13.8 | 14.8 | 13.5 | 10.2 | 3.7 | 3.2 |
| 55–64 | 35.0 | 27.5 | 10.6 | 10.8 | 12.3 | 8.0 | 2.0 | 2.6 |

*Source. Statistical Abstract of the United States: 1993* (113th edition). Washington, DC: U.S. Bureau of the Census, p. 99.

depression, hopelessness, use of a gun, social isolation, or seeing death as an escape from life problems (both young and older suicides were high on all of these suicide predictors). Also, almost all of the other leading predictors of suicide, except being male (viz., seeing death as revenge, unemployment, having a history of suicide in one's family, excessive alcohol consumption, having divorced parents, not achieving one's major life goal, dissatisfaction, irritability, low self-esteem, and making multiple suicide attempts) were more prevalent in the younger (nonmidlife) suicides.

One final midlife fact – midlife suicides generate large personal and social costs, through forgone social contributions and work products, aborted childrearing and marital disruptions, years of lost income, and so on. For example, the approximate lost income (1986 data) of midlife male suicides is about 31 (mean years of life expectancy remaining) × \$30,650 (mean income of 35- to 54-year-olds) × 6916 (number of 1986 U.S. White male suicides, ages 35 to 54) = \$6.6 billion (and in 1991 this is a cost underestimate).

## ASSESSMENT CONSIDERATIONS

Elsewhere (Maris et al., 1992) we have discussed 15 broad risk factors or predictors that need to be considered in assessing suicide potential, including the midlife age group. These risk factors are listed in Table 3. The reader is referred to our earlier book for operational definitions, scales, and instruments to be utilized in assessing suicides. Note that several of the risk factors in Table 3 peak or escalate in middle age; for example, depressive disorders, alcoholism, marital problems and divorce, hopelessness, (obviously) becoming an older male, stress, work problems, and waning physical health and energy.

One special consideration in assessing midlife suicide potential is that it tends to

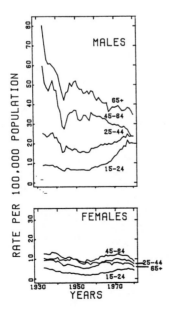

Figure 4.   Suicide rates by sex and age, 1933–1980.

Table 2
Comparison of Younger (1–29) and Older (30 +) Suicides,
Cook County, Illinois

|  | Young | Older |
|---|---|---|
| A. Young and Older Suicides' SIMILAR traits: | | |
| 1. Depression | $\bar{x} = 24$ | $\bar{x} = 21$ |
| 2. Hopelessness | 85% | 85% |
| 3. Most common method | Gun | Gun |
| 4. 0–1 close friends | 66% | 67% |
| 5. Death seen as escape | 90% | 82% |
| B. Young and Older Suicides' DIFFERENT traits: | | |
| 1. Percent female | 87% | 45% |
| 2. Death seen as revenge | 50% | 25% |
| 3. Working full time | 7% | 23% |
| 4. Suicide in family | 38% | 11% |
| 5. 3–5 drinks, when drinking | 36% | 19% |
| 6. Parents divorced | 45% | 13% |
| 7. Achieve most important goal | 0% | 61% |
| 8. Dissatisfaction | 73% | 42% |
| 9. Irritability | 75% | 61% |
| 10. Low self-esteem | 75% | 53% |
| 11. Only one suicide attempt | 29% | 68% |

Source. Maris, 1981; data reanalyzed, Maris, 1985: 107.

be invisible. For example, the middle aged are not as observable as the dependent young or the aged, nor are they usually in schools or institutions. Those of us in mid-life tend to be society's guardians, and accordingly are routinely not ourselves guarded. When the middle aged get into trouble, often no one is even watching or expecting it. One case example cited by Maris (1981) is Ernest Hemingway's routinely eating lunch in the doctors' dining room at the Mayo Clinic while receiving ECT for a serious depressive disorder.

Some subtypes of midlifers that require special assessment for their suicide potential are:

• *Executive suicides*, especially males who tend to be "control freaks," authoritarian, and rigid thinkers (including police officers; see Hendin, 1994, and the on-camera suicide of Pennsylvania state treasurer R. Budd Dwyer in January of 1987).

• *Menopausal females*, who may perceive themselves as having outlived or grown weary of their reproductive and nurturing usefulness or responsibilities (DeCatanzaro, 1986, 1992; Gilligan, 1982).

• *Younger midlife urban inner-city Blacks,*

who are often angry (rageful), drug and alcohol abusers, are estranged from their families, and are inclined to violence and impulsivity (Gibbs, 1988).

• *AIDS patients* (and others with physical

Table 3
Common Single Predictors of Suicide

1. Affective disorder, depressive illness, mental disorder
2. Alcohol and substance abuse
3. Suicide ideation, talk, preparation
4. Prior suicide attempts
5. Use of lethal methods (especially firearms)
6. Isolation, living alone, loss of social support
7. Hopelessness, cognitive rigidity
8. Being an older White male
9. Modeling, suicide in the family, genetics
10. Work problems, unemployment, occupation
11. Marital problems, family pathology
12. Stress, negative life events
13. Anger, aggression, impulsivity, low 5-HIAA
14. Physical illness
15. Repetition and comorbidity of 1–14; suicidal careers

Source: Maris et al., 1992: 9.

impasses and little future or hope; e.g., cancer and heart disease patients). Note that most of the physically ill do not resolve their life problems by suiciding.

- *The pseudodeveloped*, who tend to be stagnated and have accumulated excessive developmental debits, are chronically depressed, and are chronologically older than their achievements or emotional maturity (Farrell & Rosenburg, 1981).
- *Midlife males in crisis or burnout*, who have estranged adult children and spouses, are often substance abusers, and have work and economic problems concomitant with interpersonal and sexual problems (Levinson et al., 1978).

Of course, some of these midlife suicidal types overlap and one has to consider the 15 or so generic predictors of suicide discussed above as well as the more ad hoc characteristics of a particular midlife suicidal type. Many of these types of midlife suicide are poorly understood and are underresearched. One consequence is that some important types of midlife suicide may have been overlooked.

## MIDLIFE INTERVENTIONS, TREATMENTS, AND PREVENTION EFFORTS

Much of the treatment of suicidality at any age concerns reducing basic risk factors, such as those listed in Table 3, and at the same time embellishing and cultivating protective factors (see Maris et al., 1992: 660–667). This can be done globally and socially or, more commonly, on a case-by-case basis. The traditional approach to suicide prevention is to treat relatively ad-

vanced individual cases, not to attempt primary prevention of group risk. Refer back to Table 3 and ask yourself how each generic risk factor listed could be reversed. Obviously, some suicide factors are more treatable than others and also interact with one another in complex patterns. In a nutshell, these days one normally does a thorough evaluation and physical examination, gets a complete treatment and social history, then starts an outpatient treatment regimen of a selective serotonin reuptake inhibitor (SSRI) such as Prozac, Paxil, or Zoloft, or other antidepressant, etc., along with supportive psychotherapy. In many cases sophisticated polypharmacy (pharmacological "cocktails") is indicated. Faced with acute, serious suicide risk, the individual is often hospitalized and sometimes is given ECT series.

What about specific midlife suicide prevention? Given our "suicidal careers" concept, by ages 30 to 65 suicide potential or risk is usually well advanced (although acute risk waxes and wanes). Thus, suicide prevention in midlife tends by definition to be secondary (reducing prevalence) or tertiary (reducing disability; see Figure 1 in this paper) – that is, more treatment focused than prevention focused (although it does not have to be).

Interruptions in midlife suicidal careers probably (other things being equal) should concentrate on Levinson's relevant life-stage transition periods (see Figure 3); viz., on ages 40 to 45, and 60 to 65. In addition to dealing with specific diagnoses and conditions, treatment should help individuals adjust to the coming new demands of their next major life cycle. Much of the secret to life's persistence is appropriate flexibility. Shneidman (1992) likes to say

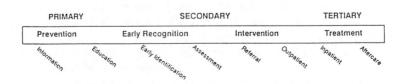

Figure 5. Generic prevention spectrum.

the "four letter word" in suicidology is "only" (as in, "It was the only thing I could do"), and Tim Beck emphasizes the cognitive rigidity of many suicidal persons (1992). If there were more pages available for this paper, we would also suggest in more detail how one might intervene in the specific midlife suicide subtypes outlined in the previous section.

Assuming that midlife suicide is a catabolic eliminative process, suicide prevention is not a goal per se. Rather, suicide prevention involves bolstering the atrophying life processes whose demise leaves suicide as the only (perceived) alternative. Like death, suicide really is not anything at all . . . just the dramatic absence of a viable life; a life devoid of ordinary work products, loving relationships, the ability to take pleasure in the common place, to avoid intolerable pain, or to be able to want to get up each morning and do something (anything). It follows that suicide prevention broadly construed is simply multifaceted "life support." This is a little like saying that panic disorder or anxiety is a rapid, irregular pulse rate, sweating, dizziness, etc. Although health is not just the absence of symptoms, it is not clear what remains of panic after beta-blockers or imipramine have removed the symptoms. In the same vein, probably almost no one would ever suicide if their intolerable life pain were removed or had the edge just taken off of it. (In Shneidman's terms, "reduce the psychache.")

In general suicide prevention should consider not just antidepressants and antipsychotics, but also diet, exercise (suicide as stopping moving), social involvement (e.g., being distracted from one's self, having others depend on you, care about you, etc.), stress management, education (in part so one can have meaningful work and attract lovers and friends), making enough money (which goes a long way in avoiding many reactive depressions), problem-solving skills (most of the time suicide is unimaginative and unresourceful, even stupid), and so on. One has to be careful here not to be naive. Sometimes there is a very specific ad hoc, ad hominem

illness, disease process, biochemical imbalance, etc., that renders life impossible in spite of having done everything else appropriately and having otherwise lived the good life.

There is more "bang for the suicide prevention buck" in broad (viz., social, economic, public health, etc.) interventions that focus on primary prevention (prevention of new cases or reducing incidence). Many of these broad social suicidologic interventions approach science fiction:

- Terrorists for mental health ("Your mission, if you decide to accept it, is to put Prozac in the water supply of every major city in the U.S.").
- Virtual reality surrogate mothers/lovers.
- Compulsory cognitive therapy for rigid thinkers (alternative = LSD therapy).
- Anesthetic water guns/darts for police, hunters, home protection.
- Male-to-female sex changes, if repeated ECT fails.
- Mint Paxil floride toothpaste with baking soda.
- Declare social isolation illegal.
- State execution for chronic suicide attempters.
- No buildings over two stories high.
- Substitute slow for fast suicide attempts (e.g., eating oneself to death).

Please do not interpret these interventions as capricious, whimsical, or out of place in a serious-minded scientific treatise. They all speak, albeit humorously, to quite serious suicidogenic factors – viz., neurotransmitter abnormalities, being unloved or unloving, rigid thinking, ready access to lethal weapons such as guns, the peculiar male proclivity for aggression and suicide, that suicides are almost always alone, environmental forces, the relation of suicide attempts to completions, that self-destruction is ubiquitous, and so on. It might also have occurred to you while reading these largely facetious interventions that suicide prevention is relatively easy. The problem, of course, is the cost. How much of what are we willing to give up to prevent suicide? It is possible, as in Huxley's *Brave New World* (1938), to imagine a society with a zero suicide rate. But few of us would want to live there; I would not.

# REFERENCES

Ahlburg, D. A., & Shapiro, M. O. (1984, February). Socioeconomic ramifications of changing cohort size: An analysis of U.S. postwar suicide rates by age and sex. *Demography, 21*(1), 97–108.

Balance, W. D. G., & Leenaars, A. A. (1991). Suicide in middle adulthood. In A. A. Leenaars (Ed.), *Life Span Perspectives of Suicide* (pp. 137–152). New York: Plenum Press.

Baltes, P. B., & Brim, O. G. (Eds.). (1979–1987). *Life-Span Development and Behavior* (Vol. 1–7). New York: Academic Press.

Baltes, P. B., Featherman, D. L., & Lerner, R. M. (Eds.). (1988). *Life-Span Development* (Vol. 8). Hillsdale, NJ: Lawrence Erlbaum.

Barraclough, B. (1987). *Suicide.* London: Croom Helm.

Beck, Aaron T. & Weishaar (1992). In R. W. Maris, et al. (eds.) *Assessment and Prediction of Suicide* (pp. 467–483). New York: Guilford Press.

Blumenthal, S. J., & Kupfer, D. J. (Eds.). (1990). *Suicide over the lifespan: Risk factors, assessment, and treatment of suicidal patients.* Washington, DC: American Psychiatric Press.

Ciernia, J. R. (1985). Myths about male mid-life crises. *Psychological Reports, 56*, 1003–1007.

de Catanzaro, D. (1986). In R. W. Maris (Ed.), *Biology of Suicide* (pp. 84–99). New York: Guilford Press.

de Catanzaro, D. (1992). In R. W. Maris et al. (Eds.), *Assessment and Prediction of Suicide* (pp. 607–624). New York: Guilford Press.

Department of Health and Human Services (DHHS) (1991). *Healthy People 2000: National Health Promotion and Disease Prevention Objectives* (DHHS Publ. no (PHS) 91-50212). Washington, DC: US Government Printing Office.

Easterlin, R. (1980). *Birth and fortune: The impact of numbers on personal welfare.* New York: Basic Books.

Erikson, E. (1950). *Childhood and society.* New York: W. W. Norton.

Farrell, M. P., & Rosensberg, S. D. (1981). *Men at midlife.* Dover, MA. Auburn House.

Gibbs, J. T. (1988). *Young, Black, and male in America.* Dover, MA: Auburn House.

Gilligan, C. (1982). *In a different voice: Psychological theory and women's development.* Cambridge, MA: Harvard University Press.

Hendin, Herbert (1994). Fall from power: Suicide of an executive. *Suicide and Life-Threatening Behavior (24)*3, 293–301.

Hendren, R. L. (1990). Suicide in the young adult and suicide in middle adulthood. In S. J. Blumenthal & D. J. Kupfer (Eds.), *Suicide Over the Lifespan: Risk Factors, Assessment, and Treatment of Suicidal Patients* (pp. 235–252). Washington, DC: American Psychiatric Press.

Humphrey, J. A., & Palmer, S. (1987, May). *Midlife suicide.* Paper presented at the annual meetings of the American Association of Suicidology in San Francisco, CA.

Jaques, E. (1965). Death and the midlife crisis. *International Journal of Psychoanalysis, 46*, 502–514.

Levinson, D. J., et al. (1978). *The seasons of a man's life.* New York: Knopf.

Maas, H. S., & Kuypers, J. A. (1974). *From thirty to seventy.* San Francisco: Jossey-Bass.

Maris, R. W. (1981). *Pathways to suicide.* Baltimore: Johns Hopkins University Press.

Maris, R. W. (1985). The adolescent suicide problem. *Suicide and Life-Threatening Behavior, 15*(2), 91–109.

Maris, R. W. (1991). The developmental perspective of suicide. In A. A. Leenaars (Ed.), *Life Span Perspectives of Suicide* (pp. 25–38). New York: Plenum.

Maris, R. W., et al. (Eds.). (1992). *Assessment and prediction of suicide.* New York: Guilford Press.

Maris, R. W. (1996, in press). The theoretical component in suicidology. In R. W. Maris et al., *Comprehensive textbook of suicidology and suicide prevention.* New York: Guilford Press.

McIntosh, J. L. (1985, April 25). Middle-age suicide: Sex and race differences. Paper presented at the annual meetings of the American Association of Suicidology, Toronto, Canada.

McIntosh, J. L. (1994). Cohort analysis of suicide: Baby boomers and 13ers. *Suicide and Life-Threatening Behavior, 24*(4), 334–342.

*New York Times* (1987, April 21). p. C1.

Robins, E. (1981). *The final months.* New York: Oxford University Press.

Sainsbury, P. (1962). Suicide in the middle and later years. In H. T. Blumenthal (Ed.), *Medical and clinical aspects of aging* (pp. 97–105). New York: Columbia University Press.

Shneidman, E. S. (1992). A conspectus of the suicidal scenario. In R. W. Maris et al. (Eds.), *Assessment and prediction of suicide* (pp. 50–64). New York: Guilford Press.

Vaillant, G. E. (1977). *Adaptation to life.* Boston: Little, Brown.

# 14

# Suicide Prevention in the Elderly (Age 65–99)

John L. McIntosh, PhD

Suicide rates by age are highest among older adults. Subpopulations of elderly adults at high risk are identified, including White males, the target of a Healthy People 2000 Objective. Several specific programs are described and a range of measures to prevent suicide in late life are suggested. These measures include primary prevention steps related to education and information dissemination, and secondary prevention involving early identification and assessment of the depressed and suicidal as well as improved referral efforts.

Pondering the topic of older adult suicide, Shneidman (1994, p. ix) suggested that "Suicide among the elderly is a double paradox. Why advertently end life toward the very end of it? Why the hurry?" These questions are indeed perplexing when attempting to understand suicide in late life. The findings of a study of college students (McIntosh, Hubbard, & Santos, 1985) imply that when the topic of suicide is mentioned, it is unlikely that death by one's own hand will be associated with older adults, but rather with the young. As suicidologists are aware, however, this general perception of risk is inaccurate.

Although the largest *number* of suicides occurs among adult populations aged 25–44 (with the highest 10-year group numbers for ages 25–34), the highest *rate* of suicide occurs among older adults (see Figure 1). For example, in 1991 (the most recent year for which official data are available; all 1991 data are derived from National Center for Health Statistics – NCHS, 1993b, or from advance data obtained directly from NCHS) Americans between the ages 25 and 44 accounted for 12,281 of the 30,810 total suicides. By comparison, the older adult population 65 years of age and above committed 6268 suicides (fewer than the total for the 25–34 age grouping alone, 6514). This apparent contradiction between the number of

suicides and the risk of suicide as measured by rates is explained by the size of the populations contributing the suicide deaths. Though elderly Americans represented 20.3% of the suicides in 1991, these suicides occurred among only 12.6% of the population (all population data for 1991 are from the U.S. Bureau of the Census, 1993). Therefore, suicide among the aged is overrepresented, that is, disproportionate to their numbers in the nation. Comparatively, young adults 25–44 years of age were 32.4% of the total United States population and their contribution to suicides was 39.9%. Once again, this young group is overrepresented among the national suicides, but not to the same degree as older adults.

Determination of risk when the sizes of population subgroups vary is more accurately portrayed by calculation of a suicide rate (the number of suicides by the group divided by its population size). The elder suicide rate in 1991 was 19.7 per 100,000 individuals in the population 65 years of age and above. The comparative rate for young adults 25–44 was 14.9 per 100,000 (with those 25–34 at 15.2 while the national rate was 12.2). Therefore, although contributing fewer deaths by suicide overall, the elderly population is at higher risk to die by their own hand. In fact, the suicide rate for each grouping

Address correspondence to the author at the Department of Psychology, Indiana University South Bend, PO Box 7111, South Bend, IN 46634.

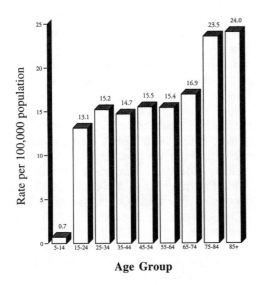

**Figure 1.** United States suicide rates by age, 1991.

combination, may provide useful information in the larger context of risk assessment and in conjunction with clinical judgment. Males are at considerably higher risk of suicide overall and particularly in old age than are women. In 1991 the suicide rate for elderly men was 40.2 per 100,000 population and only 6.0 among women 65 years and above. Additionally, whites in the United States as a whole kill themselves at higher levels than non-whites, and the same general relationship is true for elders of both groups. The rate for aged whites in 1991 was 21.0 compared to 8.3 for non-whites of the same ages.

When the factors of race and gender are combined, the relatively greater contribution of gender and the subgroups at highest risk are revealed. Substantially higher rates of suicide are observed for white elderly men, with a 1991 rate of 42.7 per 100,000 population. The nearest group rate was for elderly non-white men at 16.7, with white elder women's rates at 6.3 and non-white women only 2.9. This clear indication of high risk among elderly white men prompted the United States Department of Health and Human Services to include a mental health objective particularly for this group in its Healthy People 2000 National Health Promotion and Disease Prevention Objectives. Compared to a baseline rate of 46.7 for white men 65 years of age and above in 1987, the objective was to reduce the rate to "no more than 39.2 per 100,000" by the year 2000 (NCHS, 1993a, p. 47). While the 1991 rate shows a modest decline from the 1987 baseline, it remains, at the beginning of the decade of the 1990s, above the goal. As is discussed later, if the objective is to be realized by the year 2000, this important suicide risk group must be targeted for special intervention and prevention measures.

older than age 65 is higher than that for any other 5- or 10-year age grouping, including the often discussed youthful population aged 15–24 (1991 rate of 13.1).

Lower numbers of deaths notwithstanding, the more than 6000 adults aged 65 years and above who commit suicide each year represent an average of 17 older adults killing themselves each day, or 1 suicide death every 84 minutes (based on 1991 statistics). These deaths at or near the end of life represent premature and often preventable deaths. Following a discussion of older adults at high risk of suicide, current and potential prevention measures in suicide among the elderly are detailed.

## ELDERS AT HIGH SUICIDE RISK

Within the older adult population are subgroups that vary widely in their suicide risk. The most consistent demographic characteristics associated with suicide are gender, race, and the age of the group within the late-life total population. An appraisal of these factors singly, and in

As already noted, the suicide rate for each grouping of older adults above age 65 exceeds that for any other younger 5- or 10-year age grouping. Gerontologists (e.g., Rosenwaike, 1985) typically differentiate between the "young-old" (i.e., 65–74 years of age) and the "old-old" (75 years of age and above). These subpopulations of older adults are distinct in many ways, such as demographic characteristics, health, activity, etc. As can be seen in Figure 1, suicide rates are highest among the old-old (75 +; rate for 1991 was 23.6) and slightly lower among the young-old (65–74; 1991 rate was 16.9). The differential needs and suicide risk of these subpopulations have particularly important implications for suicide intervention and prevention in the future because the old-old subpopulation is the fastest growing among older adults.

Although no official statistics are maintained for attempted suicides (parasuicides), the elderly also differ in their levels of this suicidal behavior compared to other population subgroups. Distinct from completed suicide, rates for attempted suicide have consistently indicated peaks and high levels among the young. With increasing age, attempt rate data demonstrate declines to much lower levels among elderly males and females (e.g., Bille-Brahe, 1993; Kreitman, 1977). Therefore, older adults exhibit the lowest rates of attempted suicide across the life span. An observation that has often been made suggests that older adults who attempt suicide are more often "successful," insofar as their actions as a group end fatally more often than for younger individuals. Research findings support this contention. It is estimated from these results that the ratio of attempted to completed suicide is 8–20 : 1 in the population as a whole (Shneidman, 1969) and as high as 300 : 1 (Curran, 1987) for young people. By contrast, ratios for the elderly are estimated to be approximately 4 : 1 or lower (Stenback, 1980). One implication of this greater likelihood of death relative to the young is that taking threats of suicide seriously may be even more crucial in the case of older adults (see also McIntosh, Santos, Hubbard, & Overholser, 1994: Chap. 1).

As a final epidemiological issue, suicide rates for older adults have decreased dramatically from the levels of the 1930s. Although elderly rates increased during much of the 1980s, during the late 1980s and early 1990s they have remained mostly stable or have tended toward slight declines (see Figure 2). Future trends in suicide rates for the old are uncertain (McIntosh, 1992), and competing predictions of an arguments for both increases (Manton, Blazer, & Woodbury, 1987; Pollinger-Haas & Hendin, 1983) and decreases (Holinger, Offer, Barter, & Bell, 1994, Chapter 5; McIntosh, 1992) have been made.

While predictions of increases in rates most often focus on future growth in the size of the elderly population as well as cohort issues (see McIntosh, 1994), McIntosh (1992) contends that both near and distant future levels will depend upon many forces and factors, including future attitudes about aging, the old, and suicide; disease and health control; pain management; services for the dying and terminally ill; and economic conditions. Especially important will be the quality and nature of living in old age in the future. He contends the size of the elderly population alone will not be the deciding factor. McIntosh goes on to predict that even if suicide rates remain stable beyond the year 2000 (or even if they decline to levels targeted by the government objectives noted above)—that is, no change in risk occurs—the larger size of the elderly population will increase the *number* of older adult suicides compared to today's figures. Older adults will also comprise a larger proportion of the total U.S. population, with an accompanying increase in demand and need for services of all kinds, including mental health services. Future rate changes will only heighten or lessen somewhat the actual levels and number of suicides. They will likely not alter the probable demand and need unless measures not currently or widely in place are instituted for prevention and intervention with suicidal elders.

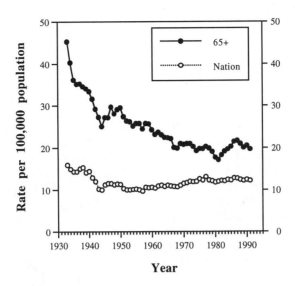

Figure 2.    United States suicide rates for older adults and the nation, 1933–1991.

## FACTORS ASSOCIATED WITH ELDERLY SUICIDE

In order to appropriately design programs to prevent elderly suicide or to intervene in suicidal crises, we must understand the forces that lead the individual to suicide, that produce what Shneidman (1993) refers to as "psychache," the cause of suicide. It is first essential to realize that suicide in all cases is the result not of any single factor, but rather of multiple factors interacting with one another. This is particularly true among older adults. Elder suicides often seem to be a response "to a total life situation more than to a single event" (Barter, 1969, p. 9). Older adulthood is itself associated with many of the more prominent forces for suicide in social, biological, health, and psychological realms. Almost necessarily an older adult will possess several high-risk conditions associated with elevated suicide risk.

The lifetime accumulation of coping methods, social supports, and other resources would usually permit the elderly individual to adapt to single factors and probably even the combination of some

factors. The breakdown or failure of these resources would likely occur when several conditions exist simultaneously and finally overwhelm or exhaust the person's ability to cope adequately. Individual levels of tolerance and resources are particularly important here. The level of psychological pain that can be tolerated is highly personal and will not be exceeded for some older adults at high levels of pain, whereas for others the threshold may be reached with many fewer stressors.

Briefly (for a detailed consideration see McIntosh et al., 1994), some of the factors that may produce suicidal behavior in older adults include: depression; alcohol or drug abuse or misuse; physical decline; physical illness; terminal illness, particularly associated with intractable pain; economic problems; social, psychological, and economic retirement-related difficulties; loneliness; social isolation; recent loss of significant others; and loss of independence. While many of these factors are common experiences in late life, each represents a potential target as part of a larger plan to prevent elderly suicide.

## PREVENTION OF ELDERLY SUICIDE

### Present Efforts: Secondary Prevention

*Intervention.* The vast majority of present suicide prevention efforts are directed at the secondary prevention level, including crisis intervention and therapy. It has often been observed that older adults generally do not seek, and therefore are seriously underrepresented in the clientele of, suicide prevention and crisis intervention centers, as well as general mental health agencies (Felton, 1982; Gatz & Smyer, 1992; Lasoski, 1986; McIntosh, Hubbard, & Santos, 1981; Redick & Taube, 1980). These programs, of course, are presently the primary services that are available in our local communities to prevent suicide among the population. The reasons for their underutilization by older persons are many. Explanations would include the lack of awareness of the existence of particular or general services, the conviction that such services are not intended for older adults, expectations regarding the cost of services and the lack of insurance coverage to pay for them, and general mistrust of agencies and institutions among the current cohorts of older adults. While elderly persons may harbor life-long negative attitudes toward mental health services in general, it is also true that the mental health delivery system has not emphasized elder care and is deficient in the number of professionals trained in geriatric areas or specialties (Santos & VandenBos, 1982).

Mercer (1989) conducted a national survey of suicide prevention resources for the elderly that revealed virtually no programs specifically established or designed for older adults. Only two suicide prevention/crisis agencies were identified that had such an objective (one in San Francisco, CA, and another in Dayton, OH). The two programs included components to confront the special problems of older adulthood and suicide (brief descriptions of these programs appear below). Although additional services to deal with elderly suicide have since been established (e.g., see Link-Plus below), the number remains small and the need is met only in a limited number of locations. It should be stressed that innovative programs will be required to reach elders who are at high risk but who do not typically use mental health services, if they are to be provided effective services.

A program developed after Mercer's survey is Link-Plus of Life Crisis Services, a St. Louis crisis intervention center. Link-Plus approaches the problem of older adult suicide largely from a conventional suicide prevention scheme but also provides a service specifically designed for and targeted to depressed elderly persons. The Link-Plus program uses traditional crisis intervention by phone. A benefit of this program is that this model is one already familiar to crisis centers. Therefore, it simply builds on skills and services most centers already provide, is cost-efficient, and is readily adopted within existing crisis center frameworks.

As commonly seen in other crisis intervention services, elderly clients (aged 60 and above) represent only approximately 3% of Life Crisis' general crisis intervention callers, despite widespread publicity of the hotline. Thus, the Link-Plus program was developed for intervention in immediate suicidal and other crises, but more descriptively and accurately, it functions as a general telephone case management program for depressed elders. Trained case managers/crisis center personnel assess the caller's physical, psychosocial, and mental health needs, and match them with community services. Following the coordination and establishment of links to agencies, availability continues to supportive counseling and problem-solving services. Ongoing telephone contact and monitoring of the client are maintained until the case manager determines them unnecessary.

The identification and referral of elderly clients for Link-Plus are made from Life Crisis hotline calls, community professionals, hospitals, and home health care agencies. Those referred to Link-Plus are most often depressed, lonely elderly persons who live alone. Typically, the clients are in contact with Link-Plus for 5 to 6 months (L. Judy, Executive Director of Life Crisis Services, personal communication, October 14, 1993).

*Early Identification.* A few programs that identify elders at risk for suicide and provide a range of services have been established. Each of these programs is a possible model for intervening with actively or potentially depressed or suicidal older adults. The Center for Elderly Suicide Prevention and Grief Related Services originated as part of the San Francisco Suicide Prevention Center. The services include two components within its Geriatric Program related to suicide intervention. This multifaceted and innovative center serves clients 60 years of age and above. One of its programs, the Friendship Line, is primarily for 24-hour crisis intervention as well as referrals and information for elders or those who call on their behalf. The telephone line functions much as any crisis intervention line, except that its advertised mission is to serve the older adult population. It is assumed that this should increase the likelihood that older adults will contact the service. For other suicide prevention and crisis intervention services, as few as 1–2% of the callers are above age 60 (e.g., McIntosh et al., 1981). During the fiscal year 1991–1992 this program, specifically for the elderly, received 8300 calls, (1254 were first-time users). Callers talk to professionally trained and supervised volunteers who provide 24-hour emotional support and human contact. It is likely that most of these callers would not contact traditional crisis intervention services.

A second component of the center's services involves the Geriatric Outreach Program that provides ongoing home visits and telephone contact to those elderly who are isolated or homebound. In fiscal year 1991–1992 the center made 14,385 calls to or on behalf of clients and 779 home visits. This component deals with the social circumstances that are often present for suicidal elders, such as living alone or in social isolation. It also provides a procedure to confront the infrequent use of traditional inpatient or outpatient mental health services. Volunteers who provide this service receive gerontological training, and, consistent with the Friendship Line approach, emotional support and counseling are the emphasis of contacts.

The Geriatric Outreach Program also calls to remind elders to take their medications on schedule. The older adult can also arrange to call the center daily, and if they fail to call, a physician or the police are alerted. Elders who are changing their residence may request a volunteer to assist with their move and to provide emotional support at this stressful time. Finally, older clients can obtain a volunteer as their advocate in negotiations with social service agencies or health care providers, or to express concerns to their families or physician. This latter service may be especially useful because the current cohort of older adults appears to be reluctant to question their physician or ask for second opinions for fear of offending or being perceived as rude.

Another program that includes strong elements of early identification, as well as the provision of intervention services, utilizes a different model of outreach, service delivery, and crisis intervention than the San Francisco program. Older adults with mental health problems who are referred by any source to the Spokane Community Mental Health Center receive an in-home evaluation in which information crucial to assessment, case management, and treatment is gathered by trained staff. Crisis intervention is available around the clock as well. The most unusual aspect of this approach for elderly suicide prevention is its Gatekeepers Program (see also Raschko, 1990). Responding to the well-established lack of self-referrals by older adults noted above, the cooperation of businesses and other organizations whose employees are in frequent contact with older adults, and especially isolated elders, has been obtained. Employees are given special training to recognize the signs and symptoms associated with a need for help and to refer such cases to Elderly Services. The diversity of gatekeepers involved is impressive and should increase the likelihood of recognition and subsequent referral. The gatekeepers include fuel oil dealers; bank and cable TV personnel; fire, police, and ambulance personnel; meter readers, credit, and repair personnel for power, electric, and gas utilities; managers and owners of apartments and mobile homes; appraisers with the tax assessor's office; pharmacists, telephone, and taxi personnel. In rural areas of the county there are also mail and newspaper carriers, grain and farm utility dealers, telephone company personnel, and ministers.

As an indication of the effectiveness of the Gatekeepers Program (R. Raschko, Director of Elderly Services, personal communication, June 25, 1992), 49% of the referrals of suicidal elders to Elderly Services during the first 6 months of 1991 were from gatekeepers. During this time 86 suicidal older adults were referred, 42 of whom were referred by gatekeepers (24% referred by hospitals and physicians, 14% by relatives, 13% by social agencies). It is possible that without the gatekeepers program these 42 suicidal elderly might not have been recognized, referred, or helped, and some might have died by suicide.

The Dayton, Ohio, Suicide Prevention Center independently developed its own Gatekeeper Program. Program offerings include a training videotape and manual designed to educate the staff of nursing homes regarding recognition of depressed and suicidal older adults. The videotape and manual may be purchased but are also loaned on request to area nursing homes (Mercer, 1992, p. 436). This resource targets another group of high-risk elders.

In addition to specific programmatic approaches, several possible changes that might improve the delivery and nature of intervention resources have been advanced. Prominent among these has been the emergence of new methods to identify and assist suicidal and troubled older persons. This might be achieved by "buddy system" phone calls and visits, or using senior centers in order to achieve early identification and referral of the potentially suicidal. It has often been suggested that older adults do not call or use crisis and suicide prevention centers because they do not identify with the service or the service providers. If true, recruiting and employing elders in these centers may increase identification and contacts. Establishing separate crisis intervention or suicide prevention centers for older adults may also prove to be an effective alternative (such as the programs described above). Any comprehensive service delivery system for the elderly, however, must include a well-organized, active outreach component with properly trained personnel who are able to identify and assist older suicidal persons. Outreach workers may need to recommend a variety of services, provide transportation to such services, or perhaps even arrange for home-based delivery of mental health services to the elderly. A similar approach has also been suggested as a model for the provision of intervention services. Support would be provided by physically traveling to the elderly person in crisis rather than requiring that the elder travel to a service site with a formal appointment. This approach, as in Alcoholics Anonymous, might utilize those who have previously been in the same circumstances (i.e., the previously suicidal). The older person in trouble may turn in time of crisis and suicidal ideation to someone with whom they identify.

Finally, an aspect of therapy that might increase its overall effectiveness involves including family members in therapy plans for elderly individuals and providing support and other training services for family caregivers of depressed older adults (similar to the case of family caregivers of those with Alzheimer's disease— see Hinrichsen, Hernandez, & Pollack, 1992; Parmelee & Katz, 1992). Interactions with depressed individuals are often difficult for those with full-time or continuing involvement. As a result, caregivers may themselves become depressed or feel overwhelmed. Support of these caregivers may not only contribute to improved care of the depressed elder but at the same time may lessen possible mental health problems among caregivers (thus, simultaneously accomplishing both secondary and primary prevention as well as potential elimination of the need for eventual tertiary prevention).

## Primary Prevention

*Information, Education, Training.* Education and training are a crucial aspect of any successful suicide prevention effort for older adults (McIntosh, 1987a). This education should be provided to the lay public, of course, and particularly those who are frequently in contact with the aged in a variety of settings. Some of the target groups include mental health professionals, health care providers (doctors, nurses, orderlies), emergency (EMTs, firefighters) and law enforcement personnel, and clergy. Of special importance would be programs for nursing home administrators and staff, senior center personnel and volunteers, nutrition center staff and Meals on Wheels volunteers, social services personnel, and those in a variety of disciplines that work with the elderly (for example, the AARP and the American Association of Suicidology developed a brochure addressing elderly suicide that is targeted for distribution to volunteers such as those who provide Meals on Wheels – McIntosh, 1993). Funeral directors should also be included as a target group since they routinely encounter the bereaved, including the survivors of suicide.

It is essential that the education and training of new professionals and volunteers in these various fields include information about suicide and aging. At the same time, provision of continuing education to those professionals who have already completed their formal training and

are working with older persons should not be overlooked. The precise depth of coverage and the inclusion of training in intervention and therapy (the latter predominantly for mental health professionals) will vary somewhat among the various disciplines involved in geriatric work, but all training should include basic aspects of suicide education (Farberow, 1969; Heilig, 1970; Maris et al., 1973) and some basic training in gerontology.

Core education and training content should include several components if it is to effectively prepare professionals and others to deal with the complex, multifactor phenomenon of elderly suicide. McIntosh (1987a) detailed such a core curriculum. A brief description of these components would include: (1) eliminating dangerous and erroneous myths about suicide and suicidal behavior; (2) discussing the identification of suicidal persons, in terms of both demographic and situational factors that are associated with high risk, and also the cognitive and other components that are important for an understanding of suicides (e.g., Shneidman, 1985); (3) training to recognize warning signs and clues to suicide (e.g., Shneidman, 1965); (4) teaching the assessment of potential lethality as a part of assessing suicidal risk; (5) conveying the availability and existence of community resources to which referrals may be made; (6) increasing awareness and knowledge of the variety of suicidal behaviors that may be exhibited by the elderly, including both direct and indirect self-destructive behaviors; and (7) sensitizing professionals to the problems associated with suicide survivorship at all ages, including possible effects that the suicide death of a loved one might produce in terms of bereavement and grief, the possibility of suicide by bereaved individuals, and the existence of community resources for the bereaved (often via bereavement support groups). A final component of such education would provide accurate knowledge about aging and old age as a basis for which the experiences and problems of suicidal elders might be compared. The development and implementation of suicide education programs would certainly offer a significant possibility for reducing the number of elders who take their own lives. Bennett (1967, p. 175), for instance, estimated that educating the public as well as professionals to recognize suicidal persons and to be knowledgeable about community resources could prevent as many as 50% of all self-destructive acts.

Meeting several of these goals, a specific program was developed for educating the general public by Pratt, Schmall, Wilson, and Benthin (1991). A 3-hour workshop was designed to convey circumstances related to depression, myths and warning signs of suicide and depression, and proper responses when depressive or suicidal inclinations are observed in an older adult. The workshop materials are presented in a film or multimedia fashion to be followed by discussion. Pratt et al. present the results of program evaluation as well for this curriculum material. The workshop is available for purchase.

*Primary Prevention and Factors in Elderly Suicide.* Primary prevention measures (similar to present interventive services) are suggested almost directly by the motivations and factors that are associated with elderly suicidal ideation and behavior. If these potential motivations were confronted early or if the conditions they represent were eliminated prior to the emergence of depression or suicidal behavior, then primary prevention would be achieved.

Health and physical factors are more often present in the suicides and suicide attempts of older adults than those of younger ages (e.g., Chynoweth, 1981; Conwell, Rotenberg, & Caine, 1990; Lyness, Conwell, & Nelson, 1992; Sainsbury, 1962; Sendbuehler & Goldstein, 1977). Regular medical examinations and early detection and treatment of even minor health problems may lessen or prevent health concerns and potential resultant depression and/or suicidal behaviors. It is, of course, essential that good medical care be accessible, available, and affordable. Regular exercise and physical activities such as sports and recreation may also improve overall physical health and functioning. The effectiveness of such programs is increased if instituted earlier in life and maintained through old age. It is clear, however, that even exercise programs begun in late life, in consultation with a physician, can have a beneficial effect for older adults.

Economic losses and related problems among the old may be lessened in a number of ways. Welfare programs do not eliminate all problems, but the availability of programmatic financial support for the aged, along with benefits that may be available to all citizens, may reduce the impact of economic factors associated with elderly suicide. Careful financial planning, savings plans for late life and retirement, and the availability of affordable catastrophic or long-term care insurance for elders would relieve some economic as well as psychological burdens on older adults who experience poor health.

Social and role losses as factors in suicide are also amenable to change. Encouragement to remain active in occupational roles as long as one is able and desires to do so, could diminish work role losses, particularly among elderly males. Relatedly, programs assisting the development of second careers, finding new roles that encourage feelings of worth and importance, and long-range emotional and economic planning for retirement, could potentially combat role losses and changes in old age.

The loss of people in the lives of older adults, both family and other relationships, is a particularly important factor in suicide. Interpersonal loss often produces loneliness, isolation, and a general lessening of social contacts and one's social network. Measures to combat these elements might include: encouraging and maintaining close family ties among living relatives, becoming involved or continuing involvement in community groups and organizations, and "recruiting" significant others on behalf of older adults, along with referral to local bereavement support and therapy resources.

Other societal and community measures that may also lower the number of elderly suicides might include more careful and responsible prescribing and dispensing of medications. Similarly, better-controlled and lessened availability of other lethal methods of suicide such as firearms would probably have an important effect. Vigorous and effective treatment and prevention of alcohol abuse and alcoholism as well as depression should be incorporated into any large-scale prevention programs to reduce geriatric suicide. Rabins (1992), for instance, has suggested that the prevention of mental health problems of older adults could be improved through more effective use of present resources and the promotion of improved communication between practitioners in the medical and mental health professions.

Although only approximately 5% of the elderly population at any one time resides in institutional settings, the risk of institutionalization for some period of time is much higher (e.g., Palmore, 1977). Osgood, Brant, and Lipman (1991) determined from a national survey that various forms of suicidal behavior are common in institutionalized elders. They (see their Chap. 8) outlined several suggestions for changes in institutions that would lead to elderly suicide prevention. Osgood et al. (1991, p. 138) have suggested that self-destructive behaviors can be prevented if institutions more adequately meet the personal needs of the residents for freedom, choice, privacy, autonomy, and space. The absence of these basic human needs as contributors to suicide are apparent in the commonalities of suicides described by Shneidman (1985). Based on survey results, they also recommended that staff development and improvement are needed if direct and indirect suicidal behaviors among institutional residents are to be reduced.

Another aspect of primary prevention relates to the personality and long-term tendencies of the individual. Shneidman (1985), Maris (1981), and Clark (1993) have contended that there are lifelong patterns that characterize the suicidal person. If they are correct, then those who may be vulnerable to the problems in old age might be identified earlier in life and taught more effective coping methods and interventions that will enable better adaptation to problems later in life.

The societal and other primary prevention measures proposed here will obviously require some time and will be expensive to implement. However, Rachlis (1970) has argued that these will be worthwhile efforts on several levels.

Helping the aging now is in a sense buying insurance for the younger generations. Supportive health and social welfare services developed today will provide security in the later years for the presently young and middle-aged. They will enter late life with assurance that help will be available to deal with the inevitable losses of aging. (p. 25)

The implications of our society's aging and the large size of the cohorts that will reach older adulthood in the future have been noted elsewhere (McIntosh, 1992, in press) and are especially relevant to Rachlis' comments.

## Tertiary Prevention

Little attention to issues of tertiary prevention has taken place in the context of elderly suicide. Although research, therapy, and support efforts have grown in recent years with respect to suicide survivors (i.e., the loved ones who survive the suicide death of a loved one), virtually none of these efforts have considered survivors of older adult suicides or older adults as survivors of suicides (see e.g., Dunne, McIntosh, & Dunne-Maxim, 1987). The one possible exception here would be studies of widows of suicides; many of these persons are themselves elders, or their deceased spouse was elderly. Some research evidence suggests that widows' suicide bereavement shares many similarities but also may differ in some ways from that associated with other causes of death (see McIntosh, 1987b; McIntosh et al., 1994, pp. 45–53), though little information specific to the old is available (an exception is research by Farberow et al.: Farberow, Gallagher, Gilewski, & Thompson, 1987; Farberow, Gallagher-Thompson, Gilewski, & Thompson, 1992).

Other frequently ignored issues of postvention involve past attempted suicides who may not be currently suicidal and the family and friends of those who have survived a nonfatal attempt. Virtually no systematic study has dealt with these groups at any age and, therefore, little is known about the problems and aftereffects that attempted but nonfatal suicide attempts may produce in their lives. The entire area of postvention with respect to issues of elderly suicide requires tremendous attention.

A final aspect of elderly suicide prevention involves another primary prevention issue. Much has been written about the negative attitudes, or ageism, toward aging and the elderly, that exist in subtle and more obvious ways in our society. The old tend to be viewed as expendable, as having lived long enough and, perhaps, as having outlived their usefulness. Daily, the high value of youth and the devaluing of old age are apparent in advertisements, television, and other media. One recent reflection of this ambivalent or even negative feeling toward aging and the aged has emerged in the debates over the rationality of suicide and assisted suicide.

Public surveys (e.g., Gallup Poll, "Fear of Dying," 1991) have indicated the general opinion that no moral right to commit suicide exists for either healthy individuals (80% = no, 16% = yes), nor those who are a heavy burden on their family (61% = no, 33% = yes). However, persons in great pain (66% = yes, 29% = no) or with incurable diseases (58% = yes, 36% = no) are felt to have a moral right to commit suicide. Other attitudinal research (e.g., Deluty, 1988–89) suggests that people regard suicide as more acceptable when the person's precipitating illness is cancer and when the person committing suicide is elderly. These attitudes are complex and will require further study as well as educational efforts to combat myths

and negative attitudes toward the old and old age as the debate over these issues continue. (See Hendin, Part V of this issue, for a fuller discussion of euthanasia.)

## CONCLUSIONS

Research investigations must be improved and expanded to provide clarification of important unanswered questions about elderly suicide and its prevention. Examples of such questions are: What can be learned by studying low-risk populations that may assist the development of preventive measures for high-risk groups such as the elderly? What therapy techniques are most effective in preventing elderly suicides? These sample questions only begin to portray the range of prevention-related aspects in late-life suicide.

The United Nations has offered a set of Principles for Older Persons that relate to the well-being of elders in societies. These principles were summarized by the statement "Add life to the years that have been added to life by assuring all older persons: independence, participation, care, self-fulfillment and dignity" ("Proposed UN Principles," 1991, p. 1). The steps to implement this statement are not clear and will require much time and effort across the world. Suicide is an extreme response to the absence or lack of these elements in the lives of older persons. Assuring that the elderly are able to realize these ingredients would go a long way in eliminating the frustrated psychological needs that Shneidman (1985) suggests are the common stressors leading to suicide. Implementation of the measures described in this paper will perhaps enable achievement of the Healthy People 2000 Objectives not only regarding elderly White male suicide, but also regarding depression and improved and expanded use of mental health services.

Death by one's own hand is premature at *any* age and the premature deaths of older adults constitute a loss of talent and resources that no society can accept. We must improve and increase our efforts to prevent and reduce such avoidable tragedies and enhance the lives of elders, both as we approach the year 2000 and as we face the challenges of the next century.

# REFERENCES

Barter, J. T. (1969). Self-destructive behavior in adolescents and adults: Similarities and differences. In U.S. Department of Health, Education, and Welfare, *Suicide among the American Indians: Two workshops* (pp. 7–10) (PHS Publication No. 903). Washington, DC: U.S. Government Printing Office.

Bennett, A. E. (1967, May). Recognizing the potential suicide. *Geriatrics, 22,* 175–181.

Bille-Brahe, U. (1993). The role of sex and age in suicidal behavior. *Acta Psychiatrica Scandinavica, 87*(Suppl. No. 371), 21–27.

Chynoweth, R. (1981). Suicide in the elderly. *Crisis, 2,* 106–116.

Clark, D. C. (1993). Narcissistic crises of aging and suicidal despair. *Suicide and Life-Threatening Behavior, 23,* 21–26.

Conwell, Y., Rotenberg, M., & Caine, E. D. (1990). Completed suicide at age 50 and over. *Journal of the American Geriatrics Society, 38,* 640–644.

Curran, D. K. (1987). *Adolescent suicidal behavior.* New York: Hemisphere.

Deluty, R. H. (1988–89). Factors affecting the acceptability of suicide. *Omega, 19,* 315–326.

Dunne, E. J., McIntosh, J. L., & Dunne-Maxim, K. (Eds.). (1987). *Suicide and its aftermath: Understanding and counseling the survivors.* New York: Norton.

Farberow, N. L. (1969). Training in suicide prevention for professional and community agents. *American Journal of Psychiatry, 125,* 1702–1705.

Farberow, N. L., Gallagher, D. E., Gilewski, M. J., & Thompson, L. W. (1987). An examination of the early impact of bereavement on psychological distress in survivors of suicide. *Gerontologist, 27,* 592–598.

Farberow, N. L., Gallagher-Thompson, D., Gilewski, M., & Thompson, L. (1992). The role of social supports in the bereavement process of surviving spouses of suicide and natural deaths. *Suicide and Life-Threatening Behavior, 22,* 107–124.

Fear of dying. (1991, January). *Gallup Poll Monthly,* No. 304, pp. 51–61.

Felton, B. J. (1982). The aged: Settings, services, and needs. In L. R. Snowden (Ed.), *Reaching the underserved: Mental health needs of neglected populations* (pp. 23–42). Beverly Hills, CA: Sage.

Gatz, M., & Smyer, M. A. (1992). The mental health system and older adults in the 1990s. *American Psychologist, 47,* 741–751.

Heilig, S. M. (1970, Spring). Training in suicide prevention. *Bulletin of Suicidology,* No. 6, pp. 41–44.

Hinrichsen, G. A., Hernandez, N. A., & Pollack, S. (1992). Difficulties and rewards in family care of the depressed older adult. *Gerontologist, 32,* 486–492.

Holinger, P. C., Offer, D., Barter, J. T., & Bell, C. C. (1994). *Suicide and homicide among adolescents.* New York: Guilford Press.

Kreitman, N. (1977). *Parasuicide.* New York: Wiley.

Lasoski, M. C. (1986). Reasons for low utilization of mental health services by the elderly. In T. L. Brink (Ed.), *Clinical gerontology: A guide to assessment and intervention* (pp. 1–18). New York: Haworth.

Lyness, J. M., Conwell, Y., & Nelson, J. C. (1992). Suicide attempts in elderly psychiatric inpatients. *Journal of the American Geriatrics Society, 40,* 320–324.

Manton, K. G., Blazer, D. G., & Woodbury, M. A. (1987). Suicide in middle age and later life: Sex and race specific life table and cohort analyses. *Journal of Gerontology, 42,* 219–227.

Maris, R. W. (1981). *Pathways to suicide: A survey of self-destructive behaviors.* Baltimore, MD: Johns Hopkins University Press.

Maris, R. W., Dorpat, T. L., Hathorne, B. C., Heilig, S. M., Powell, W. J., Stone, H., & Ward, H. P. (1973). Education and training in suicidology for the seventies. In H. L. P. Resnik & B. C. Hathorne (Eds.), *Suicide prevention in the 70s* (pp. 23–34) (DHEW Publication No. (HSM) 72-9054). Washington, DC: United States Government Printing Office.

McIntosh, J. L. (1987a). Suicide: Training and education needs with an emphasis on the elderly. *Gerontology and Geriatrics Education, 7,* 125–139.

McIntosh, J. L. (1987b). Survivors family relationships: Literature review. In E. J. Dunne, J. L. McIntosh, & K. Dunne-Maxim (Eds.), *Suicide and its aftermath: Understanding and counseling the survivors* (pp. 73–84). New York: Norton.

McIntosh, J. L. (1992). Older adults: The next suicide epidemic? *Suicide and Life-Threatening Behavior, 22,* 322–332.

McIntosh, J. L. (1993). *The suicide of older men and women: How YOU can help prevent a tragedy* [brochure]. Washington, DC: AARP and the American Association of Suicidology.

McIntosh, J. L. (1994). Generational analyses of suicide: Baby boomers and 13ers. *Suicide and Life-Threatening Behavior, 24*(4).

McIntosh, J. L., Hubbard, R. W., & Santos, J. F. (1981). Suicide among the elderly: A review of issues with case studies. *Journal of Gerontological Social Work, 4,* 63–74.

McIntosh, J. L., Hubbard, R. W., & Santos, J. F. (1985). Suicide facts and myths: A study of prevalence. *Death Studies, 9,* 267–281.

McIntosh, J. L., Santos, J. F., Hubbard, R. W., & Overholser, J. C. (1994). *Elder suicide: Research, theory and treatment.* Washington, DC: American Psychological Association.

Mercer, S. O. (1989). *Elder suicide: A national survey of prevention and intervention programs.* Washington, DC: American Association of Retired Persons.

Mercer, S. O. (1992). Suicide and the elderly. In F. J. Turner (Ed.), *Mental health and the elderly: A so-*

*cial work perspective* (pp. 425–453). New York: Free Press.

National Center for Health Statistics. (1993a). *Healthy people 2000 review, 1992* (DHHS Publication No. (PHS) 93-123211). Washington, DC: U.S. Government Printing Office.

National Center for Health Statistics. (1993b). Advance report of final mortality statistics, 1991. *NCHS Monthly Vital Statistics Report, 42*(2, Suppl.).

Osgood, N. J., Brant, B. A., & Lipman, A. (1991). *Suicide among the elderly in long-term care facilities.* New York: Greenwood.

Palmore, E. (1977). Facts on aging: A short quiz. *Gerontologist, 17,* 315–320.

Parmalee, P. A., & Katz, I. R. (1992). "Caregiving" to depressed older persons: A relevant concept? [Editorial]. *Gerontologist, 32,* 436–437.

Pollinger-Haas, A., & Hendin, H. (1983). Suicide among older people: Projections for the future. *Suicide and Life-Threatening Behavior, 13,* 147–154.

Pratt, C. C., Schmall, V. L., Wilson, W., & Benthin, A. (1991). A model community education program on depression and suicide in later life. *Gerontologist, 31,* 692–695.

Proposed UN principles for older persons. (1991, June). *Ageing International, 18*(1), 3–6.

Rabins, P. V. (1992). Prevention of mental disorder in the elderly: Current perspectives and future prospects. *Journal of the American Geriatrics Society, 40,* 727–733.

Rachlis, D. (1970, Fall). Suicide and loss adjustment in the aging. *Bulletin of Suicidology,* No. 7, pp. 23–26.

Raschko, R. (1990). The gatekeeper model for the isolated, at-risk elderly. In N. L. Cohen (Ed.), *Psychiatry takes to the streets* (pp. 195–209). New York: Guilford Press.

Redick, R. W., & Taube, C. A. (1980). Demography of mental health care of the aged. In J. E. Birren & R. B. Sloane (Eds.), *Handbook of mental health and*

*aging* (pp. 57–71). Englewood Cliffs, NJ: Prentice-Hall.

Rosenwaike, I. (1985). *The extreme aged in America: A portrayal of an expanding population.* Westport, CT: Greenwood.

Sainsbury, P. (1962). Suicide in the middle and later years. In H. T. Blumenthal (Ed.), *Aging around the world: Medical and clinical aspects of aging* (pp. 97–105). New York: Columbia University Press.

Santos, J. F., & VandenBos, G. R. (Eds.). (1982). *Psychology and the older adult: Challenges for training in the 1980s.* Washington, DC: American Psychological Association.

Sendbuehler, J. M., & Goldstein, S. (1977). Attempted suicide among the aged. *Journal of the American Geriatrics Society, 25,* 244–248.

Shneidman, E. S. (1965). Preventing suicide. *American Journal of Nursing, 65*(5), 111–116.

Shneidman, E. S. (1969). Prologue: Fifty-eight years. In E. S. Shneidman (Ed.), *On the nature of suicide* (pp. 1–30). San Francisco: Jossey-Bass.

Shneidman, E. S. (1985). *Definition of suicide.* New York: Wiley.

Shneidman, E. S. (1993). *Suicide as psychache: A clinical approach to self-destructive behavior.* Northvale, NJ: Jason Aronson.

Shneidman, E. S. (1994). Foreword. In J. L. McIntosh, J. F. Santos, R. W. Hubbard, & J. C. Overholser, *Elder suicide: Research, theory and treatment* (p. ix). Washington, DC: American Psychological Association.

Stenback, A. (1980). Depression and suicidal behavior in old age. In J. E. Birren & R. B. Sloane (Eds.), *Handbook of mental health and aging* (pp. 616–652). Englewood Cliffs, NJ: Prentice-Hall.

U.S. Bureau of the Census. (1993). U.S. population estimates, by age, sex, race, and Hispanic origin: 1980 to 1991. *Current Population Reports,* Series P-25, No. 1095.

# V. Special Topics

## 15
## Assisted Suicide, Euthanasia, and Suicide Prevention: The Implications of the Dutch Experience

### Herbert Hendin, MD

What impact would legalization of assisted suicide and euthanasia have on our ability to treat suicidal patients and to prevent suicide? Information from a study of the Dutch experience illustrates how legal sanction promotes a culture that transforms suicide into assisted suicide and euthanasia and encourages patients and doctors to see choosing death as a preferred way of dealing with serious or terminal illness. The extension of the right to euthanasia to those who are not physically ill further complicates the problem. So too does the tendency of doctors in such a culture to begin to feel that they can make decisions about ending the life of competent terminally ill patients without consulting the patient. "Normalizing" suicide as a medical option lays the groundwork for a society that turns euthanasia into a "cure" for suicidal depression.

Many of us have known situations in which a doctor would have acted humanely by helping a terminally ill person die in the final weeks of an illness. Many of us have also seen patients whose first reaction to the knowledge of serious illness and possible death is anxiety, depression and a wish to die (Hendin & Klerman, 1993). Whenever, as in the Netherlands, or in a law passed by Oregon voters in 1994 (now under a preliminary injunction pending a trial as to its constitutionality) there is legal sanction for assisted suicide for patients who are not in the last weeks of their life, and indeed who need not be experiencing severe discomfort or physical pain, the terminally ill become hopelessly confused with those who are not.

My observations in the Netherlands, where doctors following accepted guidelines, can with impunity and public acceptance practice assisted suicide and euthanasia, persuade me that legalization of these practices is not the answer to the problems of those confronted with serious illness (Hendin, 1994a). Legalization also complicates and confuses the treatment of patients who are suicidal.

De facto legalization of euthanasia and assisted suicide exists in the Netherlands (Gomez, 1991). Although the criminal law provides punishment for euthanasia and a lesser punishment for assisted suicide (Gevers, 1992), the same code stipulates that there can be exceptions to the law in special circumstances. In a series of cases over 20 years, the Dutch courts have ruled that assisted suicide and euthanasia are such special circumstances. They are permitted by a physician who found it necessary to put the welfare of his patient above the law which formally prohibits assisted suicide and euthanasia (Gomez, 1991).

The Dutch courts and the Royal Dutch Medical Association (KNMG) have established the same guidelines for physicians to follow whether in practicing assisted suicide or euthanasia: 1) voluntariness — the patient's request must be freely made, persistent, and conscious; 2) unbearable suffering that cannot be relieved by other means; and 3) consultation – the attending physician should consult with a colleague (KNMG, 1984). Doctors are expected to report cases of euthanasia as deaths due to "unnatural causes" with the understanding that prosecutors will not prosecute if the guidelines were followed.

Few cases have been brought to trial. The recommended guidelines are not fixed conditions so that even when they were not followed, judges have consistently exonerated or pardoned physicians (Gomez, 1991). A statute passed last year codifying the guidelines provides added protection for doctors – but not for patients (Hendin, 1994b).

Over the past 20 years practice in the Netherlands has moved from assisted suicide to euthanasia, from euthanasia for the terminally ill to euthanasia for patients who are chronically ill, from physical suffering to mental suffering, from voluntary euthanasia to involuntary euthanasia (called "termination of the patient without explicit request"). The Dutch government's own commissioned research documented that in more than one thousand cases a year, doctors actively caused death without the patient's request (van der Maas, van Delders, and Pijnenborg, 1992).

The rationale for such extensions has been that to deny the right to die with assistance to the chronically ill who will have longer to suffer than the terminally ill or to those who experience psychological pain not associated with physical disease is a form of discrimination. Ending patients' lives without their request has been justified as necessitated by the need to make decisions for patients not competent to choose for themselves.

## SUICIDE IN THE NETHERLANDS

The Dutch experience illustrates how social sanctions promote a culture that transforms suicide into assisted suicide and euthanasia and encourages patients and doctors to see assisted suicide and euthanasia – intended as an unfortunate necessity in exceptional cases – as almost a routine way of dealing with serious or terminal illness and more recently even with grief. The Dutch like to point out that they have a relatively low suicide rate and that since the acceptance of euthanasia that rate has not increased, but dropped. But many of the cases of euthanasia are likely to be people who would have ended their own lives if euthanasia were not available to them. This was certainly one of the justifications given by Dutch doctors for providing such help. If any significant percentage of the euthanasia cases were to be included among the suicides, the Dutch figure would rise considerably.

In fact the figures suggest that the drop in the Dutch suicide rate from a peak of 16.6 in 1983 and 1984 to 12.8 in 1992 (see Table 1) may well be due to the availability of euthanasia. More significant than the drop is the fact that it has taken place in the older age groups. In the 50-59 age group the rate dropped from a peak of 21.5 in 1984 to 14 in 1992. Among those 60-69 the rate dropped from a peak of 23.2 in 1982 to 14.5 in 1992. Among those 70 and over the rate dropped from a peak of 31.3 in 1983 to 19.9 in 1992. These are remarkable drops of about 33% in these 3 groups. Of the 1886 suicides in 1993, 940 of them were in the three older age groups. Of the 1587 suicides in 1992, 672 were in the three older age groups. The drop of 268 suicides in the three older age groups was primarily responsible for the drop in the Dutch suicide rate. Comparing the five years of 1980-1984 with the 1988-1992 years provides statistically significant evidence of a drop in the older age groups that is not due to chance. These are the age groups containing the highest numbers of euthanasia cases (86% of the men and 78% of the women) and the greatest number of suicides (see Table 2).

The period of the last decade is the period of growing Dutch acceptance of euthanasia. It seems plausible that the remarkable drop in the older age groups is due to the fact that older suicidal patients are now asking to receive euthanasia? Among an older population physical ill-

Table 1
Relative Number per 100,000 of Corresponding Community 15 Years of Age or Older

| Year | Sex[a] | | Total number | Age group[b] | | | | | | | |
|---|---|---|---|---|---|---|---|---|---|---|---|
| | Male | Female | | ≤15 | 16–19 | 20–29 | 30–39 | 40–49 | 50–59 | 60–69 | ≥70 |
| 1970 | 15.3 | 9.2 | 12.2 | 2.9 | 6.6 | 7.6 | 13.2 | 18.2 | 21.0 | 26.2 | |
| 1971 | 15.3 | 10.1 | 12.7 | 4.2 | 6.7 | 7.6 | 12.4 | 19.9 | 20.4 | 28.0 | |
| 1972 | 15.3 | 9.7 | 12.5 | 3.8 | 7.1 | 9.4 | 13.0 | 17.0 | 21.9 | 24.0 | |
| 1973 | 15.1 | 10.7 | 12.9 | 4.1 | 6.9 | 10.0 | 13.6 | 20.0 | 20.0 | 20.8 | |
| 1974 | 16.5 | 10.7 | 13.5 | 4.8 | 8.5 | 10.4 | 15.3 | 17.7 | 21.6 | 24.0 | |
| 1975 | 16.1 | 10.3 | 13.2 | 4.1 | 8.9 | 11.4 | 14.7 | 18.0 | 18.3 | 23.1 | |
| 1976 | 17.3 | 10.1 | 13.6 | 3.7 | 9.0 | 12.6 | 13.8 | 18.7 | 19.3 | 25.6 | |
| 1977 | 16.9 | 9.7 | 13.3 | 3.8 | 9.8 | 11.2 | 15.1 | 17.9 | 18.3 | 22.2 | |
| 1978 | 16.0 | 11.4 | 13.7 | 3.6 | 11.1 | 11.4 | 15.0 | 16.1 | 23.5 | 20.8 | |
| 1979 | 16.7 | 12.7 | 14.7 | 4.2 | 9.9 | 11.2 | 18.3 | 21.2 | 21.6 | 24.3 | |
| 1980 | 18.4 | 10.3 | 14.3 | 2.3 | 12.0 | 12.8 | 14.7 | 17.8 | 21.5 | 22.3 | |
| 1981 | 18.8 | 11.1 | 15.0 | 2.8 | 11.3 | 13.5 | 16.0 | 18.6 | 22.4 | 22.3 | |
| 1982 | 19.3 | 12.3 | 15.8 | 4.6 | 11.4 | 13.4 | 17.5 | 18.8 | 23.1 | 27.3 | |
| 1983 | 20.7 | 12.8 | 16.6 | 2.5 | 12.2 | 14.5 | 17.4 | 21.0 | 23.2 | 31.3 | |
| 1984 | 20.6 | 12.7 | 16.6 | 3.0 | 12.0 | 15.4 | 18.1 | 21.5 | 22.3 | 27.9 | |
| 1985 | 19.8 | 10.7 | 15.2 | 3.7 | 12.6 | 14.7 | 15.1 | 19.1 | 20.6 | 22.3 | |
| 1986 | 18.7 | 11.1 | 14.8 | 2.8 | 11.5 | 14.3 | 16.6 | 17.8 | 19.7 | 23.1 | |
| 1987 | 19.1 | 11.1 | 15.0 | 3.5 | 11.9 | 14.7 | 15.9 | 17.9 | 19.6 | 24.2 | |
| 1988 | 17.9 | 9.9 | 13.7 | 2.6 | 10.7 | 13.6 | 14.0 | 17.4 | 17.0 | 23.2 | |
| 1989 | 17.6 | 10.2 | 13.8 | 4.0 | 10.9 | 12.5 | 14.3 | 19.0 | 19.6 | 18.3 | |
| 1990 | 17.1 | 9.7 | 13.3 | 4.5 | 9.6 | 14.1 | 13.9 | 15.0 | 16.2 | 21.3 | |
| 1991 | 17.2 | 9.2 | 13.1 | 3.1 | 9.9 | 14.6 | 12.9 | 15.5 | 15.5 | 19.9 | |
| 1992 | 17.2 | 8.7 | 12.8 | 3.5 | 9.5 | 13.7 | 13.7 | 14.0 | 14.5 | 19.9 | |

*Source.* Central Bureau of Statistics, revised by Central Directory for the Development of Scientific Policy, July 1994.
[a]Unknown sex included.
[b]In the period 1970-1979, the CBS registered by the age groups of 15-20 and 21-29 years. In the period 1980-1992 the age groups became 15-19 and 20-29 years. Because of this change, the real group of 15-19 years will be slightly less and the real group 20-29 will be slightly higher in the period 1970-1979.
[c]Unknown.

ness of all types is common, and many who have trouble coping with physical illness became suicidal. In a culture accepting of euthanasia their distress may be accepted as a legitimate reason for euthanasia. It may be more than metaphorical to describe euthanasia as the Dutch cure for suicide.

Of course euthanasia advocates can maintain that making suicide unnecessary for those over 50 who are physically ill is one of the benefits of legalization, not a sign of its abuse. The acceptance of such a position depends on whether one believes that there are alternatives to assisted suicide or euthanasia in dealing with the pain, suffering, and depression of older people who become ill.

## FEAR OF DEATH

Depression, anxiety and the wish to end one's life quickly are often first reactions to the knowledge of serious illness and possible death. In studies of assisted suicide and euthanasia, most of which have been done in the Netherlands, physicians reported that loss of dignity, pain, being dependent on others were the reasons patients have for requesting euthanasia (van der Maas, van Delders and Pijnenborg, 1992). The fear of death itself is not mentioned.

Many patients and physicians displace anxieties about death onto the circumstances of dying – pain, dependence, loss of dignity, the unpleasant side effects re-

Table 2
Number of Suicides in The Netherlands from 1970 to 1992

| Year | Sex[a] | | Total number | Age group[b] | | | | | | | |
|------|------|--------|--------|------|-------|-------|-------|-------|-------|-------|------|
| | Male | Female | | ≤15 | 16–19 | 20–29 | 30–39 | 40–49 | 50–59 | 60–69 | ≥70 |
| | | | | *Absolute Number* | | | | | | | |
| 1970 | 719 | 439 | 1158 | 10 | 39 | 123 | 121 | 199 | 232 | 220 | 213 |
| 1971 | 727 | 489 | 1216 | –[c] | 56 | 130 | 122 | 188 | 259 | 216 | 242 |
| 1972 | 740 | 480 | 1220 | – | 51 | 141 | 153 | 198 | 225 | 235 | 212 |
| 1973 | 738 | 535 | 1273 | 14 | 51 | 163 | 165 | 205 | 268 | 217 | 189 |
| 1974 | 815 | 545 | 1360 | 9 | 66 | 175 | 177 | 232 | 239 | 238 | 224 |
| 1975 | 810 | 533 | 1343 | – | 57 | 187 | 199 | 223 | 246 | 203 | 219 |
| 1976 | 885 | 528 | 1413 | – | 53 | 190 | 228 | 211 | 259 | 215 | 251 |
| 1977 | 871 | 513 | 1384 | – | 55 | 206 | 210 | 232 | 249 | 205 | 221 |
| 1978 | 841 | 617 | 1458 | – | 52 | 230 | 229 | 233 | 228 | 264 | 215 |
| 1979 | 884 | 693 | 1577 | – | 61 | 206 | 229 | 284 | 301 | 242 | 254 |
| 1980 | 981 | 576 | 1557 | 4 | 32 | 281 | 269 | 231 | 257 | 241 | 242 |
| 1981 | 1023 | 627 | 1656 | 10 | 35 | 269 | 293 | 254 | 268 | 257 | 245 |
| 1982 | 1063 | 703 | 1772 | 9 | 58 | 272 | 297 | 281 | 273 | 270 | 306 |
| 1983 | 1150 | 736 | 1886 | 10 | 31 | 294 | 328 | 283 | 306 | 275 | 359 |
| 1984 | 1160 | 742 | 1902 | 9 | 37 | 293 | 353 | 302 | 313 | 268 | 327 |
| 1985 | 1127 | 633 | 1760 | 8 | 46 | 310 | 343 | 257 | 278 | 251 | 267 |
| 1986 | 1076 | 664 | 1740 | 6 | 35 | 288 | 338 | 288 | 261 | 243 | 281 |
| 1987 | 1114 | 670 | 1784 | 3 | 45 | 296 | 344 | 294 | 263 | 245 | 294 |
| 1988 | 1054 | 604 | 1658 | 8 | 31 | 270 | 317 | 271 | 257 | 214 | 290 |
| 1989 | 1045 | 629 | 1674 | 4 | 47 | 278 | 292 | 288 | 283 | 251 | 231 |
| 1990 | 1021 | 599 | 1620 | 7 | 50 | 246 | 333 | 289 | 226 | 197 | 272 |
| 1991 | 1033 | 578 | 1611 | 3 | 32 | 255 | 349 | 274 | 236 | 202 | 260 |
| 1992 | 1041 | 546 | 1587 | 3 | 35 | 245 | 333 | 299 | 216 | 190 | 266 |

*Source*. Central Bureau of Statistics, revised by Central Directory for the Development of Scientific Policy, July 1994.
[a]Unknown sex included.
[b]In the period 1970–1979, the CBS registered by the age groups of 15–20 and 21–29 years. In the period 1980–1992 the age groups became 15–19 and 20–29 years. Because of this change, the real group of 15–19 years will be slightly less and the real group 20–29 will be slightly higher in the period 1970–1979.
[c]Unknown.

sulting from medical treatments. Focusing on or becoming enraged at the process distracts from the fear of death itself.

Confronting such fear may focus a patient on what he can achieve in whatever life can still offer. A few years ago, a young professional in his early 30's who had acute myelocytic leukemia, was referred to me for consultation. With medical treatment, Tim was given a 25% chance of survival; without it, he was told, he would die in a few months.

His immediate reaction was a desperate preoccupation with suicide and a request for support in carrying it out. He was worried about becoming dependent and feared both the symptoms of his disease

and the side effects of treatment. His anxieties about the painful circumstances that would surround his death were not irrational, but all his fears about dying amplified them.

Once Tim and I could talk about the possibility or likelihood of his dying—what separation from his family and the destruction of his body meant to him—his desperation subsided. He accepted medical treatment, complained relatively little about the unpleasant side effects, and used the remaining months of his life to become closer to his wife and parents. Two days before he died, he talked of what he would have missed without the opportunity for a loving parting (Hendin, 1994a).

In the Netherlands the fear of death can lead to the premature ending of life. Even in a film intended to promote euthanasia, "Appointment with Death" that I was shown at the Dutch Voluntary Euthanasia Society (K.A. Productions, 1993), I saw such an example. A 41-year-old artist was diagnosed as HIV positive. He had no physical symptoms, but had seen others suffer with them and wanted his physician's assistance in dying. The doctor compassionately explained to him that he might live for some years symptom-free. Over time the patient repeated his request for euthanasia and eventually his doctor acceded to it. The patient was clearly depressed and overwhelmed by the news of his situation. The doctor kept establishing that the man was persistent in his request, but did not address the terror that underlay it. I was convinced that with a psychologically sensitive physician looking for more than repeated requests to die, more likely in a culture not so medically accepting of euthanasia, this man would not have needed to die when he did (Hendin, 1994a).

If the ravages of illness and the painful side effects of treatment were not accompanied by the fear of imminent death they would be more bearable and many who choose death might well not do so. Conversely, if life were so structured that we all knew that we would die on the day of our 85th birthday, but live in good health up to that time, it is likely that many people would kill themselves in the months or years prior to that time so as to avoid anxiety over the inevitability of their fate and their lack of control over it (Hendin, 1994).

Patients are not alone in their inability to tolerate situations they cannot control. Lewis Thomas (1984) has written insightfully from the physician's viewpoint of the sense of failure and helplessness that doctors may experience in the face of death. Such feelings might explain why doctors have such difficulty in discussing terminal illness with patients—a majority of doctors avoid such discussions while most patients would prefer frank talk. They might also explain both the doctor's tendency for excessive measures to maintain life in the dying as well as the need to make death a physician's decision. By deciding when patients die, by making death a medical decision, the physician has the illusion of mastery over the disease and the accompanying feelings of helplessness. The physician, not the illness, is responsible for the death. Assisting suicide and euthanasia become ways of dealing with the frustration of being unable to cure the disease (Hendin, 1994a).

## ASSISTED SUICIDE FOR DUTCH PSYCHIATRIC PATIENTS

How Dutch policies translate into practice with a psychiatric patient are evident in a case that has received a good deal of international attention. I had a chance to spend a number of hours interviewing the psychiatrist involved (Hendin, 1994a). In the spring of 1993 a Dutch court in Assen ruled that Boudewijn Chabot was justified in assisting in the suicide of his patient a physically healthy but grief-stricken 50-year-old social worker who was mourning the death of her son two months earlier.

Chabot had accepted his patient, to whom he gave the fictional name of Netty Boomsma (Chabot, 1993) into treatment in the summer of 1991 with the understanding, common in the Netherlands, that if she did not change her mind about not wanting to live, he would assist in her suicide. Netty appears to have used the agreement to mark time until Chabot felt obliged to fulfill his promise. He assisted in her suicide a little over two months after she came to see him, about four months after her younger son died of cancer at 20. Her first son had killed himself some years earlier following a rejection by his girlfriend.

Chabot told me that Netty's marriage was a disaster from the beginning. She was 23 and her husband was 28. She was not really in love but married her husband to get away from an unpleasant relationship with a domineering mother and a father who went along with whatever her mother wanted. Her husband believed a women should stay at home which she did for a while, but felt in a cage until she decided to work and earn her own money. Netty told Chabot she started to live the day her first child was born. The child made it possible for her to be something apart from her disapproving mother. Six years later she had her second son. When her children were small she went to social work school at night, while she held a job which she enjoyed during the day. Netty continued to work until January 1990 which was the start of her son's chemotherapy for his cancer.

Netty's husband blamed her for their first son's death saying she was responsible for his education so was responsible for his suicide. He would beat up Netty when he was drunk. She would leave him, but then she would have to go back because of her second son. She planned at one point to kill herself and her second son by driving into a canal, but felt she could not take his life.

Three years before Netty's death, and a few weeks after her father died, Netty left her husband and her son went with her. By then her son had become a comfort for her. He understood her grief and tried to console her. Over the years he became more important to her. Since his death Netty felt that although not a religious believer she was "pulled to her boys."

Chabot had been told by Netty's sister and brother-in-law that although Netty was somewhat better than when her first son died (she had been hospitalized at that time) her energy and interest in many activities, particularly painting, had subsided and never returned after her first son's death. Netty blamed herself for not having divorced her husband earlier, believing that had she done so, things might have been different and her son might not have killed himself.

Chabot described the case in a written account he sent a number of colleagues. Although two did not think he should go forward and felt bereavement therapy was indicated, an expert in bereavement

therapy thought it was futile and the majority agreed that Chabot should proceed. None felt it was necessary to actually see the patient.

Chabot described the scene the night he assisted in Netty's death. He went with a colleague to Netty's home and Netty had a friend with her. She said she wanted to go ahead. She asked to do it in the room of her younger son and on his bed. They all went upstairs and he gave her a liquid as well as some capsules that a pharmacist had prepared for him. She opened the capsules as she had been advised and put them in some yogurt. Jokingly she asked him if he could not have given her some capsules before to practice. She sat down on the bed and asked them to turn on the record player which played a Bach flute sonata that had been played at her son's funeral. She took the glass and drank the liquid saying that it was not too bad. While the music was playing Netty kissed a photograph of her two sons that was next to the bed. She asked her friend to sit next to her. Her friend was stroking her hair. Netty said she had made a great effort to fix her hair and her friend was messing it up. The friend replied she would make it beautiful later. To Chabot, Netty said, "why do young kids want suicide," thinking of her son. He recalled saying to her after five minutes, "think of your boys." In seven minutes she lost consciousness while being held by her friend. Then she slept. Her heart stopped in one half hour.

Chabot insisted that Netty was not depressed, was not a patient, but simply a grieving woman who wanted to die. Although Netty had not exhibited the sad affect associated with depression, patients obsessively bent on suicide often do not. In the loss of pleasure that Netty experienced in activities she previously enjoyed, Netty surely met that aspect of the criteria established for the diagnosis of depression. In the sense, however, that any therapy would have required challenging the premises under which she came, and would probably have also included some trial on medication, no therapy could be said to have been undertaken with Netty so one can understand why Chabot does not regard her as a patient.

Chabot stated that if he did not agree to her terms she would have never come back. She had also threatened to take matters into her own hands. I asked why if she did not follow his prescription for treatment, he would feel obliged to follow hers. Certainly at the end he seemed to be succumbing to blackmail.

Chabot and a number of other Dutch therapists believe there is an obligation to assist in the suicide of a suicidal patient if treatment has not succeeded. They point to cases that they had been able to involve in psychotherapy because of the promise that if treatment did not work they would assist in their patients' suicides. Most therapists, however, find that such patients can be involved in therapy without such a promise by making it clear that they accept suicidal feelings as part of the therapy, are not uncomfortable or frightened by them, and will not go to any lengths to stop the patient's suicide, conveying that ultimately the patient is responsible for being alive.

Many suicidal patients come into therapy with sometimes conscious, but often unconscious fantasies that cast the therapist in the role of their executioner. Netty seemed to be such a patient; both she and Chabot experienced a closeness in her death. A commitment on the therapist's part to become executioner if treatment fails plays into and reenforces these fantasies. It may also play into the therapist's illusion that if he cannot cure the patient no one else can either.

Some therapists also seem to have entered into the patient's fantasy of death as a reunion. Chabot's comment to Netty right before her death that she should think about her boys suggests that he too saw her death metaphorically as a return to her lost children. By metaphorizing death as something other than death, it is made to appear an attractive, fairytale-like option. But such metaphors, like fairytales, contain beneath the surface some of the most tormented and savage

emotions there are. Not treating Netty as a patient, but as a devoted mother whose desire to join her boys in death was not a sign of her disturbance but a legitimate and realizable goal makes it impossible to explore her guilt toward her children and her need for punishment.

From what Chabot was able to elicit in sessions with Netty, bereavement counseling was likely to fail with her, but psychotherapy less narrowly focused might succeed. Netty's personality problems far anteceded her bereavement. She said she became a person only when her first son was born and stayed alive only for the sake of her second son.

Netty needed someone who could tell her in a firm but kind way that she never really lived for herself and that it was not too late to try. She could always kill herself but she ought to give life a chance first. Netty's guilt over her first son's suicide had sources that were deeper than her failure to have gotten a divorce. Caring for her second son seems to have had something of the quality of an atonement. One suspects that if therapy provided her with the opportunity to understand her relationship to her sons before deciding to join them in death, it might have engaged her.

No one should underestimate the grief of a mother who has lost a beloved child, but neither should one ignore the many ways life offers to deal with the feelings of loss, guilt and pain a child's death is likely to arouse. The Dutch like to present patients with concrete alternatives. For Netty, my suggestion would be to utilize her skills as a social worker and involve her in a facility or project devoted to youth suicide prevention. Her last words to Chabot, "why do young kids want suicide," suggest that work that permitted her to deal with that question might have meaningfully engaged her in a way that would have been more positive for her as well as for those she might have helped. In any case with or without help time alone was likely to have altered her mood.

The Dutch Supreme Court which ruled on the Assen Case in June 1994 agreed with the lower courts in affirming that mental suffering can be grounds for euthanasia, but found Chabot guilty of not having had a psychiatric consultant actually see the patient. Although the court expressed the belief that a consultant's direct contact with a patient was particularly necessary in the absence of physical illness, it imposed no punishment since it felt that in all other regards Chabot had behaved responsibly. The case was seen as a triumph by euthanasia advocates since it legally established mental suffering as a basis for euthanasia. Since the consultation can easily be obtained from a sympathetic colleague, it offers the patient little protection.

In another well-publicized psychiatric case, described in a Dutch psychiatric journal (Schudel, Nolen, van Dijk and Sutorius, 1993), a patient who was chronically depressed with major depressive episodes in which he was psychotic was, between psychotic episodes, assisted in his suicide by his psychiatrist. The justification for acceding to the patient's request had been that he had not responded to treatment, that his suffering was unbearable and that in between the major depressive psychotic episodes he was competent.

The acceptance of euthanasia for psychiatric patients who are suicidal seems the inevitable consequence of allowing such criteria as "competence" and "intolerable suffering" to determine the outcome rather than sound clinical judgment. The psychiatrist in some of the psychiatric cases is in the position of working to prevent suicide until the patient asks for his assistance in committing suicide and then the rules of the game change and he negotiates with the patient as to whose approach is best.

Seriously suicidal patients want suicide. In a society that makes euthanasia accessible for them they will be harder to treat, not easier. Many of them fantasize closeness in death with a person who kills them. When psychiatrists and general practitioners have complementary fantasies, euthanasia fulfills their needs as much as the patient's.

Dutch practice ignores what we know of complex dynamics of the relation between the treatment of the suicidal and the desire of some who are seriously ill to end their lives. Suicidal patients are prone to make conditions on life that life cannot fulfill: "I won't live if I can't be in control", ... "without my husband," " ... if I lose my looks, power, prestige or health," or "if I am going to die soon" (Hendin, 1982). Depression, often precipitated by discovering a serious illness, exaggerates the tendency toward seeing problems in black-or-white terms (Hendin and Klerman, 1993). Although clinical and research experience confirm that the overwhelming majority of suicidal patients including the terminally ill suffer from a depression that can be treated (Brown, Henteleff, Barakat and Rowe, 1975), when a patient finds a doctor who shares the view that life is only worth living if certain conditions are met, the patient's rigidity is reinforced (Hendin, 1994a).

## THE REMMELINK REPORT

Despite accepting euthanasia, the Dutch did not find hard facts about it easy to come by. Estimates of the number of euthanasia cases ranged from five thousand to twenty thousand of the 130,000 deaths in the Netherlands each year. Charges that involuntary euthanasia was widespread were made.

To ascertain actual Dutch medical practice regarding euthanasia, a government commission, headed by Professor Jan Remmelink, arranged a remarkable study of the problem by investigators at Erasmus University in which physicians were granted anonymity and immunity from prosecution. The Remmelink Report found that 49,000 deaths in the Netherlands each year involve a medical decision at the end of life (MDEL). 95% of these MDEL cases involve, in equal numbers, either withholding/discontinuing life support, or the alleviation of pain and symptoms through medication that might hasten death. Frank euthanasia was the cause of death in 2,300 i.e. in 2% of all

Dutch deaths. Assisted suicide was relatively uncommon, occurring some 400 times per year. Over 50% of Dutch physicians admitted to practicing euthanasia, with cancer patients being the majority of their cases. Only 60% of doctors kept a written record of their cases, and only 29% of doctors filled out the death certificates honestly in euthanasia cases (van der Maas, van Delders, Pijnenborg, 1991).

That it is often the doctor and not the patient who determines the choice for death was underlined by the Remmelink Report's documentation of cases in which there has been "termination of the patient without explicit request" (van der Maas, van Delders and Pijnenborg, 1992). The term "involuntary euthanasia," disturbing to the Dutch, is avoided by their definition of euthanasia as the ending of the life of one person by another at the first person's request. If life is terminated without request they consider it not to be euthanasia (Borst-Eilers, 1992). "Involuntary euthanasia" seems, however, to have a far less Orwellian connotation than "termination of the patient without explicit request."

In the 1,000 cases referred to earlier where physicians admitted they had actively caused or hastened death without any request from the patient, the impossibility of treating pain effectively was given as the reason for killing the patient in only 30%. The remaining 70% were killed with a variety of different justifications ranging from "low quality of life" to "a therapy was withdrawn but the patient did not die." 27% of physicians indicated that they had terminated the lives of patients without a request from the patient to do so; another 32% could conceive of doing so (van der Maas, van Delders and Pijnenborg, 1992).

Other forms of hastening death without the patient's consent are, according to the Report, common practice in the Netherlands. In over 4,000 cases the doctor's explicit intention in administering pain medication or withdrawing or withholding treatment was to shorten life; in almost 11,000 cases this was a secondary goal." In over half of the 49,000 MDEL cases,

apart from the euthanasia cases, decisions that might or were intended to end the life of the patient without consulting the patient. In about 80% of these cases physicians gave the patient's impaired ability to communicate as their justification. This left about 5,000 cases in which physicians made decisions that might or were intended to end the lives of competent patients without consulting them.

In 13% of these cases, physicians who did not communicate with competent patients concerning MDELs that might or were intended to end their lives gave as a reason for not doing so that they previously had some discussion of the subject with the patient. Yet it seemed incomprehensible that the physician would terminate the life of a competent patient on the basis of some prior discussion without checking if the patient still felt the same way. One could only conjecture that the physician, actually knowing that the patient would not agree or had changed his mind, did not want to hear the answer because he felt it appropriate to end the patient's life and to do so after a negative reply would amount to murder. Another possibility was that the physician was justifying the death by stretching the patient's prior statement which may, according to the study, have been no more than an urgent request for pain medication.

Physicians were not challenged with regard to explanations in the study. Indeed their not being challenged was a necessary condition to secure the cooperation of the KNMG and the participating doctors. I had the impression that the study's interviewers, who were primarily physicians, were questioning their colleagues in a somewhat collegial manner, a limitation of this otherwise valuable report (Hendin, 1994a).

Some euthanasia advocates defend the need for doctors to make decisions to end the lives of competent patients without discussion with them. One euthanasia advocate gave me as an example a case where a doctor had terminated the life of a nun a few days before she would have died because she was in excruciating pain, but her religious convictions did not permit her to ask for death. He did not argue, however, when asked why she should not have been permitted to die in the way she wanted.

Other advocates admit that a system in which doctors become used to playing a predominant role in making decisions about ending life encourages some to feel entitled to make decisions without consulting patients. Many of the professionals who are advocates of euthanasia conceded that abuses were common. In their published articles, however, they do not admit this since they see the issue of euthanasia as caught in a political struggle in which conceding abuses would give ammunition to those in government who are critical of the system.

Many Dutch psychologists and psychiatrists were privately critical of Chabot's assistance in the suicide of Netty Boomsma. That assisted suicide and euthanasia are advocated and supported by both the medical and legal establishments makes it difficult for them to say so publicly or in writing; only one has done so (Koerselman 1994).

## DISCUSSION

Virtually all Dutch advocates of euthanasia familiar with the United States see our legalizing euthanasia as unwise for a variety of reasons. From their perspective, the United States is not characterized by either a legal or medical system that fosters social harmony, but instead pits one profession against the other. They believe the tendency of American patients in general to litigation would make euthanasia a nightmare for physicians. They cite social and economic disparities in health care as another source of contention and recognize that without comprehensive care for the sickly poor and the elderly, euthanasia will tend to become their only option. The Dutch believe their hospitals are not subject to the economic pressure to get rid of the terminally ill that would be present in this country. The relative absence of the family doctor, the core of medical practice

in the Netherlands, eliminates what the Dutch perceive as a major source of patient protection. Further contaminating the process in the United States would be the difficulty of preventing the profit motive from making euthanasia and assisted suicide a lucrative business.

Yet even a more equitable health care system and twenty years of experience have not protected the Dutch from the abuses of their system. In our country proposals for legislation have been hastily introduced to a public with little opportunity to develop an informed consensus.

The law recently passed in Oregon would permit doctors to prescribe lethal drugs to patients judged to be in the last six months of life. It is not just that it is impossible to predict with certainty that a patient has only six months to live, making mistaken or falsified predictions inevitable. Any law that permits assisted suicide when patients are neither in pain nor immediately about to die will encourage people who fear death to take a quicker way out.

Under the Oregon law, Tim, the patient with acute myelocytic leukemia, would probably have asked a doctor's help in taking his own life. Because he was mentally competent and did not meet the clinical criteria for a diagnosis of depression, he would have qualified for assisted suicide and would surely have found a doctor who would agree to his request.

Since the Oregon law, using guidelines like those in effect in the Netherlands, does not require an independently referred doctor for a second opinion, he would have been referred by a physician supportive of assisted suicide to a colleague who was equally supportive. The evaluation would very likely have been pro forma. He could have been put to death in an unrecognized state of terror, unable to give himself the chance of getting well or of dying in the dignified way he did.

Although the Oregon law requires counselling if the patient has a mental disorder or has his or her judgment impaired by depression, it is the doctor who determines whether such a referral is indicated. The evidence indicates that most doctors are not qualified to make such a determination (Conwell & Caine, 1991).

Nor should psychiatrists and psychologists be sanguine at being reduced to the role, advocated in most legalization proposals, of simply determining if a patient is competent to make a decision regarding euthanasia. It was the fact that I was not the arbiter of this case that permitted the patient I described with acute myelocytic leukemia to talk freely about his fears of death and eventually to change his mind about wanting an immediate end to his life.

Neither legalization of euthanasia nor opposition to it constitutes a public policy that addresses the larger problem of how to care for the terminally ill. The call for legalization is a symptom of our failure to develop a better response to death and the understandable fear of artificial prolongation of life (Hendin, 1994b).

Yet the dangers threatened by legalization of assisted suicide can be avoided. They are being avoided elsewhere in western Europe where there is no great demand for legalizing assisted suicide or euthanasia. Care for the terminally ill is better in the Scandinavian countries than in the United States and in the Netherlands. Scandinavian doctors do not accept excessive measures for prolonging life in people who are virtually dead, but neither do they encourage people to choose death prematurely.

There is a great deal of evidence that in the United States as in the Netherlands doctors are not sufficiently trained in the relief of pain and other symptoms in the terminally ill. Hospice care is in its infancy in both countries. We have not yet educated the public as to the choices they have in refusing or terminating treatment that prolongs a painful process of dying. And we have not devoted enough time in our medical schools to educating future physicians about coming to terms with the painful truth that there will be patients they will not be able to save but whose needs they must learn to address.

Psychiatrists and psychologists in the Netherlands played a relatively passive role in the growing normalization of suicide and euthanasia even though this has meant that patients who are basically suicidal, whether physically ill or not, are being assisted in death like those who seek relief in the last days of a terminal illness. We should learn from that experience to be more involved, educating the public that legalization may become a license to abuse and exploit the fears of the ill and depressed. Legalization accepts the view of those who are engulfed in suicidal despair that death is the preferred solution to the problems of illness, age, and depression. It encourages the worst tendencies of depressed patients most of whom can be helped to overcome their condition. "Normalizing" suicide as a medical option along with accepting or refusing treatment, inevitably lays the groundwork for a culture that will not only turn euthanasia into a "cure" for depression but may prove to exert a coercion to die on patients when they are most vulnerable.

## REFERENCES

Borst-Eilers, E. (1992). Euthanasia in the Netherlands: brief historical review and present situation. In R.I. Misbin (Ed.), *Euthanasia: The Good of the Patient; The Good of Society*. Frederick, Maryland: University Publishing Group.

Brown, J. H., Henteleff, P., Barakat, S. & Rowe, C. J. (1986). Is it normal for terminally ill patients to desire death? *American Journal of Psychiatry*, 143, 208–211.

Chabot, B. E. (1993). *Zelf Beschikt*. Amsterdam: Uitgeverijbalans.

Conwell, Y. & Caine E. D. (1991). Rational suicide and the right to die: reality and myth. N. Engl J Med, 15, 1100–1103

Gomez, C. (1991). *Regulating Death: Euthanasia and the Case of the Netherlands*. New York: The Free Press.

Gevers, J. K. M. (1992). What the law allows: legal aspects of active euthanasia on request in the Netherlands. In R. I. Misbin (Ed.), *Euthanasia: The Good of the Patient, the Good of Society*. Frederick, Maryland: University Publishing Group.

Hendin H. (1995) *Suicide in America*. New York: W. W. Norton and Co.

Hendin, H. and Klerman, G. (1993) Physician-assisted suicide: the dangers of legalization. *American Journal of Psychiatry*, 150, 143–145.

Hendin, H. (1994a). Seduced by death: doctors, patients and the Dutch Cure. *Issues in Law and Medicine*, 10, 1–45.

Hendin, H. (1994b) Scared to death of dying. *The New York Times Op-Ed*, December 16, 1994.

K. A. Productions (1993). "An Appointment with Death" (film).

Koerselman, G. F. (1994). Balanssuïcide als mythe: over 'Zelf Beschikt,' door B. E. Chabot MGv 5, 515–527.

KNMG, *Standpunt Inzake Euthanasie* [Standpoint on Euthanasia], 31 Medisch Contact 990 (1984), published in abridged form in KNMG, Guidelines for Euthanasia, 3 Issues in *Law and Medicine 429* (1988) (Walter Lagerwey trans.).

President's Commission for the Study of Ethical and Biomedical and Behavioral Research, *Decisions to Forego Life-Sustaining Treatment* (1983).

Schudel, W. J., Nolen, W. A., van Dijk, W. R., & Su-

torius, E. (1993). *De Zaak van de Vasthoudende Inspecteur*, Maandblad voor Geesteligke Volksgezondheid, 738–749.

Thomas, L. (1980). Dying as failure? *Journal of American Political Science*, 444, 1–4.

van der Maas, P. J., van Delders, J. J. M., & Pijnenborg, L. (1991). Euthanasia and other medical decisions concerning the end of life, *Lancet*, 338, 669–674.

van der Maas, P. J., van Delders, J. J. M., & Pijnenborg, L. (1992). Euthanasia and Other Medical Decisions Concerning the End of Life. *Health Policy Monograph*. New York: Elsevier.

# Postscript: Summary and Synthesis

Ronald W. Maris, PhD, and Morton M. Silverman, MD

A number of common themes emerge from our examination of suicide prevention in this monograph. One major theme is the need for a unified diagnostic and classification system that differentiates among the range of suicidal behaviors, actions, ideations, and related phenomena (cf., Maris, Berman, Maltsberger, & Yufit, 1992: Chap. 4). This classification schema must incorporate the clarification of existing terms such as *self-injurious behaviors, self-destructive behaviors, nonlethal suicide gestures, suicide threats*, etc. Without such a schemata, we will never be clear as to the boundaries of suicidology and suicide prevention. Many authors have called for new paradigms to understand suicide and its related phenomena, as well as to assist in developing and implementing preventive interventions in the community. Fortunately these classification issues are starting to be addressed in a workshop sponsored by the National Institute of Mental Health (Washington, DC, November 1994).

Most of the authors in this issue also recognize the need for comprehensive and coordinated community-based preventive intervention programs that address multifactorial risk and protective factors. The relationships between and among these multifactorial risk and protective factors need further elucidation. We await statistical and methodological advances to assist us in analyzing the relevant variables in a way that will allow us to derive useful profiles of individuals or groups at risk. At present so-called high-risk groups are largely a misnomer, since the risk (i.e., sensitivity and specificity) is not high enough to be very useful. Only then can we develop prediction scales and measurements that can be applied to specific suicide prevention interventions.

We still seem to be frustrated by the distinctions between those people who will eventually complete suicide and those who will make nonfatal attempts, even though we recognize their 10–15% overlap (Maris et al., 1992: Chap. 17). The frustration derives from the apparent need to develop interventions that are specific to each at-risk population (which, incidentally, includes more than just nonfatal suicide attempters and suicide completers), while recognizing the commonality of many risk factors (biological, psychological, sociocultural) that are at work in both populations. What is lacking is a continuum of preventive interventions that can be linked developmentally to the evaluation and expression of a range of specific suicidal behaviors, controlling for age, gender, race, mental disorder variables, and the like.

Most of the present authors have identified the presence of psychiatric illness as a major predictive or predisposing risk factor directly associated with suicidal behaviors. These same authors emphasize the role of biology (including neuropharmacology, neurochemistry, receptor specification, etc.) in the development of suicidal risk. At issue here is how we as a society decide to allocate our limited preventive resources. For example, is it more cost-effective to exclusively allocate the prevention dollar to medical (psychopharmacology), to clinical interventions (appropriate psychotherapies), to sociocultural (jobs and employment), or to educational (awareness, self-help) interventions?

Prevention researchers have warned us that in the absence of empirically derived knowledge on which to base social action and intervention programs, we may do well not to attempt to implement prevention programs (Garland & Zigler, 1993; Morgan, 1993).

Even if the goal of eliminating all suicidal behaviors from our society remains elusive or even undesirable (Battin, 1991), the efforts to better understand how to prevent these behaviors should continue in as many directions and domains as possible. We are not sure which efforts will provide the best insights and interventions addressing this conundrum, although it is likely that real advances will continue to occur in the fields of epidemiology and surveillance, diagnosis and classification, community and social psychology, biology and genetics, health and behavioral psychology, and clinical psychiatry; and that they will inform strategies for preventive interventions. Until such time as we have available effective preventive interventions specifically designed to address suicidal behaviors in specific populations and designed to be administered in specific settings, we need to continue to do the best we can to achieve risk reduction, drawing upon the existing knowledge base of epidemiology, risk factor research, and clinical practice.

Another theme in this monograph is the problem of possible underreporting of suicidal events in all communities. This surveillance problem is linked to the lack of internationally agreed-upon definitions and classifications. Such likely underreporting at the community, state, and national levels perpetuates the myth that suicide is such a low base rate phenomenon that it does not deserve the attention and allocation of resources necessary to mount effective and measurable preventive intervention programs.

A related issue is understanding better what differentiates the suicide rates of males and females. Assuming that the underreporting of suicidal behaviors is evenly distributed among the genders (an assumption that requires empirical investigation), we need to better understand the protective factors that are apparently at work for the female population. For example, females exceed males in rates of depressive disorder by ratios of about 2 to 1

but at the same time have suicide rate ratios 3 to 4 times *lower* than those of males.

It remains very difficult, even elusive, to move from facts and figures to well-designed, well-implemented, comprehensive, and coordinated preventive interventions. Despite being a relatively rare event, the size and scope of suicidal problems (the populations affected, the range of behaviors involved, the age span covered, the broad distribution throughout all social and economic strata) eludes simple solutions. There does not seem to be the equivalent of a straightforward antibiotic or immunization for suicidal behaviors.

Why should this be? It may well be due to how we define and understand suicidal behaviors. Alan Lipschitz (in Part IV of this issue) prefers to see these behaviors as an expression of underlying affective disorders or schizophrenia. Rene Diekstra (Part I) places emphases on the roles of unemployment, lack of social involvement and community identity, and a poor sense of future.

Canetto and Lester (Part I) see cultural values and belief systems as major contributing factors, particularly as they affect women. Kalafat and Elias (Part III) see socialization in school settings as significant contributors. Felner and Silverman (Part II) see the role of developmental trajectories and transactional relationships between people and their environments as holding the key to understanding these behaviors.

We do know that suicidal behaviors are a hybrid of the contributions of biological mechanisms (e.g., neurotransmitters, genetics), psychiatric illness and emotional dysfunction, social problems, and easy access to means for suicide. Thus, suicidal behaviors are a complex biopsychosocial behavioral problem, with varying degrees of contribution from each of the three domains on a case-by-case basis.

## PREVENTIVE INTERVENTIONS

The authors of this monograph have advocated a broad range of preventive interventions, acknowledging the diversity of behaviors, populations, and settings that comprise the field of suicide prevention. Their recommendations range from individual-focused recommendations (e.g., psychopharmacology or psychotherapy) to national legislation (i.e., gun control). All have merit within the context of specific prevention efforts designed to affect specific populations at risk for the expression or continuance of specific suicidal behaviors. The emphasis here is on the specificity of the intervention to effect change under specific conditions (population, setting, time frame) to achieve a specific outcome. We should not expect that any preventive intervention is universal in its application, reception, or predicted outcome. Assigning relative value to these efforts may be premature, in light of our knowledge base regarding the effectiveness of these interventions to prevent suicidal behaviors in specific populations.

It is no surprise that until we understand better the biopsychosocial mechanisms and processes that contribute to suicidal behaviors, our first goal perhaps should be eliminating the mechanical means for committing suicide. Hence, a strong recommendation emerging from the present contributors is to encourage gun control legislation, especially in the United States. Whether this goal is attainable by the year 2000 remains a question. In hospitals, jails, and prisons, precautions to make them hanging- or asphyxiation-proof are a major priority.

A second set of recommendations fall under the aegis of community-level and environmental interventions. Suicide education programs at the community, workplace, and school level are often cited. Both Canetto and Lester, and Lipschitz emphasize the importance of culturally sensitive interventions in order to ensure their reception and acceptance. Diekstra and McIntosh focus on essential community "infrastructures" that provide individuals and groups with social support, employment, and a sense of community. These societal-level systems can help foster self-esteem and improved self-concept,

which are known protective factors against many self-destructive behaviors. Other community-based prevention activities include access to hotlines and crisis intervention services (Berman and Jobes; McIntosh). Berman and Jobes, McIntosh, and Litman emphasize the role of early screening programs for the recognition and referral of at-risk individuals. These screening programs can function in all societal institutions but require heightened awareness and sensitivity on the part of many designated "gatekeepers" (police, clergy, teachers, physicians) to the signs and symptoms of distress and dysfunction (Maris et al., 1973).

Many recommendations remain targeted at suspected high suicide risk individuals, a reflection of the lack of our current ability to predict behaviors in unidentified individuals, groups, and communities. Berman and Jobes, McIntosh, and Lipschitz focus on modifying those predisposing risk conditions that are amenable to current interventions. The goals of such interventions might include minimizing alcohol and other substance abuse, enhancing abilities to master age-appropriate developmental tasks (cognitive and behavioral skills), and ensuring healthy family functioning. Related to these predisposing conditions are a set of precipitating risk conditions that include improving coping and affective skills, better capability to deal with sudden and painful losses, and avoiding exposure to situations that may eventuate in intolerable psychological pain. Our authors also place emphasis on strengthening protective factors, such as remaining in school, being meaningfully employed, and being involved and well-connected in one's community.

Litman, Lipschitz, Maris, and McIntosh highlight the important roles of psychotropic medications and psychotherapy (as well as other biological interventions) for those individuals demonstrating signs, symptoms, or heightened probability of increased risk for future suicidal behaviors.

In sum, many preventive strategies

have been identified that, alone or in combination, are believed to be currently effective in reducing or eliminating suicidal behaviors in specific populations and specific settings. These strategies include, but are not limited to, assessment, surveillance, information dissemination, prevention education, problem identification and referral, intervention for individuals and groups expressing early signs and symptoms of distress, and environmental manipulations and ecological approaches.

## FUTURE DIRECTIONS

Much renewed interest in the U.S. is being directed at injury control measures, particularly as they relate to the prevention of domestic and urban violence of all forms (i.e., homicide, physical assault, rape, child abuse, etc.). Such interest is in the context of public health initiatives to improve surveillance, assessment, and intervention measures.

The prevention of suicide cannot occur in a vacuum. Any effective prevention program must be comprehensive, collaborative, and coordinated with other related prevention-oriented programs. The overlap between depressive symptoms, alcohol and other substance abuse, and marital or familial disruption (e.g., widowhood, divorce, separation) is so prevalent that it is incumbent upon us all to "nest" suicide prevention efforts within substance abuse prevention programming, mental health initiatives, and social action programs. Conversely, suicide prevention efforts must incorporate messages and techniques that have proven successful in "sister" campaigns, because if we were able to deter domestic violence, alleviate depression, or reduce the prevalence of alcohol or other substance abuse, we would surely lower the incidence of suicidal behaviors in our communities. The operative concept here is community program linkages (Benard, 1990).

Another tactic is to develop a series of prevention messages and programs that are developmentally geared to different populations—for example, by age, gender, and race. If suicidal behavior is the final common behavioral pathway of many related risk factors and risk situations (unemployment, alcohol and drug abuse, personality disorder, depression, recent losses, social rejection, loss of hope in the future), then a comprehensive program geared at a target population must address each and every one of the risk factors that, when clustered, increase the overall risk for suicidal behavior. We would anticipate that a suicide prevention module would look different for middle school adolescents than for adults in the workplace. The techniques and messages need to be tailored to the audience.

One should consider the distinction between preventing a self-injurious behavior from occurring versus promoting well-being and healthy lifestyles. In some ways, these two approaches are correlated concepts and in other ways they are polar opposites. Are suicidal behaviors the consequence of the absence of health (Maris, Part IV), or are they the consequence of disease and disorder? How we answer this question will determine where we focus our efforts to reduce or eliminate suicidal behavior in our society. Obviously this is not an either/or proposition. Nevertheless, we need to clarify and better define what we are trying to accomplish, what methods we are using to do so, and what outcome criteria we will measure to monitor whether we have been successful.

Another issue is whether our goal is to prevent completed suicides or to reduce suicide attempts. Given the relatively small overlap between attempters and completers, and given the rather large ratio of attempts to suicide completions in our society, we must ask whether we should seek to reduce significant amounts of morbidity or a smaller amount of mortality. We could argue that by reducing all morbidity we will also decrease mortality by, say, 10–20%. But we know relatively little about the profiles of the attempters who eventually proceed to complete suicide at a later time, and it is unrealistic to assume that we can prevent all suicide attempts. It is conceivable that a program designed to reduce suicide attempts might not affect most of those attempters who eventually complete. The solution, in part, is to develop parallel prevention programs that address these two seemingly separate at-risk populations.

Until further notice, we must continue to actively support those "secondary" and "tertiary" prevention programs that contribute to a reduction in the prevalence of suicidal behaviors in the community. These programs include crisis intervention services (including "hotlines"), early diagnosis and treatment of psychiatric disorders (depression, schizophrenia, personality disorders, alcohol and other drug abuse), aggressive treatment of suicide attempters during and after hospitalization, postvention efforts with schools and communities after a suicide has occurred, and social service programs for the homeless and unemployed (Diekstra, 1992).

## CONCLUSION

A basic issue here is the degree to which we all see these behaviors as destructive to the individual at risk as well as to ourselves as part of a larger community. It has been suggested that a single suicide, let alone a suicide attempt, affects at least 6–8 other significant individuals dramatically—with sometimes permanent consequences related to productivity, self-esteem, self-image, general health, and mental well-being. Hence, suicide prevention is an effort not only to save individual lives or prevent a tragic loss, but also to protect every one of us from unnecessary and unintended pain, discomfort, and suffering. Our families, communities, societies, and nations cannot mature or reach their full potential and promise if we allow wanton self-destructive forces to go mindlessly unchecked. While some limited self-destruction may be necessary for individual and collective development, more often than not, rampant self-destructive forces in fact thwart our full individual and collective actualization.

## REFERENCES

Battin, M. P. (1991). Rational suicide: How can we respond to a request to help? *Crisis, 12*(2), 73–80.

Benard, B. (1990). An overview of community-based prevention. In K. H. Rey, C. L., Faegre, & P. Lowery (Eds.), *Prevention research findings: 1988* (pp. 126–147) (DHHS No. (ADM) 89-1615). Washington, DC: U.S. Government Printing Office.

Diekstra, R. F. W. (1992). The prevention of suicidal behavior: Evidence for the efficacy of clinical and community-based programs. *International Journal of Mental Health, 21*(3), 69–87.

Garland, A. F., & Zigler, E. (1993). Adolescent suicide prevention: Current research and social policy implications. *American Psychologist, 48*(2), 169–182.

Maris, R. W., et al. (1973). Education and training in suicidology for the seventies. In H. L. P. Resnik and B. C. Hawthorne (Eds.), *Suicide Prevention in the Seventies* (pp. 23–44). Washington, DC: U.S. Government Printing Office.

Maris, R. W., Berman, A. L., Maltsberger, J. T., & Yufit, R. I. (Eds.). *Assessment and prediction of suicide.* New York: Guilford Press.

Morgan, H. G. (1994). How feasible is suicide prevention? *Current Opinion in Psychiatry, 7*, 111–118.

# Index